Lecture Notes in Computer Scienc

Commenced Publication in 1973
Founding and Former Series Editors:
Gerhard Goos, Juris Hartmanis, and Jan van Leeuwen

T0238114

Henrik I. Christensen   Hans-Hellmut Nagel (Eds.)

Cognitive Vision Systems

Sampling the Spectrum of Approaches

 Springer

Volume Editors

Henrik I. Christensen
Royal Institute of Technology
Centre for Autonomous Systems
100 44 Stockholm, Sweden
E-mail: hic@nada.kth.se

Hans-Hellmut Nagel
Universität Karlsruhe
Fakultät für Informatik
Institut für Algorithmen und Kognitive Systeme
76128 Karlsruhe, Germany
E-mail: nagel@iaks.uni-karlsruhe.de

Library of Congress Control Number: 2006926926

CR Subject Classification (1998): I.4, I.2.9-10, I.2.6, I.5.4-5, F.2.2

LNCS Sublibrary: SL 6 – Image Processing, Computer Vision, Pattern Recognition, and Graphics

ISSN   0302-9743
ISBN-10   3-540-33971-X Springer Berlin Heidelberg New York
ISBN-13   978-3-540-33971-7 Springer Berlin Heidelberg New York

Springer is a part of Springer Science+Business Media

springer.com

© Springer-Verlag Berlin Heidelberg 2006
Printed in Germany

Typesetting: Camera-ready by author, data conversion by Markus Richter, Heidelberg
Printed on acid-free paper   SPIN: 11414353   06/3142   5 4 3 2 1 0

Preface

During the last decade of the twentieth century, computer vision made considerable progress towards consolidation of its fundaments, in particular regarding the treatment of geometry for the evaluation of stereo image pairs and of multi-view image recordings. Scientists thus began to look at basic computer vision solutions – irrespective of the well-perceived need to perfect these further – as components which should be explored in a larger context.

In 2000, Horst Forster, Head of Division in the Information Society Directorate-General of the European Commission, through his contacts with many computer vision researchers throughout Europe, sensed their readiness to cooperate for the exploration of new grounds in a direction subsequently to become known as 'cognitive vision.' Horst Forster succeeded in convincing the European Commission to stimulate cooperation in this direction by funding a four-year program, which encountered an unexpectedly broad response. It has been a privilege for us to have had a glimpse at the unobtrusive, effective engagement of Horst Forster to advance scientific cooperation within the European Union.

It is a particular pleasure for us to thank Colette Maloney, who closely cooperated with Horst Forster throughout the past by accompanying the many projects funded under the cognitive vision programme. Her constant encouraging support, her practically instant response to a seemingly endless series of calls for help in organizational and financial matters, and her deep commitment to advancing scientific research in this topical area across Europe made collaboration with her a truly memorable experience.

As part of the efforts to further strengthen cooperation between research groups from different countries, a seminar was organized at Schloss Dagstuhl in Germany during October 26–30, 2003. Scientists active in related areas were invited from across the world. This seminar was co-sponsored by ECVision, the Cognitive Vision network of excellence under the leadership of David Vernon. The support from ECVision was instrumental to the organization of this seminar and the creation of this volume. Presentations and associated vivid discussions at the seminar were gradually transformed into a set of contributions to this volume. The editors thank the authors for their considerable efforts to draft, refine, and cross-reference these contributions.

The editors are grateful to Alfred Hofmann from Springer for agreeing to publish this book – and for his patience while we wrestled with the 'mechanics' to put it together.

All who participated in this seminar still remember the warm hospitality and quiet efficiency of the staff at Schloss Dagstuhl who thereby contributed significantly to turning this endeavor into a stimulating and successful event.

February 2006   Henrik I. Christensen and Hans-Hellmut Nagel

Contents

1

Introductory Remarks

H.I. Christensen[1] and H.-H. Nagel[2]

[1] Kungliga Tekniska Högskolan
    100 44 Stockholm, Sweden
    hic@nada.kth.se
[2] Institut für Algorithmen und Kognitive Systeme,
    Fakultät für Informatik der Universität Karlsruhe (TH)
    76128 Karlsruhe, Germany
    nagel@iaks.uni-karlsruhe.de

The notion 'cognitive vision system (CogVS)' stimulates a wide spectrum of associations. In many cases, the attribute 'cognitive' is related to advanced abilities of living creatures, in particular of primates. In this context, a close association between the terms 'cognitive' and 'vision' appears natural, because it is well known that vision constitutes the primate sensory channel with the largest spatiotemporal bandwidth.

Since the middle of the last century, technical means were gradually developed to record and process digitized image sequences. These technical advances created a seemingly unresistable challenge to devise algorithmic approaches which explain, simulate, or even surpass vision capabilities of living creatures. In this context, 'vision' is understood to refer to a set of information processing steps which transform the light intensity distribution impinging onto the transducer surface eventually into some kind of re-action, be it an observable movement, some acoustical communication, or a change of internal representations for the union of the depicted scene and the 'vision system' itself. The common understanding of 'vision' as a kind of information processing induces the use of the word 'system' in this context for whatever performs these processing steps – be it a living creature, a familiar digital computer, or any other alternative to realize a computational device.

The premises underlying such a view have been accepted to the extent that an attribute like 'cognitive' appears applicable to technical constructs despite the fact that it has been coined originally in order to characterize abilities of living creatures. Similar to the experience with other natural language terms referring to commonsense notions – like, e. g., 'intelligence' – scientific efforts to conceive an artifact, which could be considered equivalent to living creatures regarding its input/output relations, are accompanied by efforts to define precisely the notion involved, in our case 'cognitive vision'.

It should not come as a surprise that such endeavors result in a large spectrum of definitions. This observation can be attributed to the fact that complex abilities of living creatures involve many aspects, which have to be taken into account. It sometimes is useful to ask which among these aspects have been selected – or emphasized – in order to motivate a definition of the notion 'cognitive vision system'. Three aspects in

H.I. Christensen and H.-H. Nagel (Eds.): Cognitive Vision Systems, LNCS 3948, pp. 1–4, 2006.
© Springer-Verlag Berlin Heidelberg 2006

particular appear frequently, either explicitly or implicitly, namely wide applicability, robustness, and speed. The first aspect mentioned implies that a 'true CogVS' can easily and reliably adapt to a wide variation of boundary conditions under which it is expected to operate. This implication rules out the possibility that a CogVS is endowed right from the start with 'all the knowledge' it might need in order to cope with new tasks. It is assumed instead that a CogVS can *learn* task-relevant spatiotemporal structures in its environment and can *adapt* its internal operational parameters in order to reliably estimate the current status of itself and of its environment. 'Robustness' implies that small variations of the environmental state, which are considered to be irrelevant for the execution of the current task, should not influence the performance. And 'speed' implies that the CogVS operates fast enough that task-relevant changes in the environment can be handled without endangering the desired performance level. This latter aspect became important once a 'vision system' had to provide sensory feedback for a mechanical system, in particular for the case of computer vision in the feedback loop of a moving or manipulating artifact.

Although such goals were propagated already rather early during the development of computer vision systems, it turned out that at most two of these three goals could be attained at the same time. If a system was claimed to be (more) widely applicable and robust, it was not fast enough. If it was robust and fast, it was not widely applicable (e.g. specialized machine vision systems for quality control in semi-automated manufacturing plants). And if a system approach was touted as fast and widely applicable, it usually was not robust – if it worked at all. Given our current understanding about the computational expenses required to even determine a small set of visual features reliably, this state of affairs is most plausible even almost up to present days. Ten or twenty years ago, when memory and processing capacity were smaller by three to four orders of magnitude compared to what is available at the same price today, many 'simplifications' or 'speed-ups' were simply a matter of necessity in order to be able to explore an experimental approach at all.

A frequently encountered argument in connection with a CogVS simply quotes that 'there is nothing new under the sun – in German: Alles schon dagewesen' (attributed to Rabbi Ben Akiba). As with the Delphi Oracle, the truth of such a statement can be 'proven' by choosing an appropriate point of view for the interpretation. Rather than burying the topic based on such an adage, it appears more fruitful to inquire in detail which changes or advances of the State-of-the-Art may justify to re-approach previously treated and subsequently abandoned problems. As mentioned already, the still exponential improvement of the price/performance ratio for digital memory and processors let it appear feasible that real-time processing of a video input stream does no longer compromise the quality of elementary signal processing steps to the extent that only rather brittle results could be expected. In addition, size, weight, and power consumption of today's computers and cameras allow to incorporate them into mobile experimental platforms (embodied computer vision systems). Advantages related to the fact that at least part of the system environment may 'serve as its own representation' removes many bottlenecks. A continuously updated state estimate can be used instead of time-consuming searches for the 'optimal currently appropriate hypothesis' about the state of the system and its environment.

The ability to experiment more – with the ensuing advantage of being able to study the gamut of influences in order to separate between genuinely important task conditions from mere disturbances (noise) – gradually provided a background of reproducible experiences. This in turn stimulated more theoretically oriented research which enabled to isolate critical conditions and to prepare measures to prevent them or to cope with them. Choosing a sufficiently large support area for the estimation of gray-value gradients and the exploitation of a search across a range of spatial scales may serve as examples. On top of such efforts, stochastic techniques are applied in order to cope with the unavoidable influences of noise.

In addition to these considerations, another aspect appears to become even more important. The extraction of local features (edge elements, corner points, texture elements, ...) and their aggregation to non-local descriptions (image segments, 3D-surface-facets in the scene) have matured to the point where it becomes possible to abstract from a quantitative geometric characterisation of relevant phenomena to a conceptual level of representation. At this latter level of representation, logic-based inference processes may be activated, which facilitate non-numerical consistency checks. The incorporation of such logic-based processes into a computer vision system offers three important advantages. It first allows to exploit general knowledge about spatiotemporal relations. This in turn allows to generate warnings when 'implausible' situations occur or to circumvent these altogether. And last, but not least, it simplifies the interface between the 'system' and its user – be it the developer or someone who has to supervise an operational system.

It increasingly appears justifiable, therefore, to speak about CogVS: current experimental systems begin to exhibit performance characteristics which start to reduce the qualitative difference to the performance of living creatures to a – still formidable – quantitative difference. This fact in turn opens the road for small, but effective gradual improvements of system performance. Growing familiarity with the 'real effects', which influence system performance, is likely to improve our understanding for the 'solutions' applied by living creatures. Eventually, the attribute 'cognitive' of a CogVS may become appropriate even in the sense that certain aspects of information processing by living creatures can be described in a suitable manner, quite apart from the view that 'cognitive' addresses processing at the conceptual level of representation.

The contributions collected in this volume originated in presentations at a Dagstuhl Seminar (# 03441, 26-31 October 2003) on Cognitive Vision Systems. It samples various views on what constitutes a CogVS and why. In order to preserve the wide spectrum of opinions and thereby to stimulate the debate about characteristics, means, and goals of building a CogVS, dogmatic decisions have been avoided regarding what is and is not a CogVS. The contributions have been grouped, however, with the aim to emphasize similarities in subgoals and/or approaches.

Part I (*Foundations of Cognitive Vision Systems*) collects contributions which address questions concerning the definition and overall structure of what appears to constitute a CogVS. Part II (*Recognition and Categorization*) is concerned with investigations which study the extraction and aggregation of features from video signals with the goal to establish a relation between a subset of these features and conceptual representations for observable bodies and behaviors recorded in the scene. Part III (*Learning and Adaptation*) concentrates on investigations which attempt to broaden the applicability of a system – or to reduce the necessity of interactive tuning phases – by machine learning approaches and by automatic parametric optimization. Part IV (*Representation and Inference*) collects contributions which study the exploitation of representations for inference processes, in particular inference processes based on (variants of) predicate logic. Part V (*Control and Systems Integration*) specifically addresses problem areas which become important due to the necessity to integrate a large and diverse set of processes into a coherent system. In this context, it becomes unavoidable to cope with limited resources – rather than having the system bogging down at unexpected times without reasons discernible from the outside. An attempt is made in a concluding section (Part VI) to condense the insights from this seminar into a small number of theses which could provide a starting point for future investigations.

Deliberately, no attempt is made at this point to condense even further the information formulated by authors of contributions to this volume in abstracts, introductory and concluding sections. Readers are invited to browse and most likely will find that the time spent doing this will have been worthwhile.

Part I

Foundations of Cognitive Vision Systems

The Space of Cognitive Vision

David Vernon

DIST, University of Genova, Italy
`vernon@ieee.org`

Abstract. Cognitive vision is an area that is not yet well-defined, in the sense that one can unambiguously state what issues fall under its purview and what considerations do not. Neither is there unequivocal consensus on the right approach to take in addressing these issues — there isn't a definitive universally-accepted scientific theory with 'gaps in understanding' that merely need to be plugged. On the contrary, there are clearly competing viewpoints and many poorly-understood issues (such as the point where vision stops and cognition starts). Depending on how you choose to view or define cognitive vision, there are many points of departure, some based squarely in artificial intelligence and image processing, others in developmental psychology and cognitive neuroscience, and others yet in cognitive robotics and autonomous systems theory. This paper is an attempt to sketch a framework within which the complete domain of cognitive vision can be set, a framework that embraces all of the possible approaches that can be taken and that highlights common concerns as well as fundamental differences between the approaches. Our goal here is to define cognitive vision in a way that avoids alienating any particular community and to state what the options are. While we will note in passing possible strengths and weaknesses of the various approaches, this paper will not attempt to argue in favour of one approach over another.

2.1 The Background to Cognitive Vision

It is nearly forty years since Roberts first published the results of his seminal attempts to construct a computer vision system [374]. Since then, computer vision has matured and undergone many stages in its evolution. From the blocks-world approaches of the sixties and early seventies [164, 201, 483, 419], to the knowledge-based and model-based approaches of the mid to late seventies [23, 171, 446, 54], the modular information processing approaches of the late seventies and early eighties with their strong emphasis on early vision [278, 30, 280, 283, 284, 282, 193, 281], the development of appearance-based vision in the nineties [81] – a decade that was perhaps distinguished more than anything by the creation of mathematically-sound robust early vision and the associated expansion of vision based on computational geometry [117, 175] – to the more recent probabilistic techniques and the increasingly-widespread use of machine learning [355]. On the way, computer vision has spawned a number of successful offshoots, such as machine vision for industrial inspection, the analysis of video data for remote monitoring of events, and the use of image analysis in the creation of special effects in the film

H.I. Christensen and H.-H. Nagel (Eds.): Cognitive Vision Systems, LNCS 3948, pp. 7–24, 2006.

industry. However, to date, the ultimate goal of creating a general-purpose vision system with anything close to the robustness and resilience of the human visual system remains as elusive as ever.

One of the more recent trends in computer vision research in the pursuit of human-like capability is the coupling of cognition and vision into cognitive computer vision. Unfortunately, it is apparent that the term cognitive computer vision means very different things to different people. For some, it means the explicit use of knowledge and reasoning together with sensory abstraction of data from a perceived environment; for others it implies the emergent behaviour of a physically-active system that learns to make perceptual sense of its environment as it interacts within that environment and as a consequence of that interaction. For others yet, it is a meaningless term in its own right and cannot be treated except as an intrinsic component of the process of cognition that, in turn, is an inherent feature of autonomous systems. Our goal here is to present all of these viewpoints in a single consistent framework:

1. To provide a definition of cognitive vision that is neutral with respect to possible approaches and to explain what capabilities might be provided by such a system;
2. To delineate the space of cognitive vision and characterize it in terms or dimensions that allow it to be mapped on to different approaches;
3. To highlight contentious and significant issues (*e.g.* the necessity for embodiment, the nature and need for representations, the nature and role of knowledge, the role of language, the inter-dependence of perception and action).

These are the issues to which we now turn.

2.2 Towards a Universal Definition of Cognitive Vision

There are several ways one can approach the definition of a discipline. One can take a functional approach, setting out the minimal tasks that a system should be able to carry out, or one can take an architectural approach, identifying the manner in which a system should be constructed and the functional modules that would be used in a typical system. Alternatively, one can adopt a behavioural but non-functional approach that identifies generic attributes, capabilities, and characteristics. A good definition should be neutral to any underlying model, otherwise it begs the research question and preempts the research agenda. Consequently, this rules out an architectural definition. A good definition should also be application-independent. This rules out a strictly functional definition, or at the very least necessitates that any functions be generic and typically common to all possible systems. Consequently, we will attempt to define cognitive vision using generic functionality (*i.e.* capability) and non-functional attributes.

We'll begin with the definition adopted by *ECVision* to date [12]:

> "Cognitive computer vision is concerned with integration and control of vision systems using explicit but not necessarily symbolic models of context, situation and goal-directed behaviour. Cognitive vision implies functionalities for knowledge representation, learning, reasoning about events & structures, recognition and categorization, and goal specification, all of which are concerned with the semantics of the relationship between the visual agent and its environment.'

Although this definition is useful, in that it focusses on many of the key issues, it depends a little too much on architectural issues (*e.g.* integration, control, functional modules) and it is not as neutral to underlying model(s) as perhaps it should be. That is, it strays from a definition of *what* cognitive vision is to a definition of *how* it is to be achieved. As we will see in Section 2.3, there are several competing approaches, not all of which are compatible with the one that is implicitly favoured in this definition. That said, however, it does provide us with a good starting point and the following is an attempt both to expand on it, drawing out the key issues even more, eliminating the model-dependent and architecture-specific components, and highlighting the generic functionalities and non-functional attributes.

A cognitive vision system can achieve the four levels of generic functionality of a computer vision system:[1]

1. *Detection* of an object or event in the visual field;
2. *Localization* of the position and extent of a detected entity;
3. *Recognition* of a localized entity by a labelling process;
4. *Understanding* or comprehending the role, context, and purpose of a recognized entity.[2]

It can engage in purposive goal-directed behaviour, adapting to unforeseen changes of the visual environment, and it can anticipate the occurrence of objects or events. It achieves these capabilities through:

1. a faculty for learning semantic knowledge (*i.e.* contextualized understanding of form and function), and for the development of perceptual strategies and behaviours;
2. the retention of knowledge about the environment, the cognitive system itself, and the relationship between the system and its environment;[3]
3. deliberation about objects and events in the environment, including the cognitive system itself.

This definition focusses on what constitutes a cognitive vision system, how it should behave, what it should be capable of achieving, and what are its primary characteristics. The first four points encapsulate generic functionality. The next set of issues deal with non-functional attributes, and the final three points suggest a way of spanning the space of cognitive vision.

The three non-functional characteristics of purposive behaviour, adaptability, and anticipation, taken together, allow a cognitive vision system to achieve certain goals, even in circumstances that were not expected when the system was being designed. This capacity for plastic resilient behaviour is one of the hallmarks of a cognitive vision system. The characteristic of anticipation is important as it requires the system to operate

---

[1] These four levels were suggested by John Tsotsos, York University, during the course of Dagstuhl Seminar 03441[73].

[2] Implicit in the fourth level is the concept of categorization: the assignment of an object or event to a meta-level class on some basis other than visual appearance alone.

[3] The distinction between environmental states, system states, and the environment-system relationship was introduced by Hans-Hellmut Nagel, Universität Karlsruhe, during the course of Dagstuhl Seminar 03441[73].

across a variety of time-scales, extending into the future, so that it is capable of more than reflexive stimulus-response behaviour.

The final three characteristics of cognitive vision — learning, memory, and deliberation — are all concerned with knowledge: its acquisition, storage, and usage. Knowledge is the key to cognitive vision. These three issues highlight the chief differentiating characteristics of cognitive vision *vis-à-vis* computer vision and, as we will see, allow us to define the space of cognitive vision in a way that is relevant to all the various approaches.

First, however, we must survey the different paradigms or approaches that attempt to model and effect these characteristics of cognitive vision.

2.3 A Review of Approaches to Cognition

If we are to understand in a comprehensive way what is meant by cognitive vision, we must address the issue of cognition. Unfortunately, there is no universally-accepted agreement on what cognition is and different research communities have fundamentally different perspectives on the matter.

Broadly speaking, we can identify two distinct approaches to cognition, each of which makes significantly different assumptions about the nature of cognition, the purpose or function of cognition, and the manner in which cognition is achieved. These are:

1. the *cognitivist* approach based on information processing symbolic representational systems;
2. the *emergent systems* approach, embracing connectionist systems, dynamical systems, and enactive systems.

Cognitivist approaches correspond to the classical and still prevalent view that 'cognition is a type of computation' which operates on symbolic representations, and that cognitive systems 'instantiate such representations physically as cognitive codes and ... their behaviour is a causal consequence of operations carried out on these codes' [360]. Connectionist, dynamical, and enactive systems can be grouped together under the general heading of emergent systems that, in contradistinction to the cognitivist view, argues against the information processing view of cognition as 'symbolic, rational, encapsulated, structured, and algorithmic', and argues in favour of one that treats cognition as emergent, self-organizing, and dynamical [447, 219].

2.3.1 Symbolic Information Processing Representational Cognitivist Models

Cognitive science has its origins in cybernetics (1943-53), following the first attempts to formalize what had to that point been metaphysical treatments of cognition. The intention of the early cyberneticians was to create a science of mind, based on logic. Examples of progenitors include McCulloch and Pitts and their seminal paper 'A logical calculus immanent in nervous activity' [294]. This initial wave in the development of a science of cognition was followed in 1956 by the development of an approach referred to as *cognitivism*. Cognitivism asserts that cognition can be defined as computations on symbolic representations, *i.e.* cognition is information processing [471]: rule-based manipulation of symbols. Much of artificial intelligence research is carried out on the assumption of the correctness of the cognitivist hypothesis. Its counterpart in the study of natural biologically-implemented (*e.g.* human) cognitive systems is cognitive psychology which uses 'computationally characterizable representations' as the main explanatory tool [471]. The entire discipline of cognitive science is often identified with this particular approach [219]: that cognition involves computations defined over internal representations *qua* knowledge, in a process whereby information about the world is abstracted by perception, and represented using some appropriate symbolic data-structure, reasoned about, and then used to plan and act in the world. This approach has also been labelled by many as the *information processing* (or symbol manipulation) approach to cognition [279, 176, 352, 222, 447, 219] whereby perception and cognition entail computations defined over explicit internal representations. It is undoubtedly the prevalent approach to cognition today but, as we will see, it is by no means the only paradigm in cognitive science.

For cognitivist systems, cognition is representational in a strong and particular sense: it entails the manipulation of explicit symbolic representations of the state and behaviour of the external world to facilitate appropriate, adaptive, anticipatory, and effective interaction, and the storage of the knowledge gained from this experience to reason even more effectively in the future. Vision and perception are concerned with the abstraction of isomorphic spatio-temporal representations of the external world from sensory data. Reasoning itself is symbolic: a procedural process whereby explicit representations of an external world are manipulated to infer likely changes in the configuration of the world (and attendant perception of that altered configuration) arising from causal actions.

The term *representation* is heavily laden with meaning. As Davis *et al.* noted [93], knowledge representations entail several issues. First, that the representation is a 'surrogate' or substitute for a thing itself; second, it involves a set of ontological commitments and therefore defines the way we think of or conceive of the world. Third, it is a 'fragmentary theory of intelligent reasoning' and a medium for efficient computation. Finally, representations provide a medium for human expression.

Since the representations deployed in a cognitivist system are the idealized (descriptive) product of a human designer, they can be directly accessed and understood or interpreted by a human and there is no requirement for embodiment to facilitate the development of semantic knowledge. However, one can argue that this is also the key limiting factor of cognitivist vision systems: these programmer-dependent representations effectively bias the system (or 'blind' the system [494]) and constrain it to an idealized description that is dependent on and a consequence of the cognitive requirements of human activity. This works as long as the system doesn't have to stray too far from the conditions under which these observations were made. The further one does stray, the larger the 'semantic gap' [429] between perception and possible interpretation, a gap that is normally plugged by the embedding of (even more) programmer knowledge or the enforcement of expectation-driven constraints [340] to render a system practicable in a given space of problems.

It is easy to see how this approach usually then goes hand-in-hand with the fundamental assumption that 'the world we perceive is isomorphic with our perceptions of it as a geometric environment' [416]. The goal of cognition, for a cognitivist, is to reason symbolically about these representations in order to effect intelligent, adaptive, anticipatory, goal-directed, behaviour. Typically, this approach to cognition will deploy an arsenal of techniques including machine learning, probabilistic modelling, and other techniques intended to deal with the inherent uncertain, time-varying, and incomplete nature of the sensory data that is being used to drive this representational framework.

2.3.2 Emergent Approaches

The next phase in the development of cognitive science was based on emergent systems: systems epitomized by connectionist and dynamical approaches in which cognition is viewed as an emergent property of a network of component elements. Emergence is presented as an alternative to symbol manipulation.

From the perspective of emergent systems, cognition is a process of self-organization whereby the system is continually re-constituting itself in real-time to maintain its operational identity through moderation of mutual system-environment interaction and co-determination. Vision and perception are concerned with the acquisition of visual sensory data to enable effective action and, significantly, are functionally dependent on the richness of the action interface.

Connectionist Models

Connectionist models had their genesis in the study of artificial neural networks and self-organizing systems, *e.g.* the perceptron built by F. Rosenblatt in 1958. However, it lay dormant for some 30 years until a rekindling of interest in artificial neural networks in the late '70s and '80s in the work of Grossberg, Linsker, and many others. One of the motivations for work on emergent systems was disaffection with the sequential and localized character of symbol-manipulation based cognitivism. Emergent systems, on the other hand, depend on parallel and distributed architectures which are biologically more plausible. One of the key features of emergent systems, in general, and connectionism, in particular, is that 'the system's connectivity becomes inseparable *from its history of transformations*, and related to the kind of task defined for the system' [471]. Furthermore, symbols play no role.[4] Whereas in the cognitivist approach the symbols are distinct from what they stand for, in the connectionist approach, meaning relates to the global state of the system and actually the meaning is something attributed by an external third-party observer to the correspondence of a system state with that of the world in which the emergent system is embedded.

Connectionist approaches are for the most part associative learning systems in which the learning phase is either unsupervised (self-organizing) or supervised (trained). For example, the association of proprioceptive and exteroceptive stimuli can enable a Kohonen

---

[4] It would be more accurate to say that symbols should play no role since it has been noted that connectionist systems often fall back in the cognitivist paradigm by treating neural weights as a distributed symbolic representation [465].

neural network, controlling a robot arm, to learn hand-eye coordination so that the arm can reach for and track a visually-presented target. No *a priori* model of arm kinematics or image characteristics need be assumed [210, 298]. It has also been shown that a multilayered neural network with Hebb-like connectivity update rules can self-organize to produce feature-analyzing capabilities similar to those of the first few processing stages of the mammalian visual system (*e.g.* centre-surround cells and orientation-selective cells) [260].

Dynamical Systems Models

A dynamical system is an open dissipative non-linear non-equilibrium system: a system in the sense of a large number of interacting components with large number of degrees of freedom, dissipative in the sense that it diffuses energy (its phase space decreases in volume with time implying preferential sub-spaces), non-equilibrium in the sense that it is unable to maintain structure or function without external sources of energy, material, information (hence, open). The non-linearity is crucial: dissipation is not uniform and a small number of the system's degrees of freedom contribute to behaviour. These are termed *order parameters* (or *collective variables*). It is this ability to characterize a high-dimensional system with a low-dimensional model that is one of the features that distinguishes dynamical systems from connectionist systems.

Certain conditions must prevail before a system qualifies as a cognitive dynamical system. The components of the system must be related and interact with one another: any change in one component or aspect of the system must be dependent on and only on the states of the other components: 'they must be interactive and self contained' [465]. As we will see shortly, this is very redolent of the requirement for operational closure in enactive systems, the topic of the next section.

The key position of advocates of the dynamical systems approach to cognition is that motoric and perceptual systems are both dynamical systems, each of which self-organizes into meta-stable patterns of behaviour. 'Perceiving is not strictly speaking in the animal or an achievement of the animal's nervous system, but rather is a process in an animal-environment system' [219]. Perception-action coordination can also be characterized as a dynamical system.

Proponents of dynamical systems point to the fact that they provide one directly with many of the characteristics inherent in natural cognitive systems such as multi-stability, adaptability, pattern formation and recognition, intentionality, and learning. These are achieved purely as a function of dynamical laws and consequent self-organization through bifurcations and hysteresis in behavioural states, and a number of other dynamical properties such as intermittency (relative coordination).

Significantly, dynamical systems allow for the development of higher order cognitive functions in a straightforward manner, at least in principle. For example, intentionality — purposive or goal-directed behaviour — is achieved by the superposition of an intentional potential function on the intrinsic potential function [219]. Similarly, learning is viewed as the modification of already-existing behavioural patterns in the direction to be learned. It occurs in a historical context and the entire attractor layout (the phase-space configuration) of the dynamical system is modified. Thus, learning changes the whole system as a new attractor is developed. Dynamical models can account for several non-trivial behaviours that require the integration of visual stimuli and motoric control. These include the perception of affordances, perception of time to contact, and figure-ground bi-stability [229, 147, 148, 485, 219].

The implications of dynamical models are many: as noted in [447], 'cognition is non-symbolic, nonrepresentational and all mental activity is emergent, situated, historical, and embodied'. It is also socially constructed, meaning that certain levels of cognition emerge from the dynamical interaction of between cognitive agents. Furthermore, dynamical cognitive systems are, of necessity, embodied. This requirement arises directly from the fact that the dynamics depend on self-organizing processes whereby the system differentiates itself as a distinct entity through its dynamical configuration and its interactive exploration of the environment.

One of key issues in dynamical systems is that cognitive processes are temporal processes that 'unfold' in real-time and synchronously with events in their environment. This strong requirement for synchronous development in the context of its environment again echoes the enactive systems approach set out in the next section. It is significant for two reasons. First, it places a strong limitation on the rate at which the ontogenic[5] learning of the cognitive system can proceed: it is constrained by the speed of coupling (*i.e.* the interaction) and not by the speed at which internal changes can occur [494]. Natural cognitive systems have a learning cycle measured in weeks, months, and years and, while it might be possible to collapse it into minutes and hours for an artificial system because of increases in the rate of internal adaptation and change, it cannot be reduced below the time-scale of the interaction (or structural coupling; see next section). If the system has to develop a cognitive ability that, *e.g.*, allows it to anticipate or predict action and events that occur over an extended time-scale (*e.g.* hours), it will take at least that length of time to learn. Second, taken together with the requirement for embodiment, we see that the consequent historical and situated nature of the systems means that one cannot short-circuit the ontogenic development. Specifically, you can't bootstrap an emergent dynamical system into an advanced state of learned behaviour.

Connectionist approaches differ from dynamical systems in a number of ways [219, 447, 465]. Suffice it here to note that the connectionist system is often defined by a general differential equation which is actually a schema that defines the operation of many (neural) units. That is, the differential equation applies to each unit and each unit is just a replication of a common type. This also means that there will be many independent state variables, one for each unit. Dynamical systems, on the other hand, are not made up of individual units all having the same defining equation and can't typically be so decomposed. Typically, there will be a small number of state variables that describe the behaviour of the system as a whole.

Enactive Systems Models

The last phase in the development of cognitive science comprises the study of enactive systems. Enaction is again an approach that is not based on the creation or use of representations. Significantly, cognitivism, by definition, involves a view of cognition

---

[5] Ontogeny is concerned with the development of the system over its lifetime.

that requires the representation of a given pre-determined world [471, 465]. Enaction adopts a critically different stance: cognition is a process whereby the issues that are important for the continued existence of the cognitive entity are brought out or enacted: co-determined by the entity as it interacts with the environment in which it is embedded. Thus, nothing is 'pre-given', and hence there is no need for representations. Instead there is an enactive interpretation: a context-based choosing of relevance. Enaction questions the entrenched assumption of scientific tradition that the world *as we experience it* is independent of the cognitive system ('the knower'). Instead, knower and known 'stand in relation to each other as mutual specification: they arise together' [471]. This type of statement is normally anathema to scientists as it seems to be positing a position of extreme subjectivism, the very antithesis of modern science. However, this is not what is intended at all. On the contrary, the enactive approach is an attempt to avoid the problems of both the realist (representationalist) and the solipsist (ungrounded subjectivism) positions. The only condition that is required of an enactive system is *effective action*: that it permits the continued integrity of the system involved. It is essentially a very neutral position, assuming only that there is the basis of order in the environment in which the cognitive system is embedded. From this point of view, cognition is exactly the process by which that order or some aspect of it is uncovered (or constructed) by the system. This immediately allows that there are different forms of reality (or relevance) that are dependent directly on the nature of the dynamics making up the cognitive system. Clearly, this is not a solipsist position of ungrounded subjectivism, but neither is it the commonly-held position of unique — representable — realism.

The enactive systems research agenda stretches back to the early 1970s in the work of computational biologists Maturana and Varela and has been taken up by others, even by some in the main-stream of classical AI [290, 291, 293, 470, 471, 494, 292].

The goal of enactive systems research is the complete treatment of the nature and emergence of autonomous, cognitive, social systems. It is founded on the concept of autopoiesis – literally *self-production* – whereby a system emerges as a coherent systemic entity, distinct from its environment, as a consequence of processes of self-organization. Three orders of system can be distinguished.

First-order autopoietic systems correspond to cellular entities that achieve a physical identity through structural coupling with their environment. As the system couples with its environment, it interacts with it in the sense that the environmental perturbations trigger structural changes 'that permit it to continue operating'.

Second-order systems are meta-cellular system that exhibit autopoiesis through operational closure in their organization; their identity is specified by a network of dynamic processes whose effects do not leave the network. Such systems also engage in structural coupling with their environment, this time through a nervous system that enables the association of many internal states with the different interactions in which the organism is involved.

Third-order systems exhibit (third-order) coupling between second-order (*i.e.* cognitive) systems, *i.e.* between distinct cognitive agents. These third-order couplings allow a recurrent (common) ontogenic drift in which the systems are reciprocally-coupled. The resultant structural adaptation – mutually shared by the coupled systems – gives rise to new phenomonological domains: language and a shared epistemology that reflects (but not abstracts) the common medium in which they are coupled. Such systems are capable of three types of behaviour: (i) the instinctive behaviours that derive from the organizational principles that define it as an autopoietic system (and that emerge from the phylogenic evolution of the system), (ii) ontogenic behaviours that derive from the development of the system over its lifetime, and (iii) communicative behaviours that are a result of the third-order structural coupling between members of the society of entities. Linguistic behaviours are the intersection of ontogenic and communication behaviours and they facilitate the creation of a common understanding of the shared world that is the environment of the coupled systems. That is, *language is the emergent consequence of the third-order structural coupling of a socially-cohesive group of cognitive entities.*

The core of the enactive approach is that cognition is a process whereby a system identifies regularities as a consequence of co-determination of the cognitive activities themselves, such that the integrity of the system is preserved. In this approach, the nervous system (and a cognitive agent) does not 'pick up information' from the environment and therefore the popular metaphor of calling the brain an 'information processing device' is 'not only ambiguous but patently wrong' [292].

A key postulate of enactive systems is that reasoning, as we commonly conceive it, is the consequence of recursive application of the linguistic descriptive abilities (developed as a consequence of the consensual co-development of an epistemology in a society of phylogenically-identical agents) to the cognitive agent itself. This is significant: reasoning in this sense is a descriptive phenomena and is quite distinct from the mechanism (structural coupling and operational closure) by which the system/agent develops its cognitive and linguistic behaviours. Since language (and all inter-agent communication) is a manifestation of high-order cognition, specifically structural coupling and co-determination of consensual understanding amongst phylogenically-identical and ontogenically-compatible agents, reasoning is actually an artefact of higher-order social cognitive systems.

As with dynamical systems, enactive systems operate in synchronous real-time: cognitive processes must proceed synchronously with events in the systems environment as a direct consequence of the structural coupling and co-determination between system and environment. And, again, enactive systems are necessarily embodied systems. This is a direct consequence of the requirement of structural coupling of enactive systems. There is no semantic gap in emergent systems (connectionist, dynamical, or enactive): the system builds its own understanding as it develops and cognitive understanding emerges by co-determined exploratory learning. Overall, enactive systems offer a framework by which successively richer orders of cognitive capability can be achieved, from autonomy of a system through to the emergence of linguistic and communicative behaviours in societies of cognitive agents.

While the enactive systems agenda is very compelling, and is frequently referred to by researchers in, for example, developmental psychology, it hasn't achieved great acceptance in main-stream computational cognitive science and artificial intelligence. The main reason for this is that it is more a meta-theory than a theory *per se*: it is a philosophy of science but it doesn't offer any formal models by which cognitive systems can be either analysed or synthesized. However, it does have a great deal in common with the research agenda in dynamical systems which *is* a scientific theory but is perhaps lacking the ability to prescribe how higher-order cognitive functions can be realized. The subsumption of the tenets of enactive systems into dynamical systems approaches may well provide the way forward for both communities, and for emergent approaches in general.

Finally, it is worth noting that the self-organizing constructivist approaches of both dynamical systems and enactive systems is bolstered by separate recent results which have shown that a biological organism's perception of its body and the dimensionality and geometry of the space in which it is embedded can be deduced (learned or discovered) by the organism from an analysis of the dependencies between motoric commands and consequent sensory data, without any knowledge or reference to an external model of the world or the physical structure of the organism [347, 348]. Thus, the perceived structure of reality could therefore be a consequence of an effort on the part of brains to account for the dependency between their inputs and their outputs in terms of a small number of parameters. Thus, there is in fact no need to rely on the classical idea of an *a priori* model of the external world that is mapped by the sensory apparatus to 'some kind of objective archetype'; that is, there is no need to rely on the cognitivist model of matters. On the contrary, the conceptions of space, geometry, and the world that the body distinguishes itself from arises from the sensorimotor interaction of the system. Furthermore, it is the analysis of the sensory consequences of motor commands that gives rise to these concepts. Significantly, the motor commands are *not* derived as a function of the sensory data. The primary issue is that sensory and motor information are treated simultaneously, and not from either a stimulus perspective or a motor control point of view.

2.3.3 Hybrid Models

Recently, some work has been done on approaches which combine aspects of the emergent systems and information processing & symbolic representational systems [152, 153, 155]. These hybrid approaches have their roots in strong criticism of the use of explicit programmer-based knowledge in the creation of artificially-intelligent systems [106] and in the development of active 'animate' perceptual systems [26] in which perception-action behaviours become the focus, rather than the perceptual abstraction of representations. Such systems still use representations and representational invariances but it has been argued that these representations can only be constructed by the system itself as it interacts with and explores the world. More recently, this approach has hardened even further with the work of Granlund who asserts that 'our conscious perception of the external world is in terms of the actions we can perform upon the objects around us' [152]. His is an approach of action-dependent vision in which objects should be represented as 'invariant combinations of percepts and responses where the invariances (which are not restricted to geometric properties) need to be learned through interaction rather than specified or programmed *a priori*'. Thus, a system's ability to interpret objects and the external world is dependent on its ability to flexibly interact with it and interaction is an organizing mechanism that drives a coherence of association between perception and action. There are two important consequences of this approach of action-dependent perception. First, one cannot have any meaningful access to the internal semantic representations, and second cognitive systems must be embodied (at least during the learning phase) [153]. For Granlund, action precedes perception and

Table 2.1. Attributes of different approaches to cognition (after [447] and [471])

Approaches to Cognition			
Cognitivist	**Connectionist**	**Dynamical**	**Enactive**
What is cognition?			
Symbolic computation: rule-based manipulation of symbols	The emergence of global states in a network of simple components	A history of activity that brings forth change and activity	Effective action: history of structural coupling that enacts (brings forth) a world
How does it work?			
Through any device that can manipulate symbols	Through local rules and changes in the connectivity of the elements	Through the self-organizing processes of interconnected sensori-motor subnetworks	Through a network of interconnected elements capable of structural changes
What does a good cognitive system do?			
Represent the stable truths of the real world	Develop emergent properties that yield stable solutions to tasks	Become an active and adaptive part of an ongoing and continually changing world	Become a part of an existing world of meaning (ontogeny) or shape a new one (phylogeny)

'cognitive systems need to acquire information about the external world through learning or association' ... 'Ultimately, a key issue is to achieve behavioural plasticity, *i.e.*, the ability of an embodied system to learn to do a task it was not explicitly designed for.' Thus, action-dependent systems are in many ways consistent with emergent systems while still exploiting programmer-centred representations. The identification of these representations (and processes that generate them) could be construed as being equivalent to the phylogenic specification of an emergent system, an issue that has yet to be resolved.

To summarize, Table 2.1 (after [447] and [471]) contrasts the four approaches (the cognitivist and the three emergent approaches) under three broad headings: *What is cognition? How does it work?* and *What does a good cognitive system do?*

2.4 The Space of Cognitive Vision: Knowledge & Memory, Deliberation, and Learning

It is clear from the previous section that there are several distinct and fundamentally different approaches to cognition. If we are to tackle the problem of cognitive vision in a consistent and coherent manner, we need to embed these approaches in a paradigm-independent framework that spans the entire spectrum of approaches, makes explicit their position in the spectrum, but also that highlights technical issues of mutual relevance. It is proposed that, leaving aside the four levels of generic visual functionality identified in Section 2.2, the three concerns of knowledge & memory, deliberation, and learning effectively span the space of cognitive vision.

2.4.1 Knowledge & Memory

Knowledge – its acquisition, retention, and use to deliberate about tasks and situations, and to achieve goals – is the central issue in cognitive systems. Two questions arise: where does the knowledge come from, and what relationship does it imply between the cognitive agent and its environment?

At one end of the spectrum, we have the information processing representational approach: knowledge is provided in symbolic form by human designers and possibly refined through learning, either off-line or on-line. These systems are often quite brittle: because their representations are based on the representational and processing axioms of an external designer, they often fail when their domain of discourse strays far from the domain for which they were designed.

Further along this spectrum, we have hybrid systems that use generic representational schemes (*e.g.* sub-space methods such as ISA, ICA, PCA) that are populated entirely by the agent through incremental unsupervised learning, either off-line or on-line. Deliberative cognitive behaviour is designed in, since the designer controls the link between the perceptual-motor skills and the knowledge representations. On the other hand, the system learns the actual knowledge for itself. Thus, its cognitive behaviour is a function of agent-specific and agent-acquired knowledge and pre-programmed perception-reasoning-action strategies. These types of approaches probably represent the state of the art in modern cognitive computer vision systems, both in terms of engineering maturity and functional capability.

Further along again, we move into the emergent systems space populated by, *inter alia*, connectionist approaches and dynamical systems approaches. These have no 'representations' in the sense that there are no symbols that refer to world-based objects and situations, but they do have states that encapsulate knowledge derived by the system in the historical context of its ontogenic development. In collectives or societies of cognitive agents with linguistic and communicative abilities, it is possible for a cognitive agent to describe its visual environment. These descriptions are effectively symbolic representations but they are a consequence of social cognitive behaviour, *not* the mechanism by which cognition emerges (in contradistinction to the cognitivist approach) .

2.4.2 Deliberation

Briefly, one can distinguish between 'non-thinking' cognitive agents (with reflexive autonomous behaviour), 'thinking' cognitive agents (with anticipatory adaptive behaviour), and 'thinking about thinking' cognitive agents (with the ability to explicitly reflect on their cognitive processes). At the information processing representationalist cognitivist end of the spectrum, deliberation is identical with symbolic reasoning. Deliberation *is* the operation on symbolic information representations by processes of logical reasoning. Thus thinking and thinking about thinking can be viewed as some formal process of symbol manipulation. This is exactly the cognitivist hypothesis.

On the other hand, emergent systems take a fundamentally different view. Non-thinking agents don't deliberate; their reflexive action is a consequence of their phylogenic configuration (*i.e.* their innate perceptual-motor behaviours). Thinking cognitive agents engage in weak deliberation: their anticipatory and adaptive behaviour emerges because of the evolution of its state-space as a consequence of its real-time co-development with its environment (*i.e.* ontogenic learning). Strong deliberation ("if I do this, then this will happen") arises in agents that can think about thinking (or think about thoughts, including possible actions). The emergence of this possibility arises when a society of cognitive agents with linguistic skill co-evolve and develop a common epistemological understanding of their world; the linguistic skills and the epistemological constructs give rise to the possibility of descriptions of observations, which when turned inward recursively on the cognitive agent, facilitates thinking about thinking, or exactly the reasoned discourse that we commonly identify (incorrectly) with cognition: such reasoned discourse – thinking – is an artifact of the systems socio-linguistic ontogenic development in a society of such agents and is not a causal process in the emergence of cognition.

2.4.3 Learning

The issue of learning is central to cognitive systems. Unfortunately, it is also an ill-posed concept in the sense that what learning means depends on which view of cognition you hold. Different approaches to cognition imply different assumptions and different processes. That said, one can define learning in a general way that is not specific to a given paradigm as the adaptive change in the state of the cognitive system as a result of a temporal process whereby the system uses experience to improve its performance at some defined behaviour.

For systems built around the cognitivist information processing representational view of cognition, learning typically involves the alteration of some representational data-structure. Learning can be accomplished in many ways using, for example, probabilistic (e.g. Bayesian) inference techniques or non-probabilistic approaches such as Dempster-Shafer transferrable belief models. However, there may be other approaches and the literature on machine learning is vast and growing.

For emergent systems, learning is accomplished in a manner that depends on the technique being deployed. In dynamical systems, such those advocated by developmental psychologists, the entire attractor layout of the dynamical system is modified, even in a single instance of learning. That is, learning changes the whole system. Learning moulds the intrinsic dynamics. Once learning is achieved, the memorized or learned pattern constitutes a new attractor. It is significant that learning is a specific modification of already existing behavioural patterns. This implies that learning occurs in the historical context of an individual and is dependent on the history of experiences of the learner. That is, learning is situated, historical, and developmental.

In the same way, for enactive systems, as the system couples with its environment, it interacts with it in the sense that the environmental perturbations trigger structural changes that permit it to continue operating. These changes are governed by the operational closure of autopoietic organization. An observer of the system would describe the structural changes that occur in the (nervous system) of the autopoietic entity as a learning process; however, from the perspective of the entity itself, there is just the ongoing natural structural drift: no information is picked up from the environment, but the system evolves in co-determination with the environment as it interacts with it.

Connectionist approaches distinguish several types of learning: 'learning-by-doing' or unsupervised associative learning, supervised learning (intelligent teaching with explicit input-output exemplars), unsupervised learning (clustering algorithms), and reinforcement learning (use of a cost function). 'Learning-by-doing' can be traced to Piaget, who founded the constructivist school of cognitive development in the 1940's [298]. According to this view of constructivism, knowledge is not imparted *a priori* but is discovered and constructed by a child though active manipulation of the environment.

In general, for emergent approaches, one can view learning as the ontogenic development of the cognitive agent, irrespective of how that development is achieved. Certainly, it is dependent to some extent on the phylogenic make-up of the system and the innate (reflexive) behaviours.

Winograd and Flores [494] capture the essence of developmental emergent learning very succinctly:

> 'Learning is not a process of accumulation of representations of the environment; it is a continuous process of transformation of behaviour through continuous change in the capacity of the nervous system to synthesize it. Recall does not depend on the indefinite retention of a structural invariant that represents an entity (an idea, image, or symbol), but on the functional ability of the system to create, when certain recurrent conditions are given, a behaviour that satisfies the recurrent demands or that the observer would class as a reenacting of a previous one'.

2.5 Some Implications of the Different Approaches

Two of the most important questions in cognitive vision and cognition are:

1. Can you engineer knowledge and understanding into a system, providing it with the semantic information required to operate adaptively and achieve robust and innovative goal-directed behaviour?
2. Does a cognitive system necessarily have to be embodied (in the sense of being a physical mobile exploratory agent capable of manipulative and social interaction with its environment, including other agents)?

It is clear that the answers to these questions will be different depending on who you ask. The person who subscribes to the cognitivist approach will answer respectively, 'yes, you can engineer knowledge into a system' and 'no, it doesn't need to be embodied'. Conversely, a person working with emergent systems (including connectionist systems, dynamical systems, enactive systems, and hybrid approaches) will answer respectively, 'no, you can't engineer knowledge into a system' and 'yes, it does need to be embodied'.

For those adopting the cognitivist approach, knowledge and world (scene) representations are primary: they allow explicit description of situations and structure, and of spatio-temporal behaviours. Typically, they deal with categories and categorization by focussing on form rather than function. Their tools include qualitative descriptions and conceptual knowledge, reasoning (over representations), inference over partial information, and experience/expectation driven interpretation. Interaction with humans is achievable exactly because the information representations are consistent with the (human) system designer's pre-conceptions. Motoric control is optional because these systems don't necessarily have to be embodied: knowledge, framed in the concepts of the designer, can be transplanted in and doesn't have to be developed by the system itself through exploratory investigation of the environment. Hybrid cognitivist systems, however, do exploit learning (on-line and unsupervised) to augment or even supplant the *a priori* designed-in knowledge and thereby achieve a greater degree of adaptiveness, reconfigurability, and robustness. Consequently, embodiment, while not strictly necessary in this approach, does offer an additional degree of freedom in the research agenda. In this case, agent intentions (and intentional models) require robust perception and learning to build the models, and robust reasoning capabilities to produce sensible communication with humans and/or its motoric interface. Ultimately, knowledge is used both to pre-configure a system for operation in a particular domain and to provide it with the constraints required to render the problem tractable.

It has been argued, however, that this approach to cognition is inherently limited. Since 'the essence of intelligence [*qua* cognition] is to act appropriately when there is no simple pre-definition of the problem or the space of states in which to search for a solution' [494] and since, in the cognitivist approach, the programmer sets up the system with a systematic correspondence between representations and the programmer's entities, the cognitive vision system is effectively blinded because the programmer's success as a cognitive entity in his or her own right goes far beyond the reflective conscious experience of things in the world. Thus, according to this argument, the cognitivist approach is inherently incapable of exhibiting fully-fledged cognitive capabilities, although as pointed out several times, it can of course be used to develop useful cognitive capabilities in circumstances which are well-defined and well-bounded. In this case, cognition requires either expectation-driven constraints or *a priori* programmer knowledge to render the cognitive vision problem tractable.

There are also several consequences of adopting the emergent systems approach. Phylogenic development (the evolution of the system configuration from generation to generation) gives rise to the system's innate reflexive capabilities. Ontogenic development (the adaptation and learning of the system over its lifetime) gives rise to the cognitive capabilities that we seek. Since we don't have the luxury of having evolutionary timescales to allow phylogenic emergence of a cognitive system, we must somehow identify a minimal phylogenic state of the system. Operationally, this means that we must identify and effect a mechanism for the minimal reflexive behaviours required for subsequent ontogenic development of cognitive behaviour. For dynamical systems, this is equivalent to the identification of the collective variables and the control parameters. A major research issue is how to accomplish this without falling back into conventional cognitivism: system identification based on representations derived from external observers.

A prerequisite condition for the emergence of cognitive systems (either connectionist, dynamical, or enactive) is operational (organizational) closure: the system components must be related and interact with one another and any change in one component or aspect of the system must be dependent on and only on the states of the other components. This provides some boundary conditions on the identification of admissible architectures.

The descriptions of a cognitive system are a function of its interaction with the environment and the richness of its action interface. This implies that a cognitive system must have non-trivial manipulative and exploratory capabilities.

Cognitive systems can only engage in linguistic communication with agents that have shared the same ontogenic developmental learning experience. This poses a significant hurdle for proponents of emergent systems since the overt purpose of an artificial cognitive agent is to engage in behaviours that are relevant to human users.

The requirement of real-time synchronous system-environment coupling implies strong constraints on the rate at which ontogenic learning can proceed and necessitates historical, situated, and embodied development that can't be short-circuited or interrupted. Again, this is a difficult issue for empirical research in cognitive systems: it would be more than a little frustrating to develop a cognitive system after many days of developmental learning only to have it disappear because of a power glitch.

2.6 Conclusion

Broadly speaking, there are essentially two approaches to cognition:

1. The cognitivist symbolic information processing representational approach;
2. The emergent systems approach (connectionism, dynamical systems, enactive systems).

The one thing that is common to both is the issue of knowledge and thinking. However, each approach takes a very different stance on knowledge.

The cognitivist approach:

- takes a predominantly static view of knowledge, represented by symbol systems that *refer* (in a bijective and isomorphic sense) to the physical reality that is external to the cognitive agent;
- invokes processes of reasoning on the representations (that have been provided by the perceptual apparatus);
- subsequently plans actions in order to achieve programmed goals;
- and can be best epitomized by the classical perception-reasoning-action cycle.

The emergent systems approach:

- takes a predominantly dynamic or process view of knowledge, and views it more as a collection of abilities that encapsulate 'how to do' things;
- is therefore subservient to the cognitive agent and dependent on the agent and its environmental context;
- embraces both short time-scale (reflexive and adaptive) behaviours and longer time-scale (deliberative and cognitive) behaviours, with behaviours being predominantly characterized by perceptual-motor skills;
- is focussed on the emergence (or appearance) of cognition through the co-development of the agent and its environment in real-time.

There is one other crucial difference between the two approaches. In the cognitivist symbolic information processing representational paradigm, perceptual capacities are configured as a consequence of observations, descriptions, and models of an external designer (*i.e.* they are fundamentally based in the frame-of-reference of the designer). In the emergent systems paradigm, the perceptual capacities are a consequence of an historic enactive embodied development and, consequently, are dependent on the richness of the motoric interface of the cognitive agent with its world. That is, the action space defines the perceptual space and thus is fundamentally based in the frame-of-reference of the agent. A central tenet of the enactive emergent approaches is that true cognition can only be created in a developmental agent-centred manner, through interaction, learning, and co-development with the environment.

So much for differences. There is, however, also some common ground. In our attempt at a universal definition of cognitive vision, we identified three categories of requirements for a cognitive vision system:

1. the four generic visual capabilities of detection, localization, recognition, and understanding;
2. the non-functional attributes of purposive goal-directed behaviour;
3. the three knowledge-based faculties of learning, memory, and deliberation that we subsequently used to span the space of cognitive vision.

Regarding visual capability, we noted that all emergent approaches face the problem that the evolution of a cognitive vision system *ab initio* is simply not feasible and, consequently, there is a need to identify the minimal phylogenic structure of the system, *i.e.* a minimal set of visual (and motoric) capabilities. Thus, both emergent cognitive vision and cognitivist cognitive vision, as well as the hybrid approaches, need solid robust image processing to facilitate the four generic visual capabilities and it is likely that visual processes are transferrable between paradigms.

Although the non-functional attributes are inevitably going to be paradigm-dependent, it remains to be seen how much each paradigm overlaps in the three dimensions of learning, memory, and deliberation. One thing is certain: there is a much better chance of spotting overlaps and common ground if everyone is using the same framework. The hope is that this paper will go some way towards creating that framework.

Acknowledgments

The discussions at Dagstughl seminar 03441 [73] on cognitive vision systems were pivotal in shaping the ideas presented in this paper, alerting us to the necessity of keeping open a broad research agenda without losing the focus on well-engineered computer vision systems.

Discussions with Giulio Sandini and Giorgio Metta, University of Genova, were also extremely helpful in sifting out the key issues and showing a way to actually achieve an inclusive and realistic framework that is, hopefully, relevant to all.

This work was funded by the European Commission as part of the European research network for cognitive computer vision systems — *ECVision* — under the Information Society Technologies (IST) programme, project IST-2001-35454.

3

Cognitive Vision Needs Attention to Link Sensing with Recognition

John K. Tsotsos

Dept. of Computer Science & Engineering
and
Centre for Vision Research,
York University, Toronto, Canada
tsotsos@cs.yorku.ca

Abstract. "Cognitive computer vision is concerned with integration and control of vision systems using explicit but not necessarily symbolic models of context, situation and goaldirected behaviour" (Vernon 2003 [473]). This paper discusses one small but critical slice of a cognitive computer vision system, that of visual attention. The presentation begins with a brief discussion on a definition for attention followed by an enumeration of the different ways in which attention should play a role in computer vision and cognitive vision systems in particular. The Selective Tuning Model is then overviewed with an emphasis on its components that are most relevant for cognitive vision, namely the winner-take-all processing, the use of distributed saliency and feature binding as a link to recognition.

3.1 Towards a Definition of Attention

What is 'attention'? Is there a computational justification for attentive selection? The obvious answer that has been given many times that the brain is not large enough to process all the incoming stimuli, is hardly satisfactory (Tsotsos 1987 [456]). This answer is not quantitative and provides no constraints on what processing system might be sufficient. Methods from computational complexity theory have formally proved that purely data-directed visual search in its most general form is an intractable problem in any realization (Tsotsos 1989[457]). There, it is claimed that visual search is ubiquitous in vision, and thus purely data-directed visual processing is also intractable in general. Those analyses provided important constraints on visual processing mechanisms and led to a specific (not necessarily unique or optimal) solution for visual perception. One of those constraints concerned the importance of attentive processing at all stages of analysis: the combinatorics of search are too large at each stage of analysis otherwise. Attentive selection based on task knowledge turns out to be a powerful heuristic to limit search and make the overall problem tractable (Tsotsos 1990 [458]). This conclusion leads to the following view of attention: *Attention is a set of strategies that attempts to reduce the computational cost of the search processes inherent in visual perception.* It thus plays a role in all aspects of vision.

H.I. Christensen and H.-H. Nagel (Eds.): Cognitive Vision Systems, LNCS 3948, pp. 25–35, 2006.

Many (the active/animate vision researchers) seem to claim that attention and eye movements are one and the same; certainly none of the biological scientists working on this problem would agree. That one can attend to particular locations in the visual field without eye movements has been known since Helmholtz (1924 [186]), but eye movements require visual attention to precede them to their goal (Hoffman 1998 [192] surveys relevant experimental work). Active vision, as it has been proposed and used in computer vision, necessarily includes attention as a sub-problem.

3.2 Attention in Computer Vision

What is it about attention that makes it one of the easiest topics to neglect in computer vision? The task of tracking, or active control of fixation, requires as a first step the detection of the target or focus of attention. How would one go about solving this? Knowing that with no task knowledge and in a purely-data-directed manner, this sub-task of target detection is NP-Complete means that one is attempting to solve a problem that includes known intractable sub-problems. Is the problem thought to be irrelevant or is it somehow assumed away?

Those who build complete vision application systems invoke attentional mechanisms because they must confront and defeat the computational load in order to achieve the goal of real-time processing (there are many examples, two of them being Baluja & Pomerleau 1997 [27] and Dickmanns 1992 [100]). But the mainstream of computer vision does not give attentive processes, especially task-directed attention, much consideration.

A spectrum of problems requiring attention has appeared (Tsotsos 1992 [459]): selection of objects, events, tasks relevant for domain, selection of world model, selection of visual field, selection of detailed sub-regions for analysis, selection of spatial and feature dimensions of interest, selection of operating parameters for low level operations. Take a look at this list and note how most research makes assumptions that reduce or eliminate the need for attention:

- Fixed camera systems negate the need for selection of visual field.
- Pre-segmentation eliminates the need to select a region of interest.
- 'Clean' backgrounds ameliorate the segmentation problem.
- Assumptions about relevant features and the ranges of their values reduce their search ranges.
- Knowledge of task domain negates the need to search a stored set of all domains.
- Knowledge of which objects appear in scenes negates the need to search a stored set of all objects.
- Knowledge of which events are of interest negates the need to search a stored set of all events.

The point is that the extent of the search space is seriously reduced before the visual processing takes place, and most often even before the algorithms for solution are designed! However, it is clear that in everyday vision, and certainly in order to understand vision, these assumptions cannot be made. More importantly, the need for attention is broader than simply vision as the above list shows. It touches on the relevant aspects of visual reasoning, recognition, and visual context. As such, cognitive vision systems should not include these sorts of assumptions and must provide mechanisms that can deal with the realities inherent in real vision.

3.3 The Selective Tuning Model (STM) of Visual Attention

The modeling effort described herein features a theoretical foundation of provable properties based in the theory of computational complexity (Tsotsos 1987, 1989, 1990, 1992 [456, 457, 458, 459]). The 'first principles' arise because vision is formulated as a search problem (given a specific input, what is the subset of neurons that best represent the content of the image?) and complexity theory is concerned with the cost of achieving solutions to such problems. This foundation suggests a specific biologically plausible architecture as well as its processing stages as will be briefly described in this article. A more detailed account can be found in (Tsotsos 1990 [458], Tsotsos et al. 1995 [460]).

3.3.1 The Model

The visual processing architecture is pyramidal in structure with units within this network receiving both feed-forward and feedback connections. When a stimulus is presented to the input layer of the pyramid, it activates in a feed-forward manner all of the units within the pyramid with receptive fields (RFs) mapping to the stimulus location; the result is a diverging cone of activity within the processing pyramid. It is assumed that response strength of units in the network is a measure of goodness-of-match of the stimulus within the receptive field to the model that determines the selectivity of that unit.

Selection relies on a hierarchy of Winner-Take-All (WTA) processes. WTA is a parallel algorithm for finding the maximum value in a set. First, a WTA process operates across the entire visual field at the top layer where it computes the global winner, i.e., the units with largest response (see Section 3.3.3 for details). The fact that the first competition is a global one is critical to the method because otherwise no proof could be provided of its convergence properties. The WTA can accept guidance to favor areas or stimulus qualities if that guidance is available, but operates independently otherwise. The search process then proceeds to the lower levels by activating a hierarchy of WTA processes. The global winner activates a WTA that operates only over its direct inputs to select the strongest responding region within its receptive field. Next, all of the connections in the visual pyramid that do not contribute to the winner are pruned (inhibited). The top layer is not inhibited by this mechanism. However, as a result, the input to the higher-level unit changes and thus its output changes. This refinement of unit responses is an important consequence because one of the important goals of attention is to reduce or eliminate signal interference (Tsotsos 1990 [458]). By the end of this refinement process, the output of the attended units at the top layer will be the same as if the attended stimulus appeared on a blank field. This strategy of finding the winners within successively smaller receptive fields, layer by layer, in the pyramid and then pruning away irrelevant connections through inhibition is applied recursively through the pyramid. The end result is that from a globally strongest response, the cause of that largest response is localized in the sensory field at the earliest levels. The paths remaining may be considered the

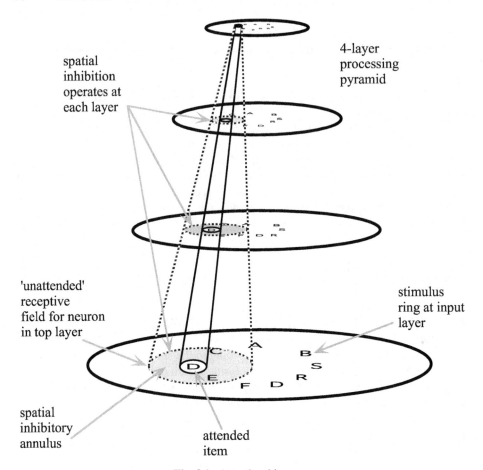

Fig. 3.1. Attentional beam

pass zone of the attended stimulus while the pruned paths form the inhibitory zone of an attentional beam. The WTA does not violate biological connectivity or relative timing constraints. Figure 3.1 gives a pictorial representation of this attentional beam.

An executive controller is responsible for implementing the following sequence of operations for visual search tasks:

1. Acquire target as appropriate for the task, store in working memory.
2. Apply top-down biases, inhibiting units that compute task-irrelevant quantities.
3. 'See' the stimulus, activating feature pyramids in a feed-forward manner.
4. Activate top-down WTA process at top layers of feature pyramids.
5. Implement a layer-by-layer top-down search through the hierarchical WTA based on the winners in the top layer.
6. After completion, permit time for refined stimulus computation to complete a second feed-forward pass. Note that this feed-forward refinement does not begin with the completion of the lowermost WTA process; rather, it occurs simultaneously with

completing WTA processes (step 5) as they proceed downwards in the hierarchy. On completion of the lowermost WTA, some additional time is required for the completion of the feed-forward refinement.

7. Extract output of top layers and place in working memory for task verification.
8. Inhibit pass zone connections to permit next most salient item to be processed.
9. Cycle through steps 4 - 8 as many times as required to satisfy the task.

This multi-pass process may seem to not reflect the reality of biological processes that seem very fast. However, it is not claimed that all of these steps are needed for all tasks. Several different levels of tasks may be distinguished, defined as:

Detection   - is a particular item present in the stimulus, yes or no?
Localization   - detection plus accurate location;
Recognition   - localization plus accurate description of stimulus;
Understanding - recognition plus role of stimulus in the context of the scene.

The executive controller is responsible for the choice of task based on instruction. If detection is the task, then the winner after step 4, if it matches the target, will suffice and the remaining steps are not needed. Thus simple detection in this framework requires only a single feed-forward pass. If a localization task is required, then all steps up to 7 are required because, as argued in below, the top-down WTA is needed to isolate the stimulus and remove the signal interference from nearby stimuli. This clearly takes more time to accomplish. If recognition is the task, then all steps, and perhaps several iterations of the procedure, are needed in order to provide a complete description. The understanding task seems to fit the concept of cognitive vision best; however, the model described here does not include all of the required functionalities for this.

3.3.2 Top-Down Selection

STM features a top-down selection mechanism based on a coarse-to-fine WTA hierarchy. Why is a purely feed-forward strategy not sufficient? There seems to be no disagreement on the need for top-down mechanisms if task/domain knowledge is considered, although few non-trivial schemes seem to exist. Biological evidence, as well as complexity arguments, suggests that the visual architecture consists of a multi-layer hierarchy with pyramidal abstraction. One task of selective attention is to find the value, location and extent of the most salient image subset within this architecture. A purely feed-forward scheme operating on such a pyramid with:

i) fixed size receptive fields with no overlap, is able to find the largest single input with local WTA computations for each receptive field but location is lost and extent cannot be considered.
ii) fixed size overlapping receptive fields, suffers from the spreading winners problem, and although the largest input value can be found, the signal is blurred across the output layer, location is lost and extent is ambiguous.
iii) all possible RF sizes in each layer, becomes intractable due to combinatorics.

While case i) might be useful for certain computer vision detection tasks, it cannot be considered as a reasonable proposal for biological vision because it fails to localize targets. Case iii) is not plausible as it is intractable. Case ii) reflects a biologically realistic architecture, yet fails at the task of localizing a target. Given this reality, a purely feed-forward scheme is insufficient to describe biological vision. Only a top-down strategy can successfully determine the location and extent of a selected stimulus in such a constrained architecture as used in STM.

3.3.3 WTA and Saliency

The Winner-Take-All scheme within STM is defined as an iterative process that can be realized in a biologically plausible manner insofar as time to convergence and connectivity requirements are concerned. The basis for its distinguishing characteristic comes from the fact that it implicitly creates a partitioning of the set of unit responses into bins of width determined by a task-specific parameter, θ. The partioning arises because inhibition between units is not based on the value of a single unit but rather on the absolute value of the difference between pairs of unit values. Further, this WTA process is not restricted to converging to single points as all other formulations. The winning bin of the partition, whose determination is now described, is claimed to represent the strongest responding contiguous region in the image (this is formally proved in Tsotsos et al. 1995 [460]).

First, the WTA implementation uses an iterative algorithm with unit response values updated by each iteration until convergence is achieved. Competition in an iteration depends linearly on the difference between unit strengths in the following way. Unit A will inhibit unit B in the competition if the response of A, denoted by $\rho(A)$, satisfies $\rho(A) - \rho(B) > \theta$. Otherwise, A will be inhibited by B. The overall impact of the competition on unit B is the weighted sum of all inhibitory effects, each of whose magnitude is determined by $|\rho(A) - \rho(B)|$. It has been shown that this WTA is guaranteed to converge, has well-defined properties with respect to finding strongest items, and has well-defined convergence characteristics (Tsotsos et al. 1995 [460]). The time to convergence, in contrast to any other iterative or relaxation-based method is specified by a simple relationship involving θ and the maximum possible value, Z, across all unit responses. The reason for this is that because the partitioning procedure uses differences of values. All larger units will inhibit the units with the smallest responses, while no units will inhibit the largest valued units. As a result the small response units are reduced to zero very quickly while the time for the second largest units to be eliminated depends only on the values of those units and the largest units. As a result, a two-unit network is easy to characterize. The time to convergence is given by

$$\log_2 \left(\frac{A - \theta}{A - B} \right)$$

where A is the largest value and B the second largest value. This is also quite consistent with behavioral evidence; the closer in response strength two units are the longer it takes to distinguish them.

Second, the competition depends linearly on the topographical distance between units, i.e., the features they represent. The larger the distance between units is, the greater the inhibition. This strategy will find the largest, most spatially contiguous subset within the winning bin. A spatially large and contiguous region will inhibit a contiguous region of similar response strengths but of smaller spatial extent because more units from the large region apply inhibition to the smaller region than inhibit the larger region from the smaller one. At the top layer, this is a global competition; at lower layers, it only takes place within receptive fields. In this way, the process does not require implausible connectivity lengths. For efficiency reasons, this is currently only implemented for the units in the winning bin. With respect to the weighted sums computed, in practice the weights depend strongly on the types of computations the units represent. There may also be a task-specific component included in the weights. Finally, a rectifier is needed for the whole operation to ensure that no unit values go below zero. The iterative update continues until there is only one bin of positive response values remaining and all other bins contain units whose values have fallen below θ. Note that even the winning bin of positive values must be of a value greater than some threshold in order to eliminate false detections due to noise.

The key question is how is the root of the WTA process hierarchy determined? The following is a conceptual description of this, and not the iterative implementation of the WTA that depends on the process described in the previous paragraphs. The "max" function used below is implemented using the iterative process just described. Let F be the set of feature maps at the output layers overall, and $F^i, i = 1$ to n, be particular feature maps. Values at each x, y location within map i are represented by $M^i_{x,y}$. The root of the WTA computation is set by a competition at the top layers of the pyramid depending on network configuration (task biases can weight each computation).

To allow full generality, define a receptive field as the set of n contiguous locations $R = \{r_i = (x_i, y_i), i = 1...n\}$. The neuron receives input from these locations from an arbitrary set of other neurons, not necessarily from the same representation. Define the receptive field of a neuron as a set of arbitrarily shaped, contiguous, sub-fields

$$F = \{f_j = \{(x_{j,a}, y_{j,a}), a = 1...b_j\}, j = 1...k\},$$

such that

$$\bigcup_{j=1,k} f_j = R.$$

Each subfield is a retinotopic representation of a particular feature. The WTA competitions are defined on the subfields f_i. For spatially overlapping parts of these subfields, the features represented can be either mutually exclusive or can co-exist. The winning value is W, and this is determined by:

1. If $k = 1$, that is, there is only a single sub-field f,

$$W = \max_{x,y} M^f_{x,y} \ . \tag{3.1}$$

2. If F contains more than one sub-field, representing mutually exclusive features (subfields are fully overlapping in location), then

$$W = \max_{x,y} \left(\max_{i \in F} M^i_{x,y} \right) . \tag{3.2}$$

3. If F contains more than one sub-field, all fully overlapping in location, representing features that can co-exist at each point, then there is more than one WTA process, all rooted at the same location but operating through different feature pyramids

$$W = \max_{x,y} \left(\sum_{i \in F} M_{x,y}^i \right) . \tag{3.3}$$

4. If F contains sub-fields representing features that are mutually exclusive (the set A, as in case 2 above) as well as complementary (the set B, as in case 3 above), the winning locations are determined by the sum of the strongest response among set B (following method 3) plus the strongest response within set A (using method 2). Thus, a combination of the above strategies is used. There is more than one WTA process, all rooted at the same location but operating through (3.4)

$$W = \max_{x,y} \left[\sum_{b \in B} M_{x,y}^b + \max_{a \in A} \left(M_{x,y}^a \right) \right] . \tag{3.4}$$

For sub-fields or portions thereof that are not spatially overlapping with any other subfield, then the WTA process operates within that region following Rule 1.

As a result, there is no single saliency map in this model as there is in all other models. Indeed, there is no single WTA process necessarily, but several simultaneous WTA threads. Saliency is a dynamic, local, distributed and task-specific determination and one that may differ even between processing layers as required. Although it is known that feature combinations of high complexity do exist in the higher levels of cortex, the above does not assume that all possible combinations must exist. Features are encoded separately in a pre-defined set of maps and the relationships of competition or cooperation among them provide the potential for combinations. The above four types of competitions then select which combinations are to be further explored. This flexibility allows for a solution (at least in part) to binding issues.

The WTA process is implemented utilizing a top-down hierarchy of units. There are two main unit types: gating control units and gating units. Gating control units are associated with each competition in each layer and at the top, are activated by the executive in order to begin the WTA process. An additional network of top-down bias units can also provide task-specific bias if it is available. They communicate downwards to gating units that form the competitive gating network for each WTA within a receptive field. Whether the competition uses Eqs. 1, 2, 3, or 4 depends on the nature of the inputs to the receptive field. Once a particular competition converges, the gating control unit associated with that unit sends downward signals for the next lower down competition to begin. The process continues until all layers have converged.

The model has been implemented and tested in several labs applying it to computer vision and robotics tasks. The current model structure is shown in Figure 3.2. The executive controller and working memory, the motion pathway (V1, MT, MST, 7a), the peripheral target area PO, the gaze WTA and gaze controller have all been implemented and examples of performance can be found in (Culhane & Tsotsos 1992 [90], Wai & Tsotsos 1994 [482], Tsotsos et al. 1995 [460], Tsotsos et al. 2002 [461]).

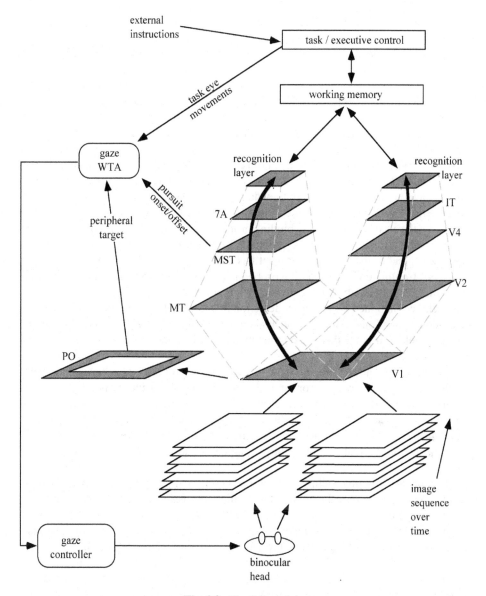

Fig. 3.2. The full model

3.3.4 Feature Binding: The Link to Recognition

A major contribution of the demonstration of how STM can operate within a complex visual hierarchy is the method of grouping features (known as the binding problem in computational neuroscience, Roskies 1999 [381]) into wholes. It is not claimed that this particular strategy has sufficient generality to solve all possible issues within the binding problem. Nevertheless, it is the first instance of such a solution and further work will investigate its generality.

Following Roskies, "the canonical example of binding is the one suggested by Rosenblatt in which one sort of visual feature, such as an object's shape, must be correctly associated with another feature, such as its location, to provide a unified representation of that object". Such explicit association is particularly important when more than one visual object is present, in order to avoid incorrect combinations of features belonging to different objects, otherwise known as "illusory conjunctions" (Treisman and Schmidt 1982 [455]). At least some authors (Ghose & Maunsell 1999 [146], von der Malsburg 1999 [481]) suggest that specialized neurons that code feature combinations (introduced as cardinal cells by Barlow 1972 [28]) may assist in binding. The STM solution does indeed include such cells; however, they do not suffice on their own as will be described because they alone cannot solve the localization problem.

Using the classical view of the binding problem, it is straightforward to show that for a purely data-directed strategy, the problem of finding the subsets of each feature map that correspond to the parts of an object has exponential complexity (it is an instance of the NP-Complete visual matching problem, Tsotsos 1989 [457]). In simple detection problems the complexity is manageable by simple strategies because there are not too many choices and the task is simply detection of a target. However, in the general case, a top-down attentional selection mechanism is needed to reduce the complexity of the search problem. It is for this reason that attention constitutes the link between sensing and recognition.

The use of localized saliency and WTA decision processes is precisely what the binding problem requires: neurons in different representations that respond to different features and in different locations are selected together, the selection being in location and in feature space, and are thus bound together via the 'pass' zone(s) of the attention mechanism. Even if there is no single neuron at the top of the pyramid that represents the concept, the WTA allows for multiple threads bound through location by definition in Eq. 1–4.

Part of the difficulty facing research on binding is the confusion over definitions and the wide variety of tasks included in binding discussions. For example, in Feature Integration Theory (Treisman and Gelade 1980 [454]), location is a feature because it assumes it is faithfully represented in a master map of locations. But this cannot be true; location precision changes layer to layer in any pyramid representation. In the cortex, it is not accurate in a Euclidean sense almost anywhere, although the topography is qualitatively preserved (Felleman & Van Essen 1991 [118]). The wiring pattern matters in order to get the right image bits to the right neurons. Thus binding needs to occur layer to layer and is not simply a problem for high-level consideration. Features from different representations with different location coding properties converge onto single cells and this seems to necessitate an active search process.

For the purposes of this argument, consider the following:

1. Location is not a feature, rather, it is the anchor that permits features to be bound together. Location is defined broadly and differently in each visual area and in practice is considered to be local coordinates within a visual area (think of an array of hypercolumns, each with its own local coordinates);

2. A grouping of features not coincident by location cannot be considered as a unitary group unless there is a unit to represent that group;

3. Features that compose a group may be in different locations and represented in different visual areas as long as they converge onto units that represent the group;

4. If the group is attended, then the WTA of Section 3.3.3 will find and attend to each of its parts regardless of their location or feature map representation.

This strategy is sufficient to handle complex recognition tasks such as multiple patterns, overlapping objects, or even transparent motions. As such, it is a solution to the aspect of binding that attends to groups and finds parts of groups.

3.4 Discussion

How can attentional selection be integrated into a cognitive computer vision system? It is certainly true that most if not all such systems have some early vision processing stages. STM provides a skeleton within which one can include layers of early vision filters and organize them into meaningful hierarchies. It is also true that somewhere in the processing stages, the need to segment an image into regions or events is important. STM's selection strategy may assist with this. If a target object is specified in advance, STM can be shown this in advance, that particular image can be processed and then stored in working memory, and used to guide visual search making search for that target more efficient than without guidance.

It is straightforward to show that for a purely data-directed strategy, the problem of finding the subsets of each feature map that correspond to the parts of an object has exponential complexity. In simple detection problems the complexity is manageable by simple strategies because there are not too many choices and the task is simply detection of a target. However, in the general case, a top-down attentional selection mechanism is needed to reduce the complexity of the search problem. Thus, attention is an important link connecting sensing and recognition for realistic images and world models.

It is clear that STM can provide selection of visual field, selection of detailed subregions for analysis, selection of spatial and feature dimensions of interest, and selection of parameters for low-level operations. It cannot select relevant objects or events from a knowledge base with respect to a particular task, select tasks relevant for a domain, select the world model appropriate for solving the current task, and so on. In other words, the machinery described seems appropriate for early and intermediate levels of visual processing but has not yet advanced to a stage to be as useful for higher levels of visual processing or for the task levels of processing. These must remain topics for future research.

4

Organization of Architectures for Cognitive Vision Systems

Goesta H. Granlund

Computer Vision Laboratory, Linkoeping University
581 83 Linkoeping, Sweden
gegran@isy.liu.se

Abstract. The purpose of cognitive systems is to produce a response to appropriate percepts. The response may be a direct physical *action* which may change the state of the system. It may be delayed in the form of a reconfiguration of internal models in relation to the interpreted *context* of the system. Or it may be to generate in a subsequent step a generalized *symbolic representation* which will allow its intentions of actions to be communicated to some other system. As important as the percepts, is the dependence upon context.

A fundamental property of cognitive vision systems is that they shall be *extendable*. This requires that systems both acquire and store information about the environment autonomously – on their own terms. The distributed organization foreseen for processing and for memory to allow learning, implies that later acquired information has to be stored in relation to earlier. The semantic character of the information which this requires, implies a storage with respect to similarity, and the availability of a metric.

The paper discusses organization aspects of such systems, and proposes an architecture for cognitive systems. In this architecture, which consists of two major parts, the first part of the system, step by step performs a mapping from percepts onto actions or states. The central mechanism is the *perception-action* feedback cycle. In a learning phase, *action precedes perception*. The reason for this reversed causal direction is that action space is much less complex than percept space. It is easy to distinguish which percepts change as a function of an action or a state change. Percepts shall be mapped directly onto states or responses or functions involving these.

The second part of the architecture deals with more invariant representations, or *symbolic* representations, which are derived mainly from system states and action states.

Through active exploration of the environment, i.e. using perception-action learning, a system builds up concept spaces, defining the phenomena it can deal with. Information can subsequently be acquired by the system within these concept spaces without interaction, by extrapolation using passive observation or communication such as language.

This structure has been implemented for the learning of object properties and view parameters in a fairly unrestricted setting, to be used for subsequent recognition purposes.

4.1 Introduction

Systems for handling and understanding of cognitive information are expected to have as great impact on society over the next decades, as what conventional computers and telecommunication have on today's society. They promise to relieve humans of many

H.I. Christensen and H.-H. Nagel (Eds.): Cognitive Vision Systems, LNCS 3948, pp. 37–55, 2006.
© Springer-Verlag Berlin Heidelberg 2006

burdens in the use and the communication with increasingly complex systems, be they technical or deriving from an increasingly complex society. They will make many new applications possible, ranging from autonomous home appliances to intelligent assistants keeping track of the operations in an office.

Up until now, systems have been built, which can operate in very restricted domains or in carefully controlled environments – i.e. in artificially constrained worlds – where models can be constructed with sufficient accuracy to allow algorithms to perform well. However, we also need systems that can respond to and act in the real world. The real world is very complex, and there is no possibility to specify all alternative actions and the decision criteria for these in the traditional way, by supplying information in some declarative form.

Cognitive systems need to acquire the information about the external world through exploratory *learning*, as the complex interrelationships between percepts and their con-textual frames can not be specified explicitly through programming with any reasonable efforts.

In the subsequent discussion, there will be several references to known properties of biological vision systems. It should be emphasized at the outset that the ambition of this paper is not to argue possible models of biological vision systems, but to propose potentially effective architectures of technical systems. In this process, however, it is deemed useful to take hints from what is known about biological vision systems.

4.2 Characteristics of Cognitive Systems

The purpose of cognitive systems is to produce a response to appropriate percepts. The response may be a direct physical *action* which may change the state of the system. It may be delayed in the form of a reconfiguration of internal models in relation to the interpreted *context* of the system. Or it may be to generate in a subsequent step a generalized *symbolic representation* which will allow its intentions of actions to be communicated. As important as the percepts, is the dependence upon context.

There is some debate as to what exactly constitutes cognitive systems especially where they start and where they end. Several terms such as perception, cognitive systems, AI, etc., may in different cultures represent partially or totally overlapping concepts, while they in others take on very specific connotations. Rather than trying to make some unambiguous definition, this document will propose areas of research which will contribute to a common goal of devising systems which can perceive and learn important information in an interaction with the environment and generate appropriate, robust actions or symbolic communication to other systems, e.g. in the form of human language. This defines the use of the term cognitive vision in this document.

The inputs to a cognitive system, or the representations of information in early stages of it, are generally referred to as percepts. They will typically be visual or auditory, as these modalities generally carry most information about the environment. However, other sensing modalities may be used, in particular for boot-strapping or other support purposes. Perception and percepts are similarly ambiguous terms, where some may say that perception is in fact the function performed by a cognitive system. However, there is generally agreement that percepts are compact, partially invariant entities representing the sensing space in question. Visual percepts will for example be some processed, more invariant, more compact representation of the information in an image, than the original iconic image obtained from the sensor.

A fundamental property of cognitive vision systems is the *extendability*. This implies that a system shall be able to deal with more situations than exactly those which the designer has foreseen, and programmed it for. This requires that systems both acquire and store information about the environment autonomously – on their own terms. The distributed organization foreseen for processing and for memory to allow learning, implies that later acquired information has to be stored in relation to earlier. The semantic character of the information implies a storage with respect to similarity, and the availability of a metric.

Building a complete vision system is a very difficult task. This difficulty results from:

- The huge amount of data to treat and the necessarily associated drastic information compression
- The necessity to combine goal driven and event driven inference mechanisms
- The necessity to design systems in a fragmented or multi-level structure

It has become increasingly apparent that classical computing architectures designed for symbol strings, are not appropriate for the processing of spatial-cognitive information. One reason is that the inevitable requirement of learning does not go well with the traditional separation of memory from processing resources. In the task to develop efficient architectures for technical vision systems, it is tempting to look at architectures of biological systems for inspirations on design [364, 68].

The views on cognitive vision architectures range between two extreme views [152]:

- Knowledge and scene representations must be supplied by the designer to the extent possible
- Knowledge about the external world has to be derived by the system through its own exploration

Proponents of the first view argue that if working systems are going to be available in some reasonable time, it is necessary to supply available information, and the modality for this is in declarative form. Proponents of the second view argue that if sufficiently complex models of the external world are going to be available to the system, it is necessary that it can explore and find these out essentially by itself.

We can assume that the economically optimal variety at the present time is somewhere between these extremes, and some combination of these. The present paper will adhere to the second view above.

The difficulty is not just to find solutions for identified sub-problems but to find a coherent, extendable and efficient architecture to combine the required functionalities. The issue is what strategies can be shown to be advantageous for different parts of cognitive systems, e.g. for the commonly assumed distinctive parts for relatively continuous perception-action mapping, versus discrete symbolic processing. This will also involve choice of preferable information representations of information and generic classes of operations, representation of memory in relation to different modes of learning, representation of uncertainty in such structurally different parts of a cognitive system.

Various alternatives for cognitive organization have been studied. One such approach is Bayesian inference and modeling [246]. Other issues are to explore particular types of information representations, which may have advantages in allowing mode separations in large systems. One such representation is the channel representation [154], which allows a fast convergence of learning structures, due to its locality property.

4.3 Overall Architectural Considerations

A vision system receives a continuous barrage of input signals. It is clear that a system cannot attempt to relate every signal to all other signals. What mechanisms make it possible to select a suitable subset for processing, which will not drown the system?

Much of the lack of success in vision for complex problems can be traced to the early view that percepts should generate a *description* of the object or the scene in question. There has traditionally been a belief that an abstraction of objects should be generated as an intermediary step, before a response is synthesized. A great deal of the robotics field has been devoted to the generation of such generalized descriptions [172]. The classical model for image analysis in robotics has been to build up a description step by step. This description has typically been in geometric terms with a conceptual similarity to CAD representations. See Figure 4.1. The ambition has usually been that the model should describe the object geometry as accurately as possible. An extreme but common form of this is the statement that ...*the best model of an object is the object itself.*

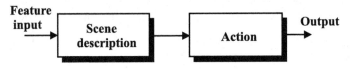

Fig. 4.1. Classical robotics model

Given this description of the image, objects shall be recognized and assigned to the proper categories, together with information about position and other relevant parameters. This description is then carried to a second unit where it is interpreted to generate appropriate actions into the physical world, e.g. to implement a robot.

This structure has not worked out very well for reasons which we will deal with in subsequent sections. In brief, it is because the leap between the abstract description and the action implementation is too large. A large number of important contextual qualifiers, of spatial and temporal nature, necessary for precise action have been lost in the abstraction process implicit in a description.

The major problem with this structure is that we primarily do not need a *description* of an object or a scene. What we need is an *interpretation*, i.e. links between actions and states that are related to an object and corresponding changes of percepts. The purpose of cognitive vision systems is consequently not primarily to build up models of the geometry of objects or of scenes. It is rather to build up model structures which relate the percept domain and the action or state domain; to associate percepts emerging from an object, to states or actions performed upon the object.

To achieve this, it turns out to be necessary to break up the big leap between percept structure and action structure into a sequence of smaller steps. In each such limited step, percepts and functions thereof are related at intermediary levels directly to corresponding states of the system itself or of the external world.

From all of this, one can conclude that the order between the parts should in fact rather be the *opposite*. See Figure 4.2.

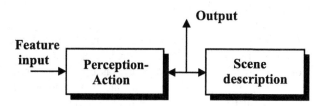

Fig. 4.2. Perception-action robotics model

From these considerations, a system structure is proposed, where the first part of the system, step by step performs a mapping from percepts onto actions or states. The central mechanism is the *perception-action* feedback cycle. The usual assumption that certain percepts shall lead to corresponding learned actions is true, for normal operation of a *trained* system. However, in the learning phase, we have the situation that *action precedes perception* for the part of the structure involved in the learning.

The crucially important reason for this inverse causal direction is that action or state space is much less complex than percept space. The number of possible combinations of perceptual primitives in an image is huge, and most combinations of these will not be of interest as they will never occur. It is necessary to identify the combinations which may occur as economically as possible. Given that the state space is less complex, and that feature combinations of interest will be specifically apparent as the system moves around in the state space, this movement of the system in the state space can be used to organize the relevant parts of the feature space, and associate them to the generative states. Although being a traditional view, the opposite could never be possible, due to the tremendous complexity of the percept space.

The system will in the early bootstrapping learning phase be driven by partly random actions, which however are known to the system itself. This will implement elements of exploration, where the system can observe how the percept structure changes, and perform an associative learning of these relations. Starting with a simple environment, it is easy to distinguish which percepts change as a function of an action or a state change. This allows the system to separate an object from its background, separate distinct parts within an object, learn how the percepts transform under manipulation, etc. Actions can likewise be used to manipulate the environment, which in consequence will modify the emergent percepts. Learning of these relations gives the system the information required for the subsequent use in the opposite direction: To use percepts to control actions in a flexible fashion.

Driving a learning system using semirandom signals for organization of the nervous system, is a well known mechanism from biology. Many low level creatures have built in noise generators, which generate muscle twitches at an early stage of development, in order to organize the sensorial inputs of the nervous system. Organization is driven from the motor side and not from the sensing side. It has been convincingly shown that noise and spontaneously generated neural activity is an important component to enable organization and coordinated behavior of organisms [216].

The major issue is that percepts shall be mapped directly onto states or responses or functions involving these, rather than onto higher level model abstractions. We will see that this step-wise relation of the percept structure to the states of the system or the external world, reduces the complexity at each interface between the two domains. This makes an association structure feasible, as the local system complexity becomes limited. The limited number of degrees of freedom allows the implementation of self-organizing or learning procedures, as there is a chance to perform fast converging optimizations. This gives a mechanism to step by step build up what finally may become a very complex processing structure, useful for the handling of a very complex niche of the external world. See also [152, 153]. In contrast, it would never be possible to build up a complex processing structure, with a large number of degrees of freedom in a single learning or optimization phase.

Driving the system using response signals has four important functions:

- *To separate different modalities of an object from each other, such that they can be separately controlled.*
- *To identify only the percepts which are related to a particular action modality.*
- *To provide action outputs from the network generated. Without a response output path, it remains an anonymous mode unable to act into the external world.*
- *Related points in the response domain exhibit a much larger continuity, simplicity and closeness than related points in the input domain.*

It is necessary that the network structure generated has an output to generate responses, which may be an activation of other structures outside the network, or to produce actions. If no such associations could be made, the network in question would have no output and consequently no meaning to the structure outside. This relates to the advantages of the *view-centered object representation*, which will be discussed in a subsequent section.

4.3.1 A Continual Learning Process

It should be emphasized that a system with this strategy will not simply switch between two modes, where it is either learning, or in operation using its acquired knowledge. Rather it will simultaneously use both strategies, and in effect learn most of the time — at some level. We have earlier emphasized that learning takes place through exploration, and in that process action precedes perception. This process only takes place in a limited part of the system, at a given instance. In that learning process, the system uses the competences it has acquired from earlier training experiences. We will use the following terminology:

By *selfgenerated action* we denote an activity of a system, which is produced without any apparent external influence. The action is assumed to be caused by a random noise signal affecting a choice or creating an activity in parts of the system.

By *reaction* we mean that the system performs an activity which is initiated or modified by a set of percepts.

It should be noted that a particular action under consideration, may typically be composed by both selfgenerated components and reactive components. This is given an intuitive illustration in Figure 4.3.

In the training to deal with a certain phenomenon, here indicated at the highest level, the system associates percepts to the states which are changing. In this process, it uses earlier acquired information in a normal mapping of percepts onto actions in the lower levels. However, at the level to be trained, the action states constitute the organizing mechanism for the associations to implement.

Different parts in the structure use either of the two mechanisms at the same time:

- **Exploratory behavior**: Selfgenerated action → Percept → Association
- **Reactive behavior**: Percept → Reaction

A selfgenerated action by the system causes a particular set of percepts to appear. The actions and percepts are linked to each other in an association process.

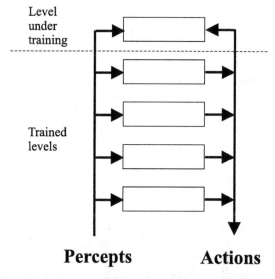

Percepts   Actions

Fig. 4.3. Intuitive illustration of hierarchical training procedure

This means that at any given time, most processes in a cognitive system implement a purposeful mapping of percepts onto actions according to the models acquired at training. However, there will generally be a (often highest) level of exploration, which is characterized by random action activities. These random components are propagated through the trained levels, where they perform purposefully within the domains of the experience acquired.

There are strong indications that the association of motor signals or actions and percepts, in the human brain, takes place in the posterior parietal cortex [206, 362, 375,

506, 288, 407]. The principle of a combination between a probing into the external space and sensing, has recently received theoretical support [347].

The mixed exploratory/reactive strategy appears to be true even for cognitive systems of the category Humans: There is always a top level which deals with phenomena hitherto unknown to us and can only be subjected to exploration, implemented as pseudo-random action components at that level. These components are propagated down through the entire multi-level perception-to-action machinery acquired from experience, and implemented as valid action sequences for a sophisticated exploration of a new domain of the environment.

4.3.2 Interface Between Percept-Action and Symbolic Representation

It is believed that the subsequent symbolic representation shall emerge from, and be organized around, the action or state representation, rather than from any descriptive, geometric representation. This does not exclude the use of static clues such as color.

There are strong indications that this is the way it is done in biological systems — it is known that our conscious perception of the external world is in terms of the actions we can perform with respect to it [431, 142, 432]. It has also been found that the perception of an object results in the generation of motor signals, irrespective of whether or not there is an intention to act upon the object [11, 158].

From an evolutionary view, lower level organisms essentially only have the perception-action mapping, while the descriptive, symbolic representation is a later development, though extremely important. The main argument for this strategy is, however, that it gives a realistic path for development of evolutionary/learning technical systems, ranging from low percept levels to high symbolic reasoning levels.

This motivates us to propose a more detailed structure for a technical cognitive vision system, as given in Figure 4.4.

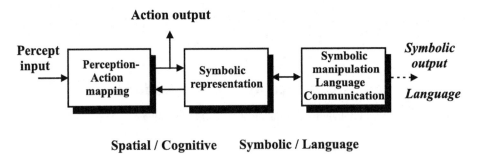

Fig. 4.4. Perception-action robotics model

The perception-action mapping part is attached to the part for symbolic processing through an interface, which will be the subject of this section. So far the discussion may have implied that we would have a sharp division between a percept side and a response side in the structure. This is certainly not the case. There will be a mixture of percept and response components to various degrees in the structure. We will for that purpose define the notion of *percept equivalent* and *response equivalent*. A response equivalent signal may emerge from a fairly complex network structure, which itself comprises a combination of percept and response components to various degree. At low levels it may be an actual response muscle actuation signal which matches or complements the low level percept signal. At higher levels, the response complement will not be a simple muscle signal, but a very complex structure, which takes into account several response primitives in a particular sequence, as well as modifying percepts. The designation implies a complementary signal to match the percept signal at various levels. Such a complex response complement, which is in effect equivalent to the system state, is also what we refer to as *context*.

A response complement also has the property that an activation of it may *not necessarily* produce a response at the time, but rather an activation of particular substructures which will be necessary for the continued processing. It is also involved in knowledge acquisition and prediction, where it may not produce any output.

The simple block structure of Figure 4.4 is obviously not fair to the assumed complexity. A variety is given in Figure 4.5, which is is intended to illustrate the fact that certain classes of percepts may map onto actions after a very brief processing path, much like what we know as reflexes in biological systems. Such direct mapped actions may however require a fairly complex contextual setup, which determines the particular mapping to use. Other actions may require a very complex processing, involving several levels of abstraction. This general, distributed form of organization is supported by findings in biological visual systems [506, 441].

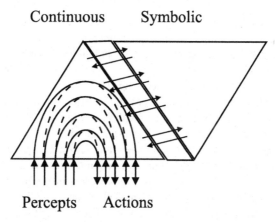

Fig. 4.5. Pyramid version of the perception-action robotics model

There are other important issues of learning such as representation of purpose, reinforcement learning, distribution of rewards, evolutionary components of learning, etc, which are important and relevant but have to be omitted in this discussion.

The number of levels involved in the generation of a response will depend on the type of stimulus input as well as of the particular input. In a comparison with biological systems, a short reflex arch from input to response may correspond to a skin touch sensor, which will act over inter-neurons in the spinal cord. A complex visual input may involve processing in several levels of the processing pyramid, equivalent to an involvement of the visual cortex in biological systems.

The assumption stated in the previous section is that the symbolic representation shall be derived from the states or actions generated from the perception-action part. From biological systems it is known that these actions may be in fact "acted out", or they may be inhibited from generating a physical action. In either case, they represent the interpretation of the set of percepts, which can be used for a symbolic processing [11, 158].

Representation of context at lower levels of a cognitive system is more complex and spatial/quantitative than we are used to for symbolic descriptions. Symbolic descriptions require the mapping into spatial-perceptual parts of a cognitive system, where references are made to its own acquired spatial knowledge and the actual state of the system.

The transition from the action or state representation to a symbolic representation, implies in principle a stripping off, of detailed spatial context to produce sufficiently invariant packets of information to be handled as symbols or to be communicated. This may require the introduction of symbolic contextual entities, derived from certain contextual attributes in the perceptual domain. What has earlier been termed a description is equivalent to a symbolic representation. This is also the part of the system where descriptions such as categories of objects should emerge.

4.4 Symbolic Representation and Processing

Subsequently follows the symbolic processing structure with its different implementations, such as for planning, language and communication. Symbolic representation and manipulation should be viewed as a domain for efficient processing of concepts in a relatively invariant format without unnecessary spatial, temporal and contextual qualifiers, which would severely complicate the processing. The invariant format makes manipulation and communication much more effective and its effects more generally applicable. While the perception-action structure deals with *here-and-now*, the symbolic structure allows the system to deal with other points in space and time in an efficient way. This is what allows *generalization*. A symbolic representation is on the other hand a too meager form for sufficiently adaptive control of actions, a sometimes overlooked characteristic of language. Language works in spite of its relatively low information content, because it maps onto a rich spatial knowledge structure at all levels, available within our surprisingly similar brain structures. This information, however, derives from the individual exploration of what are similar environments.

The output from a symbolic representation and manipulation is preferably viewed as designed for *communication*. This communication can be to another system, or to the perceptual processing part of the *own* system. This implies that the symbol structure is converted back to affect a fairly complex and detailed percept-to-action structure, where actual contextual and action parameters are reinserted in a way related to the current state of the system. In this way, symbolic information can be made to control the perception-action structure, by changing its context. The change of context may be overt or physical in commanding a different state or position bringing in other percepts, or covert affecting the interpretation of percepts. The symbolic representation must consequently be translatable back to detailed contextual parameters relating to the current state of a system, be it the own system or another system.

It is postulated that *metric* or similarity measures are only available within the spatial-cognitive part of a cognitive system and not in the symbolic part. This means that as two symbolic entities are to be compared, they are communicated from the symbolic part to the spatial-cognitive part of the system, where the comparison is implemented. One reason for this is that a relevant comparison usually requires the inclusion of actual quantitative parameters.

The output from the symbolic processing is normally (for biological systems) output over the action output interface according to Figure 4.4. For a technical system, there may be possibilities to interface directly to the symbolic processing unit, as indicated by the dashed line to the right. The reason is that the symbolic representation used in this part of the system, can be expected to be less context dependent and consequently more invariant than what is the case in the perception-action part. This will make it potentially feasible to link symbol states to an outside representation, using association or learning.

A significant trend over the last years is the recognition of the importance of *semantics* compared to *syntax*. This implies that many important relations between entities can not be described and predicted by rules. These relations simply appear as *coincidences* with no simple predictability models. Still, they are extremely important for systems intended for the real world, as the real world has this nasty unruly habit. The only way to acquire this information is through association or learning. This is true all through a cognitive system, from percepts to language, while the implementation will be different for different parts. This fact is also bringing about a shift from the traditional *declarative* representation towards the use of *procedural* representation, allowing association or learning.

The preceding strongly emphasizes the necessity for a full fledged cognitive system to have both a spatial/perceptual part and a symbolic/language part in close integration. An important issue is that the spatial/perceptual domain and the symbolic/language domain are two different worlds, where different rules and methods apply. This includes how information is represented, how learning is implemented and consequently how memory is represented. In particular, it is the difference between a very context specific world and a more invariant and generalizable world.

4.4.1 Representation in Language

Although the relation to language is not central in this document, we will make a few observations which extend the issues already dealt with. The major part of our dicourse above, is on what is postulated to happen in the spatial-cognitive or procedural part of a vision system, which for human vision is not assumed to be available to us in conscious experience, except for its effects. What is happening in the motor/language/consciousness or declarative part of the human system, on the other hand, is the generation of a normalized object-centered representation, in order to be able to communicate it in a sufficiently compact way. In this case it is necessary for compactness to cut off a major part of incidental contextual links, which are probably not necessary for the receiver, as it will not be in exactly the same state as the sender of the message, anyway. The formalism that we find in classical knowledge-based systems is oriented towards such compact, string-representable phenomena intended for communication. As for all object-centered representations, taxonomies are built up with an overview of the final outcome, rather than the type of incremental, "blind" buildup which is assumed necessary for view-centered representations.

There is a clear difference between what we represent in language as declarative statements, compared to the procedural statements required for generation of responses. While *subset-of* and *member-of* concepts are important for conscious taxonomy and organization, such as to determine a particular disease from its symptoms, it is not apparent that these concepts are useful for response generation systems. The type of grouping or abstraction which is performed here, is in fact similar to the process of increased abstraction which we will see in an object-centered representation in contrast to a view-centered representation; a number of specific action references are cut off from the representation structure.

The fact that language can communicate action, is because it is derived from action primitives as discussed earlier. The reason language works is due to the rich structure that it evokes in the receiver's cognitive system; not due to the content of the sentence itself. Language should be viewed as a pushing of buttons on the receiver. Most of the information necessary for the response has to be contained in the structure of the receiver; it can not just point to abstract references thereof. This is the major reason for the limited success of inference systems using natural language in robotics: There is too little information contained in language itself, and if there is no powerful spatial-cognitive interpretation structure available, such that language control can be implemented in a sufficiently flexible way.

4.5 Object-Centered Versus View-Centered Representation

The earlier discussion of two different domains for processing, the perception-action domain and the symbolic domain, has an important relation to two different approaches to object representation: *view-centered* and *object-centered* representation, respectively [372, 153]. See Figure 4.6.

From a real object, a number of measurements or projections are generated. They may, e.g., be images of the object, taken from different angles. See Figure 4.6a. From these measurements we can proceed along either one of two different tracks.

One of the tracks leads to the object-centered representation which combines these measurement views into some closed form mathematical object [159]. See Figure 4.6b. The image appearance of an instance of a particular orientation of the object is then obtained using separate projection mappings.

A view-centered representation, on the other hand, combines a set of appearances of an object, without trying to make any closed form representation [462, 353, 38]. See Figure 4.6c.

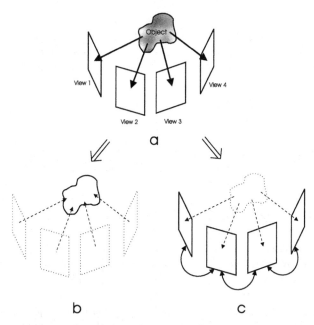

Fig. 4.6. Object-centered and view-centered representation of an object. a) Measurements produce information about different views or aspects of an object. b) Object-centered representation: The views are used to reconstruct a closed form object representation. c) View-centered representation: The views are retained as entities which linked together form a representation of the object.

4.5.1 Object-Centered Representation

The basic motive of the object-centered representation is to produce a representation which is as compact and as invariant as possible. It generally produces a closed form representation, which can subsequently be subjected to interpretation. This implies that no unnecessary information is included about details on how the information was derived. A central idea is that matching to a reference should be easier as the object description has no viewpoint-dependent properties. A particular view or appearance of the object can be generated using appropriate projection methods.

We can view the compact invariant representation of orientation as vectors and tensors [156], as a simple variety of object-centered representation. Over a window of a data set, a set of filters are applied producing a component vector of a certain dimensionality. The components of the vector tend to be correlated for phenomena of interest, which means that they span a lower dimensional sub-space. The components can consequently be mapped into some mathematical object of a lower dimensionality, to produce a more compact and invariant representation, i.e. a vector or a tensor [156].

A drawback of the object-centered representation is that it requires a preconceived notion about the object to ultimately find its mathematical and representational structure, and how the observed percepts should be integrated to support the hypothesis of the postulated object. It requires that the expected types of relations are predefined and already existing in the system, and that an external system keeps track of the development of the system such as the allocation of storage, and the labeling of information. Such a preconceived structure is not well suited for self-organization and learning. It requires an external entity which can "observe labels and structure", and take action on this observation. It is a more classical declarative representation, rather than a procedural representation.

4.5.2 View-Centered Representation

In a view-centered representation, no attempt is made to generalize the representation of the entire object into some closed form. The different parts are kept separate, but linked together using the states or responses, which correspond to or generated the particular views. This gives a representation which is not nearly as compact or invariant. However, it tells what state of the system is associated to a particular percept state. A view-centered representation in addition, has the advantage of being potentially self-organizing. This property will be shown to be crucial for the development of a learning percept-action structure. There are indications from perceptual experiments, that the view-centered representation is the one used in biological visual systems [372].

An important characteristic of the view representation is that it directly implements an *interpretation*, rather than a geometrical *description* of an object that we want to deal with. By interpretation we denote links to actions that are related to the object, and information about how the object transforms under the actions. This is what motivates the choice of structure described in earlier sections.

4.5.3 Combination of Representation Properties

An object-centered representation is by design as invariant as possible with respect to contextual specificities. It has the stated advantage to be independent of the observation angle, distance, etc. This has, however, the consequence that it cuts off all links that it has to specific contexts or response procedures which are related to that context or view. We recognize this from the preceding section as what is characterized as a *symbolic* representation. The generation of an invariant representation, implies discarding information which is essential for the system to act using the information. In order to use such information, a system has to introduce actual contextual information.

It is postulated that an interpreting system shall start out from the view-centered representation of objects. This allows the system to represent phenomena such as objects as combinations of percepts and responses. It is furthermore postulated that these can be viewed as *invariants*, i.e. there is a local region in some subspace in which small changes in the percept domain and the action or state domain are equivalent.

The structure which results from the preceding model will be of type frames-within-frames, where individual transformations of separate objects are necessary within a larger scene frame. The ability to handle local transformations is absolutely necessary, and would not be possible with a truly iconic view representation. It is postulated that the frames-within-frames partitioning is isomorphic with the response map structure. In this way, the response map "reaches" into the frame in question, to implement the percept-action invariance of a particular object aspect.

4.6 Extending and Exchanging Competences of Vision Systems

In the preceding sections, most of the attention has been paid to exploratory learning. While this modality is basic, there are other modalities available for the extension of the competences of a system. A system can acquire information using three different mechanisms, where each one is dependent upon the acquisition in the previous mechanisms:

1. Copying at the time of system generation
2. Active exploration, defining concept spaces through associative learning
3. Passive observation or communication, i.e. using language, can be used to link points in available concept spaces

4.6.1 Copying at the Time of System Generation

Any system will start with some set of basic hardware and software in some representation. It is in principle possible to copy an existing system to generate another system identical to the first one. In a given case, there may well be practical complications which may make such a procedure prohibitive. The reason why it is in principle possible, is that a copying procedure requires no *interpretation* of the structure it deals with, only a "blind" but accurate copying mechanism. A device of a similar character is a TV set, which maps the points of an image from one surface to another, not ever worrying about the content of the image, what parts relate to each other, etc.

In contrast, the task to copy *a certain item* of information from one system to another is generally not possible. Transfer of an item of information from one system to another must be made through the normal in- and outputs of the systems, and on the terms of the systems. There are two reasons for this:

1. As soon as a system takes on to explore the external world, it will proceed along a different trajectory and acquire different information than another system, even if they started out identical. Systems with the architecture proposed will store information in a *semantic* form, which means in relation or adjacency to similar information. This means that the sequence of exposure to different objects in the environment will lead to different organizations of the information. It is consequently not possible to map the information from one system to another, even if they initially were identical, which means that it is not obvious where the information should be "pushed into" the receiving system.
2. It is not clear how to identify the information belonging to a certain item or topic, as there will be attachments to references and context. All these links would be required to be identified and labeled in order to be possible to reinsert in the receiving system. It is not clear how such an establishment of correspondence could ever be made in a self-organizing knowledge structure, be it in the receiving system or in the donating system. The receiving system may in fact lack some of the contextual parameters required for attachment.

We can conclude that the only mode for transmission of information from one system to another is over the normal input and output channels, on the terms of the receiving system. The last qualification implies that the just received information has to be stored in relation to similar, earlier acquired information and context. This has the consequence that the possibility for a designer to "push in" information into an operating system, is less than traditionally desired. Such information has to go through the interpreting and organizing mechanisms of the system, as discussed above.

The way that the "practical complications" of copying have been resolved for biological systems, is that a "blueprint" of the system is copied, rather than the system itself. This has the consequence that very limited quantities of the experience of a system can be transferred.

4.6.2 Active Exploration, Defining Concept Spaces

Most of what has been discussed in earlier sections deals with the acquisition of information through active exploration. This is the fundamental mode of learning, as it establishes the basic relations between action or state and available percepts. It is postulated that this explorative perception-action mapping defines *concept spaces*, defining domains of phenomena it can deal with. The characteristics of an object are consequently the way its appearance behaves under different modes of responses. These are the different percept-response invariants referred to in [152]. The crucial issue is that these invariants are determined by the response modes of the observing system. The associative learning system will create these invariants to "match" the response effects. As a consequence, the ability of the system to understand the world is given by its ability to manipulate it. The preceding leads to the basic principle:

> *A system's ability to interpret objects and the external world is dependent upon its ability to flexibly interact with it.*

A philosophical consequence of this is that for a reasonable degree of intelligence to develop in a system, it requires a flexible machinery for a complex interaction with the external world, in addition to an effective information processing architecture. Another consequence of the necessity to disturb an object, in order to understand it, leads to a variety of the uncertainty relation [492].

4.6.3 Passive Observation or Communication

An apparent question is now: In order for the system to be able to deal with objects, is it necessary for it to interact with every such single object in every respect?

It is postulated that a response driven learning session will define sets of concept spaces. The system can then be expected to deal with objects or cases which are *sufficiently similar* to what it has experienced in the response driven learning process, through interpolation and extrapolation within the defined spaces. Exactly what sufficiently similar implies is not clear at this point. Abstractly, it must imply that an earlier defined percept-response space is valid for the phenomenon under consideration, although it may be parametrically different from what the learning trajectory defined. In some sense, it must imply that the problem structure or topology is similar. This is similar to Piaget's concepts of *assimilation* and *accommodation* in his theory of cognitive development.

It is well supported that humans are subject to the same limitations and possibilities. We can comprehend a phenomenon which we have not experienced before, as long as it contains components which are sufficiently similar to something of which we have an interactive experience; i.e. we can deal with it as an interpolation or extrapolation within an already available percept-response concept space. There are indications that at an adult age, most of the concept spaces used are already available, and that most of our knowledge acquisition after this deals with combinations of particular instances, and interpolations or extrapolations within these available spaces. This can conceivably imply that cases with the same problem structure or within the same concept space, may well appear very different, but we can handle them without considerable difficulty.

In this way, a system can comprehend a phenomenon from passively observed imagery, as long as the primitive components of it can be mapped over the association concept spaces available to the system. Similarly, language can evoke components which are familiar to the system, although the particular arrangement of them may be new.

In such a way, knowledge may be communicated in an efficient way to a system, such that it does not need to make an involved experience, but can observe passively or communicate symbolically, i.e. using some language.

4.7 Cognitive Mechanisms for Development of Vision Systems

In most of the preceding discussion, a feedback perception-action structure has been assumed, which primarily reminds of robotics applications, as it implies an embodiment which can interact with the external world. Does that mean that the preceding cognitive vision architecture is only applicable to robotics?

Not exclusively! The belief is, however, that the structure discussed is not only advantageous, but inevitable, for the development of demanding applications of vision. This also includes the interpretation of complex static imagery.

It will similarly be inevitable for cases where the output is not a physical action but the communication of a message. An example of the latter type is complex man-machine interfaces, where the actions and speech of a human are registered, interpreted and communicated symbolically to a system to implement a very sophisticated control of its functions. Sufficient flexibility and adaptation requires learning for the system to deal with all contextual variations encountered in practical situations.

The training of cognitive systems for such advanced but non-robotic applications requires the development of mixed real-virtual training environments. In these, the system will gradually build up its knowledge of its environment with objects including humans. The learning is again implemented as association, between the learning system's own state parameters, and the impinging perceptual parameters. The typical case is as discussed earlier that the system moves an object in front of its camera input. The movement parameters are known to the system and can be associated with the percepts appearing as results of the movements. This can in training environments be simulated in various ways such that corresponding state and percept information is made available to the system.

In such a way, competence can be built up step by step, in a mixture of real and virtual training environments. With a design allowing incremental learning, it shall be possible to start out with reasonably crude virtual environments, to give the system some tentative knowledge of object and environment space structure, which is refined in the real environment.

From this derives the view that the development of powerful technical vision systems inevitably has to go the path over perception-action mapping and learning, similarly to the case for robotics, even if the systems will be used for interpretation of static imagery or to generate and communicate messages to other systems. This opens up wide ranges of applications of cognitive systems at an early stage, which do not require advanced mechanical manipulators. One such important application field is in activity interpretation for man-machine interfaces. Setting up training environments for such applications is one of the research challenges in cognitive vision.

4.8 Implementation of Cognitive Mechanisms in Vision Systems

The principles discussed in this paper have been tested in a structure for unrestricted recognition of 3-D objects, documented separately in [157]. By unrestricted, we imply that the recognition shall be done independently of object position, scale, orientation and pose, against a structured background. It shall not assume any preceding segmentation and allow a reasonable degree of occlusion.

The paper [157] describes how objects can be represented. A structure is proposed to deal with object and contextual properties in a transparent manner. The method uses a hierarchy of triplet feature invariants, which are at each level defined by a learning procedure. In the feed-back learning procedure, percepts are mapped upon system states corresponding to manipulation parameters of the object. The method uses a learning architecture employing channel information representation [154].

4.9 Concluding Remarks

There is a traditional belief that percepts are in some way "understood" in a vision system, after which suitable responses are attached. This does however require simple units to have an ability of "understanding", which is not a reasonable demand upon local structures. This is a consequence of the luxury of our own capability of consciousness and verbal logical thinking. This leads to a potential danger inherent in our own process for system development, in that our conscious experience of the environment has its locus at the very end of the chain of neural processing; at a point where in fact most of the cognitive processing has already been made. It is well established that language capability, logical reasoning and conscious processing are all derivates of the motor system normally in the left half of the brain, at the end of the processing chain.

A processing in terms of such conscious object terms *inside* the cognitive processing structure is not likely to occur. Most, or nearly all of the cognitive processing has already been done when signals are available for the motor manipulation of objects to take place, or a representation in conscious terms to emerge. We are too late to see *how* it happened. We only notice *what* has happened.

Given the well known distributed nature of processing, it is apparent that there is no basis for any estimation of importance or "meaning" of percepts locally in a network, but that "blind and functional rules" have to be at work to produce what is a synergic, effective mechanism. One of these basic rules is undoubtedly to register how percepts are associated with responses, and the consequences of these. This seems at first like a very limited repertoire, which could not possibly give the rich behavior necessary for intelligent systems. Like in the case of other evolutionary processes for self-organization, there seems to be no other credible alternative. Rather, we have to look for simple and robust rules, which can be compounded into sufficient complexity to deal with complex problems in a "blind" but effective way.

Acknowledgments

The author wants to acknowledge the financial support of WITAS: The Wallenberg Laboratory For Information Technology and Autonomous Systems, SSF (The Foundation for Strategic Research) as well as the Swedish National Board of Technical Development. Considerable credit should be given to the staff of the Computer Vision Laboratory of Linkoeping University, for discussion of the contents of this paper.

5

Cognitive Vision Systems:
From Ideas to Specifications

H.-H. Nagel

Institut für Algorithmen und Kognitive Systeme,
Fakultät für Informatik der Universität Karlsruhe (TH)
76128 Karlsruhe, Germany
nagel@iaks.uni-karlsruhe.de

Abstract. A computer vision system is expected to map an image (sequence) into an appropriate description of the world section in the field of view of the recording camera(s). The resulting description will be communicated usually to animate or inanimate recipients. Alternatively, it may be exploited to influence the depicted world section directly via actuators coupled to the computer vision system. Human expectations with respect to what constitutes an 'appropriate description' expand concurrently with the processing and storage capacities of computers. As a consequence, the algorithmic processes incorporated into a computer vision system become ever more complex and the diversity of computer vision systems expands continuously.

This contribution addresses *engineering aspects* of computer vision systems. A structure is suggested for the processing steps devoted to the extraction of spatiotemporally *local signal* characterisations, their aggregation into *non-local image* descriptors, and the construction of spatiotemporal *geometric* descriptions in the scene domain. It is postulated that the association of these signal and geometric descriptions with *conceptual* descriptions facilitates the design and implementation of versatile and encompassing computer vision systems. In view of the complexity encountered in the course of such an endeavor, a set of aspects is proposed whose consideration should help to clarify the design options and to enforce precise specifications as a precondition for a viable system design and evaluation.

5.1 Introduction

It is a common experience that grass begins to grow and flowers blossom on a patch of soil without a gardener having attended to it. Much more rarely, one encounters a piece of 'garden art' – created by longlasting, meticulous attention to a fertile piece of land.

Ideas sometimes are like flowers, they apparently come out of nowhere and begin to expand within a human community without anyone explicitly tending to them. Often, they fade away as suddenly as they appeared. There are ideas, however, which take roots more permanently, possibly even attracting other ideas or transforming themselves in unexpected ways. Some people catch on and attend to such ideas more intensively – just as gardening fans begin to care about flowers, lawns, shrubbery, trees, or combinations thereof.

H.I. Christensen and H.-H. Nagel (Eds.): Cognitive Vision Systems, LNCS 3948, pp. 57–69, 2006.
© Springer-Verlag Berlin Heidelberg 2006

Given the spectacular growth of the performance/price-ratio for storage capacity, computing power, and related digital equipment like (video-)cameras during the recent decades, these technical developments serve as a fertile ground for the exploration of numerous ideas. A recurrent pattern has been the attempt to select some – more or less vaguely circumscribed – human capability and to devise an 'analogous *algorithmic*' realization. Speech understanding as well as visual perception by humans constitute prominent examples for such endeavors.

The *transmission* capacity required for uncompressed, high-fidelity speech (say, 30 KByte/s) is about three orders of magnitude smaller than that required for uncompressed color-video (about 30 MByte/s). Let us assume for the moment that the *processing* capacities required for 'understanding' of speech and video signals, respectively, are proportional to the recorded data rate. This assumption implies that video 'understanding' requires about three orders of magnitude more computing power than speech understanding. Based on the observation that the computing capacity of an integrated processor doubled about every 18 months (or roughly by a factor of ten in five years) during the last thirty years, video 'understanding' should trail speech understanding by about 15 - 20 years at a comparable level of performance. This – admittedly very coarse – estimate seems to be compatible with experience.

A short reflection on the development of speech understanding may thus be helpful to put problems of video understanding into a – hopefully clarifying – perspective. The *recognition* of '*elementary components*' of speech (phonemes, syllables, and words) has matured since about a decade or more to a state where it has become apparent that efforts at 'isolated component recognition' are confronted with a rapidly diminishing rate of further improvement. It appears more promising now to invest into the *exploitation of context* knowledge. Efforts at *speech* understanding thus approach those devoted to natural language *text* understanding. Both endeavors imply a shift towards a higher level of abstraction regarding the representation of knowledge about the discourse domain. As a consequence, questions related to knowledge representation and (commonsense) reasoning become more prominent. In order to attain a desired level of versatility, various aspects of 'learning' require increasing attention.

This contribution studies consequences of the postulate that an analogous development begins to become discernible regarding computer vision. The principal assumption underlying the following discussions can be stated quite simply: regardless of how one defines a Cognitive Vision System (CogVS), attention to (bi-directional) transitions between geometric and conceptual representations as well as details of processing at conceptual levels of representation will become a necessity in the future.

5.2 Aspects of a Cognitive Vision System (CogVS)

Many aspects will have to be taken into account in order to properly characterize a CogVS. The following selective enumeration comprises aspects which appear relevant in the context of this discussion. In principle, these aspects are introduced like a *set of axioms* in an order which proceeds from the general towards the specific – to the extent possible.

5.2.1 The Concept of a 'Single-Agent Relevant World Section (S-ARWS)'

Relevant World Section (RWS) On the one hand, a CogVS should cope with boundary conditions as they occur in the 'real world'. On the other hand, it appears to be unrealistic that a CogVS should handle *any* set of conditions which potentially might occur in the real world. It thus is postulated that a comprehensive set of conditions has to be specified which characterize the *relevant section* of the real world. This postulate implies that the relevant section of the real world is *delimited* and simultaneously *explicated*. The latter requirement will become important for the decision whether a 'failure' is due to (i) a (hardware) malfunction of the CogVS, (ii) to an error in the system implementation, or (iii) to a mistake in the system specification.

It should be noted that the preceding enumeration of alternative explanations excludes malfunctions due to incorrect user commands: these have to be detected and neutralized by an appropriate implementation, otherwise their occurrence constitutes a specification or implementation error.

'System' and environment It is postulated that the RWS can be divided into a part which henceforth will be referred to as 'the System' and its *environment*. Properties of the System will be treated in the sequel.

Sensors The System is endowed with *sensors* which enable it to record the appearance of (part of) the RWS. The System has a *memory* to store (some of) the recorded signals.

Actuators The System is endowed with *actuators* which enable it to change the appearance of the RWS.

Abstraction steps / States The System can *abstract condensed representations* from the stored signals about recorded appearances. These abstractions are denoted (RWS) *states*.

'Ego-State' vs. State of environment Note that the RWS comprises the System and its environment, i. e. the preceding postulates imply that the System can record and change (within limits still to be specified)

- the state of itself (in isolation to the extent with which the System can be separated from its environment);
- its state with respect to its environment (or vice versa);
- the state of its environment to the extent the latter can be separated from the System.

It is postulated that the System can *distinguish* between those (sub)states which

- relate only to its environment,
- relate only to itself (*'Ego'-States*), and
- refer to the relation between the System and its environment.

Elementary 'actions' Assume for a moment that *actions* of the System are the only cause of *state transitions* (a postulate which will have to be elaborated on later).

Links It is postulated that the System can build an *internal representation of potentially accessible states*. Two states are *'linked'* by a directed *'edge'* within this representation if an action by the System can cause a transition from the first to the second state.

Purpose It is postulated that the System is endowed with a *purpose*.

Goal selection Based on a purpose, the System should be able to select a 'goal' state.

Planning The System should be able to search for a chain of state transitions which transform the current state into the goal state (a '*plan*' to achieve the selected goal).

State transitions The System *can* – but need not – *condition* its actuator activation(s) on selected signals (stimulus/response).

Agent A system endowed with a purpose, the ability to select a goal and to generate a plan in order to achieve it will be referred to as an '*agent*'.

The postulates formulated up to now illustrate some of the '*specifications*' which are needed to characterize a 'Single-Agent' RWS (S-ARWS):

- the RWS;
- its division into 'the System' and its environment;
- the sensors of the System;
- the actuators of the System;
- the actions which the System can perform;
- the abstraction steps;
- the states and admissible links between states;
- the purpose of an agent (which implies the details of how goal states are selected);
- the planning capabilities.

Systematic progress regarding design and evaluation of a CogVS is unlikely to be realized unless the boundary conditions are taken into account. This requires that the boundary conditions for a system design or an evaluation experiment have to be specified explicitly – and precisely – in the first place. Usually, all these aspects have been fixed only implicitly, if at all.

5.2.2 System-Internal Representation Levels for a S-ARWS

The rather coarse discussion in the preceding section did not yet treat questions related to the type of sensor to be used nor were details given regarding how state information has to be abstracted from signals or how different states are to be represented internally within a system realizing an agent.

The subsequent treatment is based on the assumption that one or more video cameras constitute the (only) sensors of the agent to be discussed. As a consequence, state information about the agent's environment and about the agent's relations relative to its environment have to be derived by computer vision. A discussion about alternatives how to realize these computations will be greatly simplified in the case where a kind of '*reference computer vision*' system can be outlined. A coarse layer-structure such as the one given by Figure 5.1 may provide a starting point for the discussion of what will be denoted as *Core Computer Vision System (CCVS)* (the following formulations have been partially adapted from [318]).

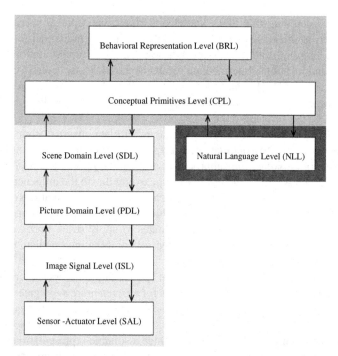

Fig. 5.1. Coarse layer structure of a 'Core Computer Vision System (CCVS). The layers underlaid in yellow constitute the 'core computer vision' subsystem for the extraction of a geometric 3-D scene representation. The 'conceptual representation' subsystem is underlaid in light blue, the 'text generation' is incorporated into the 'Natural Language Level' underlaid in light red (adapted from [318], ©2000 IEEE).

Sensor-Actuator-Level (SAL) The 'lowest' layer comprises signal capture by monocular, binocular, or multiocular (greyvalue, color, or multispectral) camera configurations. Since it can be desirable to vary *internal* and *external* camera parameters during recording, a system model has to provide signal streams *from* as well as *to* the camera(s). These *bi-directional* signal paths link the so-called *Sensor-Actuator-Level (SAL)* with the next higher level, the

Image Signal Level (ISL). The ISL provides *local signal* processing. ISL intermediate results – so-called Image Signal Descriptors (ISDs) – can be fed *back* to the SAL, for example in order to control pan, tilt, focus, or stop.

Picture Domain Level (PDL) In any case, ISDs provided by the ISL are fed *forward* to the PDL where they are selected and aggregated by *non-local* approaches based on implicit or explicit assumptions about their spatiotemporal configurations. Such assumptions can be introduced, e. g., as 2D geometric shape representations or as a particular structure (parallel, divergent, . . .) of an OF-field. The resulting Picture Domain Cues (PDCs, see [215]) are forwarded to the

Scene Domain Level (SDL) where *three*-dimensional knowledge is exploited, for example in the form of body models, illumination models, or trajectory models which represent admitted forms of body movements.

Up to and including this SDL, knowledge about the depicted scene and results obtained from image sequences appear in quantitative, numerical form, referring to spatial, temporal, and spectral attributes of *geometric* representations for bodies, surfaces, and locations. Intermediate results of the SDL – so-called Scene Domain Cues (SDCs, see [215]) – can be fed back to the PDL, for example in order to prepare for the proper handling of discontinuities due to impending occlusions. SDCs will in general be fed forward to the

Conceptual Primitives Level (CPL) where they will be converted from the quantitative, numerical form to a qualitative, *conceptual* representation. The implied *pattern recognition* or *classification* subprocesses constitute important *abstraction* steps.

In general, results will be *uncertain* to some extent due to the influence of unavoidable signal *noise*, due to *processing artefacts* related to approximations or undetected implementation errors, and due to the inherent *vagueness* of concepts. The transition to a conceptual representation facilitates to apply strict, fuzzy, or stochastic inference engines in order to further select or combine intermediate results based on *conceptual knowledge*.

The conceptual primitive representation of bodies, of their properties, relations, and movements, constitute the building blocks for an even more aggregated and thereby more abstract representation of developments in the scene, generated and maintained at the

Behavioral Representation Level (BRL). Once a suitable representational schema at the BRL has been instantiated based on results fed forward from previously mentioned system levels, it provides the data to generate a natural language text describing – in the usual sense of this word – the developments and current state in the recorded scene, at least to the extent it has been captured by image sequences.

Natural Language Level (NLL) This transformation of a representation at the CPL and the BRL into a text constitutes the task of the 'Natural Language Level'.

Obviously, the computational machinery required for such a transformation (lexica, grammars, logical inference engines, etc.) can be exploited, too, in order to translate a natural language inquiry by a user of the System into a logical representation compatible with the ones designed for the CPL and the BRL. A user may thus communicate with the System in a manner familiar to him from communication between humans.

Part of the terminology outlined in this section has been used to characterize the development of a system which transforms monocular videos recorded at an innercity road traffic intersection into textual descriptions of what happens in the recorded scenes [319]. In order to avoid repetitions, the examples reported there will not be discussed in detail here again, nor earlier publications from our group which document selected technical developments. The preliminary conclusion from these experiments for the current contribution is – not surprisingly – that the terminology is suited to capture important aspects of such a system development history. It thus appears justified to further investigate this conceptual framework in two directions, namely (i) by extensions and (ii) by applying it to other documented systems.

5.2.3 Extensions Towards a Multiple-Agent RWS (M-ARWS)

The concepts introduced so far for the characterization of a CogVS apply only to a rather strongly restricted RWS. Only a single agent is admitted whose actions are assumed to cause all appearance changes within the recorded field of view. In a strict sense, this terminology does not yet allow to treat an isolated vehicle to be tracked as an agent if the System itself is taken to be the agent: it is the system which records and interprets the recorded videos. Observable changes in the recorded field of view are implicitly assumed – according to the conceptual framework discussed so far – to have been caused by the recording system itself.

This is clearly unsatisfactory. An alternative to evade this dilemma would require that the System constitutes part of a vehicle equipped with one or more video camera(s). This vehicle is assumed to be the only one on an otherwise empty road. Such experiments have been performed indeed, albeit with different system versions designed for (near) real-time performance with respect to lane tracking (see, e. g., [321], [183, 129, 130]).

A theoretically more satisfactory alternative consists in an extension of the conceptual framework introduced so far, namely the admission of *more* than a single agent. Let us assume for the moment that the conceptual representation of a single agent is retained with the following exception: the postulate is abandoned that *all* changes can be attributed to the same *single* admitted agent. Abandoning this restriction allows to study the hypothesis that changes 'observed' by one agent are due to another agent which potentially can be observed, too, by the first agent ('the observer'). As a consequence, the 'observer-internal' representation of RWS-states has to incorporate state-configurations which reflect the 'observations' and inferences of the 'observer-agent' concerning the activities of other (observed or hypothesized, for example momentarily occluded) agents.

As a consequence of such an extension, the coarse conceptual stratification of representations discussed in Section 5.2.2 can be re-used as a scheme for each admitted agent. Each agent thus constructs a representation of the RWS *based on its own interactions with the RWS*. These interactions may occur in the form of signal sensing, of actions, or of communication-acts (assumed to constitute a particular subset of admitted actions) – both with the 'user' which is represented within an agent as just another 'agent' or as communication actions between 'observed agents'. The latter case occurs, e. g., if a vehicle switches on its direction indicators in order to signal to other vehicles at an intersection the intention to turn off.

Such an approach promises the advantage that the 'world-view' of an agent allows to model, for example, a traffic surveillance system including its operator-interactions with a minimum of additional conceptual machinery. It thus becomes perfectly conceivable within such a framework that a computer-vision-based driver-support-system eventually communicates via a cell-phone connection with a road surveillance system based on computer vision. The incorporation of additional signal modalities (radar, induction loops, infrared cameras, inertial sensors, etc.) into this conceptual framework should not constitute a fundamental obstacle. The comparison between trajectory estimates obtained from within a vehicle and from outside as reported in [321] can be looked at as a first step towards modeling such a RWS.

The admission of more than a single agent into the conceptual framework discussed so far opens another interesting avenue of research, namely the study of *interactions between observed agents*, i. e. the study of the *behaviour of agent groups*. Attempts to describe the aggregation and dissolution of vehicle queues in front of a traffic signal or an obstacle constitute an example, see [145].

5.2.4 Tools for the Creation of Schematic Representations of Behaviour

The design of schematic representations for visible bodies and body configurations – either a-priori or starting from observations by an agent – can be treated as a standard task during the conception and implementation of a computer vision system. It has been tacitly assumed so far that the same is true with respect to the design of schematic representations of agent behaviour(s). The latter task, however, still constitutes an active area of research, with many alternatives being explored. It is not the goal of this contribution to survey or even review such efforts.

It may be easier, however, to accept the justification for the hypotheses underlying this contribution if such efforts can be illustrated by an example with which the author is familiar, namely behavioural schemes in the form of so-called *Situation Graph Trees (SGTs)*. In their present form, they offer a deterministic representation of behaviour observable within a RWS. An SGT is a hierarchical structure of graphs, i. e. a special type of hypergraph. Nodes in each component graph of an SGT represent a 'situation scheme'. Such a 'situation node' *combines* the '*state*' of an agent and its environment with an '*action*' which the agent is assumed to perform when it together with its environment is found to be in this state. Both 'state' and 'action' are to be understood as introduced in Chapter 5.2.1. The state of an agent and its environment – which may well comprise other agents – is specified by a conjunction of fuzzy metric-temporal predicates (see [390]). Prioritized so-called 'prediction edges' connect a situation node to the set of admissible successor nodes. The prediction edge with highest priority often connects back to the node it came from in order to reflect the observation that a state usually prevails for more than a single time-instant. If the predicates in the state representation of a node can no longer be instantiated at a particular time on the basis of 'individual' identifiers and relations between them according to the rules of predicate logic, the situation scheme reached by the next lower prioritized prediction edge is tested for a potential instantiation. The 'universe' of such individuals and the relations between them are created at the interface between the computer vision subsystem and the conceptual subsystem when the latter 'imports' new evidence extracted by the former from the video input stream. In addition to prediction edges, another type of edge connects a situation node to a subordinated graph which *particularizes* the situation node either by adding additional predicates to the state specification ('specialisation edge') or by decomposing a situation node into an entire subgraph comprising a more detailed representation of potential agent behavior ('temporal decomposition').

A kind of tutorial introduction to the current version of the SGT-formalism can be found in [320]. A Graphical User Interface (GUI) has been designed, implemented, and made available under GNU Public License in order to facilitate design and testing of SGTs [15]. These tools have been used – amongst others – to generate SGTs in order to understand traffic videos and to create synthetic videos on the basis of an agent-internal representation of behavioural knowledge ([16, 17]). Details of this representational scheme will not be explained here because this contribution argues that it should be clarified first *which* knowledge has to be explicated within a representation before one studies *how* the required knowledge is to be represented. It thus may suffice for the moment that methods and tools are available which allow to investigate such a problem even for the case of knowledge about agent *behaviour*.

5.3 On the Specification of a Camera-Based Road Traffic Surveillance System

The model-based tracking system Xtrack (see, e.g., [166, 336]) may provide an example for what *should* have been specified, but partially happened based on intuition, more or less modified by a-posteriori 'rationalisation' (see, too, [319]). The enumeration of aspects is sometimes followed by comments on – and even a 'rationalisation' for – the current status of the system.

This – by no means exhaustive – enumeration is subdivided into three different topics. The first one is concerned with details of what constitutes the discourse domain. The next topic addresses the question how to specify admissible variations of context conditions which may potentially influence the performance of an operational CogVS. The third topic explicates some questions associated with the problem to *quantify* the performance of a CogVS.

5.3.1 Characterization of the Discourse Domain

The investigations concentrate so far on *innercity vehicular* road traffic. In the sequel, a distinction is made between *movable* and *non-movable* bodies. Among the movable bodies, the system approach is restricted to the treatment of (a subclass of) road *vehicles*. No attempt has been made to detect, track, and describe the movement of humans (pedestrians, bicycle riders, inline-skaters, etc.), animals, or other movable bodies such as carts. Among non-movable bodies, treatment is restricted to '*road(s)*' with '*lane(s)*', '*location(s)*', '*traffic signal(s)*', '*road sign(s)*', '*mast(s)*', and other (potentially occluding) '*object(s)*' such as trees or advertising columns.

Admitted road vehicles The set of admitted road vehicles will be restricted to *car(s)* and *bus(ses)*. The latter category will be understood to refer exclusively to instances of an innercity bus used for public transport, i. e. busses used for *inter*-city road traffic have been excluded. The reason is simply that busses for innercity public transport in Germany have been standardized to the extent that a single 3D-polyhedral model should be sufficient to treat all such vehicles. The category of cars is subdivided further into '*sedan(s)*', '*fastback(s)*', '*station wagon(s)*', and '*van(s)*' or '*mini-bus(ses)*' (vehicles for the transportation of up to nine persons).

Currently, *our experiments are restricted to the first three subcategories* despite the fact the Xtrack-system comprises 3D-polyhedral models, too, for innercity buses and vans. This restriction is likely to be retained until the system will be able to automatically categorize vehicle candidates at least among these three subcategories which it currently cannot yet do with sufficient reliability. The reason for this 'research challenge' (or failure, depending on the current mood) is simply that a reasonably reliable initialisation and tracking should not depend critically on details of the 3D-polyhedral model used and thus does not allow yet to differentiate between the models developped for these three subcategories.

'Agent' and 'patient' vehicles We refer to the vehicle which should constitute the subject of a descriptive sentence as the *'agent'* vehicle whereas a vehicle which appears as sentence object or within a prepositional phrase will be referred to as *'patient'*.

With a few exceptions in exploratory experiments, our investigations currently concentrate on the treatment of movements and behaviors of single agent and single patient vehicles.

Movement(s) Movements constitute the linguistic primitive descriptions for spatiotemporal changes of agents. The description of a (short-term) movement associates (part of) a vehicle trajectory in the 3D scene with one of the admitted vehicular motion verbs. They correspond to the verbs in the system dictionary.

System-internal representations have been developped *for all movements* admitted for agents in innercity road traffic scenes – see, e. g., [143] for a partial list and [144] for a more complete set.

Maneuvers A maneuver describes an elementary movement which serves as a component in a description of vehicular behavior. Linguistically, one may consider verbphrases as the corresponding concept, i. e. a verb possibly in combination with an object and propositional phrases. The notion of 'occurrence' is used to denote such building blocks. In many languages, there exist special verbs which can be 'explained' as a verbphrase using a 'primitive' verb (such as to drive).

System-internal representations have been developed for *all* single-agent maneuvers comprising single patient vehicles or a single predefined location in addition to lane references. Limitations still exist regarding desirable flexibility in the choice of locations, including reference to any non-movable body even if the system incorporates already a 3D polyhedral model for such a body.

Behavior(s) A system-internal representation, the Situation Graph Tree (SGT) formalism, enables the concatenation of single-agent maneuvers in order to generate descriptions of *goal-directed* behaviors. This formalism has been used to encode single-agent behavior at a gas station and at innercity intersections. These representations, however, are not yet considered to be comprehensive. In addition, more experience with the use of this formalism is needed for the generation of natural language textual descriptions, in particular regarding videos from other intersections than the ones with which we have experimented so far.

5.3.2 Variability of Spatiotemporal Context

Xtrack currently admits only two illumination conditions, namely *'diffuse daylight'* and *'directed sunlight'*. Up until recently, it had to be specified *interactively* which illumination condition prevailed while the camera recorded the video to be analysed. An attempt can become quite involved to endow the Xtrack system with the capability to estimate the currently prevailing illumination conditions from the video sequence to be analysed [336]).

No efforts have been started so far to extend the system towards a capability to cope with rainy weather, with fog, or with nighttime illumination.

Experience indicates that a change of camera pose or the switch to a different road intersection is not expected to generate much trouble, provided the camera can be calibrated with respect to the road plane and a polygonal model of the new lane structure will be made available.

5.3.3 Measuring System Performance

Measuring system performance will be discussed by indicating which aspects could be quantified. Other potential assessment aspects will be left open at this time.

Detection rate This can be defined as the ratio of the number of agent vehicles detected after they have entered the field of view of the recording camera and the total number of such vehicles within a given video sequence. Uncertainties in the determination of this relation could be associated with fuzziness of the degree to which a vehicle must be visible, and the delay (i. e. the number of frames) which pass before the system announces detection. On top of these questions, the relation between tolerable false alarms versus true misses has to be fixed.

Categorisation Xtrack depends on a vehicle model. It has been observed that a 'wrong' vehicle model can severely impair the initialisation and tracking steps. 'Wrong' may refer either to a general difference regarding the assigned vehicle type (e. g., truck vs. car), in the choice of an inappropriate subtype (for example, fastback vs. station wagon), or in the selection of an inappropriate size parameter (the car body, e. g., may be 0.1 m longer than the length of the 3D polyhedral body model used for tracking).

So far, selected vehicle type and length have either been selected *interactively* or, more recently, the categorisation step has been skipped entirely in favor of operation with a *single* standard car model (usually a fastback which happens to be the most frequently occurring single vehicle type in our current test video sequences).

Initialisation rate Following detection and model selection, 3D pose parameters have to be estimated for a newly detected vehicle. Experience has shown that the initialisation phase in many cases is crucial for the success of the subsequent tracking phase. It thus is important for diagnostic purposes to decide whether the initialisation occurred correctly and tracking went wrong later due to, for example, (partial) occlusion, or the problem is essentially related to an unsatisfactory initialisation.

Tracking rate Although it appears simple to define the ratio between the number of agent vehicles tracked 'correctly' vs. the total number of agent vehicles visible in the image sequence, a number of difficulties pop up here, too. Is it 'fair', though,

- to count a vehicle as a failure which has been tracked successfully for a thousand frames or more (the vehicle may have stopped in front of a traffic light or at the curb in order to allow a passenger to leave) right up to the last ten or so frames where it is lost
- when another vehicle is only visible for a small number of frames, but presented no difficulties?

The answer appears to count the number of interframe-transitions across which a vehicle has been tracked successfully. But then there may be vast differences in complexity due to (partial) occlusions, vanishing contrast against background, large shadows in part of the scene, just to name a few of the cases encountered so far. A difference in tracking rate thus can be more or less significant than it appears at first glance.

Precision Given an appropriate model, agent vehicle position can be estimated to a fraction of 0.1m even for vehicles 50m to 100m away from the camera: 0.05m correspond roughly to $1 - 2\%$ of a not too large car; if the car image extends for about 30 pixel, the quoted number requires that the vehicle position in the image is estimated to about half a pixel. This is perfectly possible given about $50 - 100$ edge elements fitted to the projected vehicle model. The question then becomes how much the projected model may be allowed to trail the vehicle image or vice versa: will a tracking result still be accepted as successful if the relative lag accumulates to $10 - 30\%$ of the vehicle length? Similar questions can be raised with respect to the tolerable differences in orientation or lateral offset.

Fine categorisation In many cases, it will not be possible to categorise a vehicle right after detection, not even for a human operator (vehicle images often cover only 20×30 pixels when a vehicle enters the field of view far away from the camera). In such situations, it may be advantageous to assign a vehicle candidate initially to a coarsely specified category (such as 'car') just to start the tracking process. It then can happen that the vehicle image becomes larger while the vehicle approaches the recording camera, or the vehicle turns, thereby exposing shape features which enable a more appropriate fine categorisation. A third alternative consists in the possibility to accumulate enough evidence for a certain categorisation option that the correct decision gradually becomes practically certain.

So far, `Xtrack` has not been operationalised to investigate coarse or fine categorisation.

5.4 Discussion and Conclusions

This may be an appropriate point to recall the main line of argumentation presented so far. Following an outline of concepts required for talking about a `CogVS`, its tasks and its internal structure, experience with an existing approach has been used to illustrate the range of alternatives which might have to be taken into account for a proper assessment of a system design and its performance.

One might be tempted to argue that the aspects discussed above and associated problems refer primarily to an engineering effort based on a drawing-board-oriented approach as opposed to the alternative to start out with a rudimentary, but mallable system which subsequently 'learns' while attempting to cope with a task. Both approaches have their merits and their inherent challenges for research. Given unavoidable limitations of time and resources, the desire will appear to compare different approaches in order to determine which one turns out to be superior under a certain set of boundary conditions.

Experience has shown that different approaches can be quite sensitive to apparently minor details of tasks, testing conditions, and assessment criteria. It thus appears worthwhile to study these influences in order to gain a balanced view. The items mentioned in the preceding enumerations illustrate how much care will be required to set up a fair comparison. A random collection of test samples is unlikely to be sufficient in the long run.

Acknowledgment

The investigations reported in this contribution have been partially supported by the European Union (FP5-project 'CogViSys', IST-2000-29404) and the Deutsche Forschungsgemeinschaft (DFG).

Part II

Recognition and Categorization

6

A System for Object Class Detection

Daniela Hall

INRIA Rhône-Alpes, 655, avenue de l'Europe,
38320 St. Ismier, France
Daniela.Hall@inrialpes.fr

Abstract. A successful detection and classification system must have two properties: it should be general enough to compensate for intra-class variability and it should be specific enough to reject false positives. We describe a method to learn class-specific feature detectors that are robust to intra-class variability. These feature detectors enable a representation that can be used to drive a subsequent process for verification. Instances of object classes are detected by a module that verifies the spatial relations of the detected features. We extend the verification algorithm in order to make it invariant to changes in scale. Because the method employs scale invariant feature detectors, objects can be detected and classified independently of the scale of observation. Our method has low computational complexity and can easily be trained for robust detection and classification of different object classes.

6.1 Introduction

Object detection is fundamental to vision. For most real world applications, object detection must be fast and robust to variations in imaging conditions such as changes in illumination, scale and view-point. It is also generally desirable that a detection system be easily trained, and be usable with a large variety of object classes. In this paper we show how to learn and use class specific features to detect objects under variations in scale and intra-class variability.

Our approach is similar to the work of Agarwal [1] who proposes a detection algorithm based on a sparse object representation. While her system is robust to occlusions, it can not deal with scale changes. She demonstrates her system on side views of cars. We extend Agarwal's idea to a larger set of object classes. We automatically construct class specific feature detectors that are robust to intra-class variability by learning the variations from a large data set and propose a representation for geometry verification with low computational complexity.

Fergus [120] has described a method to classify objects based on a probabilistic classifier that takes into account appearance, shape and scale of a small number of detected parts. His approach is robust to changes in scale, but is limited in the number of candidate parts that can be considered (≈ 30 maximum). The approaches of both Fergus

H.I. Christensen and H.-H. Nagel (Eds.): Cognitive Vision Systems, LNCS 3948, pp. 73–85, 2006.
© Springer-Verlag Berlin Heidelberg 2006

and Agarwal depend on reliable interest point detectors with a small false positive rate. Our approach is independent of such interest point detectors, and not affected by a large number of detections. Furthermore, our feature detectors are scale invariant, and thus provide object class detection under scale changes.

The article is organised as follows. Section 6.2 discusses the design of a detection and classification system. The components of this design are described in Section 6.3 and 6.4. The performance of the proposed system is demonstrated in the experimental Section 6.5.

6.2 Architecture of a Detection and Classification System

A successful detection and classification system must have two properties: it must be general enough to correctly assign instances of the same class despite large intra-class variability and it must be specific enough to reject instances that are not part of the class. Features robust to intra-class variability can be constructed by learning from examples. The result is a feature or part detector that can generalise from a small number of examples to new examples. Such a detector can provide a hypothesis about the presence of a class instance, but it is in general not specific enough for reliable detection and classification.

The relative position of distinct object features is important for classification and needs to be modeled as for example in the approaches of Fergus and Agarwal. In these approaches, the verification is computationally expensive, because the relations of all candidate parts need to be verified. A geometry verification module can provide the required specificity of the system. The flexibility of feature extraction and the specificity of spatial relations can be implemented in an elegant way by an architecture with two components (see Figure 6.1): a feature extraction module that provides features invariant to intra-class variability and a geometry verification module that introduces specificity, increases the reliability of the detection and rejects false positives.

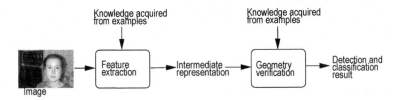

Fig. 6.1. System architecture consisting of low level feature extraction and higher level geometry verification

6.3 Low Level Feature Extraction

Our low level measurements are local image features with limited spatial extent. Local features are commonly described by neighborhood operators [227] that function as convolution masks and measure the responses to classes of local image patterns. A set of neigborhood operators provides a feature vector that measures several aspects (appearance) of a local neighborhood. Many different families of local neighborhood operators can be used, for example grey-scale invariants [397], gabor filters [495], or Gaussian derivatives [170, 266, 365].

6.3.1 Appearance Description by Gaussian Derivatives

Orthogonal families of neighborhood operators describe a local neighborhood with a minimum number of independent local features. Among the different neighborhood operators, several properties make the Gaussian derivative family an ideal candidate for appearance description of local neighborhoods. The family is orthonormal and complete. Scale is controlled by an explicit parameter. The low order Gaussian derivatives measure the basic geometry of a local neighborhood. Similarity of neighborhoods can be measured by defining a distance metric in feature space. The low dimensions of the feature space enables fast algorithms and avoids computational problems due to the curse of dimensionality.

Lindeberg [255] has proposed an algorithm to determine the intrinsic scale of local image features. Normalising features to the intrinsic feature scale enables a scale invariant description of local appearance. The intrinsic scale of a feature is characterised by a maximum in scale and space. Such a maximum can be found by sampling the response of a normalised Laplacian at different scales. Gaussian derivatives are applied successfully to various computer vision problems. The fast implementation of derivatives [467] and the algorithm for scale normalisation makes the Gaussian derivative local jet an ideal candidate for the scale invariant description of the appearance of local image neighborhoods.

In this article we focus on the detection of instances of object classes. The color information of images of the same class has a high variance. The variance of the texture in the luminance channel is less pronounced. The luminance channel is less affected by changes in illumination conditions. In our experiments, we use first and second derivatives computed from luminance and normalised to the intrinsic scale. The raw features are therefore points in a five dimensional scale invariant Gaussian derivative feature space. We do not normalise for orientation, because the absolute orientation of features is discriminant for particular features. If orientation invariance is required, a rotation invariant feature space can be used such as the one proposed by Schmid [395].

6.3.2 Features Appropriate for Classification

The raw Gaussian derivative features are appropriate for retrieval of corresponding matching candidates according to the distance in feature space that measures their similarity. This matching principle produces very good results in identification, image retrieval or other applications where the exact entity of the local neighborhood is searched, because in such cases the appearance variance between model and observed neighborhood is small. An image class is characterised by the co-occurrence of typical parts in a particular spatial arrangement. The typical parts can also have a large variance in their spatial relation. Using raw Gaussian derivatives directly for detection and classification is going to fail because the intra-class variability makes matching unreliable.

Features that can compensate for intra-class variability can be found by extracting the common parts of images of a visual class and learning the variation in appearance. Fergus [120] learns a probabilistic classifier from a large number of examples. Classification is obtained by evaluating a maximum likelihood ratio on different combination hypotheses of potential parts that are indicated by a salient region detector. This detector is essentially equivalent to a scale invariant interest point detector, such as the Harris Laplacian proposed by Mikolajczyk [300], that is also applied by Schmid and Dorko in [103, 395]. The approach depends on the detection of salient regions. No false negatives are tolerated and at the same time the number of potential candidates should be small, because the computational complexity is exponential.

Much effort is done to make interest point detectors stable and accurate. However, interest point detectors respond to image neighborhoods of particular appearance (corner features or salient features). This limits the approach to objects that can be modeled by this particular kind of features. Uniform objects can be missed because the interest point detector does not detect any points. In the following section we propose a method to compute class specific feature detectors that are robust to the feature variance of images of the same class and that are independent from general interest point detectors.

6.3.3 Computation of Class-Specific Feature Detectors

For the extraction of class-specific features, we learn the appearance of class-specific object parts from a dense, pixelwise, grid of features by clustering. Clustering of dense features is similar to Leung and Malik's approach for computation of generic features for texture classification [276]. The feature extraction is fast due to the recursive implementation of Gaussian derivatives [467]. Furthermore, the clustering produces statistically correct results, because a large amount of data points is used.

We use k-means clustering to associate close points in feature space. K-means is an iterative algorithm that is initialised with points drawn at random from the data. In each iteration, the points are associated to the closest cluster centers which are updated at the end of each cycle. An overall error is computed which converges to a minimum. The risk of returning a sub-optimal solution is reduced by running k-means several times and keeping the best solution in terms of overall error.

We assume that the data in feature space can be represented by multi-dimensional Gaussians. Non-elliptical clusters are represented by a mixture of Gaussians. Cluster C_j is characterised by its mean $\boldsymbol{\mu}_j$ (the cluster center) and covariance Σ_j (the shape of the cluster). This allows to compute the probability that a measurement belongs to cluster C_j as:

$$p_j(\mathbf{m}) = \frac{1}{(2\pi)^{d/2}|\Sigma|^{1/2}} \exp(-\frac{1}{2}(\mathbf{m} - \boldsymbol{\mu}_j)^T \Sigma_j^{-1}(\mathbf{m} - \boldsymbol{\mu}_j)) \qquad (6.1)$$

This gives rise to k probability maps where the image position (x, y) of probability map j is marked by $p_j(\mathbf{m_{xy}})$ of the extracted Gaussian derivative feature $\mathbf{m_{xy}}$. The probability maps can be condensed to a single cluster map M with k colors where the label at position (x, y) is computed as:

$$M(x, y) = \arg \max_{j=1,..,k} p_j(\mathbf{m_{xy}}) \qquad (6.2)$$

Figure 6.2 illustrates the feature extraction process. The top right graph shows an example of the probability maps (low probabilities are black, high probabilities are light grey). We observe maps which mark uniform regions, bar like regions or more complex regions such as the eyes. The corresponding clusters are the class-specific feature detectors. Many neighboring pixels are assigned to the same cluster and form connected regions. This is natural, because the local neighborhood of close pixels have a strong overlap, with a high probability that the image neighborhoods are assigned to the same cluster.

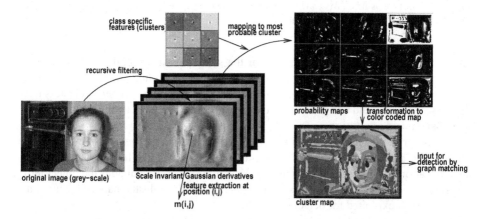

Fig. 6.2. Algorithm for raw feature extraction and mapping to most probable class specific features. The probability maps are condensed to a single color coded cluster map, where color k marks points that are assigned to cluster k.

The cluster map representation is an enormous data reduction, but at the same time, it preserves the information about class specific features and their location. This is the minimum information required for detection and classification. The cluster map representation is specific enough to provide detection and it is general enough to enable classification of images with a large intra-class variability. Evidence provide the experiments.

Another important point is that this cluster map representation is scale invariant. The scale invariance property of the raw features translates to the cluster prototypes and also to the mapping. In Figure 6.3 we show the original image at numerically scaled resolutions and the computed cluster map. Despite the resolution changes of factor 5 (left to right) corresponding face parts have the same color label, that is $M_{\sigma_1}(\sigma_1 x, \sigma_1 y) = M_{\sigma_2}(\sigma_2 x, \sigma_2 y)$.

6.3.4 Parameter Optimisation

In this section we explain how we can judge the quality of a particular clustering and select those clusters that are useful for object description. A useful object description marks the class specific features such that the description allows to generalise from

Fig. 6.3. Cluster maps M_{σ_1}, M_{σ_2}, M_{σ_3} computed from images at different resolutions. The class-specific feature detectors are scale invariant.

the training examples to unseen objects of the same class and the description allows to discriminate the object from non-objects such as background. A small number of clusters produce high generality, but bad discriminance. A high number of clusters has high discriminance and bad generalisation. This problem is related to finding the correct model and avoid overfitting.

We observe that neighboring image features are frequently assigned to the same cluster. This is a sign for the stability of the feature. Such stable features have a good generalisation ability. A good set of feature descriptors therefore divides the object into several connected regions and forms a particular pattern in the cluster map representation. This pattern is exploited for detection.

The clusters should provide a segmentation into a number of connected regions. The regions should mark particular class specific features. There should be not too few regions neither too many. We tested k in the range from 5 to 40 and selected those clusters that are stable within the region of the training objects. As stability criteria we consider the average connected component size.

6.4 Verifying Spatial Relations

The complexity of identifying the best spatial configuration of a set of parts is related to a random graph matching problem. The complexity of matching a full graph with N model parts and M candidate parts is $O(M^N)$. This exponential complexity is the reason that Fergus and Agarwal's approaches can handle only a small number of candidate parts. Labelling of graph nodes reduces the complexity to $O(\prod_{k=1}^{N} M_k)$ and M_k the number of candidate parts of model part k [250]. The complexity can be further reduced by imposing stronger constraints on the graph topology. This reduces the flexibility of the graph with the advantage of an efficient graph matching algorithm. The details of such an elastic matching of labelled graphs as proposed in [242, 345, 495] is explained in the next section where we also propose an alternative cost function that enables matching invariant to scale.

6.4.1 Elastic Matching of Labelled Graphs

Elastic graph matching has previously been applied for grouping neurons dynamically into higher order entities [242]. These entities represent a rich structure which enables the recognition of higher level objects. Model objects are represented by sparse graphs whose vertices are labelled by a local appearance description and whose edges are labelled by geometric distance vectors. Recognition is formulated as elastic graph matching, that optimizes a matching cost function, which combines appearance similarity of the vertices and geometric graph similarity computed from the geometric information of the edges.

The matching cost function consists of two parts, C_v appearance similarity of the node labels, and C_e spatial similarity of the graph edges. A sparse graph $G = (\{x_i\}, \{\mathbf{\Delta_{ij}}\})$ consists of a set of vertices $\{x_i\}$ with image positions $\mathbf{v_i}$ and labels $\mathbf{m_i}$ that measure the local image appearance. The vertices are connected by edges $\mathbf{\Delta_{ij}} = \mathbf{v_i} - \mathbf{v_j}$ which are the distance vectors of the image position of the vertices x_i, x_j.

The spatial similarity evaluates corresponding edges of the query and the model graph by a quadratic comparison function:

$$S_e(\mathbf{\Delta_{ij}}^I, \mathbf{\Delta_{ij}}^M) = (\mathbf{\Delta_{ij}}^I - \mathbf{\Delta_{ij}}^M)^2, (i,j) \in E \qquad (6.3)$$

where E is the set of edges in the model graph. The set E_{nn} containing the four nearest neighbors of a vertex is better suited to handle local distortions than the complete edge set [242].

The spatial similarity, S_e, measures the correspondence of the spatial distances between neighboring nodes. Distances are measured in pixels. The measure in (6.3) is scale dependent. This means that the measure can not distinguish between scaling and a strong distortion. We propose a normalisation by a scaling matrix, U, that can be computed from a global scale factor estimate. This normalisation makes the spatial similarity measure scale invariant.

$$U = \begin{pmatrix} \frac{w^I}{w^M} & 0 \\ 0 & \frac{h^I}{h^M} \end{pmatrix} \qquad (6.4)$$

$$S_{e,U}(\mathbf{\Delta_{ij}}^I, \mathbf{\Delta_{ij}}^M) = (\mathbf{\Delta_{ij}}^I - U\mathbf{\Delta_{ij}}^M)^2 \qquad (6.5)$$

with w^I, w^M width and h^I, h^M height of the query and the model region respectively.

Appearance similarity of labels is computed as the Mahalanobis distance of the feature vectors $\mathbf{m^I}, \mathbf{m^M} \in \mathcal{R}^d$:

$$S_v(\mathbf{m^I}, \mathbf{m^M}) = (\mathbf{m^I} - \mathbf{m^M})^T C^{-1}(\mathbf{m^I} - \mathbf{m^M}) \qquad (6.6)$$

where C is the covariance of the local feature vectors of the training data. The Mahalanobis distance has the advantage to compensate for the covariance between the dimensions of the feature space. This measure is known to be stabler than the Euclidean distance in a features space composed of Gaussian derivatives of different order [78].

The cost function C_{total} is a weighted sum of the spatial similarity and the appearance similarity.

$$C_{total}(\{x_i^I\}, \{x_i^M\}) = \lambda C_e + C_v$$
$$= \lambda \sum_{(i,j) \in E} S_{e,U}(\mathbf{\Delta_{ij}}^I, \mathbf{\Delta_{ij}}^M) - \sum_{i \in V} S_v(\mathbf{m_i^I}, \mathbf{m_i^M}) \quad (6.7)$$

The weighting factor λ controls the acceptable distortions of the query graph by penalising more or less the spatial similarity. The graph rigidity can be varied dynamically during optimization, which allows to employ a two stage algorithm that first places a rigid graph at the locally optimal position. The global cost function is then improved by allowing local distortions.

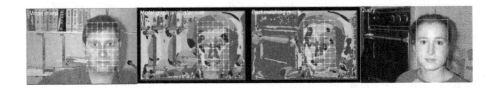

Fig. 6.4. Example of a detection by elastic graph matching on cluster map representation

The original algorithm proposed by Lades is non-deterministic. Peters has proposed a deterministic version, that proceeds as follows. First a rigid graph is placed at the best position by raster scanning the image with a coarse step size. Then the graph is distorted locally by updating each node within a small window such that the labels are the most similar. An example is shown in Figure 6.4.

When scale changes must be considered, we search the optimal position and the optimal scale in the first step of the algorithm. These parameters are kept constant for the local optimisation phase. The optimal scale is selected among a predefined range of discrete values. We envision a preprocessing module that provides a rough estimate of the global object size, and the object position. Such a module would reduce significantly the computation time of the matching algorithm.

Without the preprocessing module, the matching algorithm has a complexity of $O(k_{nodes} k_{win} N) = O(N)$ with k_{nodes} the number of nodes (typically in the range of 70 to 200), N the number of tested positions in the image (related to the image size), and k_{win} the size of the search window for the local position refinement. We use this graph matching algorithm to compare a query graph to a reference model graph.

6.5 Experiments

First we explain how the experiments are evaluated. Then the first experiment detects and classifies objects of approximately constant object size. This demonstrates the advantage of the class specific features over raw Gaussian derivative features. In the second experiment, artificially scaled objects are located by elastic graph matching using the model of the first experiment. This demonstrates the robustness to scale changes of our approach. The third experiment shows the performance of the system to detection of target objects in unconstrained images.

6.5.1 Set Up

Fergus evaluates the results by ROC (receiver operator characteristics) equal error rates against the background dataset. His system evaluates a maximum likelihood ratio $\frac{p(Obj|X,S,A)}{p(BG|X,S,A)}$ where the background is modeled from the Caltech background set. In this way, few insertions are observed for this particular background set, but an equivalent performance on a different background set is not guaranteed. As stated by Agarwal [1], the ROC measures a system's accuracy as a classifier not as a detector. To evaluate the accuracy of a detector, we are interested in how many objects are detected correctly and how often the detections are false. These aspects of a system are captured by a recall-precision curve.

$$\text{Recall} = \frac{\text{Number of correct positives}}{\text{Total number of positives in dataset}} \tag{6.8}$$

$$\text{Precision} = \frac{\text{Number of correct positives}}{\text{Number of correct positives} + \text{Number of false positives}} \tag{6.9}$$

In order to suppress multiple detections on nearby locations, Agarwal implements the scheme of a classifier activation map, that allows to return only the activation extrema within a rectangular window with parameters w_{win}, h_{win}. A point (i_0, j_0) is considered an object location if

$$\text{cost}(i_0, j_0) \leq \text{cost}(i, j), \forall (i, j) \in N \tag{6.10}$$

where $N = \{(i, j) : |i - i_0| \leq w_{win}, |j - j_0| \leq h_{win}\}$ and no other point in N has been declared an object location.

We use the image database provided by Caltech[1] and the BioID database [207], with known object position and size. Figure 6.5 shows some example images. We consider a detection correct when following constraints are fulfilled.

1. $|i_{true} - i_{det}| < \delta_{width}$ and $|j_{true} - j_{det}| < \delta_{height}$, and
2. the detection and the ground truth region have an overlap of at least θ_{area}.

The parameters are set as a function of the object size, (w^M, h^M). We use $\delta_{width} = \frac{1}{3}w^M, \delta_{height} = \frac{1}{3}h^M$ and $\theta_{area} = 50\%$. This corresponds to the parameter setting used by Agarwal.

6.5.2 Detection Without Scale Changes

Table 6.1 summarises the detection results for different object classes, evaluated with different maximum cost thresholds (rectangles mark the best results with a false detection rate of $< 10\%$). There is a tradeoff between recall and precision according to this threshold. We compare elastic graph matching on 5 dimensional Gaussian derivative features (first and second derivatives, scale invariant) and elastic graph matching on the cluster map representation. For faces, the Gaussian derivatives have a higher precision than the cluster map representation. This is due to the significant data reduction which

---

[1] available at http://www.vision.caltech.edu/html-files/archive.html

Fig. 6.5. Example Images of the Caltech databases and the BioID face database

increase the frequency of insertions. However, we obtain very good detection rates with both techniques.

For the other data bases, the cluster map representation produces superior results. Motorbikes and airplanes can be reliably localised ($\geq$ 95%) with false detection rates $<$ 10%. Elastic graph matching on Gaussian derivative features has a higher false positive rate. This confirms that the cluster map representation detects the class-specific feature robustly to intra-class variations.

The data base of rear views of cars has a much lower precision rate. This is due to the lack of structure of the target objects. Many false positives are found. The targets display a large variance in appearance and also in the spatial arrangement which explains the lower detection rate. The current non-optimised implementation requires an average of $3.3s$ for processing an image of size 252x167 pixels on a Pentium 1.4GHz (automatic scale selection, 5 Gaussian derivative filter operations on all image pixels, transformation into cluster map representation and optimising elastic graph matching function).

6.5.3 Detection Under Scale Changes

To evaluate the performance of our system to objects of different sizes, we have created artificially scaled images from the Caltech database and a database with natural scale changes (the first 99 images of the BioID database [207]). The cluster map representation is scale invariant due to the scale invariant feature extraction! (see Figure 6.3). The spatial relation model in form of a labelled graph is scale dependent. When searching a best fitting graph, we search the best position and the best scale among a set of discrete positions and scales (we test positions that are evenly spaced by 3 pixels and the tested scales are $0.56, 0.75, 1.0, 1.25$). Table 6.2 shows the detection results. We observe high detection rates. However, many more false positives are observed, elastic graph matching optimises the matching function in space, distortion and scale. As a consequence we observe more false positives which decreases the precision rate. Figure 6.6 shows an example of typical insertions. The object is detected correctly and in addition several

Table 6.1. Detection results without scale changes (rectangles mark best results with precision > 90%)

Detection by elastic graph matching using					
Cluster map			Gaussian derivatives, 5 dims		
Faces, 435 images, graph 7x10 nodes, 5 classtons					
Max cost	Recall	Precision	Max cost	Recall	Precision
25	92.2%	95.7%	160	96.4%	91.6%
35	94.3%	87.7%	180	99.5%	43.8%
45	96.4%	77.7%			
Motorbikes, 200 images, graph 9x15 nodes, 5 classtons					
50	91.5%	96%	600	69.8%	75.5%
70	97%	91.1%	1000	82.4%	66.4%
Airplanes, 200 images, graph 7x19 nodes, 5 classtons					
55	95.3%	90.3%	800	74.8%	98.8%
65	96.3%	84.4%	1000	94.4%	87.1%
75	96.3%	74.6%			
Cars (rear view), 200 images, graph 11x15 nodes, 10 classtons					
100	72%	62.1%	1000	65.5%	62.6%
120	91.2%	54.3%	1200	84%	58.3%

Table 6.2. Detection of objects on images with scale changes (method elastic graph on cluster map)

	Scale range	Recall	Precision	Max cost
Faces	0.56 - 1.0	96.2%	42.1%	35
		93.6%	54.5%	30
Motorbikes	0.56 - 1.0	82.9%	57.3%	85
		80.9%	65%	70
Airplanes	0.56 - 1.25	89.6%	58.9%	65
		83.6%	68%	55
BioID faces	natural	89.9%	75.4%	30

subparts of the motorbike are detected as well. An algorithm which removes multiple detections would help to reduce the high number of insertions and improve the detector precision.

6.5.4 Detection in Unconstrained Images

We tested our method on images with natural scale changes. For detection of faces, we use the cluster map representation that is learned from the faces of the Caltech face database. For detection we perform elastic graph matching on cluster map over different scales. Figure 6.7 shows an detection example. The model image is significantly different from the query faces. All faces are detected and we observe no false positives.

Fig. 6.6. Example of typical insertions under scale changes

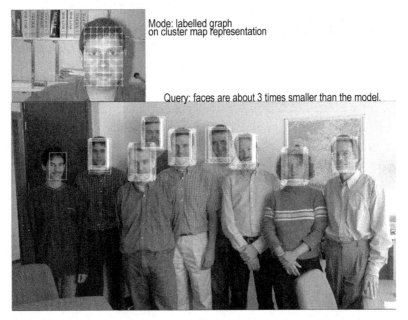

Fig. 6.7. Successful detection of faces in unconstrained images. The white rectangles mark the position and size of the graphs with lowest cost.

6.6 Conclusions and Future Work

In this article we have proposed a method to generate class-specific feature detectors that learn the intra-class variability and allows to represent an image as a cluster map, which preserves the position and the type of the class-specific feature. This is the minimum information required for detection and classification. Reliable detection is obtained by verifying spatial constraints of the features by graph matching. We proposed a method for geometry verification that has a much lower computational complexity than other algorithms. Furthermore, the proposed verification method is invariant to scale and enables successful detection of different kinds of object classes. The method allows to locate objects observed at various scales and produces good results for a selection of unconstrained images.

The strong data reduction of the cluster maps increases the probability of false positives. This is natural and caused by the information reduction of the cluster map representation. The current implementation is non-optimised and requires to search scale space for optimising the matching cost function. We are working on an additional preprocessing module that extracts candidate locations by image signal properties at very large scale. The a-priori knowledge of the location and approximate size of candidate regions is the key for a fast detection and classification system.

7

Greedy Kernel Principal Component Analysis*

Vojtěch Franc and Václav Hlaváč

Czech Technical University, Faculty of Electrical Engineering
Department of Cybernetics, Center for Machine Perception
121 35 Prague 2, Karlovo náměstí 13, Czech Republic
{xfrancv,hlavac}@cmp.felk.cvut.cz

Abstract. This contribution discusses one aspect of statistical learning and generalization. The theory of learning is very relevant to cognitive systems including cognitive vision.

A technique allowing to approximate a huge training set is proposed. The approach aims to represent data in a low dimensional space with possibly minimal representation error which is similar to the Principal Component Analysis (PCA). In contrast to the PCA, the basis vectors of the low dimensional space used for data representation are properly selected vectors from the training set and not as their linear combinations. The basis vectors can be selected by a simple algorithm which has low computational requirements and allows on-line processing of huge data sets. As the computations in the proposed algorithm appear in the form of a dot product, kernel methods can be used to cope with non-linear problems.

The proposed method was tested to approximate training sets of the Support Vector Machines and the Kernel Fisher Linear Discriminant which are known methods for learning classifiers. The experiments show that the proposed approximation can significantly reduce the complexity of the found classifiers while retaining their accuracy. On the other hand, the method is not very suitable for denoising.

7.1 Introduction

The kernel methods have become a fast developing branch of machine learning and pattern recognition in the past years. The kernel methods use kernel functions to perform a feature space straightening effectively. This technique allows to exploit the established linear classification theory to design their non-linear counterparts. Representatives of the kernel methods are for instance the Support Vector Machines (SVM) [468, 469] and the Kernel Fisher Discriminant (KFD) [299] which are learning systems for binary classifiers. The Kernel Principal Component Analysis (KPCA) is another example of the use of kernel functions to derive a non-linear version of the standard linear Principal Component Analysis (PCA).

A linear algorithm produces a solution function in the following form

---

* The authors were supported by the European Union projects ICA 1-CT-2000-70002, IST-2001-32184 ActIPret, by the Czech Ministry of Education under project MSM 212300013, by the Grant Agency of the Czech Republic project 102/03/0440.

H.I. Christensen and H.-H. Nagel (Eds.): Cognitive Vision Systems, LNCS 3948, pp. 87–105, 2006.

$$f(\boldsymbol{x}) = \langle \boldsymbol{w} \cdot \boldsymbol{x} \rangle + b \,, \tag{7.1}$$

where $\boldsymbol{x}$ and $\boldsymbol{w}$ are vectors in a space $\mathcal{X} \subseteq \mathbb{R}^n$, $b \in \mathbb{R}$ is a scalar and $\langle \boldsymbol{w} \cdot \boldsymbol{x} \rangle$ is a dot product between vectors $\boldsymbol{x}$ and $\boldsymbol{w}$. The vector $\boldsymbol{x}$ stands for the data to be processed and the pair $\boldsymbol{w}, b$ denotes the parameters of the solution function (7.1). For example, the function (7.1) can be a linear discriminant function used for classification of an object described by a feature vector $\boldsymbol{x}$. The linear algorithm usually learns the function $f(\boldsymbol{x})$ from a set of training vectors $\mathbf{X} = [\boldsymbol{x}_1, \dots, \boldsymbol{x}_l]$ (represented in a matrix for our purposes). The training set is often extended by additional information, for instance, by an assignment of the training vectors to classes.

Even though the linear algorithms are simple and well theoretically justified, they, however, cannot deal with the non-linearity in data if it is presented. A simple way how to extend linear algorithms is to use feature space straightening. The idea is to represent the training vectors $\mathbf{X} = [\boldsymbol{x}_1, \dots, \boldsymbol{x}_l]$ in a new higher dimensional feature space $\mathcal{F}$ using a non-linear mapping function $\boldsymbol{\phi} \colon \mathcal{X} \to \mathcal{F}$. Then each vector $\boldsymbol{x}$ from input space $\mathcal{X} \subseteq \mathbb{R}^n$ has its image $\boldsymbol{\phi}(\boldsymbol{x}) = [\phi_1(\boldsymbol{x}), \dots, \phi_d(\boldsymbol{x})]^T$ living in the d-dimensional feature space $\mathcal{F}$. A linear algorithm applied to images of the training vectors $\{\boldsymbol{\phi}(\boldsymbol{x}_1), \dots, \boldsymbol{\phi}(\boldsymbol{x}_l)\}$ produces a solution function

$$f(\boldsymbol{x}) = \langle \boldsymbol{\psi} \cdot \boldsymbol{\phi}(\boldsymbol{x}) \rangle + b = \sum_{i=1}^{d} \psi_i \phi_i(\boldsymbol{x}) + b \,, \qquad \boldsymbol{\psi} \in \mathcal{F} \,,$$

which is linear in the feature space $\mathcal{F}$ but is non-linear in the input space $\mathcal{X}$.

The explicit mapping of the training vectors is very often prohibitive due to the high dimensionality of the feature space $\mathcal{F}$. This problem can be overcome by so-called kernel functions. The kernel functions $k \colon \mathcal{X} \times \mathcal{X} \to \mathbb{R}$ are dot products of input vectors mapped by some mapping function $\boldsymbol{\phi}$ into a feature space $\mathcal{F}$ so that $k(\boldsymbol{x}, \boldsymbol{x}') = \langle \boldsymbol{\phi}(\boldsymbol{x}) \cdot \boldsymbol{\phi}(\boldsymbol{x}') \rangle$. The kernel functions can be often simply evaluated, unlike the computation of the dot product of the explicitly mapped input vectors. For instance, the kernel function $k(\boldsymbol{x}, \boldsymbol{x}') = \langle \boldsymbol{x} \cdot \boldsymbol{x}' \rangle^2$ corresponds to a dot product of vectors $\boldsymbol{x}, \boldsymbol{x}' \in \mathbb{R}^n$ mapped into an $n(n + 1)/2$ dimensional space. The used quadratic mapping function $\boldsymbol{\phi}$ maps the input vector $\boldsymbol{x} = [x_1, \dots, x_n]$ into the space of all unordered products of the input coordinates of the second degree. Another example is the Radial Basis Function kernel $k(\boldsymbol{x}, \boldsymbol{x}') = \exp(-c||\boldsymbol{x} - \boldsymbol{x}'||^2)$ (c is some positive real constant) which corresponds to the dot product of the input vectors mapped into an infinite dimensional feature space $\mathcal{F}$ so that the explicit mapping $\boldsymbol{\phi}(\boldsymbol{x})$ cannot even be performed in this case.

The kernel functions can be used to derive a non-linear version of the linear algorithm if all computations with data can be expressed in terms of dot products only. If this is the case then a selected kernel function k is substituted for all the dot products which is equivalent to perform the linear algorithm in the feature space $\mathcal{F}$. The solution of the kernelized linear algorithm reads

$$f(\boldsymbol{x}) = \langle \boldsymbol{\psi} \cdot \boldsymbol{\phi}(\boldsymbol{x}) \rangle + b = \langle \boldsymbol{\phi}(\boldsymbol{x}) \cdot \sum_{i=1}^{l} \alpha_i \boldsymbol{\phi}(\boldsymbol{x}_i) \rangle + b = \sum_{i=1}^{l} \alpha_i k(\boldsymbol{x}_i, \boldsymbol{x}) + b \,, \tag{7.2}$$

which means that the dot product $\langle \boldsymbol{\psi} \cdot \boldsymbol{\phi}(\boldsymbol{x}) \rangle$ can be expressed as the linear combination of the kernel functions centred in the training data $\mathbf{X} = [\boldsymbol{x}_1, \dots, \boldsymbol{x}_l]$. The kernelized linear algorithm produces the coefficients $\boldsymbol{\alpha} = [\alpha_1, \ldots, \alpha_l]^T$, $\alpha_i \in \mathbb{R}$ and the scalar $b \in \mathbb{R}$.

The kernel methods were shown to perform well in many practical problems. However, there are still several problems which can limit their use:

- *Non-sparse solution:* This occurs if many coefficients α_i in the solution function (7.2) are non-zero. This implies that the values of all the kernel functions with non-zero coefficient α_i have to be computed when the solution function (7.2) is to be evaluated. It leads to a slow evaluation (for instance, to slow classification).

- *Memory requirements:* The training vectors are represented by a kernel matrix $\mathbf{K}$ whose entries contain values of the kernel functions, i.e., $K_{i,j} = k(\boldsymbol{x}_i, \boldsymbol{x}_j)$. The size of the training data representation in terms of the kernel matrix grows quadratically with the number l of training vectors. This representation causes problems if the number l of training data is large.

Several approaches to these problems have been proposed. First, the methods which are based on approximation of the found solution (7.2), e.g., reduced set methods [60, 403]. The reduced set methods aim to find a sparse solution function close (in some sense) to the originally found solution function. Second, the approach based on sparse approximation of the kernel matrix [430]. This method selects a subset of columns of the kernel matrix which is consequently used to approximate all the dot products in the kernel matrix. The authors derived a greedy algorithm which minimises the Frobenius norm between the original kernel matrix and its approximation. The probabilistic speed up is used to overcome the computational problems connected with optimal selection of the column which best minimises the Frobenius norm.

We propose a greedy algorithm which aims to approximate the training vectors in the feature space such that the reconstruction error is minimised similarly to the Principal Component Analysis (PCA) or its kernel version (KPCA) [404]. In contrast to PCA we adopted an additional constraint on the number of training vectors used to express the basis vectors which define a new base expressing the training vectors. This is favourable in the kernel version of the algorithm as the sparseness of the solution can be controlled at the expense of the suboptimal approximation of the training data. Thus the proposed method can be seen as the greedy version of the KPCA. An preliminary version of our approach was published in [135].

Both the linear and the kernel version of the proposed greedy KPCA is derived in Section 7.2. The extensive testing of the proposed method is presented in Section 7.3. The conclusions and comparison to the standard KPCA is given in Section 7.4.

7.2 Greedy PCA Algorithm

The aim is to design a method which produces transformation of vectors to a new lower dimensional space with minimal reconstruction error similarly to PCA. In addition, the proposed method is required to overcome problems connected with the kernel version of PCA. Namely, it should produce kernel transformation with lower complexity than the KPCA returns and computational and memory requirements should be reduced as well. In the following lines, the linear version of the proposed method is described and it is consequently extended to its kernel variant.

The idea of the method is to express the training data $\mathbf{X} = [\boldsymbol{x}_1, \ldots, \boldsymbol{x}_l]$ as a linear combination of vectors[2] $\mathbf{S} = [\boldsymbol{s}_1, \boldsymbol{s}_2, \ldots, \boldsymbol{s}_m]$ which are properly selected from the training data themselves, i.e., $\mathbf{S} \subseteq \mathbf{X}$. The new approximated representation of training data $\tilde{\mathbf{X}} = [\tilde{\boldsymbol{x}}_1, \tilde{\boldsymbol{x}}_2, \ldots, \tilde{\boldsymbol{x}}_l]$ is computed as

$$\tilde{\boldsymbol{x}} = \mathbf{S}\boldsymbol{\beta}, \tag{7.3}$$

where $\boldsymbol{\beta}$ is a vector $[m \times 1]$ of real coefficients for a particular training vector $\boldsymbol{x} \in \mathbf{X}$. The objective function minimises the mean square reconstruction error

$$\varepsilon_{MS} = \frac{1}{l} \sum_{i=1}^{l} ||\boldsymbol{x}_i - \tilde{\boldsymbol{x}}_i||^2. \tag{7.4}$$

In addition, the set $\mathbf{S}$ should be as small as possible which is important for the kernel variant. Notice that PCA minimises the error ε_{MS} but at the expense of the set $\mathbf{S}$ containing all training data, i.e., PCA produces solution which is the best with respect to the first goal and the worst with respect to the second goal. The proposed method searches for the solution which lies somewhere in between. If the size m of the set $\mathbf{S}$ is fixed in advance then the problem of the set $\mathbf{S}$ selection such that error ε_{MS} is minimised leads to a combinatorial problem as there exist $\binom{l}{m}$ possible selections. This suggests to use a greedy iterative algorithm to solve this problem. The proposed algorithm iteratively selects new vectors from the training set to become new basis vectors such that the error ε_{MS} is decreased.

It is easy to see that given a set $\mathbf{S}$ the computation of the optimal coefficient vector $\boldsymbol{\beta}$, which minimises the reconstruction error $||\boldsymbol{x} - \tilde{\boldsymbol{x}}||^2$ for a vector $\boldsymbol{x} \in \mathbf{X}$, has the following analytical solution

$$\boldsymbol{\beta} = \operatorname*{argmin}_{\boldsymbol{\beta}'} ||\boldsymbol{x} - \mathbf{S}\boldsymbol{\beta}'||^2 = (\mathbf{S}^T\mathbf{S})^{-1}\mathbf{S}^T\boldsymbol{x}. \tag{7.5}$$

The coefficient vectors $\boldsymbol{\beta}_i$, $i = 1, \ldots, l$, can be seen as a new representation of training data $\boldsymbol{x}_i$, $i = 1, \ldots, l$, in the base $\mathbf{S}$. Using (7.3) and (7.5) yields the formula for reconstruction error of a single vector $\boldsymbol{x} \in \mathbf{X}$,

$$\varepsilon_R(\boldsymbol{x}) = ||\boldsymbol{x} - \tilde{\boldsymbol{x}}||^2 = \langle \boldsymbol{x}, \boldsymbol{x} \rangle - \boldsymbol{x}^T\mathbf{S}^T(\mathbf{S}^T\mathbf{S})^{-1}\mathbf{S}\boldsymbol{x}. \tag{7.6}$$

It is obvious that the reconstruction error for the vectors in the set $\mathbf{S}$ is zero as they can be perfectly represented by themselves.

Let $\mathbf{S}^{(t)} = [\boldsymbol{s}_1, \ldots, \boldsymbol{s}_t]$ denote the set of selected basis vectors in t-th iteration of the algorithm. Similarly $\varepsilon_{MS}^{(t)}$ is the mean square reconstruction error and $\tilde{\mathbf{X}}^{(t)} = [\tilde{\boldsymbol{x}}_1^{(t)}, \ldots, \tilde{\boldsymbol{x}}_l^{(t)}]$ the approximated training data when using the set $\mathbf{S}^{(t)}$.

A naive greedy algorithm looks as follows:

---

[2] $\mathbf{S} = [\boldsymbol{s}_1, \boldsymbol{s}_2, \ldots, \boldsymbol{s}_m]$ (similarly as $\mathbf{X} = [\boldsymbol{x}_1, \boldsymbol{x}_2, \ldots, \boldsymbol{x}_l]$) is referred to as both the matrix and the set of vectors. This is a slight abuse of the notation which, however, simplifies the description.

Algorithm 1: **Naive greedy PCA**

---

1. Initialisation $t = 0$, $\mathbf{S}^{(0)} = \{0\}$.
2. Iterate until desired stopping condition is satisfied:
   a) Set $t = t + 1$.
   b) For all vectors $\boldsymbol{x} \in \mathbf{X} \setminus \mathbf{S}^{(t-1)}$
      i. Compute error $\varepsilon_R(\boldsymbol{x}_i)$, $i = 1, \ldots, l$ for all training vectors using the set $\mathbf{S}^{(t-1)} \cup \boldsymbol{x}$ as a new base.
      ii. Compute mean square error $\varepsilon_{MS}(\boldsymbol{x}) = \frac{1}{l} \sum_{i=1}^{l} \varepsilon_R(\boldsymbol{x}_i)$.
   c) Select a vector which yields the biggest decrease of the mean square error as

$$s_t = \underset{\boldsymbol{x} \in \mathbf{X} \setminus \mathbf{S}^{(t-1)}}{\operatorname{argmax}} \varepsilon_{MS}(\boldsymbol{x}) .$$

   d) Set $\mathbf{S}^{(t)} = \mathbf{S}^{(t-1)} \cup s_t$.

Algorithm 1 implements an optimal greedy strategy, however, its computational complexity is too high since it requires $O(l^2 m)$ operations, where l is a number of training vectors and m is a number of selected basis vectors. Algorithm 1 has the following bottlenecks: (i) evaluation of the mean square error ε_{MS} depends for all possible candidates on a new basis vector which is of complexity $O(l^2)$ and (ii) the computation of the reconstruction error (7.6) for a single vector has complexity $O(m^2)$ provided complexity of dot product computation is $O(1)$ and Sherman-Woodbury formula (see [151]) is used for efficient matrix inversion with complexity $O(m^2)$.

The following adjustments are proposed to make the algorithm computationally efficient: (i) Efficiently computable upper bound on the mean square reconstruction error ε_{MS} which is used and (ii) the basis vectors $\mathbf{S}$ are gradually orthonormalized which further speeds up computations as will be seen below. Following lines describe these two adjustments more in detail.

The mean square error $\varepsilon_{MS}^{(t)}$ in the t-th iteration can be upper bounded using the following inequality,

$$\varepsilon_{MS}^{(t)} = \frac{1}{l} \sum_{i=1}^{l} ||\boldsymbol{x}_i - \tilde{\boldsymbol{x}}_i^{(t)}||^2 \leq \frac{1}{l}(l - t) \max_{\boldsymbol{x} \in \mathbf{X} \setminus \mathbf{S}^{(t)}} ||\boldsymbol{x} - \tilde{\boldsymbol{x}}^{(t)}||^2 . \qquad (7.7)$$

The upper bound (7.7) is decreased if the vector $s_{t+1} = \max_{\boldsymbol{x} \in \mathbf{X} \setminus \mathbf{S}^{(t)}} ||\boldsymbol{x} - \tilde{\boldsymbol{x}}^{(t)}||^2$ with the currently biggest approximation error is selected as the new basis vector. It is obvious since including the vector s_{t+1} to the set $\mathbf{S}^{(t+1)} = \mathbf{S}^{(t)} \cup s_{t+1}$ ensures that the approximation error of the corresponding training vector $\boldsymbol{x} = s_{t+1}$ is zero. In addition, the term $(l - t)$ decreases by 1 as t is increased. If individual reconstruction errors $\varepsilon_R(\boldsymbol{x})$ are given then selection of the new basis vector requires $O(l)$ operations.

It is computationally wise to use orthonormalised base $\mathbf{W} = [\boldsymbol{w}_1, \ldots, \boldsymbol{w}_m]$, which spans the same space as the selected base $\mathbf{S}$, to represent the training data as

$$\tilde{\boldsymbol{x}} = \mathbf{W}\boldsymbol{z} ,$$

where z is a new representation of x in the base $\mathbf{W}$. If $\mathbf{W}$ is an orthonormal base, i.e., $\mathbf{W}^T\mathbf{W} = \mathbf{E}$ ($\mathbf{E}$ is identity matrix), then the optimal z minimising the reconstruction error (7.6) is computed simply as

$$z = \mathbf{W}^T x\,,$$

which directly follows from (7.5). The reconstruction error can be also simply evaluated as

$$\varepsilon_R(x) = ||x - \tilde{x}||^2 = \langle x \cdot x \rangle - \langle z \cdot z \rangle\,, \tag{7.8}$$

which follows when using $\tilde{x} = \mathbf{W}\mathbf{W}^T x$. There remains only to derive the procedure for orthonormalisation of the set $\mathbf{S}^{(t)} = [s_1, \ldots, s_t]$. The orthonormalisation is done gradually as new basis vectors s_i, $i = 1, \ldots, t$, appear. The $\mathrm{Span}(\mathbf{S}^{(t)})$ is required to be equal to $\mathrm{Span}(\mathbf{W}^{(t)})$ and $\langle w_i \cdot w_j \rangle = \delta(i,j), i = 1, \ldots, t, j = 1, \ldots, t$. The procedure is based on the Gram-Schmidt orthogonalisation process

$$\begin{aligned} w_1 &= \tfrac{s_1}{r_1}\,, \\ w_t &= \tfrac{1}{r_t}\left(s_t - \textstyle\sum_{i=1}^{t-1}\langle w_i \cdot s_t \rangle w_i\right)\,, \quad \text{for} \quad t > 1\,, \end{aligned} \tag{7.9}$$

where r_t is the normalisation constant ensuring $||w_t|| = 1$. In fact, only the projections $\langle x \cdot w_t \rangle$, $t = 1, \ldots, m$, of a vector x onto the basis vectors w_t are needed in the algorithm. Moreover, in the kernel version derived below the explicit evaluation of w_t is impossible. The formula for the dot product $\langle x \cdot w_t \rangle$ can be simply derived from (7.9) as

$$\langle x \cdot w_t \rangle = \langle \alpha_t \cdot \mathbf{S}^T x \rangle = z_t(x)\,,$$

where $\mathbf{S} = [s_1, \ldots, s_m]$ and the recursive formula for α_t $[m \times 1]$ reads

$$\begin{aligned} \alpha_1 &= \tfrac{1}{r_1}\delta(1)\,, \\ \alpha_t &= \tfrac{1}{r_t}\left(\delta(t) - \textstyle\sum_{i=1}^{t-1}\langle w_i \cdot s_t \rangle \alpha_i\right)\,, \quad \text{for} \quad t > 1\,. \end{aligned}$$

The vector $\delta(i)$ of size $[m \times 1]$ has all entries 0 except the i-th entry equal to 1. It follows from (7.8) that the reconstruction error $\varepsilon_R^{(t)}(x)$ of a vector $x \in \mathbf{X}$ in t-th iteration is determined by

$$\varepsilon_R^{(t)}(x) = \langle x \cdot x \rangle - \sum_{i=1}^{t}(\langle x \cdot w_i \rangle)^2\,.$$

The equations (7.9) give the formula for the normalisation constant $r^{(t)}$ which is equal to the square root of the reconstruction error $\sqrt{\varepsilon_R^{(t)}(s_{t+1})}$.

Putting all items introduced above together yields the following greedy PCA algorithm:

Algorithm 2: **Greedy PCA**
---

1. Initialise $t = 0$, $\mathbf{S}^{(0)} = \{0\}$, $\varepsilon_R^{(0)}(x) = \langle x \cdot x \rangle, \forall x \in \mathbf{X}$, $z_0(x) = 0, \forall x \in \mathbf{X}$.
2. Iterate until desired reconstruction error is achieved:
   a) Set $t = t + 1$.

b) Select $s_t = \text{argmax}_{x \in \mathbf{X} \setminus \mathbf{S}} \varepsilon_R^{(t-1)}(x)$.

c) Compute $z_t(x) = \frac{1}{\sqrt{\varepsilon_R^{(t-1)}(s_t)}} \left(\langle x \cdot s_t \rangle - \sum_{i=1}^{t-1} z_i(s_t) z_i(x) \right)$ for all $x \in \mathbf{X}$.

d) Compute $\varepsilon_R^{(t)}(x) = \varepsilon_R^{(t-1)} - z_t(x) z_t(x)$ for all $x \in \mathbf{X}$.

e) Set $\mathbf{S}^{(t)} = \mathbf{S}^{(t-1)} \cup s_t$.

The greedy PCA Algorithm 2 requires $O(lm^2)$ operations if m basis vectors were selected (the inner loop was performed m times): Step (b) is of complexity $O(l)$. Step (c) requires $O(lt)$, $1 \leq t \leq m$, operations thus in total it gives $O(l\frac{m(m+1)}{2}) \approx O(lm^2)$. In Step (d), the error $\varepsilon_R(x)$ is updated for all $x \in \mathbf{X}$ which is of complexity $O(l)$. The computation of a dot product $\langle x \cdot s_t \rangle$ as well as an insertion of the vector to the set are assumed to be $O(1)$.

The inner loop of the algorithm can be enriched by the computation of vectors α_t, $t = 1, \ldots, m$ which does not increase the complexity. Let $\mathbf{A} = [\alpha_1, \ldots, \alpha_t]$ and $\mathbf{S} = [s_1, \ldots, s_m]$ be matrices of vectors computed by Algorithm 2. The representation of a vector x in the base $\mathbf{W}$ is computed as

$$z = \mathbf{A}^T \mathbf{S}^T x. \tag{7.10}$$

It is interesting that Algorithm 2 tries to represent $\text{Span}(\mathbf{X})$ by selecting the outer vertices of the convex hull of the data $\mathbf{X}$ as the set $\mathbf{S}$. Therefore it can be expected that the method is sensitive to outliers. This predetermines the method for applications for which the extremal data are important, e.g., Support Vector Machines which describe the decision rule just by the vectors lying on the boundary of the convex hull. On the other hand, the method can be less suitable where outliers are to be suppressed, e.g., in application of the PCA to denoising.

7.2.1 Stopping Conditions

The number of iterations of the algorithm equals to the number m of selected basis vectors. The number m can be equal to the number of all training vectors l at most. In this case, the reconstruction error ε_{MS} must be zero, however, it is reasonable to stop the algorithm earlier. It is natural to stop the algorithm if the one of the following conditions is satisfied:

1. Mean square reconstruction error $\varepsilon_{MS} = \frac{1}{l} \sum_{i=1}^{l} ||x_i - \tilde{x}_i||^2$ falls below prescribed limit.

2. Maximal reconstruction error $\max_{x \in \mathbf{X}} ||x - \tilde{x}||^2$ falls below prescribed limit.

3. The number of basis vectors achieves prescribed limit m.

Use of a particular stopping condition depends on the application for which the algorithm is desired. For instance, the stopping condition 3 is particularly useful for kernel version of the Algorithm (see below) as it allows to control complexity of the final kernel projection.

7.2.2 Kernel Greedy PCA Algorithm

In this section the greedy PCA algorithm is extended to its kernel variant. The kernel variant can be derived readily since Algorithm 2 uses data in terms of dot products only.

It is assumed that the greedy PCA algorithm is applied to the training vectors $\mathbf{X} = [\boldsymbol{x}_1, \ldots, \boldsymbol{x}_l]$ non-linearly mapped to a feature space $\mathcal{F}$ by a function $\boldsymbol{\Phi} \colon \mathbb{R}^n \to \mathcal{F}$. Let $\{\phi(\boldsymbol{x}_1), \ldots, \phi(\boldsymbol{x}_l)\}$ be a set of non-linearly mapped training vectors $\mathbf{X} = [\boldsymbol{x}_1, \ldots, \boldsymbol{x}_l]$ and $\{\phi(\boldsymbol{s}_1), \ldots, \phi(\boldsymbol{s}_m)\}$ a set of non-linearly mapped vectors of the set $\mathbf{S} \subseteq \mathbf{X}$.

The greedy KPCA algorithm is:

Algorithm 3: Kernel greedy PCA

1. Initialise $t = 0$, $\mathbf{S}^{(0)} = \{0\}$, $\varepsilon_R^{(0)}(\boldsymbol{x}) = k(\boldsymbol{x}, \boldsymbol{x})$, $\forall \boldsymbol{x} \in \mathbf{X}$, $z^{(0)}(\boldsymbol{x}) = 0$, $\forall \boldsymbol{x} \in \mathbf{X}$, $\boldsymbol{\alpha}_0 = \mathbf{0}$.
2. Iterate until desired reconstruction error is achieved:
   a) $t = t + 1$.
   b) Select $\boldsymbol{s}_t = \operatorname{argmax}_{\boldsymbol{x} \in \mathbf{X} \setminus \mathbf{S}} \varepsilon_R^{(t-1)}(\boldsymbol{x})$.
   c) Compute $z^{(t)}(\boldsymbol{x}) = \dfrac{1}{\sqrt{\varepsilon_R^{(t-1)}(\boldsymbol{s}_t)}} \left(k(\boldsymbol{x}, \boldsymbol{s}_t) - \sum_{i=1}^{t-1} z^{(i)}(\boldsymbol{s}_t) z^{(i)}(\boldsymbol{x}) \right)$ for all $\boldsymbol{x} \in \mathbf{X}$.
   d) Compute $\boldsymbol{\alpha}_t = \dfrac{1}{\sqrt{\varepsilon_R^{(t-1)}(\boldsymbol{s}_t)}} \left(\delta(t) - \sum_{i=1}^{t-1} z^{(i)}(\boldsymbol{s}_t) \boldsymbol{\alpha}_i \right)$.
   e) Compute $\varepsilon_R^{(t)}(\boldsymbol{x}) = \varepsilon_R^{(t-1)} - z^{(t)}(\boldsymbol{x}) z^{(t)}(\boldsymbol{x})$ for all $\boldsymbol{x} \in \mathbf{X}$.
   f) Set $\mathbf{S}^{(t)} = \mathbf{S}^{(t-1)} \cup \boldsymbol{s}_t$.

The kernel greedy PCA Algorithm 3 has the same computational complexity $O(lm^2)$ as its linear counterpart provided the evaluation of the kernel function is of complexity $O(1)$. The number of kernel evaluations (dot product evaluations in linear case) equals to $\text{KerEval} = \frac{(m+1)(2l-m)}{2}$. In the limit case $m = l$, the number of kernel evaluations equals to $\text{KerEval} = \frac{l(l+1)}{2}$ which is the same as evaluations required to compute full kernel matrix when standard kernel PCA is used.

The output of Algorithm 3 is a subset $\mathbf{S} \subseteq \mathbf{X}$ and the vectors $\mathbf{A} = [\boldsymbol{\alpha}^{(1)}, \ldots, \boldsymbol{\alpha}^{(m)}]$. A projection of $\phi(\boldsymbol{x})$ onto non-linear images of found orthonormal base is given by

$$z = \mathbf{A}^T \boldsymbol{k}_S(\boldsymbol{x}), \tag{7.11}$$

where $\boldsymbol{k}_S(\boldsymbol{x}) = [k(\boldsymbol{x}, \boldsymbol{s}^{(1)}), \ldots, k(\boldsymbol{x}, \boldsymbol{s}^{(m)})]^T$. Because the z is obtained by projecting $\phi(\boldsymbol{x})$ onto orthonormal base the dot product of reconstructed vectors $\tilde{k}(\boldsymbol{x}, \boldsymbol{x}') = \langle \phi(\tilde{\boldsymbol{x}}) \cdot \phi(\tilde{\boldsymbol{x}'}) \rangle$ is directly computed as the dot product $\langle z \cdot z' \rangle$.

Algorithm 3 can be seen as a method which computes decomposition of kernel matrix $K_{[i,j]} = k(\boldsymbol{x}_i, \boldsymbol{x}_j)$. Let

$$\tilde{\mathbf{K}} = \mathbf{Z}^T \mathbf{Z},$$

be approximated kernel matrix $[l \times l]$ decomposed to rectangular matrix $\mathbf{Z} = [\boldsymbol{z}_1, \ldots, \boldsymbol{z}_l]$ of size $[m \times l]$ which containing projections (7.11) of the training vectors $\mathbf{X}$.

7.3 Experiments

In most of our experiments the benchmark repository of the Intelligent Data Analysis (IDA) group[3] was used to evaluate the proposed greedy KPCA algorithm. The IDA repository contains both the real life and synthetic data of moderate size. The repository contains 13 different data sets. There are 100 realisations splitting each data set into training and testing data. The presented results are mean values computed over 100 realizations. The Radial Basis Functions (RBF) kernel function $k(x, x') = \exp(-c||x - x'||^2)$ was used in all experiments. All the algorithms were implemented in Matlab 6 and run on the 2.4 GHz PC under Linux OS.

7.3.1 Reconstruction Error Experiment

In this experiment, the greedy KPCA algorithm is compared to the standard KPCA in terms of the mean square reconstruction error. The aim is to investigate how fast the greedy version decreases the reconstruction error compared to the optimal solution.

The limit on the mean square reconstruction error

$$\varepsilon_{MS} = \frac{1}{l} \sum_{i=1}^{l} ||\phi(x_i) - \tilde{\phi}(x_i)||^2$$

was used as the stopping condition. The sets of training vectors were approximated with $\varepsilon_{MS} = [0.1, 0.01, 0.001]$. Notice that when using the RBF kernel then the ε_{MS} range between 0 and 1. The following quantities were measured: (i) the number of basis vectors required to achieve approximation error $\varepsilon_{MS} = [0.1, 0.01, 0.001]$, (ii) the training CPU time required to achieve the approximation with $\varepsilon_{MS} = 0.001$ and (iii) the speed up in projection of testing vectors when using the greedy KPCA. The speed up is proportional to the ratio between the number of kernel evaluations required by the standard KPCA and greedy KPCA to project the testing vectors. The Matlab function eig was used to solve the eigenvalue problem of the standard KPCA. The width of the RBF kernel which yields the best classification performance of the SVM classifier was used in this experiment (cf. Section 7.3.2).

The results obtained are enlisted in Table 7.1. It can be seen that the greedy KPCA obviously needs more basis vectors to achieve desired error ε_{MS} than the standard KPCA. This is especially apparent at the first stages (for $\varepsilon_{MS} = 0.1$). However, this difference decreases as the number of basis vectors grows. The greedy KPCA algorithm required on average 30% more basis vectors than the optimal KPCA to achieve the reconstruction error $\varepsilon_{MS} = 0.001$. The training time of the greedy kernel PCA is considerably faster than the standard KPCA especially when number of basis vectors m is much smaller than the number of training data l. If m comes closer to l then this difference vanishes. This is obvious as the greedy KPCA has complexity proportional to $O(lm^2)$ while the standard KPCA has complexity $O(l^3)$. The speed up in the projection of the testing vectors obtained when using greedy KPCA is of factor 400 on the average.

---

[3] http://ida.first.fraunhofer.de/projects/bench/benchmarks.htm

Table 7.1. Comparison between the greedy KPCA and the standard KPCA in terms of ability to decrease the mean square reconstruction error and the time of projection of the testing vectors

| | KPCA | | | | Greedy KPCA | | | | Test |
| | ε_{MS} | | | CPU | ε_{MS} | | | CPU | speed |
	0.1	0.01	0.001	time [s]	0.1	0.01	0.001	time [s]	up
Banana	13	30	47	4.8	22	41	60	0.2	331
Breast	3	14	41	0.1	7	27	61	0.1	134
Diabetes	3	19	51	7.2	8	37	84	0.3	284
German	27	210	458	27.8	91	313	525	14.3	611
Heart	6	33	84	0.1	11	53	104	0.1	137
Image	13	81	185	188.7	59	146	262	7.7	917
Ringnorm	246	360	393	4.3	279	373	396	3.7	397
Flare	1	5	12	13.2	1	13	31	0.1	258
Splice	558	897	956	76.6	667	920	963	66.9	993
Thyroid	10	31	49	0.2	25	42	60	0.1	114
Titanic	4	9	11	0.1	10	11	12	0.0	138
Twonorm	30	210	347	5.0	76	263	366	3.3	379
Waveform	28	195	342	5.1	66	251	365	3.3	375

Figure 7.3.1 shows four examples of comparison between standard KPCA and greedy KPCA in terms of training and testing reconstruction error ε_{MS} with respect to the number of used basis vectors.

7.3.2 Non-linear Feature Extraction Experiment

The greedy KPCA algorithm is used for a non-linear feature extraction step. The non-linear feature extraction can serve as the preprocessing step for linear algorithms. In this case, the extracted features are used as an input to a linear algorithm. It is actually another way how to extend the linear algorithms to produce non-linear solution functions. Let $f(z) = \langle w \cdot z \rangle + b$ be the linear discriminant function produced by a linear algorithm. The greedy KPCA algorithm finds the non-linear kernel projection $z = \mathbf{A}^T k_S(x)$ of input data $x \in \mathcal{X}$. If the non-linearly projected data are brought into the input of the linear discriminant function then it results to the kernel discriminant function of SVM type, i.e,

$$f(x) = \langle w \cdot z(x) \rangle + b = \langle w \cdot \mathbf{A}^T k_S(x) \rangle + b = \sum_{i=1}^{m} \alpha_i k(s_i, x) + b,$$

where the vector $\alpha = \mathbf{A}w$ combines both parameters of the feature extraction and the linear classifier.

In this particular experiment, the linear Support Vector Machines (linear SVM) and the Fisher Linear Discriminant (FLD) were used as the linear algorithms. The kernel versions of these algorithms can have problems with the high complexity of resulting solution functions which are, in this case, discriminant functions of a binary classifier. Even thought the SVM selects just a subset of training data to determine the classifier this subsets can be too big especially when overlapping data are present. The Kernel

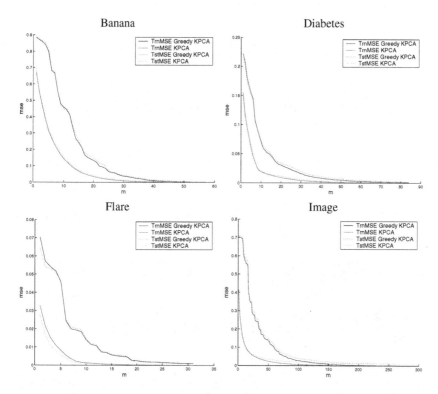

Fig. 7.1. Comparison of the greedy KPCA and KPCA algorithm on four data sets of the IDA benchmark repository. The training and testing mean square reconstruction error ε_{MS} with respect to the number of basis vectors m is plotted.

Fisher Discriminant (KFD) requires all the training data to determine the classifier thus it leads always to non-sparse classifier. Moreover, the complexity of training KFD scales with $O(l^3)$ which limits this approach to modest problems only.

The combination of the greedy kernel PCA algorithm and the linear variants of these methods can avoid the mentioned problems. The complexity of the resulting classifier can be controlled before its training by means of prescribing the number of basis vectors. The combination of the greedy KPCA and the linear SVM or FLD is referred to as greedy SVM or greedy KFD, respectively.

A toy example of classifiers found by the proposed greedy SVM and greedy KFD on the Riply's data set can be seen in Figure 7.2. This figure shows the classifiers found by the standard SVM and KFD in comparison to their greedy variants. It is visible that the decision boundaries are almost identical while the complexity (number of support vectors or basis vectors in greedy case) of the greedy variants is reduced considerably.

Next, a more detailed comparison performed on the IDA benchmark repository is presented. The algorithms tested are denoted as follows:

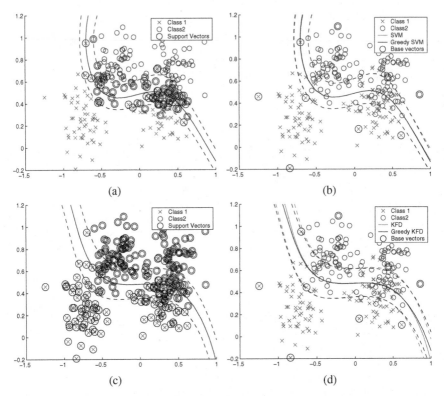

Fig. 7.2. Comparison between Support Vector Machines, Kernel Fisher Discriminant and their greedy variants on the Riply's data set. Figure (a) shows classifier found by standard SVM and Figure (b) shows the greedy SVM and standard SVM for comparison. Figure (c) shows standard KFD classifier and Figure (b) shows the greedy KFD and standard KFD for comparison.

SVM	Standard kernel Support Vector Machines.
KFD	Standard Kernel Fisher Discriminant.
Greedy SVM	Combination of kernel greedy PCA and the linear SVM.
Greedy KFD	Combination of kernel greedy PCA and the FLD.

The parameters of SVM and KFD were obtained using grid search and 5-fold cross validation. The precision of the approximation found by the greedy PCA is determined by the used stopping condition (cf. Section 7.2.1). Limits on the maximal number m of basis vectors and the maximal reconstruction error $\varepsilon_{\max} = \max_{x \in \mathbf{X}} \varepsilon_R(x)$ were used as the stopping condition. The following setting were used: (i) number of basis vectors $m = 0.2l$ was equal to 20% of training data, $\varepsilon_{\max} = 0.05$ and (ii) number basis vectors $m = 0.5l$ was equal to 50% of training data, $\varepsilon_{\max} = 0.001$. The kernel functions and their parameters obtained from tuning of the standard SVM and KFD were adopted to the greedy SVM and KFD.

The following statistics were measured:

- Number of support vectors n_{sv} was recorded as the measure of complexity of the resulting classifier. This number equals to the number of training vectors $n_{sv} = l$ in the case of KFD.
- The testing classification error was measured to assess the accuracy of resulting classifiers. The errors are recorded on all the 100 realizations for each data set. The results enlisted in tables are mean values.

The results for SVM and the greedy SVM are enlisted in Table 7.2. In 3 cases (23%) the standard SVM outperformed the greedy SVM and in 5 cases (38%) the standard SVM were worse in terms of classification error. This result is surprising as the greedy SVM uses in fact only approximated training data. A possible explanation is that enforcing smaller number of support vector in the greedy SVM is a kind of regularisation which increases the generalisation ability of the resulting classifier. However, the differences in classification errors were small – in order of 1%. In terms of the complexity of resulting classifier, the greedy SVM won significantly as in 11 cases (85%) the number of support vectors were smaller than the standard SVM used. The reduction of number of support vectors ranged from 2% to 80%.

The results for KFD and the greedy KFD are enlisted in Table 7.3. In 5 cases (40%), the standard KFD outperformed the greedy KFD and in 6 cases (46%), the standard KFD was worse in terms of classification error. However, the differences are again in order of 1%. The number of support vectors used by greedy KFD were always smaller. The variant of greedy KFD with higher number of basis vectors (50% of training data) was better than the sparser one. This indicates that the KFD needs more accurate approximation of training data than in the case of SVM. This observation supports common sense as the greedy PCA concentrates on approximation of outliers which can deteriorate the first and second order statistics used by the KFD.

Table 7.2. Comparison of SVM and greedy SVM on IDA benchmark data sets

	SVM		Greedy SVM			
			$m = 0.2l, \varepsilon_{\max} = 0.05$		$m = 0.5l, \varepsilon_{\max} = 0.001$	
	TstErr [%]	n_{sv}	TstErr [%]	n_{sv}	TstErr [%]	n_{sv}
Banana	10.4	139	10.4	41	10.5	72
Breast	26.1	113	26.3	19	26.1	82
Diabetes	23.2	255	23.3	30	23.1	115
German	23.7	402	24.2	30	23.5	350
Heart	15.7	98	15.6	34	15.9	85
Image	3.0	147	5.9	118	3.1	348
Ringnorm	1.6	131	3.0	80	2.0	200
Flare solar	32.4	473	34.0	11	32.3	35
Splice	11.1	594	14.2	200	12.9	500
Thyroid	4.7	20	4.9	28	4.7	70
Titanic	22.4	69	22.4	11	22.4	11
Twonorm	3.6	57	2.6	80	3.2	200
Waveform	10.1	129	10.3	80	10.1	200

Table 7.3. Comparison of KFD and greedy KFD on IDA benchmark data sets

| | KFD | | Greedy KFD | | | |
| | | | $m = 0.2l$, $\varepsilon_{max} = 0.05$ | | $m = 0.5l$, $\varepsilon_{max} = 0.001$ | |
	TstErr [%]	n_{sv}	TstErr [%]	n_{sv}	TstErr [%]	n_{sv}
Banana	10.4	400	10.5	41	10.5	72
Breast	25.4	200	25.9	17	26.0	76
Diabetes	23.1	468	23.2	35	22.9	129
German	24.0	700	24.6	140	24.0	350
Heart	16.2	170	17.2	24	16.1	85
Image	3.5	1300	5.0	260	3.6	650
Ringnorm	2.0	400	2.5	80	1.7	200
Flare solar	34.5	666	34.5	59	34.4	87
Splice	10.8	1000	14.2	200	12.3	500
Thyroid	4.8	140	5.3	28	4.4	56
Titanic	22.5	150	22.3	11	22.4	11
Twonorm	2.6	400	2.7	80	2.6	200
Waveform	9.7	400	9.8	80	9.7	200

7.3.3 Greedy Kernel Least Squares Experiment

The greedy KPCA algorithm is applied to make tractable kernel least squares (LS) function approximation. A problem of the linear least squares approximation is the following: given a matrix of training vectors $\mathbf{X} = [\boldsymbol{x}_1, \ldots, \boldsymbol{x}_l]^T$ with an associated vector of output values $\boldsymbol{y} = [y_1, \ldots, y_l]^T$ the task is to find parameters $(\boldsymbol{w}, b)$ of a linear function $f(\boldsymbol{x}) = \langle \boldsymbol{w} \cdot \boldsymbol{x} \rangle + b$ such that the criterion

$$\varepsilon_{LS} = \sum_{i=1}^{l} (y_i - f(\boldsymbol{x}_i))^2 ,$$

is minimised. This problem has a known analytical solution: Let the vector

$$\hat{\boldsymbol{x}}_i = [x_{i[1]}, \ldots, x_{i[n]}, 1]^T$$

($x_{i[j]}$ is used to denote the j-th coordinate of the vector $\boldsymbol{x}_i$) be an extended training vector and $\hat{\mathbf{X}} = [\hat{\boldsymbol{x}}_1, \ldots, \hat{\boldsymbol{x}}_l]$ be a matrix of extended training vectors. Similarly let $\hat{\boldsymbol{w}} = [w_1, \ldots, w_n, b]^T$ be the extend solution vector. The least squares criterion can be rewritten in compact form as

$$\varepsilon_{LS} = ||\boldsymbol{y} - \hat{\mathbf{X}}^T \hat{\boldsymbol{w}}||^2 . \tag{7.12}$$

Since the criterion (7.12) defines unconstrained convex problem, the optimal solution for $\hat{\boldsymbol{w}}$ is obtained by setting the derivative $\partial \varepsilon_{LS} / \partial \hat{\boldsymbol{w}}$ to zero. This yields

$$\hat{\boldsymbol{w}} = (\hat{\mathbf{X}} \hat{\mathbf{X}}^T)^{-1} \hat{\mathbf{X}} \boldsymbol{y} . \tag{7.13}$$

An extension to the non-linear least squares can be simply derived using the kernel trick. The extended solution vector is assumed to be determined as a linear combination of vectors $\hat{\mathbf{X}}$ which follows from (7.13), that is

$$\hat{w} = \hat{\mathbf{X}}\alpha. \tag{7.14}$$

The optimal coefficients α are obtained by substituting (7.14) to the criterion (7.12) and the solution for α yields

$$\begin{aligned}\alpha &= (\hat{\mathbf{X}}^T\hat{\mathbf{X}}\hat{\mathbf{X}}^T\hat{\mathbf{X}})^{-1}\hat{\mathbf{X}}^T\hat{\mathbf{X}}y \\ &= ((\mathbf{X}^T\mathbf{X}+1)(\mathbf{X}^T\mathbf{X}+1))^{-1}(\mathbf{X}^T\mathbf{X}+1)y. \end{aligned} \tag{7.15}$$

The resulting solution function can be thus written using α as

$$f(\boldsymbol{x}) = \langle \boldsymbol{x} \cdot \mathbf{X}\alpha \rangle + b, \tag{7.16}$$

where $b = \sum_{i=1}^{n} \alpha_i$. It can be seen that both in the computation of parameters (7.15) and in the expression of resulting function (7.16) data appear as the dot products only. Therefore substituting the kernel functions for these dot products yields the kernel least squares (KLS):

$$\alpha = (\hat{\mathbf{K}}\hat{\mathbf{K}})^{-1}\hat{\mathbf{K}}y,$$
$$f(\boldsymbol{x}) = \langle \alpha \cdot \boldsymbol{k}(x) \rangle + b,$$

where $\boldsymbol{k}(\boldsymbol{x}) = [k(\boldsymbol{x}_1, \boldsymbol{x}), \dots, k(\boldsymbol{x}_l, \boldsymbol{x})]^T$ and modified kernel matrix $\hat{\mathbf{K}} = \mathbf{K} + 1$ (matrix 1 has all entries equal to 1).

However, the computational complexity of KLS scales with $O(l^3)$ as the matrix of size $[l \times l]$ has to be inverted. Moreover, the solution is non-sparse as all the training vectors appear in the solution (7.16). Both the mentioned facts limit the use of the KLS to moderate problems only.

The greedy KPCA algorithm offers a solution how to find an approximated sparse version of the KLS. The greedy KPCA is first applied onto the training data $\mathbf{X}$ and, consequently, the linear LS are used. This actually means that two approximations are performed. The first approximation reduces dimensionality of the non-linear images $\{\phi(\boldsymbol{x}_1), \dots, \phi(\boldsymbol{x}_l)\}$ of the training vectors $\mathbf{X} = [\boldsymbol{x}_1, \dots, \boldsymbol{x}_l]$. This reduction is performed by the greedy KPCA which yields a new representation of data given by $\boldsymbol{z} = \mathbf{A}k_S(\boldsymbol{x})$. Let $\mathbf{Z} = [\boldsymbol{z}_1, \dots, \boldsymbol{z}_l]$ be the training vectors processed by the greedy KPCA. The second approximation is a linear function fitted to the vectors $\mathbf{Z}$ using the linear LS. Combining both the approximations the greedy KLS fit is obtained

$$f(\boldsymbol{x}) = \langle \boldsymbol{w} \cdot \mathbf{A}^T k_S(\boldsymbol{x}) \rangle + b = \sum_{i=1}^{m} \alpha_i k(\boldsymbol{s}_i, \boldsymbol{x}) + b,$$

where the coefficient matrix $\mathbf{A}$ and vectors $\mathbf{S} = [\boldsymbol{s}_1, \dots, \boldsymbol{s}_m]$ are returned by the kernel greedy PCA Algorithm 3. As the RBF kernel was used, the fitted function reads

$$f(\boldsymbol{x}) = \sum_{i=1}^{m} \alpha_i \exp(-c||\boldsymbol{s}_i - \boldsymbol{x}||^2) + b. \tag{7.17}$$

The performance of the proposed greedy KLS was tested on two synthetic and on one real data set. The width of the used RBF kernel was set experimentally to achieve smooth fitted function.

The first and the second experiment use synthetically generated data from known model corrupted with the Gaussian noise. In the first experiment, the following 1-dimensional model

$$f(\boldsymbol{x}) = \sin(2\pi x) + N(\sigma, \mu), \quad \boldsymbol{x} \in \mathbb{R},$$

was used. Parameters of the Gaussian noise were $\sigma = 0.2$ and $\mu = 0$. The domain $\mathcal{X}$ was randomly sampled in $l = 100$ points according to the identical distribution. This results in the training sample $\mathbf{X} = [\boldsymbol{x}_1, \ldots, \boldsymbol{x}_l]$ and corresponding function values $\boldsymbol{y} = [y_1, \ldots, y_l]$ corrupted with the noise. Figure 7.3.3 shows the ground truth function, the function by the KLS and the greedy KLS algorithm, respectively. Notice that the KLS requires all the sample data to determine the solution in contrast to greedy KLS which in this case uses only a subset of $m = 5$ basis vectors.

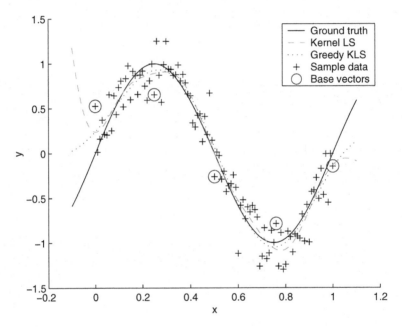

Fig. 7.3. Comparison of Kernel LS and greedy Kernel LS algorithm

In the second example, the proposed method was used with larger data set. The following 2-dimensional function

$$f(\boldsymbol{x}) = x_1 \exp(-(x_1)^2 - (x_2)^2) + N(\sigma, \mu), \quad \boldsymbol{x} = [x_1, x_2]^T \in \mathbb{R}^2,$$

corrupted again with the Gaussian noise ($\sigma = 0.2$, $\mu = 0$) was used. The number of sample data $l = 160801$ were generated to demonstrate the usefulness of the method for large data. The ground truth function is depicted in Figure 7.4(a) and the cloud of sample data can be seen in Figure 7.4(b). A subset of $m = 40$ basis vectors selected by the greedy KLS algorithm is shown in Figure 7.4(c). The fitted function is depicted

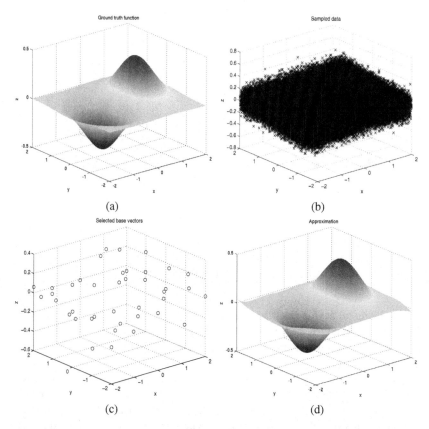

Fig. 7.4. Example of using the greedy KLS to fit a non-linear function to the set of 160801 points in $3D$

in Figure 7.4(d). The KLS was not computed as it would require inversion of matrix of size $[160801 \times 160801]$ which is infeasible.

In the third experiment face model is build by fitting the non-linear function (7.17) to points obtained from 3D scan of a human face [508]. The function domain $\mathcal{X} \subset \mathbb{R}^2$ is approximated by a subset of $m = 900$ basis vectors out of the total number of $l = 3994$ training vectors. The result can be seen in Figure 7.5.

7.4 Conclusions

The greedy PCA algorithm and its kernel variant (greedy KPCA) was proposed. The objective is to find a new lower dimensional base in which the training vectors are represented with possibly minimal mean square reconstruction error. In addition the complexity of the projection function is minimised. This complexity does not play a role in the linear case but is crucial when the non-linear kernel variant is derived. The standard KPCA finds the new representation with the minimal mean square error but at

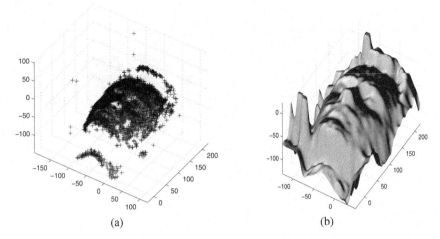

Fig. 7.5. Fitting face surface using greedy KLS. Figure (a) shows cloud of points obtained from 3D scan. Figure (b) shows the face surface computed by the greedy KLS.

the expense of using all training data to represent the projection function. On the other hand, the proposed greedy KPCA algorithm searches for a suboptimal solution with respect to the mean square reconstruction error but the projection function is determined by a small subset of training data.

The key idea of the greedy KPCA is to use individual training vectors as the basis vectors. The greedy algorithm selects such a vector in each step the inclusion of which into the basis vectors causes the maximal decrease in the optimised criterion. The bottleneck is the evaluation of the optimised mean squared error. An upper bound on the mean squared error is proposed which can be efficiently evaluated. The upper bound is given by the maximal reconstruction error over all training vectors. This can be a very pessimistic estimate especially for noisy data but it is quite simple to optimise by the vector with currently the biggest reconstruction error. Further speed up is gained by gradual orthogonalisation of the basis vectors. An implementation of these ideas leads to a simple iterative algorithm with low computational complexity.

The following summary compares the standard KPCA and the greedy KPCA algorithm:

Reconstruction error. The standard KPCA always finds the optimal projection which minimises the mean square reconstruction error with respect to the number of basis vectors. The greedy version offers suboptimal solution which gets closer to the optimal one as the number of basis vectors grows. It is obvious that the reconstruction error of both these methods falls to zero if the basis vectors span the training data. The efficiency of the greedy algorithm substantially depends on the nature of the training data and can deteriorate if too many outliers are present. Therefore the greedy KPCA algorithm is not suitable for the applications in which the outliers should be suppressed (e.g., denoising). By contrast, the greedy KPCA algorithm is suitable if the extremal data are to be described well, e.g., in SVM techniques, which was supported in our experiments.

Complexity of projection function. The standard KPCA algorithm requires all training data l to represent the projection function regardless of the number of extracted features. The greedy KPCA requires only m selected training data to represent the kernel projection where m equals the number of extracted features.

Computational complexity. The computation of the standard version of KPCA is dominated by the eigenvalue decomposition of matrix. Its size grows quadratically with the number of training data and l dominates in the computations of the standard KPCA. The complexity of eigenvalue decomposition is $O(l^3)$. The greedy algorithm requires $O(lm^2)$ operations where m is the number of extracted features (basis vectors). Therefore the greedy algorithm can be much faster if large training data are processed and the number of extracted features $m << l$ is small.

Memory requirements. The matrix of size $[l \times l]$ has to be stored in the standard KPCA therefore the space complexity is $O(l^2)$. The space complexity of the greedy algorithm is $O(lm)$. The space complexity is closely related to the number of required kernel evaluations: the standard KPCA requires $\mathrm{KerEval} = l(l+1)/2 \approx O(l^2)$ evaluations while the greedy algorithm requires only $\mathrm{KerEval} = (m+1)(2l-m)/2 \approx O(ml)$ evaluations.

8

Many-to-Many Feature Matching in Object Recognition

Ali Shokoufandeh[1], Yakov Keselman[2], Fatih Demirci[1], Diego Macrini[3], and Sven Dickinson[3]

[1] Computer Science Department, Drexel University, 3200 Chestnut St., Philadelphia, PA 19104
[2] School of Computer Science, DePaul University, 243 S. Wabash Ave., Chicago IL 60604
[3] Department of Computer Science, University of Toronto, 6 King's College Rd., Toronto, Ontario M5S 3G4

Abstract. One of the bottlenecks of current recognition (and graph matching) systems is their assumption of one-to-one feature (node) correspondence. This assumption breaks down in the generic object recognition task where, for example, a collection of features at one scale (in one image) may correspond to a single feature at a coarser scale (in the second image). Generic object recognition therefore requires the ability to match features many-to-many. In this paper, we will review our progress on three independent object recognition problems, each formulated as a graph matching problem and each solving the many-to-many matching problem in a different way. First, we explore the problem of learning a 2-D shape class prototype (represented as a graph) from a set of object exemplars (also represented as graphs) belonging to the class, in which there may be no one-to-one correspondence among extracted features. Next, we define a low-dimensional, spectral encoding of graph structure and use it to match entire subgraphs whose size can be different. Finally, in very recent work, we embed graphs into geometric spaces, reducing the many-to-many graph matching problem to a weighted point matching problem, for which efficient many-to-many matching algorithms exist.

8.1 Introduction

One of the fundamental obstacles to generic object recognition is the common assumption that saliency in the image implies saliency in the model. Alternatively, for every salient image feature (e.g., a long, high-contrast edge, a homogeneous region, a perceptual group of lines, a patch of pixel values, or even a neighborhood-encoded interest point), there's a corresponding salient model feature. Under this one-to-one correspondence assumption, object models are constrained to be 2-D or 3-D templates of the object, and recognition is constrained to be exemplar-based.

When image features are represented as graphs, this one-to-one feature correspondence assumption translates into a one-to-one correspondence (or isomorphism) assumption. However, there are a variety of conditions that may lead to graphs that represent visually similar image feature configurations yet do not contain a single one-to-one node correspondence. For example, due to noise or segmentation errors, a single feature (node) in one graph may map to a collection of broken features (nodes) in another graph. Or, due to scale differences, a single, coarse-grained feature in one graph may

H.I. Christensen and H.-H. Nagel (Eds.): Cognitive Vision Systems, LNCS 3948, pp. 107–125, 2006.
© Springer-Verlag Berlin Heidelberg 2006

map to a collection of fine-grained features in another graph. In general, we seek not a one-to-one correspondence between image features (nodes), but rather a many-to-many correspondence.

In this paper, we review three of our approaches to the problem of many-to-many graph matching for object recognition. In the first approach, in material drawn from [220], we explore the problem of generic model acquisition from a set of images containing exemplars belonging to a known class. Specifically, we present to the system a set of region adjacency graphs, representing region segmentations of the exemplar images, for which a single region (node-to-node) correspondence may not exist across the input graphs. The goal is to search the space of abstractions of these input graphs for the most informative abstraction common to all the input exemplars.

In the second approach, in material drawn from [424], we explore the problem of graph matching based on a spectral embedding of hierarchical graph structure. We map a directed acyclic graph (DAG) to a low-dimensional vector, or signature, that characterizes the topological properties of the DAG. This signature allows us to compute the distance between two graphs without insisting on isomorphism or one-to-one node correspondence. Finally, in material drawn from [221], we explore the problem of many-to-many graph matching using low-distortion graph embedding techniques. By embedding the nodes of a graph into a geometric space, we can reformulate the many-to-many graph matching problem as a many-to-many point matching problem, for which the Earth Mover's Distance (EMD) algorithm is ideal.

The ability to match features (or graphs) many-to-many is essential for generic object recognition, in which shape similarity between two objects exists not in the form of low-level features that appear explicitly in the image, but rather in the form of feature (graph) abstractions. The three approaches reviewed in this paper provide three different perspectives on the problem. The abstraction of image data is an important problem that's been largely unaddressed by the object recognition community, and the three methods reported here can be seen as generating and matching graph abstractions.

8.2 Generic Model Acquisition from Examples

Assume that we are presented with a collection of images, such that each image contains a single exemplar, all exemplars belong to a single known class, and the viewpoint with respect to the exemplar in each image is similar. Fig. 8.1(a) illustrates a simple example in which three different images, each containing a block in a similar orientation, are presented to the system. Our task is to find the common structure in these images, under the assumption that structure that is common across many exemplars of a known class must be definitive of that class. Fig. 8.1(b) illustrates the class "abstraction" that is derived from the input examples. In this case, the domain of input examples is rich enough to "intersect out" irrelevant structure (or appearance) of the block. However, had many or all the exemplars had vertical stripes, the approach would be expected to include vertical stripes in that view of the abstracted model.

Any discussion of model acquisition must be grounded in image features. In our case, each input image will be region-segmented to yield a region adjacency graph. Similarly, the output of the model acquisition process will yield a region adjacency graph containing

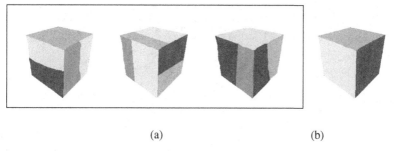

(a)   (b)

Fig. 8.1. Illustrative example of generic model acquisition: (a) Input exemplars belonging to a single known class; (b) generic model abstracted from examples

the "meta-regions" that define a particular view of the generic model. Other views of the exemplars would similarly yield other views of the generic model. The integration of these views into an optimal partitioning of the viewing sphere, or the recovery of 3-D parts from these views, is beyond the scope of this paper. For now, the result will be a collection of 2-D views that describes a generic 3-D object. This collection would then be added to the view-based object database used at recognition time.

8.2.1 Problem Formulation

Returning to Fig. 8.1, let us now formulate our problem more concretely. As we stated, each input image is processed to form a region adjacency graph (we employ the region segmentation algorithm of Felzenzwalb and Huttenlocher [119]). Let us now consider the region adjacency graph corresponding to one input image. We will assume, for now, that our region adjacency graph represents an oversegmentation of the image. In [220], we discuss the problem of undersegmentation, and how our approach can accommodate it. The space of all possible region adjacency graphs formed by any sequence of merges of adjacent regions will form a lattice, as shown in Fig. 8.2. The lattice size is exponential in the number of regions obtained after initial oversegmentation.[4]

Each of the input images will yield its own lattice. The bottom node in each lattice will be the original region adjacency graph. In all likelihood, if the exemplars have different shapes (within-class deformations) and/or surface markings, the graphs forming the bottom of their corresponding lattices may bear little or no resemblance to each other. Clearly, similarity between the exemplars cannot be ascertained at this level, for there does not exist a one-to-one correspondence between the "salient" features (i.e., regions) in one graph and the salient features in another. On the other hand, the top of each exemplar's lattice, representing a silhouette of the object (where all regions have been merged into one region), carries little information about the salient surfaces of the object.

We can now formulate our problem more precisely, recalling that a lattice consists of a set of nodes, with each node corresponding to an entire region adjacency graph. Given

---

[4] Indeed, considering the simple case of a long rectangular strip subdivided into $n + 1$ adjacent rectangles, the first pair of adjacent regions able to be merged can be selected in n ways, the second in $n - 1$, and so on, giving a lattice size of $n!$.

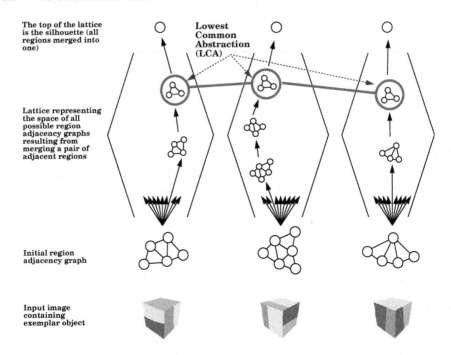

Fig. 8.2. The Lowest Common Abstraction (LCA) of a set of input exemplars (see, too, Figure 13.3)

N input image exemplars, $E_1, E_2, \ldots, E_N$, let $L_1, L_2, \ldots, L_N$ be their corresponding lattices, and for a given lattice, L_i, let $L_i n_j$ be its constituent nodes, each representing a region adjacency graph, G_{ij}. We define a *common abstraction*, or CA, as a set of nodes (one per lattice) $L_1 n_{j_1}, L_2 n_{j_2}, \ldots, L_N n_{j_N}$ such that for any two nodes $L_p n_{j_p}$ and $L_q n_{j_q}$, their corresponding graphs G_{pj_p} and G_{qj_q} are isomorphic. Thus, the root node (whose graph consists of one node representing the silhouette region) of each lattice is a common abstraction. We define the *lowest common abstraction*, or LCA, as the common abstraction whose underlying graph has maximal size (in terms of number of nodes). Given these definitions, our problem can be simply formulated as finding the LCA of N input image exemplars.

Intuitively, we are searching for a node (region segmentation) that is common to every input exemplar's lattice and that retains the maximum amount of structure common to all exemplars. Unfortunately, the presence of a single heavily undersegmented exemplar (a single-node silhouette in the extreme case) will drive the LCA toward the trivial silhouette CA. In a later section, we will relax our LCA definition to make it less sensitive to such outliers.

8.2.2 The LCA of Two Examples

For the moment, we will focus our attention on finding the LCA of two lattices, while in the next section, we will accommodate any number of lattices. Since the input lattices are exponential in the number of regions, actually computing the lattices is intractable.

Clearly, we need a means for focusing the search for the LCA that avoids significant lattice generation. Our approach will be to restrict the search for the LCA to the *intersection* of the lattices. Typically, the intersection of two lattices is much smaller than either lattice (unless the images are very similar), and leads to a tractable search space. But how do we generate this new "intersection" search space without enumerating the lattices?

Our solution is to work top-down, beginning with a node known to be in the intersection lattice – the root node, representing a single region (silhouette). If the intersection lattice contains only this one node, i.e., one or both of the region segmented images contain a single region, then the process stops and the LCA is simply the root (silhouette). However, in most cases, the root of each input lattice is derived from an input region adjacency graph containing multiple regions. So, given two silhouettes, each representing the apex of a separate, non-trivial lattice, we have the opportunity to search for a lower abstraction (than the root) common to both lattices. Our approach will be to find a decomposition of each silhouette region into two subregions, such that: 1) the shapes of the corresponding subregions are similar (for this, we employ the shape matching method outlined in Section 8.3 [424]), and 2) the relations among the corresponding regions are similar. Since there is an infinite number of possible decompositions of a region into two component regions, we will restrict our search to the space of decompositions along region boundaries in the original region adjacency graphs. Note that there may be multiple 2-region decompositions that are common to both lattices; each is a member of the intersection set.

Assuming that we have some means for ranking the matching decompositions (if more than one exist), we pick the best one (the remainder constituting a set of backtracking points), and recursively apply the process to each pair of isomorphic component subregions.[5] The process continues in this fashion, "pushing" its way down the intersection lattice, until no further decompositions are found. This lower "fringe" of the search space represents the LCA of the original two lattices. The specific algorithm for choosing the optimal pair of decompositions is given in [220], and can be summarized as follows:

1. Map each region adjacency graph to its dual *boundary segment graph*, in which boundary segments become nodes and edges capture segment adjacency.
2. Form the product graph (or association graph) of the two boundary segment graphs. Nodes and arcs in the product graph correspond to pairs of nodes and arcs, respectively, in the boundary segment graphs. Therefore, a path in the product graph corresponds to a pair of paths in the boundary segment graphs which, in turn, correspond to a pair of decompositions of the region adjacency graphs.
3. With appropriate edge weights, along with a suitable objective function, the optimal pair of corresponding decompositions corresponds to the shortest path in the product graph.
4. The optimal pair of decompositions is verified in terms of satisfying the criteria of region shape similarity and region relation consistency.

---

[5] Each subregion corresponds to the union of a set of regions corresponding to nodes belonging to a connected subgraph of the original region adjacency graph.

8.2.3 The LCA of Multiple Examples

So far, we've addressed only the problem of finding the LCA of two examples. How, then, can we extend our approach to find the LCA of multiple examples? Furthermore, when moving toward multiple examples, how do we prevent a "noisy" example, such as a single, heavily undersegmented silhouette, from driving the solution toward the trivial silhouette? To extend our two-exemplar LCA solution to a robust, multi-exemplar solution, we begin with two important observations. First, the LCA of two exemplars lies in the intersection of their abstraction lattices. Thus, both exemplar region adjacency graphs can be transformed into their LCA by means of sequences of region merges. Second, the total number of merges required to transform the graphs into their LCA is minimal among all elements of the intersection lattice, i.e., the LCA lies at the lower fringe of the lattice.

Our solution begins by constructing an approximation to the intersection lattice of multiple examples. Consider the closure of the set of the original region adjacency graphs under the operation of taking pairwise LCA's. In other words, starting with the initial region adjacency graphs, we find their pairwise LCA's, then find pairwise LCA's of the resulting abstraction graphs, and so on (note that duplicate graphs are removed). We take all graphs, original and LCA, to be nodes of a new *closure* graph. If graph H was obtained as the LCA of graphs G_1 and G_2, then directed arcs go from nodes corresponding to G_1, G_2 to the node corresponding to H in the closure graph.

Next, we will relax the first property above to accommodate "outlier" exemplars, such as undersegmented, input silhouettes. Specifically, we will not enforce that the LCA of multiple exemplars lies in the intersection set of all input exemplars. Rather, we will choose a node in our approximate intersection lattice that represents a "low abstraction" for many (but not necessarily all) input exemplars. More formally, we will define the LCA of a set of exemplar region adjacency graphs to be that element in the intersection of two or more abstraction lattices that minimizes the total number of edit operations (merges or splits) required to obtain the element from *all* the given exemplars. If a node in the intersection lattice lies along the lower fringe with respect to a number of input exemplars, then its sum distance to all exemplars is small. Conversely, the sum distance between the silhouette outlier (in fact, the true LCA) and the input exemplars will be large, eliminating that node from contention. Our algorithm for computing this "median" of the closure graph, along with an analysis of its complexity, is given in [220].

8.2.4 Demonstration

In Figure 8.3, we illustrate the results of our approach applied to a set of three coffee cup images, respectively. The lower row represents the original images, the next row up represents the input region segmented images (with black borders), while the LCA is shown with an orange border. The closure graph consists of only four members, with the same pairwise LCA emerging from all input pairs. The solution captures our intuitive notion of the cup's surfaces, with a handle, a body, a top, and the hole in the handle (the algorithm cannot distinguish a surface from a hole). Additional examples can be found in [220].

Fig. 8.3. Computed LCA (orange border) of three examples

8.3 Graph Matching Using a Spectral Encoding of Graph Structure

We now turn to the problem of inexact graph matching where, due to noise and occlusion, two graphs representing very similar objects may not be isomorphic. In a coarse-to-fine feature hierarchy, we'd like to find correspondences in a coarse-to-fine fashion, requiring that we have some way of compactly, robustly, and efficiently describing the underlying structure rooted at a node. Given such a low-dimensional encoding of DAG structure, we would compare the "shapes" of two graphs by comparing their encodings. Although correspondence may be established between two nodes in two graphs, according to the similarity of their encodings, it is important to note that these encodings describe the *entire* underlying structures rooted at these two nodes. Since these structures may have different numbers of nodes and may have slight variation in branching structure, the resulting matching can be seen as many-to-many, effectively matching two graph abstractions.

8.3.1 An Eigen-Decomposition of Structure

To describe the topology of a DAG, we turn to the domain of eigenspaces of graphs, first noting that any graph can be represented as an antisymmetric $\{0, 1, -1\}$ node-adjacency matrix (which we will subsequently refer to as an adjacency matrix), with 1's (-1's) indicating a forward (backward) edge between adjacent nodes in the graph (and

0's on the diagonal). The eigenvalues of a graph's adjacency matrix encode important structural properties of the graph. Furthermore, the eigenvalues of the adjacency matrix A are invariant to any orthonormal transformation of the form $P^t A P$. Since a permutation matrix is orthonormal, the eigenvalues of a graph are invariant to any consistent re-ordering of the graph's branches. In recent work [421], we established the stability of a graph's eigenvalues to minor perturbation due to noise and occlusion.

8.3.2 Formulating an Index

We can now proceed to define an index based on the eigenvalues. We could, for example, define a vector to be the sorted eigenvalues of a DAG, with the resulting index used to retrieve nearest neighbors in a model DAG database having similar topology. However, for large DAGs, the dimensionality of the index (and model DAG database) would be prohibitively large. Our solution to this problem will be based on eigenvalue sums rather than on the eigenvalues themselves.

Specifically, let T be a DAG whose maximum branching factor is $\Delta(T)$, and let the subgraphs of its root be $T_1, T_2, \ldots, T_S$, as shown in Figure 8.4. For each subgraph, T_i, whose root degree is $\delta(T_i)$, we compute the eigenvalues of T_i's submatrix, sort them in decreasing order by absolute value of their magnitude, and let S_i be the sum of the $\delta(T_i) - 1$ largest magnitudes. The sorted S_i's become the components of a $\Delta(T)$-dimensional vector, called a *Topological Signature Vector, or TSV*, assigned to the DAG's root. If the number of S_i's is less than $\Delta(T)$, then the vector is padded with zeroes. We can recursively repeat this procedure, assigning a TSV to each nonterminal node in the DAG, computed over the subgraph rooted at that node. The reasons for computing a description for each node, rather than just the root, will become clear in the next section.

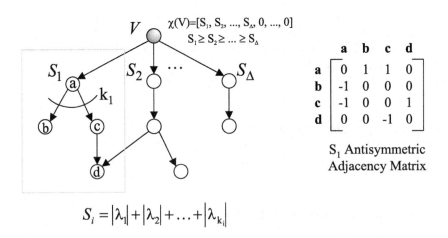

$$S_i = \left|\lambda_1\right| + \left|\lambda_2\right| + \ldots + \left|\lambda_{k_i}\right|$$

Fig. 8.4. Forming a low-dimensional vector description (TSV) of graph structure

Although the eigenvalue sums are invariant to any consistent re-ordering of the DAG's branches, we have given up some uniqueness (due to the summing operation) in order to reduce dimensionality. We could have elevated only the largest eigenvalue from each subgraph (non-unique but less ambiguous), but this would be less representative of the subgraph's structure. We choose the $\delta(T_i) - 1$ largest eigenvalues for two reasons: 1) the largest eigenvalues are more informative of subgraph structure, and 2) by summing $\delta(T_i) - 1$ elements, we effectively normalize the sum according to the local complexity of the subgraph root.

8.3.3 Matching Hierarchical Structures

Each of the top-ranking candidates emerging from the indexing process must be verified to determine which is most similar to the query. If there were no clutter, occlusion, or noise, our problem could be formulated as a graph isomorphism problem. If we allowed clutter and limited occlusion, we would search for the largest isomorphic subgraphs between query and model. Unfortunately, with the presence of noise, in the form of the addition of spurious graph structure and/or the deletion of salient graph structure, large isomorphic subgraphs may simply not exist. It is here that we call on our eigen-characterization of graph structure to help us overcome this problem.

Each node in our graph (query or model) is assigned a TSV, which reflects the underlying structure in the subgraph rooted at that node. If we simply discarded all the edges in our two graphs, we would be faced with the problem of finding the best correspondence between the nodes in the query and the nodes in the model; two nodes could be said to be in close correspondence if the distance between their TSVs (and the distance between their domain-dependent node labels) was small. In fact, such a formulation amounts to finding the maximum cardinality, minimum weight matching in a bipartite graph spanning the two sets of nodes. At first glance, such a formulation might seem like a bad idea (by throwing away all that important graph structure!) until one recalls that the graph structure is really encoded in the node's TSV. Is it then possible to reformulate a noisy, largest isomorphic subgraph problem as a simple bipartite matching problem?

Unfortunately, in discarding all the graph structure, we have also discarded the underlying hierarchical structure. There is nothing in the bipartite graph matching formulation that ensures that hierarchical constraints among corresponding nodes are obeyed, i.e., that parent/child nodes in one graph don't match child/parent nodes in the other. This reformulation, although softening the overly strict constraints imposed by the largest isomorphic subgraph formulation, is perhaps too weak. We could try to enforce the hierarchical constraints in our bipartite matching formulation, but no polynomial-time solution is known to exist for the resulting formulation. Clearly, we seek an efficient approximation method that will find corresponding nodes between two noisy, occluded DAGs (a DAG that encodes the graph structure of an object and an occluder, i.e. portions of the DAG may not represent the target object but that of an occluder), subject to hierarchical constraints.

Our algorithm, a modification to Reyner's algorithm [371], combines the above bipartite matching formulation with a greedy, best-first search in a recursive procedure to compute the corresponding nodes in two rooted DAGs. As in the above bipartite matching formulation, we compute the maximum cardinality, minimum weight matching in the bipartite graph spanning the two sets of nodes. Edge weight will encode a function of both topological similarity (TSV) as well as domain-dependent node similarity. The result will be a selection of edges yielding a mapping between query and model nodes. As mentioned above, the computed mapping may not obey hierarchical constraints. We therefore greedily choose only the best edge (the two most similar nodes in the two graphs, representing in some sense the two most similar subgraphs), add it to the solution set, and recursively apply the procedure to the subgraphs defined by these two nodes. Unlike a traditional depth-first search which backtracks to the next statically-determined branch, our algorithm effectively recomputes the branches at each node, always choosing the next branch to descend in a best-first manner. In this way, the search for corresponding nodes is focused in corresponding subgraphs (rooted DAGs) in a top-down manner, thereby ensuring that hierarchical constraints are obeyed.

8.3.4 Demonstration

To demonstrate our approach to matching, we turn to the domain of 2-D object recognition [422, 424]. We adopt a representation for 2-D shape that is based on a coloring of the shocks (singularities) of a curve evolution process acting on simple closed curves in the plane [223]. Any given 2-D shape gives rise to a rooted *shock tree*, in which nodes represent parts (whose labels are drawn from four qualitatively-defined classes) and arcs represent relative time of formation (or relative size). Figure 8.5 illustrates a 2-D shape, its shock structure, and its resulting shock graph, while Figures 8.6 illustrates a matching example of two similar shapes, showing part correspondences. Extensive examples and performance evaluation can be found in [424, 271, 270].

8.4 Many-to-Many Graph Matching Using Graph Embedding

Several existing approaches to the problem of many-to-many graph matching suffer from computational inefficiency and/or from an inability to handle small perturbations in graph structure. We seek a solution to this problem while addressing drawbacks of existing approaches. Drawing on recently-developed techniques from the domain of low-distortion graph embedding, we have explored an efficient method for mapping a graph's structure to a set of vectors in a low-dimensional space. This mapping not only simplifies the original graph representation, but it retains important information about both local (neighborhood) as well as global graph structure. Moreover, the mapping is stable with respect to noise in the graph structure.

Armed with a low-dimensional, robust vector representation of an input graph's structure, many-to-many graph matching can now be reduced to the much simpler problem of matching weighted distributions of points in a normed vector space, using a *distribution-based* similarity measure. We consider one such similarity measure, known as the Earth Mover's Distance (EMD), and show that the many-to-many vector mapping that realizes the minimum Earth Mover's Distance corresponds to the desired many-to-many matching between nodes of the original graphs. The result is a more efficient

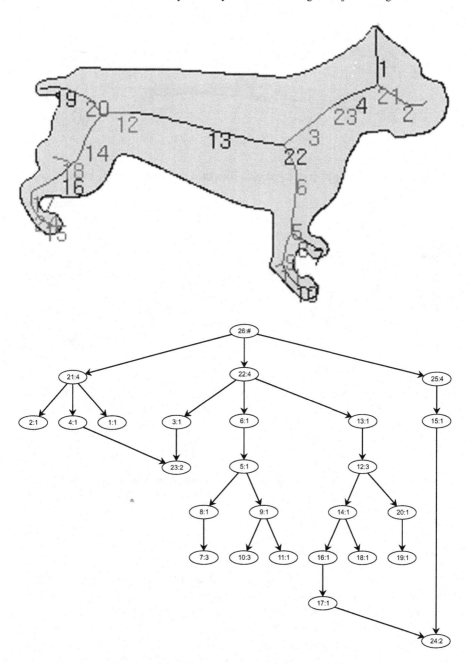

Fig. 8.5. An illustrative example of a shape and its corresponding shock graph

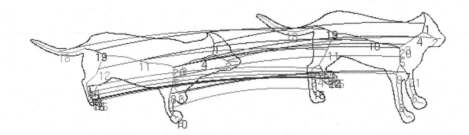

Fig. 8.6. Example part correspondences computed by the matching algorithm

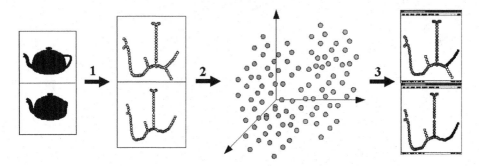

Fig. 8.7. Overview of many-to-many matching procedure. a pair of views are represented by undirected, rooted, weighted graphs (transition 1). The graphs are mapped into a low-dimensional vector space using a low-distortion graph embedding (transition 2). A many-to-many point (graph node) correspondence is computed by the earth mover's distance under transformation (transition 3).

and more stable approach to many-to-many graph matching that, in fact, includes the special case of one-to-one graph matching. The overview of the approach is presented in Figure 8.7.

8.4.1 Low-Distortion Embedding

Our interest in low-distortion embedding is motivated by its ability to transform the problem of many-to-many matching in finite graphs to geometrical problems in low-dimensional vector spaces. Specifically, let $G_1 = (\mathcal{A}_1, E_1, \mathcal{D}_1)$, $G_2 = (\mathcal{A}_2, E_2, \mathcal{D}_2)$ denote two graphs on vertex sets $\mathcal{A}_1$ and $\mathcal{A}_2$, edge sets E_1 and E_2, under distance metrics $\mathcal{D}_1$ and $\mathcal{D}_2$, respectively ($\mathcal{D}_i$ represents the distances between all pairs of nodes in G_i). Ideally, we seek a single embedding that can map each graph to the same vector space, in which the two embeddings can be directly compared. However, in general, this is not possible without introducing unacceptable distortion.

We will therefore tackle the problem in two steps. First, we will seek low-distortion embeddings f_i that map sets $\mathcal{A}_i$ to normed spaces $(\mathcal{B}_i, ||.||_k)$, $i \in \{1, 2\}$. Next, we will align the normed spaces, so that the embeddings can be directly compared. Using

. these mappings, the problem of many-to-many vertex matching between G_1 and G_2 is therefore reduced to that of computing a mapping $\mathcal{M}$ between subsets of $\mathcal{B}_1$ and $\mathcal{B}_2$.

In practice, the robustness and efficiency of mapping $\mathcal{M}$ will depend on several parameters, such as the magnitudes of distortion of the $\mathcal{D}_i$'s under the embeddings, the computational complexity of applying the embeddings, the efficiency of computing the actual correspondences (including alignment) between subsets of $\mathcal{B}_1$ and $\mathcal{B}_2$, and the quality of the computed correspondence. The latter issue will be addressed in Section 8.4.2.

The problem of low-distortion embedding has a long history for the case of planar graphs, in general, and trees, in particular. More formally, the most desired embedding is the subject of the following conjecture:

Conjecture 1. [162] Let $G = (\mathcal{A}, E)$ be a planar graph, and let $M = (\mathcal{A}, \mathcal{D})$ be the shortest-path metric for the graph G. Then there is an embedding of M into $||.||_p$ with $O(1)$ distortion.

This conjecture has only been proven for the case in which G is a tree. Although the existence of such a distortion-free embedding under $||.||_k$-norms was established in [258], no deterministic construction was provided. One such deterministic construction was given by Matoušek [287], suggesting that if we could somehow map our graphs into trees, with small distortion, we could adopt Matoušek's framework.

The Shortest Path Metric

Before we can proceed with Matoušek's embedding, we must choose a suitable metric for our graphs, i.e., we must define a distance between any two vertices. Let $G = (\mathcal{A}, E)$ denote an edge-weighted graph with real edge weights $\mathcal{W}(e)$, $e \in E$. We will say that $\mathcal{D}$ is a metric for G if, for any three vertices $u, v, w \in \mathcal{A}$, $\mathcal{D}(u, v) = \mathcal{D}(v, u) \geq 0$, $\mathcal{D}(u, u) = 0$, and $\mathcal{D}(u, v) \leq \mathcal{D}(u, w) + \mathcal{D}(w, v)$. In general, there are many ways to define metric distances on a weighted graph. The best-known metric is the shortest-path metric $\delta(., .)$, i.e., $\mathcal{D}(u, v) = \delta(u, v)$, the shortest path distance between u and v for all $u, v \in \mathcal{A}$. In fact, if the weighted graph G is a tree, the shortest path between any two vertices is unique, and the weights of the shortest paths between vertices will define a metric $\mathcal{D}(., .)$.

In the event that G is not a tree, $\mathcal{D}(., .)$ can be defined through a special representation of G, known as the *centroid metric tree* $\mathfrak{T}$ [2]. The path-length between any two vertices u, v in $\mathfrak{T}$ will mimic the metric $\delta(u, v)$ in G. A metric $\mathcal{D}(., .)$ on n objects $\{v_1, \ldots, v_n\}$ is a centroid metric if there exist labels $\ell_1, \ldots, \ell_n$ such that for all $i \neq j$, $\mathcal{D}(v_i, v_j) = \ell_i + \ell_j$. If G is not a tree, its centroid metric tree $\mathfrak{T}$ is a star on vertex-set $\mathcal{A} \cup \{c\}$ and weighted edge-set $\{(c, v_i) | \mathcal{W}(c, v_i) = \ell_i, v_i \in \mathcal{A}\}$. It is easy to see that the path-lengths between v_i and v_j in $\mathfrak{T}$ will correspond to $\mathcal{D}(v_i, v_j)$ in G. For details on the construction of a metric labeling ℓ_i of a metric distance $\mathcal{D}(., .)$, see [2].

Path Partition of a Graph

The construction of the embedding depends on the notion of a path partition of a graph. In this subsection, we introduce the path partition, and then use it in the next subsection to construct the embedding. Given a weighted graph $G = (\mathcal{A}, E)$ with metric distance $\mathcal{D}(.,.)$, let $\mathfrak{T} = (\mathcal{A}, \mathfrak{E})$ denote a tree representation of G, whose vertex distances are consistent with $\mathcal{D}(.,.)$. In the event that G is a tree, $\mathfrak{T} = G$; otherwise $\mathfrak{T}$ is the centroid metric tree of G. To construct the embedding, we will assume that $\mathfrak{T}$ is a rooted tree. It will be clear from the construction that the choice of the root does not affect the distortion of the embedding.

The dimensionality of the embedding of $\mathfrak{T}$ depends on the caterpillar dimension, denoted by $\mathrm{cdim}(\mathfrak{T})$, and is recursively defined as follows [287]. If $\mathfrak{T}$ consists of a single vertex, we set $\mathrm{cdim}(\mathfrak{T}) = 0$. For a tree $\mathfrak{T}$ with at least 2 vertices, $\mathrm{cdim}(\mathfrak{T}) \leq k + 1$ if there exist paths $P_1, \ldots, P_r$ beginning at the root and otherwise pairwise disjoint, such that each component $\mathfrak{T}_j$ of $\mathfrak{T} - \mathfrak{E}(P_1) - \mathfrak{E}(P_2) - \cdots - \mathfrak{E}(P_r)$ satisfies $\mathrm{cdim}(\mathfrak{T}_j) \leq k$. Here $\mathfrak{T} - \mathfrak{E}(P_1) - \mathfrak{E}(P_2) - \cdots - \mathfrak{E}(P_r)$ denotes the tree $\mathfrak{T}$ with the edges of the P_i's removed, and the components $\mathfrak{T}_j$ are rooted at the single vertex lying on some P_i. The caterpillar dimension can be determined in linear time for a rooted tree $\mathfrak{T}$, and it is known that $\mathrm{cdim}(\mathfrak{T}) \leq \log(|\mathcal{A}|)$ (see [287]).

The construction of vectors $f(v)$, for $v \in \mathcal{A}$, depends on the notion of a *path partition* of $\mathfrak{T}$. The path partition $\mathfrak{P}$ of $\mathfrak{T}$ is empty if $\mathfrak{P}$ is a single vertex; otherwise $\mathfrak{P}$ consists of some paths $P_1, \ldots, P_r$ as in the definition of $\mathrm{cdim}(\mathfrak{T})$, plus the union of path partitions of the components of $\mathfrak{T} - \mathfrak{E}(P_1) - \mathcal{M}(P_2) - \cdots - \mathfrak{E}(P_r)$. The paths $P_1, \ldots, P_r$ have level 1, and the paths of level $k \geq 2$ are the paths of level $k - 1$ in the corresponding path partitions of the components of $\mathfrak{T} - \mathfrak{E}(P_1) - \mathfrak{E}(P_2) - \cdots - \mathfrak{E}(P_r)$. Note that the paths in a path partition are edge-disjoint, and their union covers the edge-set of $\mathfrak{T}$.

To illustrate these concepts, consider the tree shown in Figure 8.8. The three darkened paths from the root represent three level 1 paths. Following the removal of the level 1 paths, we are left with 6 connected components that, in turn, induce seven level 2 paths, shown with lightened edges.[6] Following the removal of the seven level 2 paths, we are left with an empty graph. Hence, the caterpillar dimension ($\mathrm{cdim}(\mathfrak{T})$) is 2. It is easy to see that the path partition $\mathfrak{P}$ can be constructed using a modified depth-first search in $O(|\mathcal{A}|)$ time.

Construction of the Embedding

Given a path partition $\mathfrak{P}$ of $\mathfrak{T}$, we will use m to denote the number of levels in $\mathfrak{P}$, and let $P(v)$ represent the unique path between the root and a vertex $v \in \mathcal{A}$. The first segment of $P(v)$ of weight l_1 follows some path P^1 of level 1 in $\mathfrak{P}$, the second segment of weight l_2 follows a path P^2 of level 2, and the last segment of weight l_α follows a path P^α of level $\alpha \leq m$. The sequences $\langle P^1, \ldots, P^\alpha \rangle$ and $\langle l_1, \ldots, l_\alpha \rangle$ will be referred to as the *decomposition sequence* and the *weight sequence* of $P(v)$, respectively.

To define the embedding $f : \mathcal{A} \to \mathcal{B}$ under $||.||_2$, we let the relevant coordinates in $\mathcal{B}$ be indexed by the paths in $\mathfrak{P}$. The vector $f(v)$, $v \in \mathcal{A}$, has non-zero coordinates corresponding to the paths in the decomposition sequence of $P(v)$. Returning to Figure 8.8, the vector $f(v)$ will have 10 components (defined by three level 1 paths and seven level 2 paths). Furthermore, every vector $f(v)$ will have at most two non-zero components.

---

[6] Note that the third node from the root in the middle level 1 branch is the root of a tree-component consisting of five nodes that will generate two level 2 paths.

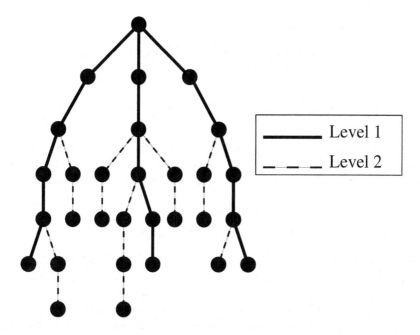

Fig. 8.8. Path partition of a tree

Consider, for example, the lowest leaf node in the middle branch. Its path to the root will traverse three level 2 edges corresponding to the fourth level 2 path, as well as three level 1 edges corresponding to the second level 1 path.

Such embedding functions have become fairly standard in the metric space representation of weighted graphs [259, 287]. In fact, Matoušek [287] has proven that setting the i-th coordinate of $f(v)$, corresponding to path P^k, $1 \leq k \leq \alpha$, in decomposition sequence $\langle P^1, \ldots, P^\alpha \rangle$, to

$$f(v)_i = \sqrt{l_k \left[l_k + \sum_{j=1}^{\alpha} \max\left(0, l_j - l_k/2m\right) \right]}$$

will result in a small distortion of at most $\sqrt{\log \log |\mathcal{A}|}$. It should be mentioned that although the choice of path decomposition $\mathfrak{P}$ is not unique, the resulting embeddings are isomorphic up to a transformation. Computationally, constructions of $\mathfrak{T}$, $\mathfrak{P}$, and $\mathcal{B}$ are all linear in terms of $|\mathcal{A}|$ and $|\mathfrak{E}|$.

The above embedding has preserved both graph structure and edge weights, but has not accounted for node information. To accommodate node information in our embedding, we will associate a weight w_v to each vector $f(v)$, for all $v \in \mathcal{A}$. These weights will be defined in terms of vertex labels which, in turn, encode image feature values. Note that nodes with multiple feature values give rise to a vector of weights assigned to every point. We will present an example of one such distribution in Section 8.4.3.

8.4.2 Distribution-Based Matching

By embedding vertex-labeled graphs into normed spaces, we have reduced the problem of many-to-many matching of graphs to that of many-to-many matching of weighted distributions of points in normed spaces. However, before we can match two point distributions, we must map them into the same normed space. This involves reducing the dimensionality of the higher-dimensional distribution and aligning the two distributions. Given a pair of weighted distributions in the same normed space, the Earth Mover's Distance (EMD) framework [384] is then applied to find an optimal match between the distributions. The EMD approach computes the minimum amount of work (defined in terms of displacements of the masses associated with points) it takes to transform one distribution into another.

Embedding Point Distributions in the Same Normed Space

Embeddings produced by the graph embedding algorithm can be of different dimensions and are defined only up to a distance-preserving transformation (a translated and rotated version of a graph embedding will also be a graph embedding). Therefore, in order to apply the EMD framework, we perform a PCA-based "registration" step, whose objective is to project the two distributions into the same normed space. Intuitively, the projection of the original vectors associated with each graph embedding onto the subspace spanned by the first K right singular vectors of the covariance matrix retains the maximum information about the original vectors among all projections onto subspaces of dimension K. Hence, if K is the minimum of the two vector dimensions, projecting the two embeddings onto the first K right singular vectors of their covariance matrices will equalize their dimensions while losing minimal information [221]. The resulting transformation is expected to minimize the initial EMD between the distributions.

The Earth Mover's Distance

The Earth Mover's Distance (EMD) [384, 74] is designed to evaluate the dissimilarity between two multi-dimensional distributions in some feature space. The EMD approach assumes that a distance measure between single features, called the *ground distance*, is given. The EMD then "lifts" this distance from individual features to full distributions. Computing the EMD is based on a solution to the well-known *transportation problem* [4], whose optimal value determines the minimum amount of "work" required to transform one distribution into the other. Moreover, if the weights of the distributions are the same, and the ground distance is a metric, EMD induces a metric distance [384].

Recall that a translated and rotated version of a graph embedding will also be a graph embedding. To accommodate pairs of distributions that are "not rigidly embedded", Cohen and Guibas [74] extended the definition of EMD, originally applicable to pairs of fixed sets of points, to allow one of the sets to undergo a transformation. They also suggested an iterative process (which they call **FT**, short for "an optimal **F**low and an optimal **T**ransformation") that achieves an infimum of the objective function for EMD. The iterative process stops when the improvement in the objective function value falls below a threshold. For our application, the set of allowable transformations consists of only those transformations that preserve distances. Therefore, we use a weighted version of the Least Squares Estimation algorithm [464] to compute an optimal distance-preserving transformation given a flow between the distributions. The main advantage of using EMD lies in the fact that it subsumes many histogram distances and permits partial and many-to-many matches under transformation in a natural way. This important property allows the similarity measure to deal with uneven clusters and noisy datasets.

8.4.3 Demonstration

To demonstrate our approach to many-to-many matching, we turn to the domain of view-based object recognition using silhouettes. For a given view, an object's silhouette is first represented by an undirected, rooted, weighted graph, in which nodes represent *shocks* [424] (or, equivalently, skeleton points) and edges connect adjacent shock points.[7] We will assume that each point p on the discrete skeleton is labeled by a 4-dimensional vector $v(p) = (x, y, r, \alpha)$, where (x, y) are the Euclidean coordinates of the point, r is the radius of the maximal bi-tangent circle centered at the point, and α is the angle between the normal to either bitangent and the linear approximation to the skeleton curve at the point.[8] This 4-tuple can be thought of as encoding local shape information of the silhouette.

To convert our shock graphs to shock trees, we compute the minimum spanning tree of the weighted shock graph. Since the edges of the shock graph are weighted based on Euclidean distances of corresponding nodes, the minimum spanning tree will generate a suitable tree approximation for shock graphs. The root of the tree is the node that minimizes the sum of distances to all other nodes. Finally, each node is weighted proportionally to its average radius, with the total tree weight being 1. An illustration of the procedure is given in Figure 8.9. The left portion shows the initial silhouette and its shock points (skeleton). The right portion depicts the constructed shock tree. Darker, heavier nodes correspond to fragments whose average radii are larger. Figure 8.10 illustrates the many-to-many correspondences that our matching algorithm yields for two adjacent views (30° and 40°) of the TEAPOT. Corresponding clusters (many-to-many mappings) have been shaded with the same color. Note that the extraneous branch in the left view was not matched in the right view, reflecting the method's ability to deal with noise. Further details and additional experiments can be found in [221].

8.5 Conclusions

Successful object recognition requires overcoming the restrictive assumption of one-to-one feature correspondence. We introduce three different graph theoretic frameworks for many-to-many feature matching. The first, addressing the problem of generic model acquisition, searches the space of all possible abstractions of an image, and uses support

---

[7] Note that this representation is closely related to Siddiqi et al.'s *shock graph* [424], except that our nodes (shock points) are neither clustered nor are our edges directed.

[8] Note that this 4-tuple is slightly different from Siddiqi et al.'s shock point 4-tuple, where the latter's radius is assumed normal to the axis.

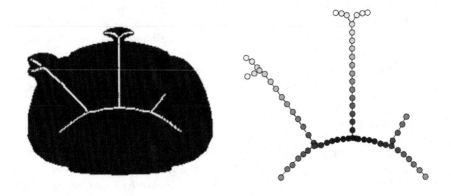

Fig. 8.9. Left: The silhouette of a TEAPOT and its medial axis. Right: the medial axis tree constructed from the medial axis. darker nodes reflect larger radii.

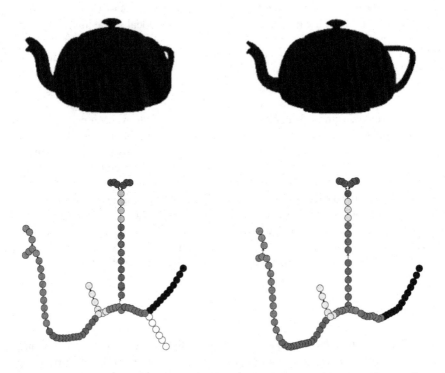

Fig. 8.10. Illustration of the many-to-many correspondences computed for two adjacent views of the TEAPOT. Matched point clusters are shaded with the same color.

from other objects drawn from the same class to help constrain the search. The second, addressing the problem of graph matching, draws on spectral graph theory to generate and match abstractions of directed acyclic graphs. The third, addressing the problem of many-to-many graph matching, attempts to map the graphs into a geometric domain, in which effective algorithms for many-to-many point matching exist. In current work, we are pushing each of these three fronts in order to improve matching in the presence of increased noise, occlusion, articulation, and deformation.

Acknowledgements

The authors gratefully acknowledge the support of NSERC, IRIS, NSF, ONR, and PREA.

9

Integrating Video Information over Time. Example: Face Recognition from Video*

Volker Krüger[1], Shaohua Zhou[2], and Rama Chellappa[2]

[1] Aalborg University Esbjerg, Departement for Computer Science
Niels Bohrs Vej 8
6700 Esbjerg, Denmark
vok@cs.aue.auc.dk

[2] University of Maryland, Center for Automation Research
A.V. Williams Building
College Park, MD 20742, USA
{shaohua|rama}@cfar.umd.edu

9.1 Introduction

The ability to integrate information over time in order to come to a conclusion is a strength of cognitive systems. It allows the system, e.g., to

1. verify insecure observations: This is the case when data is noisy or of low-quality, or if conditions in general are non-optimal.
2. exploit general knowledge about spatio-temporal relations: This allows the system to exploit the specific dynamics of an object as an additional feature for, e.g., recognition, interpretation and prediction of actions of other agents.
3. In general, using dynamics allows the system to recursively generate and verify hypotheses for object and scene interpretation and to generate warnings when 'implausible' hypotheses occur or to circumvent them altogether.

We have studied the effectiveness of temporal integration for recognition purposes by using the face recognition as an example study case. Face recognition is a prominent problem and has been studied more extensively than almost any other recognition problem. An observation is that face recognition works well in ideal conditions. If those conditions, however, are not met, then all present algorithms break down disgracefully. This problem appears to be general to all vision techniques that intend to extract visual information out of low-SNR image data. It is exactly a strength of cognitive systems that they are able to cope with non-ideal situations. In this chapter we will deal with this problem.

Most approaches that claim to do video-based recognition, (e.g., [71]), apply a tracking method to track the face under consideration. If a frame is being detected that meets a certain quality requirement, it is extracted and then forwarded to the recognition method.

---

* This work was partially supported by the DARPA HumanID Grant N00014-00-1-0908.

H.I. Christensen and H.-H. Nagel (Eds.): Cognitive Vision Systems, LNCS 3948, pp. 127–144, 2006.
© Springer-Verlag Berlin Heidelberg 2006

Such a *tracking-then-recognition* approach considers uncertainty in tracking and recognition to be independent, which, of course, they are not.

There are several unresolved issues in the *tracking-then-recognition* approach: criteria for selecting good frames and estimation of parameters for registration. Also, still-to-still recognition does not effectively exploit temporal information. A common strategy that selects several good frames, performs recognition on each frame and then votes on these recognition results for a final solution might be *ad hoc*.

To overcome these difficulties, we present the *still-to-video* based face recognition approach. This approach attempts to resolve uncertainties in tracking and recognition *simultaneously* in a unified probabilistic framework. To fuse temporal information, the time series state space model is adopted to characterize the evolving kinematics and identity in a probe video. Three basic components of the model are:

- a *motion equation* governing the kinematic behavior of the tracking motion vector,
- an *identity equation* governing the temporal evolution of the identity variable,
- an *observation equation* establishing a link between the motion vector and the identity variable.

Using the sequential importance sampling (SIS) [202, 224, 263, 104] technique, the joint posterior distribution of a motion vector α and an identity variable i, i.e., $p(i_t, \alpha_t | Z_1 \ldots Z_t)$, is estimated at each time instant and then propagated to the next time instant governed by motion and identity equations. The marginal distribution of the identity variable, i.e., $p(i_t | Z_1 \ldots Z_t)$, is estimated to provide a recognition result. An SIS algorithm is used to approximate the distribution $p(i_t | Z_1 \ldots Z_t)$.

The still templates in the gallery can be generalized to video sequences in order to realize *video-to-video* recognition. In video-to-video recognition, exemplars and their prior probabilities are learned from the gallery videos to serve as still templates in the still-to-video scenario. A person i may have a collection of several exemplars, say $\mathcal{C}^i = \{c_1^i, c_2^i, \ldots, c_{K_i}^i\}$ indexed by k. The likelihood is modified as a mixture density with exemplars as mixture centers. We first compute the joint distribution $p(i_t, k_t, \alpha_t | Z_1 \ldots Z_t)$ using the SIS algorithm and marginalize it to yield $p(i_t | Z_1 \ldots Z_t)$. In the experiments reported, the subject walks in outside environments and indoors on a tread-mill with his/her face moving naturally, giving rise to significant variations in illumination and across poses. However, the proposed method successfully copes with these pose variations as evidenced by the experimental results.

The organization of the paper is as follows: Section 9.2 reviews some related studies on video-based tracking and recognition in the literature. Section 9.3 introduces preliminaries. Section 9.4 briefly reviews the SIS principles from the viewpoint of a general state space model. Section 9.5 describes the still-to-video based approach and illustrates it with experiments on data collected as part of the HumanID effort. In Section 9.6, the exemplar-based learning algorithm and the SIS algorithm to accommodate video-to-video recognition are presented. Experimental results for the video-to-video recognition problem using the CMU data are also included in this section. Section 9.7 concludes the paper with discussions.

9.2 Related Literature

Nearly all video-based recognition systems apply still-image-based recognition to selected good frames. The face images are warped into frontal views whenever pose and depth information about the faces is available [71].

In [200, 296, 488] RBF (Radial Basis Function) networks are used for tracking and recognition purposes. In [200], the system uses an RBF (Radial Basis Function) network for recognition. Since no warping is done, the RBF network has to learn the individual variations as well as possible transformations. The performance appears to vary widely, depending on the size of the training data but has not been thoroughly evaluated. In [296] face tracking is based on a RBF network to provide feedback to a motion clustering process. Good tracking results were demonstrated, but person authentication results were referred to as future work. [488] present a fully automatic person authentication system. The system uses video break, face detection, and authentication modules and cycles over successive video images until a high recognition confidence is reached. During operation, the face is tracked, face images are normalized and then used for authentication with an RBF network. This system was tested on three image sequences; the first was taken indoors with one subject present, the second was taken outdoors with two subjects, and the third was taken outdoors with one subject in stormy conditions. Perfect results were reported on all three sequences, as verified against a database of 20 still face images.

In [251], a generic approach to simultaneous object tracking and verification is proposed. The approach is based on posterior probability density estimation using sequential Monte Carlo methods [104, 203, 224, 263]. Tracking is formulated as a probability density propagation problem and the algorithm also provides verification results. However, no systematic recognition evaluation was done.

In [434], a system called *PersonSpotter* is described. This system is able to capture, track and recognize a person walking toward or passing a stereo CCD camera. It has several modules, including a head tracker, and a landmark finder. The landmark finder uses a dense graph consisting of 48 nodes learned from 25 example images to find landmarks such as eyes and nose tip. An elastic graph matching scheme is employed to identify the face.

A multimodal based person recognition system is described in [71]. This system consists of a face recognition module, a speaker identification module, and a classifier fusion module. The most reliable video frames and audio clips are selected for recognition. 3D information about the head is used to detect the presence of an actual person as opposed to an image of that person. Recognition and verification rates of 100% were achieved for 26 registered clients.

9.3 Preliminaries

Before delving into details about video-based recognition and exemplar learning, we will introduce some terminology borrowed from the FERET evaluation protocol [349].

A *Gallery* $\mathcal{V} = \{V_1, V_2, \ldots, V_N\}$ is here either a set of images or a set of videos, depending on the considered application. Each V_i is associated with a single individual, i.e., N individuals $\mathcal{N} = \{1, 2, \ldots, N\}$, are represented in the Gallery $\mathcal{V}$.

A *Probe set* $\mathcal{P} = \{P_1, P_2, \ldots, P_M\}$ is a set of M probe videos which are used for testing.

9.3.1 Objects, Faces and Exemplars

In our framework a *face* is defined to be a gray value image that has been suitably processed. We therefore treat faces in an appearance-based 2D manner. An *exemplar* is a selected "representative", extracted directly from raw video.

9.3.2 Geometric and Photometric Transformations

An image Z may undergo a geometrical or photometrical transformation

$$\tilde{Z} = \mathcal{T}_\alpha\{Z\} \tag{9.1}$$

for $\alpha \in \mathcal{A}$, where $\mathcal{A}$ is the set of possible transformations.

For example, $\mathcal{T}_\alpha$ represents the similarity transforms, if with $\alpha = (\mathbf{c}, \theta, s)$

$$\mathcal{T}_\alpha\{Z(\mathbf{x})\} = Z(\mathcal{T}_\alpha(\mathbf{x})) = Z(s\mathbf{R}(\theta)\mathbf{x} + \mathbf{c}) . \tag{9.2}$$

The set of possible transformations $\mathcal{A}$ has to be pre-defined in our framework.

9.3.3 Likelihood Measure

Let $F = \{f_1, f_2 \ldots, f_N\}$ be a set of faces, with $\mathcal{N} = \{1, 2, \ldots, N\}$.

Let further $X \in \mathcal{A} \times \mathcal{N}$ be a random variable. This random variable defines the transformation $\mathcal{T}_\alpha$ and the number i of a face $f_i \in F$. Thus, having observed a video image Z, the observation likelihood for a hypothesis $X = (\alpha, i)$, is given by

$$\begin{aligned} p(Z|X) &\equiv p(Z|\alpha, i) \\ &\propto z \exp -\frac{1}{2\sigma^2} d(Z, \mathcal{T}_\alpha\{f_i\}) , \end{aligned} \tag{9.3}$$

Eq. (9.3) computes the probability that the observation Z shows the face of an individual i, while the face f_i undergoes the transformation α. Here, $d(\cdot, \cdot)$ is a suitable distance function. In face recognition, one usually deals with the inner face region of the subject, rather than the entire image. We therefore interpret Eq. (9.3) such that $\mathcal{T}_\alpha\{f_i\}$ is compared to a subimage of Z where the position and scale of the subimage is specified by α.

Clearly, the computation of this posterior joint probability does not depend on the specific choice of certain distance function d. The choice of a suitable d depends rather on the choice of image representation which may be chosen from a large variety (PCA, LDA, bunchgraph) that have proven to be useful for face recognition. σ and the normalizing constant z have do be chosen with respect to the chosen distance measure d. In addition, also other likelihood measures may be used such as the one introduced in [305] that facilitates the *intra-personal* and the *extra-personal* variations for recognition (see also Sec.9.5).

9.3.4 Tracking and Recognition in the Bayesian Framework

Given an input image sequence $\mathcal{Z} = Z_1, Z_2, \ldots, Z_N$ we can now compute the observation likelihoods as in Eq. 9.3 and we can track and identify individuals in the video: Let $X_t = (\alpha_t, i_t) \in \mathcal{A} \times \mathcal{N}$ be a random variable. We want to estimate the joint distribution

$$p(X_t | Z_1, \ldots, Z_t) \; . \tag{9.4}$$

Using the classical Bayesian propagation over time, we get

$$p(X_t | Z_1, Z_2, \ldots, Z_t) \equiv p_t(\alpha_t, i_t)$$
$$= \sum_{i_{t-1}} \int_{\alpha_{t-1}} p(Z_t | \alpha_t, i_t) p(\alpha_t, i_t | \alpha_{t-1}, i_{t-1}) p_{t-1}(\alpha_{t-1}, i_{t-1}) \; . \tag{9.5}$$

Here, $p(Z_t | \alpha_t, i_t)$ denotes the likelihood measure, $p(\alpha_t, i_t | \alpha_{t-1}, i_{t-1})$ the propagation or motion function and $p_{t-1}(\alpha_{t-1}, i_{t-1})$ the prior. Marginalizing the posterior over the possible transformations $\alpha \in \mathcal{A}$ we get a probability mass function for the identity:

$$p(i_t | Z_1, \ldots, Z_t) = \int_{\alpha_t} p(\alpha_t, i_t | Z_1, \ldots, Z_t) \; . \tag{9.6}$$

Maximizing (9.6) leads to the desired identity.

9.4 Sequential Importance Sampling Algorithm

We solve Eq. 9.5 with a particle filtering method. The essence of particle filters or Monte Carlo methods is to represent an arbitrary probability distribution $\pi(x)$ closely by a set of discrete samples $\{x^{(m)}\}_{m=1}^M$ from $\pi(x)$. It is ideal to draw i.i.d. samples $\{x^{(m)}\}_{m=1}^M$ from $\pi(x)$. However, it is often difficult to implement, especially for non-trivial distributions. Instead, a set of samples $\{x^{(m)}\}_{m=1}^M$ is drawn from an *importance function* $g(x)$ which is easy to sample from, then a weight

$$w^{(m)} = \pi(x^{(m)})/g(x^{(m)}) \tag{9.7}$$

is assigned to each sample. This technique is called *Importance Sampling* (IS). It can be shown[263] that the *importance sample set* $\mathcal{S} = \{(x^{(m)}, w^{(m)})\}_{m=1}^M$ is *properly weighted* to the target distribution $\pi(x)$. To accommodate a video, importance sampling is used in a sequential fashion, which leads to *Sequential Importance Sampling* (SIS). SIS propagates $\mathcal{S}_{t-1}$ according to the *sequential importance function*, say $g(x_t | x_{t-1})$, and calculates the weight using

$$w_t = w_{t-1} p(Z_t | x_t) p(x_t | x_{t-1})/g(x_t | x_{t-1}). \tag{9.8}$$

In the Condensation algorithm [202], $g(x_t | x_{t-1})$ is taken to be $p(x_t | x_{t-1})$ and Eq. (9.8) becomes

$$w_t = w_{t-1} p(Z_t | x_t), \tag{9.9}$$

In fact, Eq. (9.9) is implemented by first resampling the sample set $\mathcal{S}_{t-1}$ according to w_{t-1} and then updating the weight w_t using $p(Z_t|x_t)$. For a complete description of the SIS method, we refer the reader to [263, 104].

The following two propositions are useful for guiding the development of the SIS algorithm.

Proposition 1. *When $\pi(x)$ is a PMF defined on a countably finite sample space, the proper sample set should exactly include all samples in the sample space.*

Proposition 2. *If a set of weighted random samples $\{(x^{(m)}, y^{(m)}, w^{(m)})\}_{m=1}^{M}$ is proper with respect to $\pi(x, y)$, then a new set of weighted random samples $\{(y'^{(k)}, w'^{(k)})\}_{k=1}^{K}$, which is proper with respect to $\pi(y)$, the marginal of $\pi(x, y)$, can be constructed as follows:*
1) Remove the repetitive samples from $\{y^{(m)}\}_{m=1}^{M}$ to obtain $\{y'^{(k)}\}_{k=1}^{K}$, where all $y'^{(k)}$'s are distinct;
2) Sum the weight $w^{(m)}$ belonging to the same sample $y'^{(k)}$ to obtain the weight $w'^{(k)}$, i.e.,

$$w'^{(k)} = \sum_{m=1, y^{(m)}=y'^{(k)}}^{M} w^{(m)}. \tag{9.10}$$

In the context of this framework, the posterior probability $p(i_t, \alpha_t|Z_1 \ldots Z_t)$ is represented by a set of *indexed and weighted* samples

$$\mathcal{S}_t = \{(i_t^{(m)}, \alpha_t^{(m)}, w_t^{(m)})\}_{m=1}^{M} \tag{9.11}$$

with i_t as the identity index. By Proposition 2, we can sum the weights of the samples belonging to the same index i_t to obtain a proper sample set $\{i_t, \beta_{i_t}\}_{i_t=1}^{N}$ with respect to the posterior PMF $p(i_t|Z_1 \ldots Z_t)$.

9.5 Still-to-Video Based Face Recognition

To illustrate the theory explained above, and to verify and show its effectiveness we have applied it to the still-to-video based face recognition scenario. In this case, the gallery $\mathcal{V} = \{V_1, V_2, \ldots, V_N\}$ is a set of face images, one for each individual.

9.5.1 Likelihood Measure

As likelihood measurement (Eq. (9.3)) we used the *intra-personal* space, as introduced by Moghaddam et al. [305], multiplied by a "truncated Laplacian".

The intra-personal space (IPS) considers the possible image variations between different facial images of a single individual, given, e.g., as the respective difference images.

At least two images per individual are needed for this. In addition to the given gallery, a second image per individual was therefore cropped from the available videos (see Fig. 9.1) while ensuring no overlap between gallery and probe video images during testing. As in [305], we apply PCA to compute a probabilistic subspace density for each individual

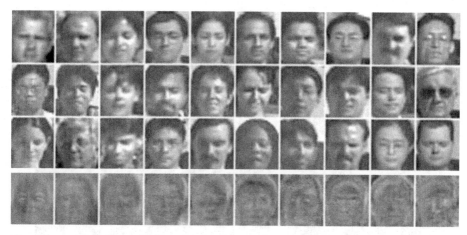

Fig. 9.1. Top rows: the second facial images for training probabilistic density. Bottom row: top 10 Eigenvectors for the IPS.

IPS. Suppose the eigensystem for the IPS is $\{(\lambda_i, e_i)\}_{i=1}^{N}$, where N is the number of training images and $\lambda_1 \geq ... \geq \lambda_N$. Only top M principal components corresponding to top M eigenvalues are then kept while the residual components are considered as isotropic. Fig. 9.1 (bottom row) show the eigenvectors from the IPS.

The density is written as follows:

$$p(z_t | i_t, \alpha_t) = PS(\mathcal{T}_{\alpha_t}\{z_t\} - I_{i_t}) \cdot LAP(\|\mathcal{T}_{\alpha_t}\{z_t\} - I_{i_t}\|; \sigma_1, \tau_1). \qquad (9.12)$$

Here,

$$PS(x) = \left[\frac{\exp(-\frac{1}{2}\sum_{i=1}^{M} \frac{y_i^2}{\lambda_i})}{(2\pi)^{M/2} \prod_{i=1}^{M} \lambda_i^{1/2}} \right] \left[\frac{\exp(-\frac{\epsilon^2}{2\rho})}{(2\pi\rho)^{(N-M)/2}} \right],$$

where $y_i = e_i^T x$ for $i = 1, ..., M$ is the ith principal component of x, $\epsilon^2 = \|x\|^2 - \sum_{i=1}^{s} y_i^2$ is the reconstruction error, and $\rho = (\sum_{i=s+1}^{N} \lambda_i)/(N - M)$. Please see the original paper [305] for full details.

The truncated Laplacian LAP in Eq. 9.12 is given as

$$LAP(x; \sigma, \tau) = \begin{cases} \sigma^{-1} \exp(-x/\sigma) & \text{if } x \leq \tau\sigma \\ \sigma^{-1} \exp(-\tau) & \text{otherwise} \end{cases} \qquad (9.13)$$

9.5.2 Experiments

For the experiments we have used a database, that was collected, as part of the HumanID project, by researchers at the National Institute of Standards and Technology and the University of South Florida. The database consists of video sequences with subjects walking in a slant path towards the camera. There are 30 different subjects in the database, each having one face template. These templates define the face gallery that is shown in Fig. 9.2. The probe set consists of 30 video sequences, one for each subject. Fig. 9.2

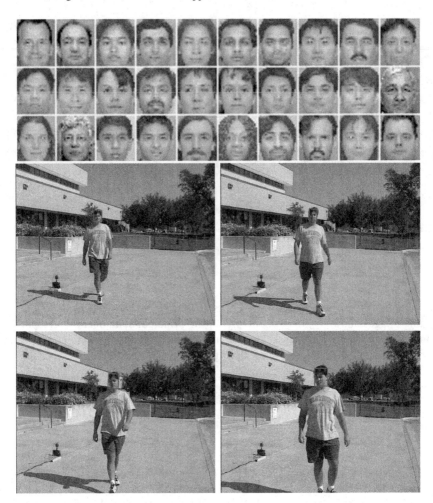

Fig. 9.2. Top three rows: the face gallery with image size being 30x26. Two bottom rows: 4 example frames in one probe video with image size being 720x480 while the actual face size ranges approximately from 20x20 in the first frame to 60x60 in the last frame. Notice the significant illumination variations between the probe and the gallery.

shows example frames extracted from one of the probe video. Concerning the scenario, this database is very interesting because the imaging conditions of the gallery are very different from those in the probe videos, especially in lighting. This is similar to the 'FC' test protocol of the FERET test [349].

First, general face tracking was tested which was successfull all the time. Then, recognition rates were estimated: 93% of the correct matches scored as top matches while 100% of the correct matches were within the top 3 matches. Interestingly, using the intra-personal space measure without the truncated Laplacian, top match recognition performance degraded to 83% while tracking failed in 7% of the cases.

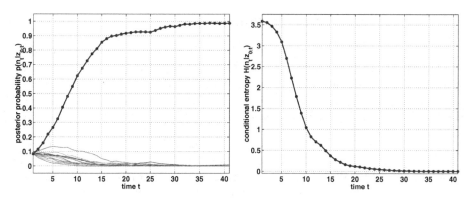

Fig. 9.3. Posterior probability $p(i_t|Z_1 \ldots Z_t)$ against time t, obtained by the SIS algorithm (left) and the conditional entropy $H(i_t|Z_1 \ldots Z_t)$ (right)

It is interesting to see, how the posterior probabilities develop over time. Examples for this can be seen in Fig. 9.3. The thick line refers to the correct hypothesized identity, the other curves refer to the probabilities of the top matching identities other than the true one. One can see in the left plot that the thick line (true hypothesis) increases quickly to one. The right curve plots the conditional entropy H for the posterior density. For comparison, we have also tested the still-to-still face recognition scenario with this database. Here, we manually selected the frames with the best frontal face view from the probe video, cropped out the facial region and normalized them with respect to the eye coordinates. This collection of images (Fig. 9.4), is fed as probes into a still-to-still face recognition system with the same probabilistic subspace as used in the still-to-video experiment. The top match recognition result is 57%, and 83% of the correct matches were within the top 3 matches.

Fig. 9.4. The facial images cropped out from the largest frontal view

9.6 Video-to-Video Based Recognition

In this chapter we illustrate how the above theory can be further applied for the video-to-video based face recognition scenario. In this case, the gallery $\mathcal{V} = \{V_1, V_2, \dots, V_N\}$ is a set of face video sequences, one for each individual.

9.6.1 Learning Exemplars from Video

In order to realize *video-to-video* recognition, a probabilistic model needs to be learned from each gallery video V. Being inspired by the probabilistically interpreted RBF neural network approach [265], we propose an online technique to learn the exemplars: At each time step t, $p(Z_t|\alpha, c)$ of Eq. (9.14) is maximized. If $p(Z_t|\alpha, c) < \rho$ for some ρ (which depends on the choice of d) then Z_t is added to the set of exemplars.

This approach is similar to the ones proposed in [453, 136]. The approaches have in common that they try to find a set of exemplars that describe the set of training images best, i.e., that minimize the expected distance $E\{d(\mathcal{Z}, \mathcal{C})\}$ between the given set of images $\mathcal{Z} = \{Z_1, Z_2, \dots, Z_N\}$ and a set of exemplars (cluster centers) $\mathcal{C} = \{c_1, c_2, \dots, c_K\}$.

In other words let $\mathcal{Z} = \{Z_1, Z_2, \dots, Z_N\}$ be the sequence of video images. It is being searched for a set of exemplars $\mathcal{C} = \{c_1, c_2, \dots, c_K\}$ for that video such that

$$p(Z_t) = \sum_{c \in \mathcal{C}} \int_{\mathcal{A}} p(Z_t|\alpha, c)p(\alpha|c)p(c)d\alpha \tag{9.14}$$

is maximal for all t.

Learning Algorithm

For this let $\mathcal{Z} = \{Z_1, Z_2, \dots, Z_N\}$ be the training images, and $\mathcal{C} = \{c_1, \dots, c_K\}$ be a set of already located exemplars.

1. The first step is the alignment or tracking step: a cluster i and a deformation $\alpha \in \mathcal{A}$ is found such that $d(\mathcal{T}_\alpha\{c_i\}, Z_t)$ is minimized:

$$\alpha_t \longleftarrow \arg\min_{\alpha} \min_i d(\mathcal{T}_\alpha^{-1}\{Z_t\}, c_i) \text{ and} \tag{9.15}$$

$$i_t \longleftarrow \arg\min_i d(\mathcal{T}_{\alpha_t}^{-1}\{Z_t\}, c_i)$$

2. The second step generates a new cluster center, if necessary: if

$$p(Z_t|\alpha_t, c_{i_t}) < \rho$$

then

$$\mathcal{C} \longleftarrow \mathcal{C} \cup \{\widehat{\mathcal{T}_\alpha^{-1}\{Z_t\}}\},$$

where $\widehat{\mathcal{T}_\alpha^{-1}\{Z_t\}}$ is the subimage of $\mathcal{T}_\alpha^{-1}Z_t$ on which the computation of the distance d in the first step of (9.15) was based.
Count the number of times, $count(i_t) = count(i_t) + 1$, that cluster c_{i_t} approximated image Z_t best.

3. Repeat steps one and two until all video frames are processed.
4. Compute the mixture weights $\pi_i \propto count(i)$.

The result of this learning procedure is

1. a set $C = \{c_1 \ldots, c_K\}$ of aligned exemplars c_i,
2. a prior π_i for each of the exemplars c_i.

Clearly, the more careful the set A is chosen, the fewer exemplars are generated. Allowing A, e.g., to compensate only for translations, exemplars are generated to compensate changes in scale and rotation.

Given a gallery V of videos, the above has to be carried out for each video.

During recognition, as will be explained below, the exemplars are used as centers of mixture models.

The above learning algorithm is motivated by the online learning approaches for artificial neural networks (ANNs) [137, 285] and clearly, all kinds of enhancements can be imagined (topology preserving maps, neighborhood relations, etc.). An online learning algorithm for exemplars used during testing could allow, in a bootstrapping manner, to learn new exemplars from probe videos.

In [488] a similar learning approach was presented. In contrast to our work, face images are not normalized with respect to A which results in a far larger number of clusters. In [200] a 'Unit Face' RBF model is proposed where for each individual, a single RGF network is trained. The authors have also investigated different geometrical normalizations and have tested preprocessing such as the application of a 'difference of Gaussians' or Gabor wavelets.

The goal of both above works was to build a representation of a face intensity by using an RBF network. We want to make clear once more, that this is exactly what we do not want! Our intention is, to chose a well-known face representation in *advance* (such as, e.g., PCA). *Then*, we learn the different exemplars of a single face. The advantage is that this way we inherit the "face recognition capabilities" of the PCA, LDA, etc. techniques and recognition rates can thus be predicted. This representation can be viewed as an "appearance-based 3D model", where affine tracking is used to compensate for the missing calibration information.

9.6.2 Exemplars as Mixture Centers

After the application of the learning algorithm in the previous section, we have a set of exemplars C^i for each individual $i \in \mathcal{N}$ in the Gallery V.

We can now compute the observation likelihoods as in Eq. 9.3 and apply Bayesian propagation (Eq. 9.5) to compute the joint distribution $p(X_t|Z_1, \ldots, Z_t)$. To take into account a set of exemplars $C^i = \{c_1^i, \ldots, c_{K_i}^i\}$ for each individual i, we refine Eq. (9.3):

$$p(Z|X) \equiv p(Z|\alpha, i)$$

$$\propto \sum_{c \in \mathcal{C}^i} p(Z|\alpha, i, c) p^i(c) \tag{9.16}$$

$$\propto \sum_{c \in \mathcal{C}^i} z \exp\left[-\frac{1}{2\sigma^2} d(Z, T_\alpha\{c\})\right] \pi_c^i . \tag{9.17}$$

The *exemplars* in $\mathcal{C}^i$ are used as the mixture center of a joint distribution and $p^i(c) = \pi_c^i$ is the prior for mixture center c of individual i.

9.6.3 Propagation Model

In Eq. (9.5)

$$p(X_t|X_{t-1}) \equiv p(\alpha_t, i_t|\alpha_{t-1}, i_{t-1})$$

defines the probability of the state variable to change from X_{t-1} to X_t. The transformation α_t may change according to a motion model. The identity i, however, is assumed to be constant over time, i.e., it is assumed that the identity of the tracked person does not magically change.

9.6.4 Computation of Posterior Distribution

We have used a particle method to efficiently compute $p_t(i_t, \alpha_t|Z_t)$ [505, 104, 203, 224, 263], where i_t, α_t depicts the hypothesized identity and transformation of the individual in the video. In Sec. 9.5 each individual is presented by only a single exemplar. Here, we have a Gallery of $N = |\mathcal{N}|$ persons and each person i is represented by a set of exemplars $\mathcal{C}_i = \{c_1^i, \ldots, c_{K_i}^i\}$.

In order to efficiently use the Condensation method, it needs to be adapted. Using Condensation the posterior probability distribution $p_t(i_t, k_t, \alpha_t|Z_t)$ (where i refers to the individual and k to the exemplar number) is represented by a set of M indexed and weighted particles

$$\left\{\left(i^{(m)}, j^{(m)}, \alpha^{(m)}, w^{(m)}\right)\right\}_{m=1\ldots M}^t . \tag{9.18}$$

Here, $i^{(m)}$ refers to the identity, $j^{(m)}$ to the exemplar, $\alpha^{(m)}$ to the deformation and $w^{(m)}$ to the weight. Note that we have, for better readability, indexed the entire set with t, instead of each component. Since all exemplars per person are aligned, we do not have to treat the different exemplars for a single person separately. We can therefore increase efficiency if we rewrite set (9.18):

$$\left\{\begin{bmatrix} i^{(m)}, 1, \alpha^{(m)}, w_1^{(m)} \\ \vdots \\ i^{(m)}, K_{i^{(m)}}, \alpha^{(m)}, w_{K_i}^{(m)} \end{bmatrix}\right\}_{m=1..M'}^t . \tag{9.19}$$

Set (9.19) is a set of $K_{i^{(m)}} \times 4$ dimensional matrices, and each matrix represents one particle, where $K_{i^{(m)}} = \left|\mathcal{C}^{i^{(m)}}\right|$. We can now easily marginalize over $\mathcal{C}^{i^{(m)}}$ to compute the posteriori probability $p_t(i_t, \alpha_t|Z_t)$: We get with

$$\hat{w}^{(m)} = \sum_{k=1}^{K_{i(m)}} \pi_k^{i^{(m)}} w_k^{(m)} \qquad (9.20)$$

a new set of weighted sample vectors:

$$\left\{ \left(i^{(m)}, \alpha^{(m)}, \hat{w}^{(m)} \right) \right\}_{m=1...M'}^{t} . \qquad (9.21)$$

In Eq. (9.20), $\pi_k^{i^{(m)}}$ is the prior of exemplar k of person $i^{(m)}$.

To compute the identity from the particle set (9.21) we marginalize over α in the same manner. See [505] for a detailed discussion of convergence speed and convergence properties of this particle method.

9.6.5 Experiments

We have tested our *video-to-video*-based approach on 99 video sequences of 25 different individuals.

The video sequences show the individuals walking on a tread-mill. We simulated different walking styles to assure a variety of conditions that are likely to appear in real life: *Walking slowly, walking fast, inclining* and *carrying an object*. Therefore, four videos per person are available. The subjects were not aware that their images were being acquired for face recognition studies and so did not move their heads unnaturally. During recording of the videos, illumination conditions were not altered. Each video consists of 300 frames (480×640 pixels per frame) captured at 30 Hz.

Some example images of the videos (*slowWalk*) are shown in Fig. 9.5.

The inner face regions in these videos are between 30×30 and 40×40 pixels.

In the experiments we used one of the video types as gallery videos for training while the remaining ones were used as probes for testing.

For each gallery video, a first face sample was cropped by hand. Based on this sample, the training process was started. Four examples of automatically extracted exemplar sets are shown in Fig. 9.6 (extracted from the videos *slowWalk*). The top row shows the exemplars of subjects 04006 and 04079 (six exemplars each). The leftmost exemplars of each of the two sets are the handextracted ones. Rows three and four of Fig. 9.6 show the exemplars of subject 04015, rows five and six the exemplars of subject 04022. The top left exemplars of each of the two sets are again the handextracted ones. Clearly, the number of generated exemplars depends on the variety of different views that are apparent in the gallery video. To generate these exemplars, we set $\rho = 0.65$ and standard deviation per pixel to $\sigma = 0.4$. Increase of σ to $\sigma = 0.5$ roughly decreased the number of exemplars by a factor of two.

During testing, these exemplar galleries were used to compute, over time, the posteriori probabilities $p_t(i_t|Z_t)$. In order to consider *all* the frames of the video, we restart the algorithm after the SIS has converged to one identity. Recognition is established by that identity to which the SIS converged most often.

Examples illustrating the robustness as well as the limits of our approach are shown in Figs. 9.6, 9.8 and 9.9: Due to the severe differences between the gallery exemplars (derived from "slowWalk") in Fig. 9.6 (5th and 6th row) and the sample images from

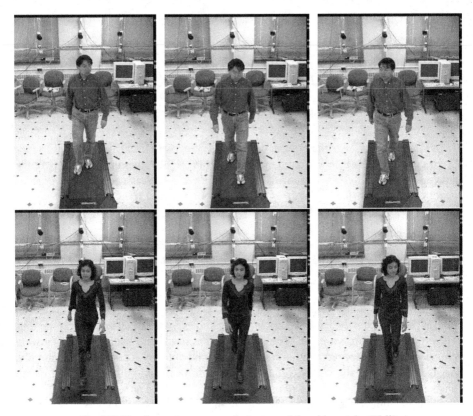

Fig. 9.5. The figure shows example images of the videos (*slowWalk*)

the probe video in Fig. 9.8, the recognition of subject 04022 was not successful. On the other hand, in spite of the differences between the gallery exemplars and the probe video, subject 04079 was always recognized successfully. Fig. 9.7 shows the development of the posteriori density for subject 04079. One can observe that for frames between 200 and 240, recognition failed. Frame 230 of that sequence is shown to the right in Fig. 9.9. The major problems that we encountered during our experiments were:

1. Subjects appear severely different in the gallery video and in the probe videos: This was the case for about 50% of the failed experiments.
2. Subjects looked down while walking: This was the case for roughly 10 subjects (Fig. 9.10). In some cases, where the subject looked down in the Gallery as well as in the Probe, this wasn't necessarily a problem. However, in cases, where this happened in either the probe or the gallery (see Fig. 9.10, left), this led to mis-classification.

Clearly, both problems can be solved by using more gallery videos. We have therefore done a second set of experiments, where two videos were used in the gallery, while the testing was carried out on the remaining two videos. The overall recognition results for one and two gallery videos are summarized in Table 9.1. The '**g**' indicates which videos

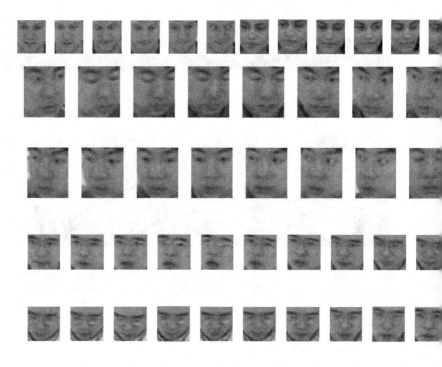

Fig. 9.6. The figure shows the exemplars of a person in a gallery video. In this example, *slowW* videos were used as gallery videos.

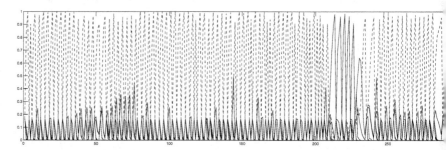

Fig. 9.7. The figure shows a typical probability evolutions of a successful recognition. The x-refers to the time t. The graph (subject 04079) shows the curve for the entire video (gal slowWalk; probe: fastWalk).

were used in the gallery. The gallery contained 25 different individuals, however, for "carrying" video set, only 24 different individuals were available.

In addition to the exemplars, it is natural to also learn and extract dynamic data f the training videos. This concerns the dynamics of the deformation vector α as we the dynamics between the exemplars. Such a dynamic model can be used directl extend the propagation model in Eq. 9.5. However, it can be observed, that the dyna

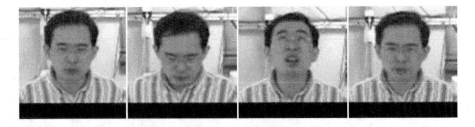

Fig. 9.8. The figure shows sample frames 1, 35, 81, 100 of a probe video. One observes large differences to the gallery. In this case recognition was *not* successful.

Fig. 9.9. The figure shows sample frames 1, 9, 40, 230 of a probe video. One observes large differences to the gallery. In this case, however, recognition *was* successful.

Table 9.1. Overall recognition rates in percent for $\sigma = 0.4$ (left), and $\sigma = 0.5$ (right). The 'g' indicates the video used as gallery.

slow	fast	incline	carrying		slow	fast	incline	carrying
g	100%	96%	92%		g	96%	92%	88%
92%	g	100%	96%		92%	g	92%	92%
100%	96%	g	96%		96%	96%	g	96%
88%	96%	92%	g		88%	88%	83%	g
g	g	100%	96%		g	g	96%	92%
g	100%	g	100%		g	100%	g	100%
g	100%	96%	g		g	96%	96%	g
100%	g	g	96%		100%	g	g	96%
100%	g	100%	g		92%	g	96%	g
100%	100%	g	g		100%	96%	g	g

information of individuals changes severely with walking speed, shoe-type, and even with daytime and mood. Available video databases are too limited so that learning approaches tend to memorize the dynamics. In our experiments using the dynamics between the exemplars in Eq. 9.5 has lead to a significant decrease in recognition results.

Video images from our test data were converted from color to gray value images and histogram equalized. To receive the above results, we used the Euclidean distance

Fig. 9.10. Images show failure examples, where the galleries were not sufficient to recognize the subjects.

measure. The set of deformations $\mathcal{A}$ included scale and translation. Shear and rotation were not considered.

For comparison we have applied also our still-to-video approach to the MoBo database. Due to the large pose variations, a single frontal view was not sufficient to represent all the appearances under different poses and the recognition rates are relatively low with 56% of correct top matches and 88% when top 3 matches are considered.

9.7 Conclusion

We have presented a systematic method for face recognition from a probe video, compared with a gallery of still templates. A time series state space model is used to accommodate the video and SIS algorithms provide the numerical solutions to the model. This probabilistic framework, which overcomes many difficulties arising in conventional recognition approaches using video, is registration-free and poses no need for selecting good frames. It turns out that an immediate recognition decision can be made in our framework due to the degeneracy of the posterior probability of the identity variable. The conditional entropy can also serve as a good indication for the convergence. In addition, the still templates in the gallery are generalized to videos by learning exemplars from the gallery video. However, in order to show that our approach is capable of recognizing faces in practice, one needs to work with much larger face databases.

The following issues are worthy of investigation in the future.

1. *Robustness.* Generally speaking, our approach is more robust than the still-image-based approach since we essentially compute the recognition score based on all video frames and, in each frame, all kinds of transformed versions of the face part corresponding to the sample configurations that are considered. However, since we take no explicit measure when handling frames with outlier or other unexpected factors, recognition scores based on those frames might be low. But, this is a problem for other approaches too. The assumption that the identity does not change as time proceeds, i.e., $p(i_t|i_{t-1}) = \delta(i_t - i_{t-1})$, could be relaxed by having nonzero transition probabilities between different identity variables. Using nonzero transition probabilities will enable us an easier transition to the correct choice in case that the initial choice is incorrectly chosen, making the algorithm more robust.

2. *Resampling.* In the recognition algorithm, the marginal distribution $\{(\alpha_{t-1}^{(j)}, w_{t-1}^{'(j)})\}_{j=1}^{J}$ is sampled to obtain the sample set $\{(\alpha_t^{(j)}, 1)\}_{j=1}^{J}$. This may cause problems in principle since there is no conditional independence between α_t and n_t given $Z_1 \ldots Z_t$. However, in a practical sense, this is not a big disadvantage because the purpose of resampling is to 'provide chances for the good streams (samples) to amplify themselves and hence rejuvenate the sampler to produce better results for future states as the system evolves' [263]. The resampling scheme can either be simple random sampling with weights (like in Condensation), residual sampling, or local Monte Carlo methods.

10

Interleaving Object Categorization and Segmentation

Bastian Leibe and Bernt Schiele

Multimodal Interactive Systems
TU Darmstadt, FB 20
D-64289 Darmstadt, Germany
{leibe,schiele}@informatik.tu-darmstadt.de

Abstract. In this chapter, we aim to connect the areas of object categorization and figure-ground segmentation. We present a novel method for the categorization of unfamiliar objects in difficult real-world scenes. The method generates object hypotheses without prior segmentation, which in turn can be used to obtain a category-specific figure-ground segmentation. In particular, the proposed approach uses a probabilistic formulation to incorporate knowledge about the recognized category as well as the supporting information in the image to segment the object from the background. This segmentation can then be used for hypothesis verification, to further improve recognition performance. Experimental results show the capacity of the approach to categorize and segment object categories as diverse as cars and cows.

10.1 Introduction

Object recognition has reached a level where we can identify a large number of previously seen and known objects. However, the more general task of object categorization, that is of recognizing a-priori unknown objects of a given category and assigning the correct category label, is less well-understood. Obviously, this task is more difficult, since it requires a method to cope with large within-class variations of object colors, textures, and shapes, while retaining, at the same time, enough specificity to yield only a small number of misclassifications. This is especially true for recognition in cluttered real-world scenes, where objects are often partially occluded and where similar-looking background structures can act as additional distractors. Here, it is not only needed to assign the correct category label to an image, but also to find the objects in the first place and to separate them from the background.

Historically, this step of figure-ground segmentation has often been seen as an important and even necessary precursor for object recognition [281]. In that context, segmentation is mostly defined as a data driven, that is bottom-up, process. However, except for cases where additional cues, such as motion or stereo, could be used, purely bottom-up approaches have so far been unable to yield figure-ground segmentations of sufficient quality for object categorization. This is in part due to the fact that the notion and definition of what constitutes an object is largely task-specific and can thus not be answered in an uninformed way. Indeed, recent results from human vision indicate that for humans,

H.I. Christensen and H.-H. Nagel (Eds.): Cognitive Vision Systems, LNCS 3948, pp. 145–161, 2006.

recognition and segmentation are heavily intertwined processes [346, 472, 323]. It has thus been argued that top-down knowledge from object recognition can and should be used for guiding the segmentation process.

This motivates us to explore how high-level knowledge can be used for grouping image regions belonging to the same object. In this paper, we present a local approach that combines the processes of object categorization and segmentation into a common framework. In particular, we derive a probabilistic formulation of the problem that allows us to incorporate knowledge about the recognized category, as well as the supporting information in the image. As a result, our approach can detect categorical objects in real-world scenes and automatically obtain segmentation masks for them, together with a per-pixel confidence estimate specifying how much this segmentation can be trusted. Thus, figure-ground segmentation is achieved as a result of object recognition.

The chapter is structured as follows. We first present a review of the current state of the art in object categorization, with specific attention paid to the basic features and structural representations that are used by current algorithms. Section 10.3 then introduces our object categorization approach. This approach uses a learned codebook of local appearance for individual object categories to generate probabilistic object hypotheses. Based on these hypotheses, Section 10.4 then derives a probabilistic formulation of the segmentation problem. Finally, Section 10.5 presents experimental results.

10.2 State of the Art in Object Recognition/Categorization

Early approaches to "generic" object recognition represented objects by 3D models or by a decomposition into parametric surfaces or volumetric primitives [41, 281, 40]. A central element of these approaches was the use of an object-centered coordinate system, which should enable view-invariant recognition. However, the difficulty of reliably extracting the postulated geometric representations from real-world images and of finding viewpoint-invariant yet discriminative descriptions restricted their success.

The object-centered paradigm was challenged in the early 90's by the success of view-based approaches, which showed that the use of a viewer-centric coordinate system and fast image-comparison methods made it possible to identify a large number of known objects [443, 313, 366, 396, 324, 392]. A main focus of those efforts was to achieve robustness to deteriorated viewing conditions caused by changes in viewpoint, scale, and image plane rotation; and the introduction of noise, clutter, and occlusion. However, the robustness to these influences was often just tested for individual objects and under laboratory conditions. In contrast, object detection approaches concentrated on the task of finding instances of a single object class under real-world conditions. Impressive results, both in terms of accuracy and run-time, have been achieved for object classes such as pedestrians, faces, and cars [383, 400, 401, 338, 478, 480], even though often only for single viewpoints.

Still, the more general task of multi-class object categorization under real-world conditions is yet largely unsolved. In recent years, renewed interest in the topic has sparked many new approaches, including [486, 247, 120]. Nevertheless, many questions are still open. While it is generally agreed that the underlying features should be local in order to cope with noise and occlusion, it is not yet clear which features are best for object categorization, nor in what kind of structural representation they should be combined. The rest of this section therefore aims to give an overview of the design choices that have been used in various systems so far.

The history of figure-ground segmentation is closely connected to that of recognition. In early approaches, segmentation was often seen as a necessary preprocessing step for recognition, for which a solution could be assumed. While the difficulty of segmentation was generally acknowledged, it was still assumed that a separation into object and non-object regions could be achieved by a series of purely bottom-up grouping steps of corner, line, and region primitives. The general failure to achieve this goal, together with the success of appearance-based methods to provide recognition results without prior segmentation, led to the separation of the two areas and the further development of recognition independent from segmentation. In recent years, however, the areas have converged again by the growing insight that recognition and segmentation are indeed interleaved processes and that intermediate recognition results can be used to drive a top-down segmentation process [48, 502, 248].

In the following, we give an overview of features and structural representations that are used in current approaches to object categorization. In addition, we document the recent transition from recognition to top-down segmentation, which has been developing into an area of active research. In accordance with the current state of the field, we concentrate on view-based object categorization, with a focus on local appearance-based methods. This overview will set the context for the introduction of our combined object categorization and segmentation approach in Section 10.3.

10.2.1 Features

The design choice which features to use for recognition can be divided into two separate questions. The first question is which image locations shall be sampled, that is which subset of the available image information shall actually be used. The second question is then how to represent the sampled image information and which descriptors to compute.

Of course, these questions are closely interrelated. Many early appearance-based methods rely on relatively simple features that are sufficiently low-dimensional that they can be computed (and stored) over the full image. [443] represent an object by its color histogram (approximating its color distribution). Objects are identified by matching a color histogram from a test image region with the histograms from training objects. Other authors use multidimensional combinations of derivatives. [366] represent objects (or object patches) by a high-dimensional "iconic" feature vector, consisting of 45 responses of nine oriented Gaussian filters at five different scales ($9 \times 5 = 45$). Using the steerability of Gaussian derivatives, the feature vector is made rotational invariant. [396] propose instead to describe an image by a nine-dimensional rotational invariant vector of local characteristics based on Gaussian derivatives computed at interest points. [392] generalize the color histogram approach to represent objects by multidimensional histograms of greyvalue derivatives over multiple scales. [170] again generalize this approach to include a combination of color and grayvalue derivatives in an eight-dimensional feature vector. In previous work, we have analyzed the suitability of various simple feature descriptors for the task of object categorization [247]. Our results indicate that while the simple features allow for a surprising degree of generalization, the more important information for categorization seems to be the (global or local) object shape.

In contrast to these relatively low-dimensional representations, the following local descriptors are so high-dimensional that they are typically only evaluated at certain specific locations, such as those returned by interest point detectors. The interest point detectors themselves have a long history. The underlying idea is to search for locations that are distinctive enough that they can be reliably extracted under various image transformations. Depending on the application, this can be boundary concavities or curvature extrema [243], corner-like structures [174], or extrema of local operators optimized for scale-invariant [256, 300, 213] or even affine-invariant extraction [301, 286]. The use of interest point detectors allows to represent objects by a relatively small set of local descriptors, such as the ones described below.

Perhaps the simplest local descriptor for matching interest points is just a raw image patch, as used in [62, 486, 487, 1, 120, 248]. The advantages of such a representation are its simplicity of implementation and the ability to directly visualize what has been matched, which may be very helpful during algorithmic design. A disadvantage is the higher dimensionality. However, this problem may be alleviated by performing matching in a truncated eigenspace with a significantly reduced number of dimensions (see [120] for an example). Typically, some kind of lighting normalization is also performed prior to matching. The idea to just extract patches from the input image can also be augmented by other preprocessing steps. In addition to raw image patches, [487] also propose a representation based on high-pass filtered patches. [324, 325] go one step further and extract local windows of edge-like structures (based on a robust computation of curvature extrema) as basic features.

[266, 267, 268] introduces a local feature representation inspired by the response properties of complex neurons in the human visual cortex. His so-called SIFT descriptors are defined as 4×4 grids of localized histograms of gradient orientations computed at multiple scales. [303] extend this idea and compute a similar descriptor based on localized edge direction histograms.

Although a recent study has compared a representative selection of local descriptors for the task of finding exact correspondences between image pairs [302], it is not yet clear which of them are best suited for object categorization, where a generalization to certain within-class variations is needed. In our experience, however, the exact choice of descriptor is not as important as how their combination is performed and how the object structure is represented.

10.2.2 Shape/Structure Representations

Over the years, the term *shape* has been connotated with many meanings. We therefore find it important to make a clear distinction between the concepts of *shape* and *structure*. Many early papers have argued for the need to find an object representation that is both invariant to variations in the imaging process and mathematically simple to model. In their context, *pure shape* denotes the information which remains when the effects of color, texture, and illumination are discarded. In practice, the term is often equated with the object contour or silhouette, or with an edge-based representation. In order to avoid confusions with this definition, we will use the term *object structure* to denote a set of spatial relations between local appearances[1]. The two concepts represent different strategies for dealing with the inherent problem of imaging variations in computer vision. While shape-based methods try to cope with these variations by building a representation that is invariant to them, structure-based methods are trying to use them to build a more realistic object model. In this chapter, we will only focus on representations for object structure – for a detailed discussion of shape-based methods, we refer to Chapter 8.

A large class of methods match object structure by computing a cost term for the deformation needed to transform a prototypical object model to correspond with the image. Prominent examples of this approach include *Deformable Templates* [503, 409], *Morphable Models* [211, 212, 149], or *Shape Context Matching* [33, 34]. The main difference between them lies in the way point correspondences are found and in the choice of an energy function for computing the deformation cost (e.g. Euclidean distances, strain energy, thin plate splines, etc.). [81] go one step further and characterize objects by means and modes of variation for both shape and texture. Their *Active Appearance Models (AAM)* first warp the object to a mean shape, so that the texture variations can be computed on corresponding object pixels. Since there may be correlations between the shape and greylevel variations, they then estimate the combined modes of variation of the concatenated shape and texture models. For matching the resulting AAMs to a test image, they learn the relationship between model parameter displacements and the induced differences in the reconstructed model image. This allows them to learn an inverse mapping from residual matching errors to the parameter changes that lead to a better fit. Provided that the method is initialized with a close estimate of the object's position and size, a good overall match to the object is typically obtained in a few iterations, even for deformable objects. [44] generalize this approach further to use densely sampled 3D models obtained by a laser scanner instead of 2D shape models.

[496] propose a different structural model known as *Bunch Graph*. The original version of this approach represents object structure as a graph of hand-defined locations, at which local jets (multidimensional vectors of simple filter responses) are computed. The method learns an object model by storing, for each graph node, the set ("bunch") of all jet responses that have been observed in this location on a hand-aligned training set. During recognition, only the strongest response is taken per location, and the joint model fit is optimized by an iterative elastic graph matching technique. This approach has achieved impressive results for face identification tasks, but an application to more object classes has been restricted by the need to hand-model a set of suitable graph locations. A recent generalization of the method, however, alleviates this restriction by automatically learning a suitable graph structure [264]. Chapter 6 presents an object categorization method that uses a similar elastic graph matching technique for comparing the spatial arrangement of a set of learned prototypical region detectors.

In contrast to those deformable representations, most classic object detection methods either use a monolithical object representation [383, 338] or look for local features in fixed configurations [400, 401, 478]. [400, 401] express the likelihood of object and non-object appearance using a product of localized histograms, which represent the joint statistics of subsets of wavelet coefficients and their position on the object. The detection

---

[1] Note that this explicitly includes the above-mentioned effects of color, texture, and illumination. In particular, *structure* can also be defined on top of (local) *shape*, but not vice versa.

decision is made by a likelihood-ratio classifier. Multiple detectors, each specialized to a certain orientation of the object, are used to achieve recognition over a variety of poses, including frontal and profile faces and various views of passenger cars. Their approach achieves very good detection results on standard databases, but is computationally still relatively costly. [478] instead focus on building a speed-optimized system for face detection. They achieve this by building a cascade of simple classifiers, each of which is based only on the differences between average grayvalues summed over fixed image regions. The classifiers themselves are simple threshold functions, but their ensemble allows to learn complex appearance variations. In more recent work, [480] extend this approach to pedestrian detection using a combination of appearance and motion features. In recent years, this class of approaches has been shown to yield fast and accurate object detection results under real-world conditions. However, a drawback of these methods is that since they do not explicitly model local variations in object structure (e.g. from body parts in different articulations), they typically need a large number of training examples in order to learn the allowed changes in global appearance.

One way to model these local variations is by representing objects as an assembly of parts. Early approaches that tried to model objects by a set of hand-defined or postulated geometric parts with a rule-based combination scheme [281, 40] were not too successful, mainly because of the difficulty of reliably extracting the geometric representations from real-world images. Even though some later approaches had more success with (human and horse) body parts modeled as cylinders [133], the geometric part definition typically restricts them to a small application domain. For this reason, many current methods use appearance-based parts instead and try to learn as much as possible about the object model instead of postulating it.

[306] still use a set of hand-defined appearance parts, but learn an SVM-based configuration classifier for pedestrian detection. The resulting system performs significantly better than the original full-body person detector by [338]. In addition, its component-based architecture makes it more robust to partial occlusion. [184] use a similar approach for component-based face detection. As an extension of Mohan et al.'s approach, their method also includes an automatic learning step for finding a set of discriminative components from user-specified seed points.

[324, 325] propose to recognize objects by an approach based on the assembly of local "context frames". The algorithm extracts contour segments from intensity images based on a robust computation of curvature extrema. Extracted segments are stored together with their context, i.e. the relative position of other segments in their surroundings, in a local reference frame, which is brought to a canonical orientation. For recognition, matches between these local context regions are searched, which are then combined to single object views in a global skeleton. Experimental results show that the method achieves good results for object recognition in cluttered scenes and under partial occlusions. Although the original system was only intended for the identification of known, rigid objects, later results indicate also good generalization performance for object categories, such as cups, toy cars, toy airplanes, and snakes.

[62] learn the assembly of hand-selected (appearance) object parts by modelling their joint spatial probability distribution. [487, 486] build on the same framework, but also learn the local parts and estimate their joint distribution. [120] extend this approach

to scale-invariant object parts and estimate their joint spatial and appearance distribution. Their approach has been successfully demonstrated on several object categories. However, the complexity of the combined estimation step restricts their methods to a relatively small number of parts. [1] keep a larger number of object parts and apply a feature-efficient classifier for learning spatial configurations between pairs of parts. However, their learning approach relies on the repeated observation of cooccurrences between the same parts in similar spatial relations, which again requires a large number of training examples.

[463] and [475] represent objects by a set of fragments that were chosen to maximize the information content with respect to an object class. Candidate fragments are extracted at different sizes and from different locations of an initial set of training images. From this set, their approach iteratively selects those fragments that add the maximal amount of information about the object class to the already selected set, thus effectively resulting in a cover of the object. In addition, the approach automatically selects, for each fragment, the optimal threshold such that it can be reliably detected. For recognition, however, only the information which model fragments were detected is encoded in a binary-valued feature vector (similar to Agarwal & Roth's), onto which a simple linear classifier is applied without any additional shape model. The main problem of this approach is, however, that the complexity of the fragment selection process restricts the method to very low image resolutions (e.g. 14×21 pixels), which severely limits its applicability in practice.

Another large group of approaches, the *Geometric Methods*, represent object structure only implicitly for computationally efficient matching. The basic idea behind these approaches is to avoid costly grouping operations of local features in the image space and instead transform them into a space where whole object configurations can be described by single points. In the *Generalized Hough Transform* [198, 25, 159], matching feature pairs between a model and test image are translated into votes for a rigid transformation which would align the two objects under the assumption that the matches are correct. As the same procedure is independently applied to a large number of feature pairs, consistent votes for the same transformation reinforce each other and result in distinct peaks in the voting space, while false votes from random mismatches are uniformly spread over the possible transformations. As a result, the Hough Transform is robust to a high percentage of outliers [268]. *Geometric Hashing* [243, 244, 497] follows a similar principle, but stores votes in a one-dimensional hash table. In the original approach, triplets of feature points define an affine basis for calculating the coordinates of all remaining points, which are used as entries to the hash table (together with the associated object label). In an offline learning step, the hash table is precomputed for all such triplets from all training objects. During recognition, only a small number of triplets need to be taken as affine bases for querying the hash table with the transformed coordinates of the remaining points. The method then accumulates the votes from accessed hash table entries to determine the object identity and its location in the scene. Originally, geometric methods have been introduced and motivated for the identification of specific, solid objects. Successful applications for this purpose include [267, 268]. However, in Section 10.3 of this chapter, we will describe how the Hough Transform can be generalized to recognize object categories.

10.2.3 From Recognition to Top-Down Segmentation

The traditional view of object recognition has been that prior to the recognition process, an earlier stage of perceptual organization occurs to determine which features, locations, or surfaces most likely belong together [281]. As a result, the segregation of the image into a figure and a ground part has often been seen as a prerequisite for recognition. In that context, segmentation is mostly defined as a bottom-up process, employing no higher-level knowledge. State-of-the-art segmentation methods combine grouping of similar image regions with splitting processes concerned with finding most likely borders [418, 413, 276]. However, grouping is mostly done based on low-level image features, like color or texture statistics, which require no prior knowledge. While that makes them universally applicable, it often leads to poor segmentations of objects of interest, splitting them into multiple regions or merging them with parts of the background [48].

Results from human vision indicate, however, that object recognition processes can operate before or intertwined with figure-ground organization and can in fact be used to drive the process [346, 472, 323]. In consequence, the idea to use object-specific information for driving figure-ground segmentation has recently developed into an area of active research. Approaches, such as Deformable Templates [503], or Active Appearance Models [81] are typically used when the object of interest is known to be present in the image and an initial estimate of its size and location can be obtained. Examples of successful applications include tracking and medical image analysis.

[48] represent object knowledge using image fragments together with their figure-ground labeling (as known from a training set). Class-specific segmentations are obtained by fitting fragments to the image and combining them in jigsaw-puzzle fashion, such that their figure-ground labels form a consistent mapping. While the authors present impressive results for segmenting sideviews of horses, their approach includes no global recognition process. As only the local consistency of adjacent pairs of fragments is checked, there is no guarantee that the resulting cover really corresponds to an object and is not just caused by background clutter resembling random object parts.

[502] also present a parallel segmentation and recognition system. They formulate the segmentation problem in a graph theoretic framework that combines patch and pixel groupings. A set of 15 known objects is represented by local color, intensity and orientation histograms obtained from a number of different viewpoints. During recognition, these features are matched to patches extracted from the image to obtain object part hypotheses, which are combined with pixel groupings based on orientation energy. A final solution is found using the Normalized Cuts criterion [418]. This method achieves good segmentation results in cluttered real-world settings. However, their system needs to know the exact objects beforehand in order to extract their most discriminant features.

In our application, we do not require the objects to be known beforehand – only familiarity with the object category is needed. This means that the system needs to have seen some examples of the object category before, but those do not have to be the ones that are to be recognized later. Obviously, this makes the task more difficult, since we cannot rely on any object-specific feature, but have to compensate for large in-class variations. The following section describes how our algorithm achieves this by learning a codebook of local appearance.

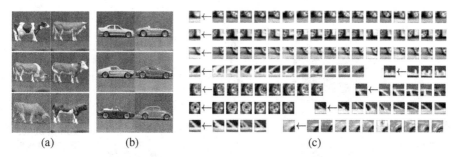

Fig. 10.1. (a,b) Some of the training objects used for cows and cars (from the ETH-80 database [247]). From each object, 16 views were taken from different orientations. (c) Example codebook clusters for cars with their corresponding patches.

10.3 A Codebook of Local Appearance for Object Categorization

In this section, we present a new local approach to combined object categorization and segmentation (originally published in [248]). The approach is based on a Generalized Hough Transform [198, 25], which has been originally introduced only for the identification of specific objects. In order to make it applicable to the more general task of recognizing objects of a specific category, we introduce several ways of representing the uncertainty stemming from intra-class variations. In a first step, we replace specific object features by a codebook of category-specific local appearances. Using this codebook, we represent uncertainty both on the matching level and on the level of the resulting transformation votes by storing, for each codebook part, the spatial probability distribution where it can be found on the object category. As a result, we obtain a probabilistic formulation of the Hough Transform, which allows us to recognize categorical objects. As shown in the next section, this probabilistic framework also provides the basis for deriving a category-specific segmentation.

In order to generate a codebook of local appearances of a particular object category, we use an approach inspired by the work of [1]. From a variety of images (in our case 160 images corresponding to 16 views around the equator of each of the 10 training objects shown in Figure 10.1(a,b)), image patches of size 25×25 pixels are extracted with the Harris interest point detector [174]. Starting with each patch as a separate cluster, agglomerative clustering is performed: the two most similar clusters C_1 and C_2 are merged as long as the average similarity between their constituent patches (and thus the cluster compactness) stays above a certain threshold t:

$$similarity(C_1, C_2) = \frac{\sum_{p \in C_1, q \in C_2} NGC(p, q)}{|C_1| \times |C_2|} > t, \qquad (10.1)$$

where the similarity between two patches is measured by Normalized Greyscale Correlation (NGC):

$$NGC(p, q) = \frac{\sum_i (p_i - \overline{p_i})(q_i - \overline{q_i})}{\sqrt{\sum_i (p_i - \overline{p_i})^2 \sum_i (q_i - \overline{q_i})^2}} \qquad (10.2)$$

This clustering scheme guarantees that only those patches are grouped which are visually similar, and that the resulting clusters stay compact, a property that is essential

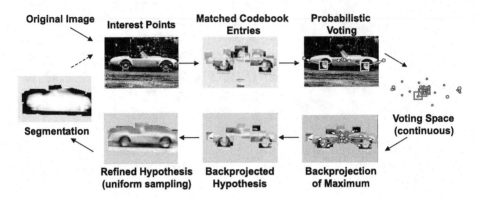

Fig. 10.2. The Recognition Procedure. Image patches are extracted around interest points and compared to the codebook. Matching patches then cast probabilistic votes, which lead to object hypotheses that can later be refined. Based on the refined hypotheses, we compute a category-specific segmentation.

for later processing stages. From each resulting cluster, we compute the cluster center and store it in the codebook.

Figure 10.1(c) shows some of the codebook entries, together with the patches they were derived from. With a value of $t = 0.7$, the 8'269 extracted car image patches are reduced to a codebook of size 2'519. While the resulting number of clusters is still high, the most interesting property of the clustering scheme is that all clusters are compact and only contain image patches that are visually similar.

Rather than to use this codebook directly to train a classifier as in [1], we propose to use a probabilistic voting scheme which produces comparable results. For this, the extracted image patches are matched to the codebook using the NGC measure. In contrast to [1], though, we do not activate the best-matching codebook entry only, but all entries whose similarity is above t, the threshold already used during clustering. For every codebook entry, we store all the positions it was activated in, relative to the object center.

During recognition, we use this information to perform a Generalized Hough Transform [25, 266]. Given a test image, we extract image patches and match them to the codebook to activate codebook entries. Each activated entry then casts votes for possible positions of the object center. Figure 10.2 illustrates this procedure. We search for hypotheses as maxima in the continous vote space using Mean-Shift Mode Estimation [69, 80]. For promising hypotheses, all patches that contributed to it are collected (Fig. 10.2(bottom)), therefore visualizing what the system reacts to. Moreover, we can refine the hypothesis by sampling all the image patches in its surroundings, not just those locations returned by the interest point detector. As a result, we get a representation of the object including a certain border area.

In the following, we cast this recognition procedure into a probabilistic framework. Let **e** be our evidence, an extracted image patch. Each image patch may have several valid interpretations I_i, namely the matching codebook clusters. Each interpretation is

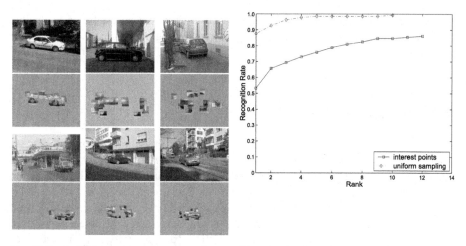

Fig. 10.3. (left) Example car images and recognition results from the test set (images 1-5: 1st hypothesis; image 6: 7th hypothesis). (right) Quantitative recognition results if all hypotheses up to a certain rank are considered.

weighted with the probability $p(I_i|\mathbf{e})$. If a codebook cluster matches, it can cast its votes for different object positions. That is, for every I_i, we can obtain votes for several object identities o_n and positions x_j, which we weight with $p(o_n, x_j|I_i)$. Thus, any single vote has the weight $p(o_n, x_j|I_i)p(I_i|\mathbf{e})$, and the patch's contribution to the hypothesis can be expressed by the following marginalization:

$$p(o_n, x_j|\mathbf{e}) = \sum_i p(o_n, x_j|I_i)p(I_i|\mathbf{e}). \qquad (10.3)$$

By basing the decision on single-patch votes and assuming a uniform prior for the patches, we obtain

$$p(o_n, x_j) \sim \sum_k p(o_n, x_j|\mathbf{e}_k). \qquad (10.4)$$

From this probabilistic framework, it immediately follows that the $p(I_i|\mathbf{e})$ and $p(o_n, x_j|I_i)$ should both sum to one. In our experiments, we assume a uniform distribution for both (meaning that we set $p(I_i|\mathbf{e}) = \frac{1}{|I|}$, with $|I|$ the number of matching codebook entries), but it would also be possible, for example, to let the $p(I_i|\mathbf{e})$ distribution reflect the relative matching scores.

In order to evaluate the system's recognition capability, we have applied it to a database of 137 images of real-world scenes containing one car each in varying poses. Based on interest points, the system is able to correctly recognize and localize 53.3% of the cases with its first hypothesis and up to 86.1% with the first 12 hypotheses. Taking all available patches by uniform sampling, performance improves to 87.6% with the first hypothesis and 98.5% with the first 5 hypotheses[2]. Figure 10.3 shows the quantitative recognition results and some example images from the test set. These results show the

---

[2] Since the object size in our images is roughly twice that of Agarwal & Roth's [1], we double the tolerances used in their evaluation and accept a hypothesis if $\delta_x \leq 56$, $\delta_y \leq 28$, and bounding box overlap is above 50%.

system's ability to recognize objects in a variety of different poses. In the following, we want to extend the approach to obtain pose-specific segmentations of objects. In the context of this paper, we explore in particular the possibility to segment side views of cars and cows.

10.4 Object Segmentation

In this section, we derive a probabilistic formulation for the segmentation problem. As a starting point, we take a refined object hypothesis (o_n, x) obtained by the algorithm from the previous section. Based on this hypothesis, we want to segment the object from the background.

Up to now, we have only dealt with image patches. For segmentation, we now want to know whether a certain image pixel $\mathbf{p}$ is *figure* or *ground*, given the object hypothesis. More precisely, we are interested in the probability $p(\mathbf{p} = figure|o_n, x)$. The influence of a given patch $\mathbf{e}$ on the object hypothesis can be expressed as

$$p(\mathbf{e}|o_n, x) = \frac{p(o_n, x|\mathbf{e})p(\mathbf{e})}{p(o_n, x)} = \frac{\sum_I p(o_n, x|I)p(I|\mathbf{e})p(\mathbf{e})}{p(o_n, x)} \qquad (10.5)$$

where the patch votes $p(o_n, x|\mathbf{e})$ are obtained from the codebook, as described in the previous section. Given these probabilities, we can obtain information about a specific pixel by marginalizing over all patches that contain this pixel:

$$p(\mathbf{p} = figure|o_n, x) = \sum_{\mathbf{p} \in \mathbf{e}} p(\mathbf{p} = figure|\mathbf{e}, o_n, x)p(\mathbf{e}|o_n, x) \qquad (10.6)$$

where $p(\mathbf{p} = figure|\mathbf{e}, o_n, x)$ denotes patch-specific segmentation information, which is weighted by the influence $p(\mathbf{e}|o_n, x)$ the patch has on the object hypothesis. Again, we can resolve patches by resorting to learned patch interpretations I stored in the codebook:

$$p(\mathbf{p} = figure|o_n, x) = \sum_{\mathbf{p} \in \mathbf{e}} \sum_I p(\mathbf{p} = figure|\mathbf{e}, I, o_n, x)p(\mathbf{e}, I|o_n, x) \qquad (10.7)$$

$$= \sum_{\mathbf{p} \in \mathbf{e}} \sum_I p(\mathbf{p} = figure|I, o_n, x)\frac{p(o_n, x|I)p(I|\mathbf{e})p(\mathbf{e})}{p(o_n, x)}. \qquad (10.8)$$

This means that for every pixel, we build a weighted average over all segmentations stemming from patches containing that pixel. The weights correspond to the patches' respective contributions to the object hypothesis. For the *ground* probability, the result can be obtained in an analogue fashion.

The most important part in this formulation is the per-pixel segmentation information $p(\mathbf{p} = figure|I, o_n, x)$, which is only dependent on the matched codebook entry, no longer on the image patch. If we store a fixed segmentation mask for every codebook entry (similar to Borenstein & Ullman's approach [48]), we obtain a reduced probability $p(\mathbf{p} = figure|I, o_n)$. In our approach, we remain more general by keeping a separate segmentation mask for every stored *occurrence position* of each codebook entry. We thus take advantage of the full probability $p(\mathbf{p} = figure|I, o_n, x)$. The following section describes in more detail how this is implemented in practice.

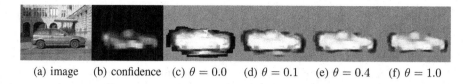

(a) image   (b) confidence   (c) $\theta = 0.0$ (d) $\theta = 0.1$ (e) $\theta = 0.4$ (f) $\theta = 1.0$

Fig. 10.4. *Segmentation Results with Different Confidence Levels θ*

10.4.1 Implementation

For learning segmentation information, we make use of a figure-ground segmentation mask that is available for each of our training images. We can thus obtain a figure-ground mask for any image patch from the training data. In this chapter, we have experimented with two different ways of integrating segmentation information into the system, corresponding to the different interpretations of the probability $p(\mathbf{p} = figure | I, o_n, x)$ described above.

In the first approach, as inspired by [48], we store a segmentation mask with every image patch obtained from the training images. When the patches are clustered to form codebook entries, the mask coherence is integrated into the similarity measure used for clustering. Thus, it is ensured that only patches with similar segmentation masks, in addition to similar appearance, are grouped together. Whenever a codebook entry is matched to the image during recognition, its stored segmentation mask is applied to the image. The entry may cast votes for different object identities and positions, but whatever it votes for, the implied segmentation mask stays the same. When an object hypothesis is formed as a maximum in vote space, all patch interpretations contributing to that hypothesis are collected, and their associated segmentation masks are combined to obtain the per-pixel probabilities $p(\mathbf{p} = figure | o_n, x)$.

In the second approach, pioneered in this chapter, we do not keep a fixed segmentation mask for every codebook entry, but we store a separate mask for every location it occurs in on the training images. With the 2'519 codebook entries used for the car category, we thus obtain 20'359 occurrences, with one segmentation mask stored for each. For the cow category, the codebook contains only 2'244 clusters, but these occur in a total of 50'792 locations on the training images, owing to the larger texture variability on the cow bodies. Whenever a codebook entry is matched to the image using this approach, a separate segmentation mask is associated with every object position it votes for. As such, the same vertical structure can indicate a solid area if it is in the middle of a cow's body, and a strong border if it is part of a leg. Which option is finally selected depends on the winning hypothesis and its accumulated support from other patches. In any case, the feedback loop of only taking the votes that support the winning hypothesis ensures that only consistent interpretations are used for the later segmentation.

In our experiments, we obtained much better results with the occurrence masks, even when edge information was used to augment matches. In the following, we therefore only report results for occurrence masks. In addition, we assume uniform priors for $p(\mathbf{e})$ and $p(o_n, x)$, so that these elements can be factored out of the equations. In order to obtain a segmentation of the whole image from the figure and ground probabilities, we build the likelihood ratio for every pixel:

$$L = \frac{p(\mathbf{p} = \textit{figure}|o_n, x)}{p(\mathbf{p} = \textit{ground}|o_n, x)}. \tag{10.9}$$

Figure 10.4 shows an example segmentation of a car, together with $p(\mathbf{p} = \textit{figure}|o_n, x)$, the system's confidence in the segmentation result. The lighter a pixel, the higher its probability of being *figure*. The darker it is, the higher its probability of being *ground*. The uniform gray region in the background does not contribute to the object hypothesis and is therefore considered neutral. By only considering the pixels where

$$\max(p(\textit{figure}), p(\textit{ground})) > \theta,$$

the computed probability can be used to set a certain "confidence level" for the segmentation and thus limit the amount of missegmentation. Figures 10.4(c)-(f) show segmentation results with different confidence levels (The confidences are not in the range $[0, 1]$ because we omitted a normalization factor in the implementation). As can be observed, the segmentation with the lowest confidence level still contains some missegmented areas, while higher confidence levels ensure that only trusted segmentations are made, although at the price of leaving open some uncertain areas. This estimate of how much the obtained segmentation can be trusted is especially important when the results shall later be combined with a bottom-up segmentation method, e.g. based on contour grouping.

10.5 Results

The enlargement shown in Figures 10.5(a)-(e) demonstrates an advantage of the proposed approach compared to gradient-based methods. At the bottom of the car, there is no visible border between the black car body and the dark shadow underneath. Instead, a strong shadow line extends much further to the left of the car. The proposed algorithm can compensate for that since it "knows" that if a codebook entry matches in this position relative to the object center, it must contain the car's border. Since at this point only those patch interpretations are considered that are consistent with the object hypothesis, the system can infer the missing contour.

Figures 10.5(f)-(j) show another interesting case. Even though the car in the image is partially occluded by a pedestrian, the algorithm finds it with its second hypothesis. Refining the hypothesis yields a good segmentation of the car, without the occluded area. The system is able to segment out the pedestrian, because it contributes nothing to the car hypothesis. This is something that would be very hard to achieve for a system purely based on pixel-level discontinuities.

More segmentation results for cars and cows can be seen in Figures 10.6 and 10.7. All the cars and the first three cows have been correctly found with the recognition system's first hypothesis (The last cow was found with the second hypothesis). Next to each test image, the gradient magnitude is shown to illustrate the difficulty of the segmentation task. Even though the images contain low contrast and significant clutter, the algorithm succeeds in providing a good segmentation of the object. Confidence and segmentation quality are especially high for the bottom parts of the cars, including the cars' shadows (which were labeled *figure* in the training examples). Most difficulties arise with the car

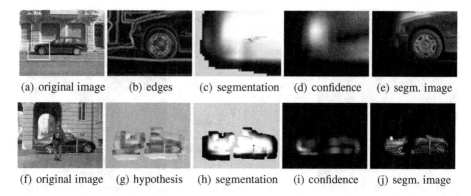

(a) original image   (b) edges   (c) segmentation   (d) confidence   (e) segm. image

(f) original image   (g) hypothesis   (h) segmentation   (i) confidence   (j) segm. image

Fig. 10.5. (top) Example where object knowledge compensates for missing edge information. (bottom) Segmentation result of a partially occluded car. The system is able to segment out the pedestrian, because it contributes nothing to the car hypothesis.

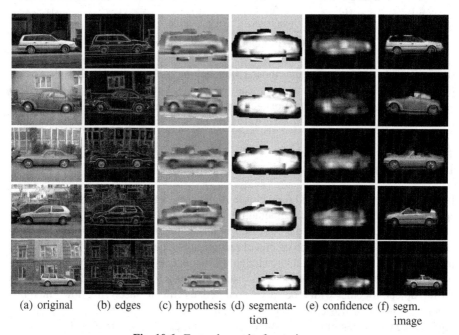

(a) original   (b) edges   (c) hypothesis (d) segmenta-   (e) confidence (f) segm.
                                                     tion   image

Fig. 10.6. Example results for car images

roofs and cow heads. These regions contain a lot of variation (e.g. caused by (semi-) transparent windows or different head orientations), which is not sufficiently represented in the training data. What is remarkable, though, is that the cows' legs are captured well, even though no single training object contained exactly the same leg configuration. The local approach can compensate for that by combining elements from different training objects.

Another interesting effect can be observed in the cow images 1 and 4. Even though there are strong edge structures on the cows' bodies, no borders are introduced there,

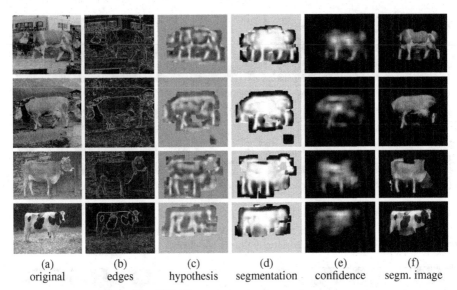

| (a) | (b) | (c) | (d) | (e) | (f) |
| original | edges | hypothesis | segmentation | confidence | segm. image |

Fig. 10.7. Example results for cow images

since the system has learned that those edges belong to the body. On the other hand, relatively weak edges around the legs lead to strong segmentation results. The system has learned that if a certain structure occurs in this region, it must be a leg. No heuristics are needed for this behavior – it is entirely learned from training data.

10.6 Conclusion

In this chapter, we have argued for a closer connection between the areas of object categorization and figure-ground segmentation. Following a review of the state-of-the-art in this field, we have proposed a novel algorithm that achieves figure-ground segmentation as a result and extension of object recognition. The method uses a probabilistic formulation to integrate learned knowledge about the recognized category with the supporting information in the image. As a result, it returns a figure-ground segmentation for the object, together with a per-pixel confidence estimate specifying how much this segmentation can be trusted. We have applied the method to the task of categorizing and segmenting unfamiliar objects in difficult real-world scenes. Experiments show that it is applicable for categories as diverse as cars and cows and that it can cope with cluttered backgrounds and partial occlusions.

For more accurate segmentation results, obviously, the combination with traditional contour or region based segmentation algorithms is required. The result images show that edges are quite prominent in those regions where our proposed algorithms has problems, such as on the car roofs or cow heads. On the other hand, category-specific knowledge can serve to resolve ambiguities between low-level image structures in those regions where our algorithm is confident. In short, both kinds of methods are mutually beneficial and should be combined, ideally in an iterative process. The probabilistic formulation of our algorithm lends itself to an easy integration with other segmentation methods.

Acknowledgments

This work is part of the CogVis project, funded in part by the Commission of the European Union (IST-2000-29375), and the Swiss Federal Office for Education and Science (BBW 00.0617).

Part III

Learning and Adaptation

11

Learning an Analysis Strategy for Knowledge-Based Exploration of Scenes

H. Niemann[1], U. Ahlrichs[1], and D. Paulus[1,2]

[1] Lehrstuhl für Mustererkennung
Universität Erlangen-Nürnberg
Martensstraße 3
91058 Erlangen, Germany
`niemann@informatik.uni-erlangen.de`

[2] *current address*
Institut für Computervisualistik
Universitätsstraße 1
56070 Koblenz, Germany

Abstract. A system is presented which searches with an active camera for known objects, constrained to lie on a table, in an otherwise unknown office using color images. Both camera actions and image processing methods are represented as concepts of a semantic network. Image processing methods comprise depth computation to find a table, generation of object hypotheses in an overview image, and object verification in a close-up view. Camera actions are pan, tilt, zoom, and motion on a linear sledge. System actions, either image processing or camera actions, are initialized by a graph search based control algorithm which tries to compute the best scoring instance of a goal concept. The sequence of actions for computing an instance is determined by precedences which are either adjusted manually or computed from reinforcement-learning. Results are presented comparing the two approaches.

11.1 Introduction

In knowledge–based vision as understood in this contribution we have a knowledge base which contains both declarative and procedural knowledge and a mainly task–independent control strategy which computes a processing strategy, that is, it determines which algorithms to activate at a certain time with which subset of the available data. The processing strategy should be optimal with respect to a predefined criterion, e.g., it should maximize the score (or reliability) of a computed result with a minimum number of processing steps. Approaches to knowledge–based processing are presented, e.g., in [108, 252, 289, 330, 329, 334, 341, 387, 448].

In active vision the recorded image is selected with respect to space, time, and resolution in order to find in the image the information necessary to perform a certain

---

[b] This work was partially supported by the "Deutsche Forschungsgemeinschaft (DFG)" under grant NI 191/12–1. Only the authors are responsible for the content.

H.I. Christensen and H.-H. Nagel (Eds.): Cognitive Vision Systems, LNCS 3948, pp. 165–180, 2006.

Fig. 11.1. The objects used in the experiments (from left to right: 3 red, 2 blue, 1 yellow)

task [9, 24, 43, 97, 95]. Selection in space and resolution need camera actions like pan, tilt, and zoom. This is useful in tasks to be solved by autonomous robots and assistance systems which have to work in a fairly uncontrolled environment [82, 217]. An important capability of such systems is to explore the environment, for example, in order to find a save path or to find interesting objects which are to be fetched and carried.

An interesting and important question is how to determine a camera action in a systematic way. In [96, 95] an information theoretic criterion is used to determine an action which is optimal with respect to mutual information. In [3] a knowledge–based system is developed which can *learn* an analysis strategy based on a training sequence of images. In this contribution we present an outline of this approach.

In view of the sentence "nothing happens in the universe which does not have the meaning of a well–defined maximum or minimum" (due to LEIBNIZ) one may treat and solve problems like (human) perception and (machine) analysis of images (or image understanding, active vision, cognitive vision, or ...) as *optimization problems*. This opens a theoretically well-founded and systematic approach to diverse problems. Different optimization criteria were developed for different tasks, e.g., pattern classification [72, 402], classification and localization of objects [194, 195], knowledge–based image analysis [241], selection of camera parameters in active vision [96], or energy minimization [185, 344].

In this paper we present an operational knowledge–based system for the general task to *find* (known) objects in an (unknown, static) office scene using color images. There are six objects shown in Fig. 11.1, three red, two blue, and one yellow; they are constrained to be on a table. A hypothezise–and–test approach is used. If no known object is visible in an overview image, a scene exploration is done by performing a camera search for an object by taking another viewpoint. If an object is visible but too small for verification, the camera zooms in on an object hypothesis; and finally, the object hypothesis is verified. Knowledge about the scene *and* about camera actions is represented in a semantic network. Possible camera actions are pan, tilt, and zoom; in addition, the camera may move on a linear sledge fixed in the upper part of a room. We compare a hand–designed processing strategy to one computed by reinforcement–learning. The emphasis is on the system aspect, knowledge representation and use for this task, and the learning of a strategy. Two typical office scenes are shown in Fig. 11.2.

The approach to knowledge–based exploration of a scene is the following. A model

$$\mathcal{M} = \langle C_j \rangle \qquad (11.1)$$

represents both declarative and procedural knowledge about the task–domain; in our case it is a (semantic) network of concepts C. An account of this is given in Sect. 11.2. Results of knowledge–based processing are (possibly competing) instances $I_i(C_j)$ of concepts C_j. The interface between the image, i.e. the pixel or numerical data, and the model,

Fig. 11.2. Two typical office scenes used in the experiments

i.e. the concepts or symbolic data, is established via an initial segmentation $\mathcal{A}$. This is computed by image processing algorithms presented in Sect. 11.3. The goal of processing is, of course, also represented by a concept, the *goal concept* C_g. Each concept, including the goal concept, has an attached *judgment function* G which computes a score — which may be a value of goodness or of cost — of an instance of this concept. Therefore, knowledge–based image understanding in this framework amounts to the computation of an *optimal instance* of the goal concept, that is, an instance having maximal value (or minimal cost)

$$I^*(C_g) = \underset{\{I(C_g)\}}{\operatorname{argmax}} \left\{ G(I(C_g) \mid \mathcal{M}, \mathcal{A}) \right\} . \tag{11.2}$$

An optimal instance may be computed, for example, by a *graph search algorithm* as described in Sect. 11.4 or by combinatorial optimization [127, 329]. Since there are many design choices in a control algorithm and during processing, promising intermediate results should be identified, directions for guiding the control algorithm must either be provided manually or by automatic learning as described in Sect. 11.5. Results and a conclusion are given in Sect. 11.6 and Sect. 11.7, respectively.

11.2 Knowledge Representation

As mentioned above, a semantic network formalism is used for knowledge representation. Since detailed descriptions of this formalism are available in references like [331, 387], we only summarize the main points here; related work is found in [52].

A semantic network is basically a *graph* with a restricted number of node types and link types. We use *three types of nodes*, the concept C, the modified concept M, and the instance I. A concept is the computer representation of some (colloquial) conception, e.g. "car", "hole punch", "zoom", or "explore". It is mainly defined by its attributes, relations, and links to other concepts. Each attribute A has an attached function F to compute an attribute value for an instance $I(C)$ of the concept. A relation may hold between attributes A_C of the concept, attributes A_P of its parts, and attributes A_K of concretes of the concept. Each relation has an attached function which computes a score for the degree of fulfillment of the defined relation. In addition, a concept has a judgment function for scoring of its instances. A modified concept contains intermediate results for not yet fully instantiated concepts and allows, together with an appropriate control algorithm, the top–down and bottom–up propagation of constraints resulting from intermediate results. This improves the efficiency of processing. An instance contains results of image processing and scene interpretation which meet the specifications of the concept. Every instance has a judgment of its reliability. The structure of an instance is the same as that of a concept. The functions attached to a concept are replaced by computed values in an instance.

There are four types of links, the specialization V, the part P, the concrete K, and the instance link L. In order to handle also camera actions in this formalism we added a special *action link* to cope with camera actions. Parts and concretes may be labeled obligatory or optional. Two types of parts are distinguished, the context–independent parts and the context–dependent parts. This allows the representation and use (by the control algorithm) of context–sensitive relations. In order to instantiate a concept at least partially, there must be instances of all of its obligatory concretes and of all of its obligatory context–independent parts; in order to instantiate a concept C_1 which is a context–dependent part of another concept C_2, there must be at least a partial instance of C_2, where the partial instance may even be empty, if no further information is currently available. The full definition of an instantiation rule is given below in Fig. 11.10. To allow compact knowledge bases, sets of modalities H have been introduced which contain subsets of parts and concretes and allow the definition of slightly different versions of a concept within the same data structure; the alternative would be to provide a separate concept for every slightly different version. No relations like "is on" or "left of" are put into links, but they are represented in concepts in order to facilitate the specification of a control algorithm which is *independent* of the content (or meaning) of a knowledge base and only dependent on its syntax, i.e. the defined node and link types; hence it is essential to strictly limit the number of link types.

A semantic network contains both *declarative knowledge*, that is, the network of concepts, and *procedural knowledge* attached to concepts, that is, procedures for image processing, camera actions, computation of attribute values and scores of instances. The basic structure of a concept is

$$
\begin{aligned}
C = (\qquad & \\
D : T_C, \qquad\qquad & \text{name} \\
(P_{\text{ci}} : C)^* \qquad\qquad & \text{context--indep. parts} \\
(P_{\text{cd}} : C)^* \qquad\qquad & \text{context--dep. parts} \\
(K : C)^* \qquad\qquad & \text{concretes} \\
(V : C)^*, \qquad\qquad & \text{specializations} \\
(H : C)^*, \qquad\qquad & \text{modalities} \\
(L : I)^*, \qquad\qquad & \text{instances} \\
(A : (T_A \mapsto F))^*, \qquad\qquad & \text{attributes} \\
(S(A_C, A_P, A_K) \mapsto F)^*, \qquad\qquad & \text{relations} \\
G \mapsto F, \qquad\qquad & \text{judgment} \\
P \qquad\qquad & \text{priorities} \\
) &
\end{aligned}
\qquad (11.3)
$$

A section of the model of the task domain is shown in Fig. 11.3. It shows both concepts for objects, for example, "gluestick" or "table", and for actions, for example, "explore hole punch" or "zoom on region".

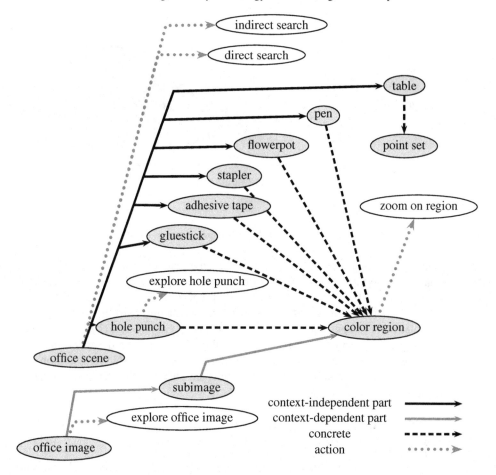

Fig. 11.3. A Model of the Task Domain

11.3 Image Processing

The routines for image processing are an important part of the procedural knowledge in the semantic network outlined above. In order to find objects, not every detail in an image is important, but only the sections containing known objects. Hypotheses for object locations are generated in an *overview image*. If an object hypothesis is generated in an overview image, a subimage (cf. the concept "subimage" in Fig. 11.3) is generated such that the center of the subimage and of an object hypothesis coincide. If the object is too small to be verified, the camera zooms in on this image region (cf. the concept "zoom on region" in Fig. 11.3). The close–up view is segmented by split-and-merge [196] or by the color structure code (CSC) [356] (cf. the concept "color region" in Fig. 11.3). Then it is tried to verify the object hypothesis by evaluating the fit between the segmented region (image) and the region concept (a priori knowledge). If no objects are visible, either an *indirect* or a *direct* search (cf. concepts for these two actions in Fig. 11.3) is performed. In an indirect search it is tried to find a table in the current overview image; in

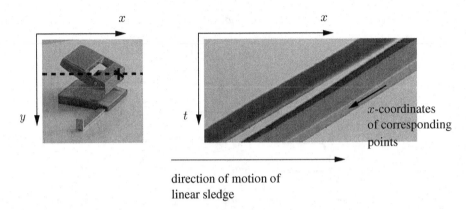

Fig. 11.4. An object (left) and tracked points (right)

a direct search another view of the scene is recorded. In the following we describe depth computation, recognition of a table, generation of an object hypothesis, segmentation of a close–up view, and verification of an object hypothesis.

A color camera can move under computer control on a linear sledge. This generates a monocular color image sequence $\boldsymbol{f}(\boldsymbol{x}, t) = (f_1(x, y, t), \ f_2(x, y, t), \ f_3(x, y, t))^\mathsf{T}$ in which conspicuous points are detected and tracked. The approach described in [451] was extended to color images in [182]. By using color images faster computation due to smaller window size and better tracking results are obtained. For depth computation the disparity $\boldsymbol{d}$ is needed

$$\boldsymbol{d}(x, y, t) = (d_1(x, y, t), \ d_2(x, y, t))^\mathsf{T} = \boldsymbol{x}_t - \boldsymbol{x}_{t+\tau}$$
$$= b(x, y, t) \boldsymbol{r}(x, y, t) \tag{11.4}$$

where r is the directional constraint due to the linear camera motion on the sledge. The value of b minimizing the mean square error is obtained from

$$b(x, y, t) = \frac{\underset{W}{\iint} \boldsymbol{h}^\mathsf{T}(u, v, t) \, \boldsymbol{J}^\mathsf{T}(u, v, t) \, \boldsymbol{r}(x, y, t) \, du \, dv}{\underset{W}{\iint} |\boldsymbol{J}^\mathsf{T}(u, v, t) \boldsymbol{r}(x, y, t)|^2 \, du \, dv} \tag{11.5}$$

$$\boldsymbol{h}(u, v, t) = \boldsymbol{f}(u, v, t) - \boldsymbol{f}(u, v, t + \tau)$$
$$\boldsymbol{J}(u, v, t) = (\nabla f_1, \ \nabla f_2, \ \nabla f_3)_{(u,v,t)} \quad \text{(JACOBI matrix)}$$

Points with a large value of the denominator are tracked, and hence one need not care for a small or zero denominator. The camera is moved on the sledge in small steps to record 20 images, and corresponding image points are tracked. An example is shown in Fig. 11.4.

Using depth information from points which can be tracked in at least ten images, a table is assumed if points lie within a "plane" of 10 cm tolerance. A result is shown in Fig. 11.5.

Objects are assumed to lie on a table. Object hypotheses are generated by histogram backprojection [443]. The basic algorithm is given in Fig. 11.6, and a result in Fig. 11.7.

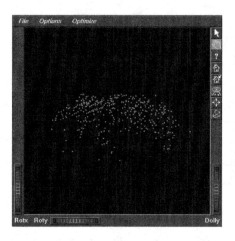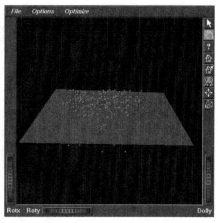

Fig. 11.5. A set of points obtained from depth computation and its approximation by a plane (right)

input: color histogram $H^{(o)} = [h_k^{(o)}]_{k=1...K}$ of an object $\boldsymbol{o}$
compute color histogram $H^{(f)} = [h_k^{(f)}]_{k=1...K}$ of given image $\boldsymbol{f}$
FOR each histogram bin $k \in \{1, \ldots, K\}$
$\quad h_k^{(r)} = \min\{\frac{h_k^{(o)}}{h_k^{(f)}}, 1\}$ (compute ratio histogram $H^{(r)} = [h_k^{(r)}]_{k=1...K}$)
FOR all positions (i, j) in the image
$\quad A_{i,j} := h_{\phi(\boldsymbol{f}_{i,j})}^{(r)}$, where $\boldsymbol{f}_{i,j}$ denotes the color vector at position (i, j) and ϕ maps color vector to histogram bin
$\boldsymbol{B} := \boldsymbol{D}_r * \boldsymbol{A}$, where $*$ denotes convolution
output: object position $(i_o, j_o) := \operatorname{argmax}_{i,j}(B_{i,j})$

Fig. 11.6. Algorithm for histogram backprojection

Different color spaces were tried, and finally the rg color space, i.e. RG values normalized by the intensity, was used for red and blue objects, the RGB space for the yellow object.

After region segmentation a postprocessing is done by a morphological opening operation using a 10×10 mask; on average, 14 regions are obtained per close–up view. Results for two close–up images are shown in Fig. 11.8.

The verification of an object hypothesis employs geometric models of 2–D views. They contain the features color, height, width of the object. Rotation invariance of a color region in an image is achieved by normalizing the moments. Height and width are normalized by using the focal length and the distance of the camera to the object center. The probability of observing features is approximated by GAUSS distributions and they are also the basis for classification by BAYES rule. Fig. 11.9 shows the histogram of an object height and its approximation by a normal distribution.

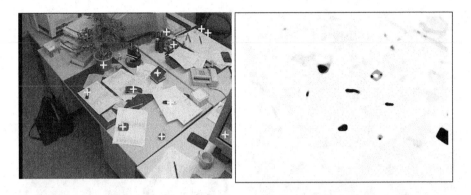

Fig. 11.7. Result of histogram backprojection

close–up image   color–structure–code   split–and–merge

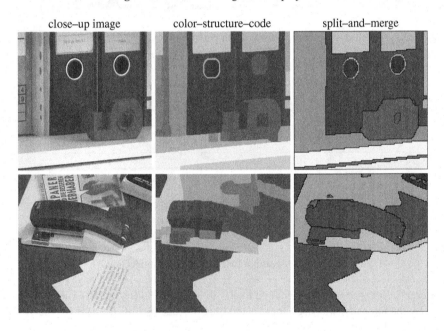

Fig. 11.8. Examples of segmentation results

11.4 Control

The sequence of operations in our system is not "hard–wired" but depends on the input and on intermediate results. The task of the control algorithm is to compute a processing strategy which finally yields an optimal instance $I^*(C_g)$ of the goal concept C_g (i.e. "office scene") as specified in (11.2). This basically amounts to solving a *search problem* in an implicitly defined search tree. The root node v_0 of the search tree contains the initial data, that is, the input image. A set of transformations, specified by six inference rules, is defined which generates new nodes in the search tree. They are the rules for the computation of modified concepts and instances given the model $\mathcal{M}$ as a semantic

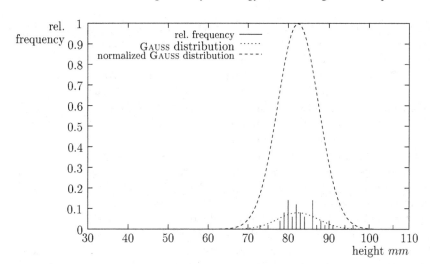

Fig. 11.9. Approximation of the distribution of height values of the object "adhesive tape" by a normal distribution

IF: for a concept C_i *or* a modified concept $M_j(C_i)$ *and* a modality description of C_i there are already instances for
  • all obligatory concretes
  • all obligatory parts which are not context–dependent on C_i
  and there is a partial instance of a concept of which C_i is a context–dependent part

THEN: generate partial instances $I_k^P(C_i)$ by the following steps
  • generate an empty instance for $I_k^P(C_i)$ and enter the current modality
  • link $I_k^P(C_i)$ to related instances, concepts, and modified concepts
  • activate functions attached to C_i for $I_k^P(C_i)$ in the order
    – scoring of links
    – computation of attribute values
    – computation of attribute scores
    – computation of relation scores
    – computation of the score of instance $I_k^P(C_i)$

Fig. 11.10. The inference rule for computation of a partial instance of a concept

network. There are three rules for the computation of partial instances, of full instances, and of extended instances, two rules for data–driven and for model–driven computation of modified concepts, and one rule for the generation of modified concepts from segmentation results. As an example the full definition of the first inference rule is given in Fig. 11.10, for the details of the other rules the reader is referred to [387].

In analogy to the conflict set in rule–based systems there may be several rules which can be activated at a certain time, and there may be different concepts, modified concepts, and instances to which a rule may be applied. In addition, more than one instance of a concept may be created due to ambiguities of results or constraints in the knowledge base. This results in competing search tree nodes which are treated by the A* algorithm

[332, 328]. The basic prerequisite for A* to be admissible is a scoring function for search tree nodes (which should not be confused with the scoring functions for instances, relations, and so on) which is monotone in the sense that the estimate of the cost of a sequence of search tree nodes along a search path is non–decreasing. An example of such a scoring function is given in (11.6). Of course, the better the cost estimate approximates the actual cost of a search tree node, the better will be the efficiency of search. It is known that the complexity of A* is exponential in the worst case, but may be reduced if suitable scoring functions are available [342].

Using the A* algorithm the search starts at the root node v_0 of the search tree which is labeled as an "open" node. At every processing step A* scores the open search tree nodes and determines the best scoring node. If this contains an instance of the goal concept, the search is finished successfully, and from the properties of A* it is known that no better scoring instance can be found. If the best scoring node does not contain an instance of the goal concept, it is labeled as "finished" and it is expanded, that is, all possible successor nodes are generated by the application of rules $T\{v_k\}$ for generating further nodes; the generated successor nodes are scored and labeled open. The process of selecting the best scoring open node, inspection for an instance of a goal concept, and generation of successors is repeated until the search finishes successfully or until no further successors can be generated; in this case the search stops with a failure, that is, no result can be computed.

The basic idea for scoring a search tree node v is to estimate the score $G(I(C_g))$ of an instance $I(C_g)$ of the goal concept C_g which might be computed by extending the search path through v. This results in a scoring function which always looks for the expected score of a final result. Since at a certain stage of analysis not all results will be available which are necessary to compute the score G, the scores of missing results are replaced by optimistic estimates. Let C be some concept having the set $D_i, i = 1, \ldots, n$ of parts and concretes. Let the scoring function G be a measure of cost normalized to $0 \leq G \leq 1$. Then an estimate of the cost of an instance of the goal concept C_g associated with a node v in the search tree and denoted by $\widehat{G}(I_v(C_g))$ can be computed at every stage of analysis from the recursive definition of the score of an instance $I_v(C)$ associated with v by

$$
\widehat{G}(I_v(C)) = \begin{cases} G(I_v(C)) & \text{if } C \text{ is instantiated and } I_v(C) \text{ is the instance} \\ & \text{associated with } v; \\ 0 & \text{if } C \text{ is primitive and still uninstantiated;} \\ \widehat{G}(\widehat{G}(I_v(D_1)), \ldots, \widehat{G}(I_v(D_n)) \mid C) \\ & \text{if } C \text{ is still uninstantiated and instances } I_v(D_1), \\ & \ldots, I_v(D_n) \text{ are associated with } v. \end{cases} \quad (11.6)
$$

Due to the requirements of the A* algorithm we then use $\widehat{G}(I_v(C_g))$ as an optimistic estimate of the cost of an instance of the goal concept associated with node v.

Conceptually, a search tree node v_k represents a state of analysis, that is, the concepts of the model and all so far computed modified concepts and instances. If A* selects a search tree node for expansion, computation of instances or modified concepts is done on *an element* of this node — but the question is on which one? One solution is to attach a problem–dependent *precedence* value plus a problem–independent *priority* value to each concept. During analysis, concepts in the search tree node with the highest precedence value are processed first. If several have the same precedence, they are ordered by priority. The priority is a measure of the length of a path from the concept along concrete links to a primitive concept (i.e. one having no parts and concretes). The precedence may be specified by the designer of the system or it may be learned from examples as described in Sect. 11.5. Proper specification of precedences is important for the goal directed operation of the control strategy, but it needs a thorough understanding of and ample experience with the operation of the control algorithm. Hence, automatic learning is very desirable.

11.5 Learning

It was mentioned in the preceding section that the determination of the precedence values is not a straightforward task. Techniques known from reinforcement learning (RL) [442] can be used to learn precedence values during the operation of the system. In Fig. 11.11 the control problem is shown in terms of a reinforcement learning problem. Basically, the problem of determining problem–dependent precedence values is replaced by finding a suitable criterion or reward function for judging the success of learning. If this reward can be formulated problem–independent, a significant progress is achieved to simplify the problem of finding an efficient control strategy. Fig. 11.12 compares the terminology of RL and knowledge based processing (KBP) showing the direct correspondence of the two problems.

Starting in a certain state of KBP, represented in the current search tree node v_k, the control algorithm selects at time t the next action a_t, that is, one of the six inference rules applied to one of the elements in the search tree node (i.e. a concept, a modified concept, or an instance). This generates a new state of analysis. This is precisely what also RL does, where an agent at time step t selects an action a_t based on an observation of the state s_t of the environment. After execution of a_t the environment gives a reward r_{t+1} and the state of the environment is changed to s_{t+1}. The goal of RL is to maximize the total reward.

In RL the decision for an action by the agent is based on the *policy*

$$\pi_t(s, a) = p(a_t = a | s_t = s) \tag{11.7}$$

which is the probability to select action $a_t = a \in A$ if the environment is in state $s_t = s \in S$. The total reward (or return) is defined by

$$R_t = \sum_k \beta^k r_{t+k+1} , \quad 0 \le \beta \le 1 \tag{11.8}$$

In the above equation $\beta = 1$ is allowed only for a finite sequence of action–state pairs. Assuming the properties of a MARKOV decision process the action value function or Q–function, which is the expected total reward for action a in state s, is given by

$$Q^\pi(s, a) = E_\pi\{R_t | a_t = a, s_t = s\} = E_\pi\left\{\sum_k \beta^k r_{t+k+1} | a_t = a, s_t = s\right\} \tag{11.9}$$

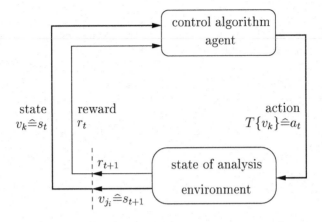

Fig. 11.11. The action of the control module depicted as a reinforcement learning problem

RL	KBP
agent	control algorithm
action a_t	transformation $T(v_k) = \{v_j\}$, $j = 1, \ldots, m$ to generate new search tree nodes
environment	the states of analysis $\{v\}$
	A^* selects best scoring v_{j_i}
reward r_{t+1} of agent	criterion for search efficiency
policy $\pi_t(s, a)$ to select action	basis for learning precedence values

Fig. 11.12. The direct correspondence between Reinforcement Learning (RL) and Knowledge-Based Processing (KBP)

Then the *optimal policy* is defined by

$$\forall a \in A_t(s) : \pi(s, a) = \begin{cases} 1 & \text{if } a = \text{argmax}_{a'} \, Q(s, a') \\ 0 & \text{otherwise} \end{cases} , \tag{11.10}$$

where $A_t(s)$ is the set of actions possible in state s.

For the purpose of KBP the reward is measured by the number $|\text{STN}|$ of search tree nodes. This is a problem–independent reward function which ensures an efficient control strategy, regardless of the knowledge represented in the semantic network. The reward is defined by

$$r_t = \begin{cases} \dfrac{1000 - |\text{STN}|}{1000} & : |\text{STN}| \leq 1000 \\ -1 & : \text{ELSE} \end{cases} \tag{11.11}$$

The number of search tree nodes varies significantly with the control strategy and hence is an important measure of system performance. In one experimental evaluation we found that about 200 search tree nodes were generated for a model–driven strategy and about 1.000 nodes for a data–driven strategy.

We initialize Q by the priorities described in Sect. 11.4 and then use a MONTE CARLO method to estimate values of Q in a *policy iteration* cycle. It generates an

				hole punch	adhesive tape disp.	gluestick	stapler	pen	flower pot	others
	red	blue	yellow	red	red	red	blue	yellow	blue	avg./im.
total	**rg**	**rg**	**RGB**	90 %	96 %	62 %	78 %	92 %	94 %	5.8
	rg	UV	RGB	60 %	72 %	44 %	40 %	54 %	56 %	8.3
	UV	UV	RGB	56 %	62 %	50 %	38 %	50 %	54 %	8.6
	UV	rg	RGB	52 %	60 %	38 %	48 %	42 %	66 %	8.8

Fig. 11.13. Number of Correct Object Hypotheses for Different Color Spaces

	hole punch	adhesive tape	gluestick	stapler	pen	flower pot
office 1	18	15	10	15	15	12
office 2	18	18	6	4	19	13
total	72 %	66 %	32 %	38 %	68 %	50 %

Fig. 11.14. Success Rate of the Overall System on 25 Images per Office Scene (no camera zoom allowed)

episode, i.e. an instantiation of the complete semantic net, by using π_ν in iteration step ν and computes $Q^{\pi_\nu}(s, a)$. Given Q^{π_ν}, it computes a new policy $\pi_{\nu+1}$ from (11.10). Finally, the *precedence* values of concepts are the learned Q values.

11.6 Results

Generation of Object Hypotheses

The evaluation of object hypothesis generation uses two types of office scenes and 25 images per office; two examples were given in Fig. 11.2. In each image all 6 objects, shown in Fig. 11.1, are present. We used different backgrounds and object locations per image. A result of histogram backprojection was shown in Fig. 11.7. In Fig. 11.13 the success rate for different color spaces is shown per object. It turns out that the rg color space for red and blue objects and the RGB space for the yellow object is the best choice.

User Defined Control Strategy

Next, the overall system was evaluated again for 25 images in 2 types of office scenes. All 6 objects were visible in the first overview image; hence, there were 25 occurrences per object and type of office scene. Fig. 11.14 shows the success rate if no zooming of the camera is allowed and Fig. 11.15 shows the number of changes if zooming is included. The two segmentation algorithms mentioned in Sect. 11.3 are investigated, and only the split–and–merge segmentation gives a net improvement. The control strategy is user–defined in both cases.

The number of camera actions per image is shown in Fig. 11.16. It shows that the camera is quite busy which is mainly due to instable image segmentation. The problems

		hole punch		adhesive tape		glue stick		stapler		pen		flower pot		total	
		+	-	+	-	+	-	+	-	+	-	+	-	+	-
off. 1	csm	0	0	3	1	2	3	3	4	1	1	0	0	9	9
	csc	0	0	2	0	1	6	3	4	0	2	0	0	6	12
off. 2	csm	1	0	3	3	3	0	5	3	2	1	0	2	14	9
	csc	1	3	2	3	0	2	5	1	1	4	0	2	9	15

Fig. 11.15. Changes of System Performance on 25 Images per Office Scene with Camera Zoom (csm: color split–and–merge; csc: color structure code for segmentation of a close–up view)

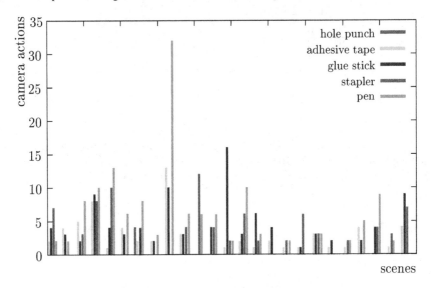

Fig. 11.16. The Number of Camera Actions for Different Images and Different Objects

of image segmentation are also the reason for the only few improvements of object verification in Fig. 11.15. The problems in image segmentation, in particular for office scene 2, mainly result from inhomogeneous illumination which can be seen in the right image of Fig. 11.2. We deliberately avoided to influence the illumination since this is hard to do in a natural environment.

Learned Control Strategy

We now consider the usefulness of a control strategy defined by automatically learned precedence values. Ten different overview images of office scenes were recorded. A policy π_j is learned from one overview image j and tested on the remaining 9 images. In addition, a policy π_{all} is learned from all 10 images and tested on another 10 images. The analysis was stopped if more than 1.000 search tree nodes were generated. New search tree nodes were generated only for instances having a score above a threshold. One complete scene interpretation needs on average 67.3 sec if 1.000 search tree nodes are generated (computation on a 683 MHz Pentium III).

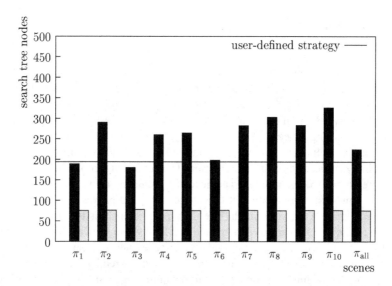

Fig. 11.17. Comparison of the user–designed and the automatically learned control strategy. The black bars show the average of the mean number of search tree nodes for eleven learned policies π (black bars), the minimum possible number of search tree nodes (light gray bars), and the average number of search tree nodes of a user–defined strategy (horizontal line).

It is possible to compute the minimal number of search tree nodes to analyze one image, if the number of concepts in the semantic network is known and if the number of object hypotheses for this image is known. Without going into details it is only mentioned that for the implemented system this minimal number equals 14 plus six times the number of object hypotheses. This minimal number as computed from the analysis strategy is shown per image in Fig. 11.17 as the light gray bars.

The mean number of search tree nodes was computed on each image. It is obtained from 20 tests per image resulting from different start states of analysis. Different start states are possible since in the semantic network there are 20 modified concepts which can be used as a starting point of processing. Since policy π_j is evaluated on all 9 images, this mean number is averaged over the 9 images and is shown as the black bar in Fig. 11.17.

Finally, the number of search tree nodes is also computed per image for the purely user–defined strategy. Its mean value is shown as the horizontal bar in Fig. 11.17.

Since the user–defined strategy was designed by a person having a lot of experience with the implemented system, it is not surprising that this strategy is fairly good. It is a significant success that by using reinforcement learning a control strategy can be learned automatically with a problem–independent reward function which performs almost as good as the user–defined strategy. For a discussion of the influence of the different parameters of RL on the learning process (e.g. β in (11.8) or ϵ in (11.10)) we refer the reader to [3].

11.7 Conclusion

A knowledge–based system which searches for known objects in an unknown office scene by handling an active camera was described. The objects are constrained to lie on a table. Basically, a hypothesize–and–test approach is used. The camera actions as well as the knowledge about objects and the scene is integrated into a knowledge base which is a semantic network. An important point was to improve the efficiency of processing by an automatic learning process. During the analysis of a scene there may be ambiguous and competing results due to ambiguities in the knowledge base and due to imperfect results of image processing and segmentation. The control algorithm must be guided by suitable preference values in order to achieve an efficient analysis strategy.

It was shown experimentally that the active camera improves the results of object verification, although not very much. The main problem here is the instability of segmentation results during various camera actions. It was also shown experimentally that by reinforcement learning precedence values can be learned automatically which result in an efficient processing strategy. The efficiency is measured by the number of search tree nodes, and this number is comparable to the number generated by a strategy which is manually designed after a lot of experience with the system. Thus, the tedious procedure of hand–designing an analysis strategy can be automated. Since the principle of reinforcement learning and the quality measure (number of search tree nodes) are problem–independent, this approach can be used also in other task domains.

Part IV

Representation and Inference

12

Things That See: Context-Aware Multi-modal Interaction

James L. Crowley

Laboratoire GRAVIR, INRIA Rhône Alpes
655 Avenue de l'Europe
F-38330 Montbonnot, France

Abstract. Human activity is extremely complex. Current technology allows us to handcraft real-time perception systems for a specific perceptual task. However, such an approach is inadequate for building systems that accommodate the variety that is typical of human environments. In this paper we define a framework for context aware observation of human activity. A context in this framework is defined as a network of situations. A situation network is interpreted as a specification for a federation of processes to observe humans and their actions. We present a process-based software architecture for building systems for observing activity. We discuss methods for building systems using this framework. The framework and methods are illustrated with examples from observation of human activity in an "Augmented Meeting Environment".

12.1 Introduction

This paper presents a framework for context aware observation of human activity. Within this framework, contexts are modeled as a network of situations. Situation models are interpreted to dynamically configure a federation of processes for observing the entities and relations that define a situation. We propose a software architecture based on dynamically assembled process federations [125], [116]. Our model builds on previous work on process-based architectures for machine perception and computer vision [84], [367], as well as on data flow models for software architecture [415].

Within this framework, a situation is described by a configuration of relations for observed entities. Changes in relations correspond to events that signal a change in situation. Such events can be used to trigger actions by the system. Situation models are used to specify an architecture in which reflexive processes are dynamically composed to form federations for observing and predicting situations. We believe that this architecture provides a foundation for the design of systems that act as a silent partner to assist humans in their activities in order to provide appropriate services without explicit commands and configuration. In the following section we review the use of the term "context aware" in different domains. This leads us to a situation-based approach to modeling context.

H.I. Christensen and H.-H. Nagel (Eds.): Cognitive Vision Systems, LNCS 3948, pp. 183–198, 2006.

12.2 A Brief History of Context

The word "context" has come to have many uses. Winograd [493] points out that the word "Context" has been adapted from linguistics. Composed of "con" (with) and "text", context refers to the meaning that must be inferred from the adjacent text. Such meaning ranges from the references intended for indefinite articles such as "it" and "that" to the shared reference frame of ideas and objects that are suggested by a text. Context goes beyond immediate binding of articles to the establishment of a framework for communication based on shared experience. Such a shared framework provides a collection of roles and relations with which to organize meaning for a phrase.

Early researchers in both artificial intelligence and computer vision recognized the importance of a symbolic structure for understanding. The "Scripts" representation [391] sought to provide just such information for understanding stories. Minsky's Frames [304] sought to provide the default information for transforming an image of a scene into a linguistic description. Semantic Networks [361] sought to provide a similar foundation for natural language understanding. All of these were examples of what might be called "schema" [47]. Schema provided context for understanding, whether from images, sound, speech, or written text. Recognizing such context was referred to as the "Frame Problem" and became known as one of the hard unsolved problems in AI.

In computer vision, the tradition of using context to provide a framework for meaning paralleled and drew from theories in artificial intelligence. The "Visions System" [171] expressed and synthesized the ideas that were common among leading researchers in computer vision in the early 70's. A central component of the "Visions System" was the notion of a hierarchical pyramid structure for providing context. Such pyramids successively transformed highly abstract symbols for global context into successively finer and more local context terminating in local image neighborhood descriptions that labeled uniform regions. Reasoning in this system worked by integrating top-down hypotheses with bottom-up recognition. Building a general computing structure for such a system became a grand challenge for computer vision. Successive generations of such systems, such as the "Schema System" [105] and "Condor" [128] floundered on problems of unreliable image description and computational complexity. Interest in the 1990's turned to achieving real time systems using "active vision" [24], [10]. Many of these ideas were developed and integrated into a context driven interpretation within a process architecture using the approach "Vision as Process" [86]. The methods for sensing and perceiving context for interaction described below draw from this approach.

Context awareness has become very important to mobile computing where the term was first introduced by Schilit and Theimer [393]. In their definition, context is defined as "the location and identities of nearby people and objects and changes to those objects". While this definition is useful for mobile computing, it defines context by example, and thus is difficult to generalize and apply to other domains. Other authors, such as [55] [376] and [484] have defined context in terms of the environment or situation. Such definitions are essentially synonyms for context, and are also difficult to apply operationally. Cheverest [70] describes context in anecdotal form using scenarios from a context aware tourist guide. His system is considered one of the early models for a context aware application.

Pascoe [339] defines context to be a subset of physical and conceptual states of interest to a particular entity. This definition has sufficient generality to apply to a recognition system. Dey [98] reviews definitions of context, and provides a definition of context as "any information that can be used to characterize situation". This is the sense in which we use the term context. Situation refers to the current state of the environment. Context specifies the elements that must be observed to model situation. However, to apply context in the composition of perceptual processes, we need to complete a clear definition with an operational theory. Such a foundation is provided by a process-based software architecture.

12.3 Perceptual Components for Context Awareness

In this section we describe a process-based software architecture for real time observation of human activity. The basic component of this architecture is a perceptual process. Perceptual processes are composed from a set of modules controlled by a supervisory controller. We describe several common classes of modules, and describe the operation of the controller. We also present several classes of perceptual processes and discuss how they can be combined into process federations according to a network of expected situations.

12.3.1 Perceptual Processes

A system's view of the external world is driven by a collection of sensors. These sensors generate observations that may have the form of numeric or symbolic values. Observations may be produced in a synchronous stream or as asynchronous events. In order to determine meaning from observations, a system must transform observations into some form of action. Such transformations may be provided by perceptual processes.

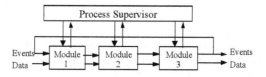

Fig. 12.1. A perceptual process integrates a set of modules to transform data streams or events into data streams or events

Perceptual processes are composed from a collection of modules controlled by a process supervisor, as shown in Figure 12.1. Processes operate in a synchronous manner within a shared address space. In our experimental system, the process supervisor is implemented as a multi-language interpreter [269] equipped with a dynamic loader for precompiled libraries. This interpreter allows processes to receive and interpret messages containing scripts, to add new functions to a process during execution. The modules that compose a process are formally defined as transformations applied to a certain class of data or event. Modules are executed in cyclic manner by the supervisor according to a process schedule. We impose that transformations return an auto-critical report that describes the results of their execution (see Figure 12.2). Examples of information contained in an auto-critical report include elapsed execution time, confidence in the result, and any exceptions that were encountered. The auto-critical report enables a supervisory controller to adapt parameters for the next call in order to maintain an execution cycle time, or other quality of service.

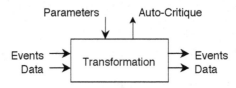

Fig. 12.2. Modules apply a transformation to an input data stream or events and return an auto-critical report

12.3.2 Examples: Modules for Observing, Grouping and Tracking

A typical example of a module is a transformation that uses table look-up to convert a color pixel into a probability of skin, as illustrated in Figure 12.3. Such a table can easily be defined using the ratio of a histogram of skin colored pixels in a training image, divided by the histogram of all pixels in the same image [408]. Skin pixels for an individual in a scene will all exhibit the same chrominance vector independent of surface orientation and thus can be used to detect the hands or face of that individual [439]. This technique has provided the basis for a very fast (video rate) process that converts an RGB color image into image of the probability of detection based on color using a look-up table.

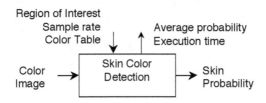

Fig. 12.3. A module for detecting skin colored pixels with a region of interest

A color observation module applies a specified look-up table to a rectangular "Region of Interest" or ROI using a specified sample rate. The sample rate, S, can be adapted to trade computation time for precision. The output from the module is an image in which pixels inside the ROI have been marked with the probability of detection. The auto-critical report returns the average value of the probabilities (for use as a confidence factor) as well as the number of microseconds required for execution. The average probability can be used to determine whether a target was detected within the ROI. The execution time can be used by the process supervisor to assure that the overall execution time meets a constraint. This module can be used either for initial detection or for tracking, according to the configuration specified by the supervisor. The color observation module is one example of a pixel level observation module. Pixel level observation modules provide the basis for inexpensive and controllable perceptual processes. In our systems, we use pixel level observation modules based on color, motion, background subtraction [350], and receptive field histograms [170]. Each of these modules applies a specified transformation to a specified ROI at a specified sample rate and returns an average detection probability and an execution time. Interpretation requires that detected regions be grouped into "blobs". Grouping is provided by a grouping module, defined using moments, as shown in Figure 12.4.

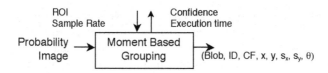

Fig. 12.4. A module for grouping detected pixels using moments

Let $w(i, j)$ represent an image of detection probabilities provided by a pixel level observation process. The detection mass, M, is the sum of the probabilities within the ROI. The ratio of the sum of probability pixels to the number of pixels, N, in the ROI provides a measure of the confidence that a skin colored region has been observed.

The first moment of the detected probabilities is the center of gravity in the row and column directions (x, y). This is a robust indicator of the position of the skin colored blob.

The second moment of $w(i, j)$ is a covariance matrix. Principal components analysis of the covariance matrix formed from σ_{ii}^2, σ_{ij}^2, and σ_{jj}^2 yield the length and breadth (σ_x, σ_y), as well as the orientation (θ) of the blob of detected pixels.

Tracking is a cyclic process of recursive estimation applied to a data stream. The Kalman filter provides a framework for designing tracking processes [214]. A general discussion of the use of the Kalman filter for sensor fusion is given in [89]. The use of the Kalman filter for tracking faces is described in [85].

Tracking provides a number of fundamentally important functions for a perception system. Tracking aids interpretation by integrating information over time. Tracking makes it possible to conserve information, assuring that a label applied to an entity at time T_1 remains associated with the entity at time T_2. Tracking provides a means to focus attention, by predicting the region of interest and the observation module that should be applied to a specific region of an image. Tracking processes can be designed to provide information about position, speed, and acceleration that can be useful in describing situations.

In perception systems, a tracking process is generally composed of three phases: predict, observe, and estimate as illustrated in Figure 12.5. Tracking maintains a list of entities, known as "targets". Each target is described by a unique ID, a target type, a confidence (or probability of existence), a vector of properties and a matrix of uncertainties (or precisions) for the properties.

The prediction phase uses a temporal model (called a "process model" in the tracking literature) to predict the properties that should be observed at a specified time for each target. For many applications of tracking, a simply linear model is adequate for such prediction. A linear model maintains estimates of the temporal derivatives for each target property and uses these to predict the observed property values. For example, a first order temporal model estimates the value for a property, X_{T_1}, at time T_1 from the value X_{T_0} at a time T_0 plus the temporal rate of change multiplied by the time step, $\Delta T = T_1 - T_0$:

$$X_{T_1} = X_{T_0} + \Delta T \cdot (dX/dt).$$

Higher order linear models may also be used provided that the observation sample rate is sufficiently fast compared to the derivatives to be estimated. Non-linear process models are also possible. For example, articulated models for human motion can provide important constraints on the temporal evolution of targets. The prediction phase also updates the uncertainty (or precision model) of properties. Uncertainty is generally represented as a covariance matrix for errors between estimated and observed properties. These uncertainties are assumed to arise from imperfections in the process model as well as errors in the observation process. Restricting processing to a region of interest (ROI) can greatly reduce the computational load for image analysis. The predicted position of a target determines the position of the ROI at which the target should be found. The predicted size of the target, combined with the uncertainties of the size and position, can be used to estimate the appropriate size for the ROI. In the tracking literature, this ROI is part of the "validation gate", and is used to determine the acceptable values for properties.

Observation is provided by the observation and grouping modules described above. Processing is specific for each target. A call to a module applies a specified observation procedure for a target at a specified ROI in order to verify the presence of the target and to update its properties. When the detection confidence is large, grouping the resulting pixels provides the information to update the target properties. The estimation process combines (or fuses) the observed properties with the previously estimated properties for each target. If the average detection confidence is low, the confidence in the existence of a target is reduced, and the predicted values are taken as the estimates for the next cycle. If the confidence of existence falls below a threshold, the target is removed from the target list.

The detection phase is used to trigger creation of new targets. In this phase, specified observation modules are executed within a specified list of "trigger" regions. Trigger regions can be specified dynamically, or recalled from a specified list. Target detection is inhibited whenever a target has been predicted to be present within a trigger region.

A simple zero-th order Kalman filter may be used to track bodies, faces, and hands in video sequences. In this model, target properties are represented by a "state vector"

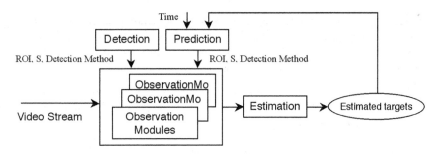

Fig. 12.5. Tracking is a cyclic process of four phases: Predict, Observe, Detect and Estimate. Observation is provided by the observation and grouping modules described above.

composed of position, spatial extent, and orientation $(x, y, \sigma_x, \sigma_y, \theta)$. A 5x5 covariance matrix is associated with this vector to represent correlations in errors between parameters. Although prediction does not change the estimated position, it does enlarge the uncertainties of the position and size of the expected target. The expected size provides bounds on the sample rate, as we limit the sample rate so that there are at least 8 pixels across an expected target.

12.3.3 A Supervisory Controller for Perceptual Processes

The supervisory component of a process provides four fundamental functions: command interpretation, execution scheduling, parameter regulation, and reflexive description. The supervisor acts as a programmable interpreter, receiving snippets of code script that determine the composition and nature of the process execution cycle and the manner in which the process reacts to events. The supervisor acts as a scheduler, invoking execution of modules in a synchronous manner. The supervisor regulates module parameters based on the execution results. Auto-critical reports from modules permit the supervisor to dynamically adapt processing. Finally, the supervisor responds to external queries with a description of the current state and capabilities. We formalize these abilities as the autonomic properties of auto-regulation, auto-description and auto-criticism.

A process is auto-regulated when processing is monitored and controlled so as to maintain a certain quality of service. For example, processing time and precision are two important state variables for a tracking process. These two may be traded off against each other. The process controllers may be instructed to give priority to either the processing rate or precision. The choice of priority is dictated by a more abstract supervisory controller.

An auto-critical process maintains an estimate of the confidence for its outputs. Such a confidence factor is an important feature for the control of processing. Associating a confidence factor to every observation allows a higher-level controller to detect and adapt to changing circumstances. When supervisor controllers are programmed to offer "services" to higher-level controllers, it can be very useful to include an estimate of the confidence of their ability to "play the role" required for the service. A higher-level controller can compare responses from several processes and determine the assignment of roles to processes.

An auto-descriptive controller can provide a symbolic description of its capabilities and state. The description of the capabilities includes both the basic command set of the controller and a set of services that the controller may provide to a more abstract supervisor. Such descriptions are useful for the dynamic composition of federations of controllers.

12.3.4 Classes of Perceptual Processes

We have identified several classes of perceptual processes. The most basic class is composed of processes that detect and track entities. Entities may generally be understood as spatially correlated sets of properties, corresponding to parts of physical objects. However, correlation may also be based on temporal location or other, more abstract, relations. From the perspective of the system, an entity is any association of correlated observable variables. Formally, an entity is a predicate function of one or more observable variables.

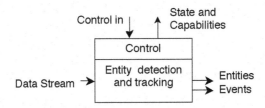

Fig. 12.6. Entities and their properties are detected and described by a special class of perceptual processes

Entities may be composed by entity detection and tracking processes, as shown in Figure 12.6. The input to an entity detection process is typically a stream of numeric or symbolic data. The output of the transformation is a stream including a symbolic token to identify the class of the entity, accompanied by a set of numerical or symbolic properties. These properties allow the system to define relations between entities. The detection or disappearance of an entity may, in some cases, also generate asynchronous symbolic signals that are used as events by other processes. A fundamental aspect of interpreting sensory observations is determining relations between entities. Relations can be formally defined as a predicate function of the properties of entities. Relations may be unary, binary, or N-ary. For example, Visible(Entity1), On(Entity1, Entity2), and Aligned(Entity1, Entity2, Entity3) are examples of relations.

Relations that are important for describing situations include 2D and 3D spatial relations, as well as temporal relations [8]. Other sorts of relations, such as acoustic relations (e.g. louder, sharper), photometric relations (e.g. brighter, greener), or even abstract geometric relations may also be defined. As with entity detection and tracking, we propose to observe relations using perceptual processes. Relation-observation processes are defined to transform a list of entities into a list of relations based on their properties, as shown by Figure 12.7. Relation observation processes read in a list of entities tracked by an entity detection and tracking process and produce a list of relations that are true along with the entity or entities that render them true. Relation observation uses tracking to predict and verify relations. Thus they can generate an asynchronous event when a new relation is detected or when a previously detected relation becomes false.

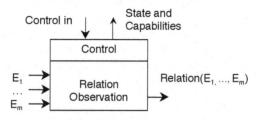

Fig. 12.7. Relations are predicates defined over one or more entities. Relation observation processes generate events when relations become true or false.

Composition processes assemble sets of entities into composite entities. Composition processes are similar to relation observation entities, in that they operate on a list of entities provided by an entity observation process. However, entity observation processes produce a list of composite objects satisfying a set of relations. They can also measure properties of the composite object. As with relation observation processes, composition processes can generate asynchronous events when a composite object is detected or lost.

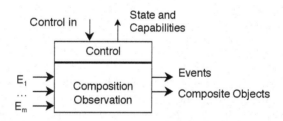

Fig. 12.8. Composition processes observe and track compositions of entities

12.3.5 Process Federations

Perceptual processes may be organized into software federations [116]. A federation is a collection of independent processes that cooperate to perform a task. We have designed a middleware environment that allows us to dynamically launch and connect processes on different machines. In our system, processes are launched and configured by a "meta-supervisor". The meta-supervisor configures a process by sending snippets of a control script to be interpreted by the controller. Each control script defines a command that can be executed by a message from the meta-supervisor. Processes may be interrogated by the meta-supervisor to determine their current state and the current set of commands.

Meta-supervisors can also launch and configure other meta-supervisors so that federations can be built up hierarchically. Each meta-supervisor invokes and controls lower level supervisors that perform the required transformation. At the lowest level are perceptual processes that observe and track entities and observe the relations between entities. These are grouped into federations as required for to observe the situations in a context.

As a simple example of a federation of perceptual processes, consider a system that detects when a human is in the field of view of a camera and tracks his hands and face. We say that observed regions can be selected to "play the role" of torso, hands and faces. We call this a FaceAndHand observer. The system uses an entity and detection tracking process that can use background difference subtraction and color modeling to detect and track blobs in an image stream. The set of tracked entities are sent to a composition process that labels likely blobs as a torso, face or a left or right hand.

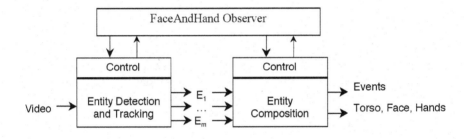

Fig. 12.9. A simple process federation composed of an entity detection process, a composition process and a meta-supervisor

The control for this process federation works as follows. The meta-supervisor begins by configuring the entity detection and tracking processes to detect a candidate for torso by looking for a blob of a certain size using background subtraction in a pre-configured "detection region". The acceptance test for torso requires a blob detected by background subtraction in the center region of the image, with a size within a certain range. Thus the system requires an entity detection process that includes an adaptive background subtraction detection.

When a region passes the torso test, the composition process notifies the meta-supervisor. The meta-supervisor then configures new trigger regions using color detection modules in the likely positions of the hands and face relative to the torso. The acceptance test for face requires a skin colored region of a certain range of sizes in the upper region of the torso. Hands are also detected by skin color blob detection over regions relative to the torso. Sets of skin colored regions are passed to the composition process so that the most likely regions can be assigned to each role. We say that the selected skin-colored regions are assigned the "roles" of face, left hand and right hand. The assignments are tracked so that a change in the entity playing the role of hand or face signals an event. Such role assignment is a simple example of a more general principle developed in the next section.

12.3.6 Context and Situation

Perceptual processes provide a means to detect and track compositions of entities and to verify relations between entities. The design problem is to determine which entities to detect and track and which relations to verify. For most human environments, there is a potentially infinite number of entities that could be detected and an infinite number of possible relations for any set of entities. The appropriate entities and relations must be determined with respect to a task or service to be provided. In this section we discuss the methods for specifying context models for human activity. We define the concept of a "role" and explain how roles can help simplify context models. We define three classes of events in such systems, and describe the system reaction to each class. We then present two examples of simple context models. An early version of the concepts discussed in this section was presented in [88]. This paper refines and clarifies many aspects of this framework in the light of experience with implementing systems based on this model.

12.3.7 Specifying a Context Model

A system exists in order to provide some set of services. Providing services requires the system to perform actions. The results of actions are formalized by defining the output "state" of the system. Simple examples of actions for interactive environments include adapting the ambient illumination and temperature in a room, or displaying a users "availability for interruption". More sophisticated examples of tasks include configuring an information display at a specific location and orientation, or providing information or communication services to a group of people working on a common task.

The "state" of an environment is defined as a conjunction of predicates. The environment must act so as to render and maintain each of these predicates to be true. Environmental predicates may be functions of information observed in the environment, including the position, orientation and activity of people in the environment, as well as position, information and state of other equipment. The information required to maintain the environment state determines the requirements of the perception system.

The first step in building a context model is to specify the desired system behavior. For an interactive environment, this corresponds to the environmental states, defined in terms of the variables to be controlled by the environment, and predicates that should be maintained as true. For each state, the designer then lists a set of possible situations, where each situation is a configuration of entities and relations to be observed. Although a system state may correspond to many situations, each situation must uniquely belong to one state. Situations form a network, where the arcs correspond to changes in the relations between the entities that define the situation. Arcs define events that must be detected to observe the environment.

In real examples, we have noticed that there is a natural tendency for designers to include entities and relations that are not really relevant to the system task. Thus it is important to define the situations in terms of a minimal set of relations to prevent an explosion in the complexity of the system. This is best obtained by first specifying the system output state, then for each state specifying the situations, and for each situation specifying the entities and relations. Finally for each entity and relation, we determine the configuration of perceptual processes that may be used.

12.3.8 Simplifying Context Models with Roles

The concept of role is an important (but subtle) tool for simplifying the network of situations. It is common to discover a collection of situations for an output state that have the same configuration of relations, but where the identity of one or more entities is varied. A role serves as a "variable" for the entities to which the relations are applied, thus allowing an equivalent set of situations to have the same representation. A role is played by an entity that can pass an acceptance test for the role. In that case, it is said that the entity can play or adopt the role for that situation.

In our framework, the relations that define a situation are defined with respect to roles, and applied to entities that pass the test for the relevant roles. For example, in a group discussion, at any instant, one person plays the role of the speaker while the other persons play the role of listeners. Dynamically assigning a person to the role of speaker allows a video communication system to transmit the image of the current speaker at each instant. Detecting a change in roles allows the system to reconfigure the transmitted image. Entities and roles are not bijective sets. One or more entities may play a role. A role may be played by one or several entities. The assignment of entities to roles may (and often will) change dynamically. Such changes provide the basis for an important class of events : role-events. Role events signal a change in assignment of an entity to a role, rather than a change in situation. Roles and relations allow us to specify a context model as a kind of "script" for activity in an environment. However, unlike theater, the script for a context is not necessarily linear. Context scripts are networks of situations where a change in situations is determined based on relations between roles.

12.3.9 Context and Situation

To summarize, a context is a composition of situations that concerns a set of roles and relations. A context determines the configuration of processes necessary to detect and observe the entities that can play the roles and the relations between roles that must be observed. The roles and relations should be limited to the minimal set required for recognizing the situations necessary for the environmental task. All of the situations in a context are observed by the same federation.

$$Context \rightarrow \{Role_1, Role_2, ..., Role_n; Relation_1, ..., Relation_m\}$$

A situation is a kind of state, defined by a conjunction of relations. Relations are predicate functions evaluated over the properties of the entities that have been assigned to roles. A change in the assignment of an entity to a role does not change the situation, unless a relation changes in value.

Entities are assigned to roles by role assignment processes. The context model specifies which roles are to be assigned and launches the necessary role assignment processes. A meta-supervisor determines what kind of entities can play each role, and launches processes to detect and observe these entities. A description of each detected entity is returned to the role assignment process where it is subjected to the acceptance test to determine its suitability for the role based on type, properties, and confidence factor. The most suitable entity (or entities) is (are) assigned to the roles. Relations are then evaluated, and the set of relations determines the situation.

The situation is a set of relations computed on the entities assigned to roles. Situation changes when the relations between entities change. If the assignment of entities to situations changes, the situation remains the same. However, the system may need to act in response to a change in role assignment. For example, if the person playing the role of speaker changes, then a video communication system may need to change the camera view to center on the new speaker.

12.3.10 Classes of Events

From the above, we can distinguish three classes of events: Role Events, Relation events and Context events.

Role events signal a change in the assignment of entities to roles. Such a Role event may result in a change in the system output state and thus requires that the system acts so as to bring the state back to the desired state. For example, the change in speaker (above) renders a predicate Camera-Aimed-At(Speaker) false, requiring the system to selected the appropriate camera and orient it to the new speaker. Situation events or (relation events) signal changes in relations that cause a change in situation. If the person playing the role of speaker stops talking and begins writing on a blackboard, then the situation has changed. Context events signal changes in context, and usually require a reconfiguration of the perceptual processes.

Role events and Situation-Events are data driven. The system is able to interpret and respond to them using the context model. They do not require a change in the federation of perceptual processes. Context events may be driven by data, or by some external system command .

12.3.11 Simple Example: An Interuptibility Meter

As first simple example, consider a system whose task is to display the level of "interruptibility" of a user in his office environment. Such a system may be used to automatically illuminate a colored light at the door of the office, or it may be used in the context of a collaborative tool such as a media-space [87]. The set of output actions is very simple. The environment should display one of a set of interruptibility states. For example, states could be "Not in Office", "Ok for Interruptions", "Urgent Interrupts Only" and "Do not Disturb".

Suppose that the user has decided that his four interruptibility states depend on the following eight situations, labeled S_1 to S_8: (S_1) The user is not in office when the user is not present. He is interruptible when (S_2) alone in his office or (S_3) not working on the computer or (S_4) talking on the phone. He may receive urgent interruptions when (S_5) working at his computer, or when (S_6) visitors are standing in the office. The user should not be interrupted (S_7) when on the phone, or (S_8) when the visitors are sitting in his office.

The roles for these situations are <User>, <Visitor>, <Computer>, <Phone>. The <User> role may be played by a human who meets an acceptance test. This test could be based on an RFID badge, a face recognition system, a spoken password, or a password typed into a computer. A <Visitor> is any person in the office who has not met the test for <User>. A person is a class of entity that is detected and tracked by a person observation process. For example, this can be a simple visual tracker based on subtraction from an adaptive background.

The predicate "Present(User)" would be true whenever a person observed to be in the office has been identified as the <User>. The fact that entities are tracked means that the person need only be identified once. Evaluating the current situation requires applying a logical test for each person. These tests can be applied when persons enter the office, rather then at each cycle.

Situation S_1 would be true if no person being tracked in the office passes the test for user. Situation S_2 also requires a predicate to know if a person is playing the role of visitor. States S_4 and S_7 require assigning an entity to the role <Phone>. This can be done in naïve manner by assigning regions of a certain color or texture at a certain location. However, if we wish to include cellular phones we would need more sophisticated vision processes for the role assignment. For assigning an object to the role of <Computer> a simple method would be to consider a computer as a box of a certain color at a fixed location. The <User> could then be considered to be using the computer if a face belonging to his torso is in a certain position and orientation. Facing would normally require estimating the position and orientation of a person's face. The test would be true if the orientation of the position of the face was within a certain distance of the computer and the orientation of the face were opposite the computer screen. Again, such tests could be arbitrarily sophisticated, arbitrarily discriminant and arbitrarily costly to develop. Situations S_6 and S_8 require tests for persons to be sitting and standing. These can be simple and naïve or sophisticated and expensive depending on how the system is to be used.

12.3.12 Second Example: A Video-Based Collaborative Work Environment

As a second example, consider a video-based collaborative work environment. Two or more users are connected via high bandwidth video and audio channels. Each user is seated at a desk and equipped with a microphone, a video communication monitor and an augmented work surface. Each user's face and eyes are observed by a steerable pan-tilt-zoom camera. A second steerable camera is mounted on the video display and maintains a well-framed image of the user's face. The augmented workspace is a white surface, observed by a third video camera mounted overhead.

The system task is to transmit the most relevant image of the user. If the user is facing the display screen, then the system will transmit a centered image of the users face. If the user faces his drawing surface, the system will transmit an image of the drawing surface. If the user is facing neither the screen nor the drawing surface then the system will transmit a wide-angle image of the user within the office. This can be formalized as controlling two functions: transmit(video-stream) and center(camera, target). For each function, there is a predicate that is true when the actual value corresponds to the specified value.

The roles that compose the context are:

1. the user,
2. the display screen,
3. a writing surface.

The user is a composite entity composed of a torso, face and hands.

The system's task is to determine one of three possible views of the user: a well-centered image of the user's face, the user's workspace, and an image of the user and his environment. Input data include the microphone signal strength, and a coarse resolution estimation of the user's face orientation. The system context includes the roles "speaker" and "listener". At each instant, all users are evaluated by a meta-supervisor to determine assignment to one of the roles "speaker" and "listener". The meta-supervisor assigns one of the users to the role speaker based on recent energy level of his microphone. Other users are assigned the role of listener. All listeners receive the output image of the speaker. The speaker receives the mosaic of output images of the listeners.

The user may place his attention on the video display, or the drawing surface or "off into space". This attention is manifested by the orientation of his face, as measured by positions of his eyes relative to the center of gravity of his face (eye-gaze direction is not required). When the user focuses attention on the video display, his output image is the well-framed image of his face. When a user focuses attention on the work surface, his output image is his work-surface. When the user looks off "into space", the output image is a wide-angle view of the user's environment. This system uses a simple model of the user's context completed by the system's context to provide the users with the appropriate video display. Because the system adapts its display based on the situation of the group of users, the system, itself, fades from the user's awareness.

12.4 Conclusions

A context is a network of situations concerning a set of roles and relations. Roles are services or functions relative to a task. Roles may be "played" by one or more entities. A relation is a predicate defined over the properties of entities. A situation is a configuration of relations between entities.

This ontology provides the basis for a software architecture for the perceptual components of context aware systems. Observations are provided by perceptual processes defined by a tracking process or transformation controlled by a reflexive supervisor. Perceptual processes are invoked and organized into hierarchical federations by reflexive meta-supervisors. A model of the user's context makes it possible for a system to provide services with little or no intervention from the user.

Acknowledgment

This work has been partly supported by the EC project IST FAME project (IST-2000-28323) and IST CAVIAR (IST 2001-37540) as well as French national project RNTL/ProAct CONTACT. This work has been performed in active collaboration with Joelle Coutaz, Gaetan Rey, Patrick Reignier, Dave Snowdon, Jean-Luc Meunier and Alban Caporossi.

13

Hierarchies Relating Topology and Geometry

Walter G. Kropatsch[1], Yll Haxhimusa[1], and Pascal Lienhardt[2]

[1] Pattern Recognition and Image Processing Group 183/2,
   Institute for Computer Aided Automation, Vienna University of Technology, Austria
   {krw,yll}@prip.tuwien.ac.at
[2] SIC, FRE CNRS 2731 University of Poitiers, France
   lienhardt@sic.sp2mi.univ-poitiers.fr

Abstract. Cognitive Vision has to represent, reason and learn about objects in its environment it has to manipulate and react to. There are deformable objects like humans which cannot be described easily in simple geometric terms. In many cases they are composed of several pieces forming a "structured subset" of $\mathbb{R}^n$ or $\mathbb{Z}^n$. We introduce the potential topological representations for structured objects: plane graphs, combinatorial and generalized maps. They capture abstract spatial relations derived from geometry and enable reconstructions through attributing the relations by e.g. coordinates. In addition they offer the possibility to combine both topology and geometry in a hierarchical framework: irregular pyramids. The basic operations to construct these hierarchies are edge contraction and edge removal. We show preliminary results in using them to hold a whole set of segmentations of an image that enable reasoning and planning actions at various levels of detail down to a single pixel in a homogeneous way. We further speculate that the higher levels map the inherent structure of objects and can be used to integrate (and "learn") the specific object properties over time by up-projecting individual measurements. The construction of the hierarchies follows the philosophy to reduce the data amount at each higher level of the hierarchy by a reduction factor > 1 while preserving important topological properties like connectivity and inclusion.

13.1 Introduction

Handling "structured geometric objects" is important for many applications related to Geometric Modeling, Computational Geometry, Image Analysis, etc.; one has often to distinguish between different parts of an object, according to properties which are relevant for the application (e.g. mechanical, photometric, geometric properties). For instance for geological modeling, the sub-ground is made of different layers, maybe split by faults, so layers are sets of (maybe not connected) geological blocks. For image analysis, a region is a (structured) set of pixels or voxels, or more generally a (structured) set of lower-level regions. At the lowest level, such an object is a subdivision[3], i.e. a partition of the object into cells of dimensions 0, 1, 2, 3 ... (i.e. vertices, edges, faces, volumes ...).

---

[3] For instance, a Voronoi diagram in the plane defines a subdivision of the plane

H.I. Christensen and H.-H. Nagel (Eds.): Cognitive Vision Systems, LNCS 3948, pp. 199–220, 2006.
© Springer-Verlag Berlin Heidelberg 2006

The structure, or the topology, of the object is related to the decomposition of the object into sub-objects, and to the relations between these sub-objects: basically, topological information is related to the cells and their adjacency or incidence relations. Other information (embedding information) are associated to these sub-objects, and describe for instance their shapes (e.g. a point, resp. a curve, a part of a surface, is associated with each vertex, resp. each edge, each face), their textures or colors, or other information depending on the application.

Many topological models have been conceived for representing the topology of subdivided objects, since different types of subdivisions have to be handled: general complexes [67, 83, 115, 490] or particular manifolds [14, 32, 489], subdivided into any cells [160, 101] or into regular ones (e.g. simplices, cubes, etc.) [123, 337]. Few models are defined for any dimensions [36, 382, 53, 254]. Some of them are (extensions of) incidence graphs or adjacency graphs. So, their principle is often simple, but:

- they cannot deal with any subdivision without loss of information, since it is not possible to describe the relations between two cells precisely if they are incident in several locations;
- operations for handling such graphs are often complex, since they have to handle simultaneously different cells of different dimensions.

Other structures are "ordered" [53, 254, 115], and they do not have the drawbacks of incidence or adjacency graphs. A comparison between some of these structures is presented in [253]. A subdivided object can be described at different levels: for instance a building is subdivided into floors, each floor is subdivided into wings, each wing is subdivided into rooms, etc. So several works deal with hierarchical topological models and topological pyramids [94, 36, 233]. For geometric modeling, levels are often not numerous. For image analysis, more levels are needed since the goal is to rise up information which is not known a priori (cf. below).

Since a geometric object is represented by a topological structure and its embedding in a geometric space we distinguish: (i) topological operations which modify the structure; (ii) embedding operations which modify the embedding; and (iii) geometric operations which modify both topology and embedding. For instance for animation of articulated objects, the object structure is not modified: so it can be performed by applying embedding operations. A main interest is the fact that local operations can be easily defined and performed, for instance chamfering, contraction, removal, extrusion, split, etc. It is important for instance in order to simultaneously apply local operations in parallel when an image is analyzed.

Moreover, topological features can be computed from the topological structure (e.g. orientability for pseudo-manifolds, genus for surfaces, homology groups which provide information about the "holes" in the object for any dimension, etc.). Such information can be used in order to control the (construction of the) object. For instance when simplifying an image (for constructing a pyramid for instance), one often wants to keep some properties invariant, as connectedness, etc. When an object is made of many parts, one need some tools in order to check it. Topology and shape (as curvature, etc.) are complementary, and it is very useful to compute both types of information.

13.1.1 Visual Abstraction

Recognition, manipulation and representation of visual objects can be simplified significantly by "abstraction". By definition abstraction extracts essential features and properties while it neglects unnecessary details. Two types of unnecessary details can be distinguished:

- redundancies and
- data of minor importance.

Details may not be necessary in different contexts and under different objectives which reflect in different types of abstraction. In general, three different types of abstraction are distinguished:

isolating abstraction: important aspects of one or more objects are extracted from their original context.

generalizing abstraction: typical properties of a collection of objects are emphasized and summarized.

idealizing abstraction: data are classified into a (finite) set of ideal models, with parameters approximating the data and with (symbolic) names/notions determining their semantic meaning.

These three types of abstraction have strong associations with well known tasks in computer vision: recognition and object detection tries to **isolate** the object from the background; perceptual grouping needs a high degree of **generalization**; and classification assigns data to **"ideal"** classes disregarding noise and measurement inaccuracies.

In all three cases abstraction drops certain data items which are considered less relevant. Hence the **importance** of the data needs to be computed to decide which items to drop during abstraction. The importance or the relevance of an entity of a (discrete) description must be evaluated with respect to the purpose or the goal of processing. The system may also change its focus according to changing goals after knowing certain facts about the actual environment, other aspects that were not relevant at the first glance may gain importance. Representational schemes must be flexible enough to accommodate such attentional shifts in the objectives.

13.1.2 Overview

The paper is organized as follows. A short introduction to regular and irregular (graph) pyramid is summarized in Sec. 13.2. In Sec. 13.3 we discuss closing the representation gap, and introduce a novel method based on extended region adjacency graph hierarchy. The method to build a hierarchy of partitions is given in Sec. 13.4. We discuss in detail the question of preserving the topology and the robustness of a graph pyramid in Sec. 13.5. In Sec. 13.6 optimal graph contraction of homogeneous regions leads to a concept of top-down construction of an "optimal" hierarchy. The conclusion summarizes the main results and gives an outlook of future research issues.

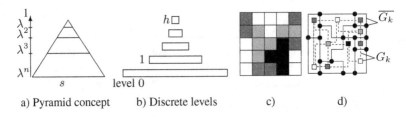

a) Pyramid concept   b) Discrete levels   c)   d)

Fig. 13.1. (a,b) Multiresolution pyramid, (c) Partition of pixel set into cells, (d) Representation of the cells and their neighborhood relations by a dual pair $(G_k, \overline{G_k})$

13.2 Pyramids

In this section we summarize the concepts developed for building and using a multiresolution pyramid [209, 237] and put the existing approaches into a general framework. The focus of the presentation is the representational framework, its components and the processes that transfer data within the framework.

A pyramid (Fig. 13.1a,b) describes the contents of an image at multiple levels of resolution. The base level is a high resolution input image. Many processes on regular pyramids [233] have a parallel computational complexity that depends on the number of levels of the pyramid. The number of levels of a regular pyramid is determined by a constant **reduction factor** [209, 379]. It is 4 for a pyramid with levels of $2^i \times 2^i, 2^{i-1} \times 2^{i-1}, \ldots, 2^0 \times 2^0$ pixels.

Generally, successive levels reduce the size of the data by a constant reduction factor $\lambda > 1.0$ while local **reduction windows** relate one cell at the reduced level with a set of cells in the level directly below. Thus local independent (and parallel) processes propagate information up and down in the pyramid. The contents of a lower resolution cell is computed by means of a **reduction function** the input of which are the descriptions of the cells in the reduction window. Sometimes the description of the lower resolution needs to be extrapolated to the higher resolution. This function is called the **refinement** or **expansion function**. It is used in Laplacian pyramids [63] and wavelets [277] to identify redundant information in the higher resolution and to reconstruct the original data. The number of levels n is limited by the reduction factor λ: $n \leq \log(image\_size)/\log(\lambda)$. The main computational advantage of image pyramids is due to this logarithmic complexity. The reduction window and the reduction factor relate two successive levels of a pyramid. In order to interpret a derived description at a higher level this description should be related to the original input data in the base of the pyramid. This can be done by means of the **receptive field** (RF) of a given pyramidal cell c_i: $RF(c_i)$ collects all cells (pixels) in the base level of which c_i is the ancestor. This is the base of several pyramidal approaches, one of which is chosen as representative: irregular graph pyramids.

13.2.1 Irregular Pyramid

In irregular pyramids, each level represents an arbitrary partition of the pixel set into cells, i.e. connected subsets of pixels. The construction of an irregular pyramid is **iteratively**

local [297, 178]: **i)** the cells have no information about their global position, **ii)** the cells are connected only to (direct) neighbors, and **iii)** the cells cannot distinguish the spatial positions of the neighbors.

This means that we use only local properties to build the hierarchy of the pyramid. On the base level (level 0) of an irregular image pyramid the cells represent single pixels and the neighborhood of the cells is defined by the connectivity of the pixels. A cell on level $k + 1$ (parent) is a union of neighboring cells on level k (children). This union is controlled by so called **contraction kernels** (decimation parameters [233]). Every parent computes its values independently of other cells on the same level. This implies that an image pyramid is built in $O[log(image\_diameter)]$ parallel steps. Neighborhoods on level $k + 1$ are derived from neighborhoods on level k. Two cells c_1 and c_2 are neighbors if the base level contains pixels p_1 in c_1 and p_2 in c_2 such that p_1 and p_2 are neighbors (Fig. 13.1c). In the base level (level 0) pixels are the vertices and two vertices are related by an edge if the two corresponding pixels are neighbors. On each level $k + 1$ ($k \geq 0$) there exists at least one cell not contained in level k. In particular, there exists a highest level h. In general the top of the pyramid can have one vertex, i.e. an apex.

A graph pyramid is a pyramid where each level is a graph $G(V, E)$ consisting of vertices V and of edges E relating two vertices. In order to correctly represent the embedding of the graph in the image plane [150] we additionally store the dual graph $\overline{G}(\overline{V}, \overline{E})$ at each level. We represent the levels as **dual pairs** $(G_k, \overline{G_k})$ of plane graphs G_k and $\overline{G_k}$ (Fig. 13.1d). The vertices of G_k represent the cells and the edges of G_k represent the neighborhood relations of the cells on level k, depicted with square vertices and dashed edges in Figure 13.1d. This graph is also called the **region adjacency graph**. The edges of $\overline{G_k}$ represent the borders of the cells on level k, depicted with solid lines in Figure 13.1d, possibly including so called pseudo edges needed to represent the neighborhood relation to a cell completely surrounded by another cell. Finally, the vertices of $\overline{G_k}$, the circles in Figure 13.1d, represent meeting points of at least three edges from G_k, solid lines in Figure 13.1d. Let us denote the original graph as the **primal graph**. The sequence $(G_k, \overline{G_k})$, $0 \leq k \leq h$ is called (dual) **graph pyramid** (Figure 13.1b). Moreover the graph is attributed, $G(V, E, attr_v, attr_e)$, where $attr_v : V \rightarrow \mathbb{R}^+$ and $attr_e : E \rightarrow \mathbb{R}^+$, i.e. content of the graph is stored in attributes attached to both vertices and edges. Initially only the attributes of the vertices receive the gray values of the pixels. In Sec. 13.4.2 we use a weight for $attr_e$ measuring the difference between the two end points.

13.2.2 Dual Graph Contraction

In general a graph pyramid can be generated bottom-up as in Alg. 1. The complete formalism of **dual graph contraction** is described by Kropatsch et al. [237]. Let us explain it here by means of our image example (Fig. 13.1c).

Algorithm 1 – Constructing Graph Pyramid

Input: Graphs $(G_0, \overline{G_0})$
   1: $k := 0$.
   2: **while** further abstraction is possible **do**

3:     determine contraction kernels, $N_{k,k+1}$.
4:     perform dual graph contraction and simplification of dual graph, $(G_{k+1}, \overline{G_{k+1}}) = C[(G_k, \overline{G_k}), N_{k,k+1}]$.
5:     apply reduction functions to compute content $attr : G_{k+1} \to \mathbb{R}^+$ of new reduced level.
6:     $k := k + 1$.
Output: Graph pyramid $- (G_k, \overline{G_k}), 0 \le k \le h$.

The 3rd step determines what information in the current top level is important and what can be dropped. A contraction kernel is a (small) sub-tree which is chosen to survive (rooted trees in Fig. 13.2b). Fig. 13.2a shows the window and Fig. 13.2b the selected contraction kernels $N_{0,1}$. Selection criteria in this case contract only edges inside connected components having the same gray value.

All the edges of the contraction kernels are dually contracted during step 4. Dual contraction of an edge e (formally denoted by $G/\{e\}$) consists of contracting e and removing the corresponding dual edge $\bar{e}$ from the dual graph (formally denoted by $\overline{G} \setminus \{\bar{e}\}$). In our example the graph G_1 shown in Fig. 13.2c is created. This preserves duality and the dual graph needs not be constructed from the contracted primal graph G' at the next level. Since the contraction of an edge may yield multi-edges and self-loops there is a second phase of step 4 which removes all redundant multi-edges and self-loops (edges $S_{0,1}$ in Fig. 13.2d). Note that not all such edges can be removed without destroying the topology of the graph: if the cycle formed by the multi-edge or the self-loop surrounds another part of the data its removal would corrupt the connectivity! Fortunately this can be decided locally by the dual graph since **faces of degree two** (having the double-edge as boundary) and **faces of degree one** (boundary = self-loop) of a connected graph cannot contain any further elements in its interior. Since removal and contraction are dual operations, the removal of a self-loop or a double edge can be done by contracting the corresponding dual edges in the dual graph, which are not depicted in our example for the simplicity of figures. The dual contraction of our example graph G_0 remains a simple graph G_1 without self-loops and multi-edges. Step 4 generates a reduced pair of dual graphs. Their contents is derived in step 5 from the level below using the reduction

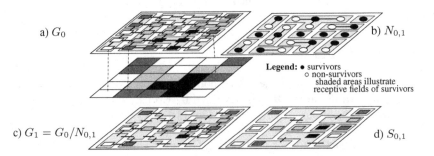

a) G_0

b) $N_{0,1}$

Legend: ● survivors
○ non-survivors
shaded areas illustrate
receptive fields of survivors

c) $G_1 = G_0/N_{0,1}$

d) $S_{0,1}$

Fig. 13.2. a) Neighborhood graph G_0, b) Contraction kernel $N_{0,1}$, c) Edge contraction $G_0/N_{0,1}$ and d) Redundant edges $S_{0,1}$

function. In our example reduction is very simple: the surviving vertex inherits the color of its son. The result of the dual contraction is also a graph, which can be used to generate another level. The procedure is repeated up to the highest possible abstraction.

There are lots of useful properties of the resulting graph pyramids. If the plane graph is transformed into a combinatorial map the transcribed operations form the combinatorial pyramid [57, 56]. This framework allowed us to prove several of the above mentioned properties and link dual graph pyramids with topological maps which extend the scope to three dimensions. The following table summarizes dual graph contraction in terms of the control parameters used for abstraction and the conditions to preserve topology:

level	representation	contract / remove	conditions
0	$(G_0, \overline{G_0})$		
	$\downarrow$	contraction kernel $N_{0,1}$	forest, depth 1
	$(G_0/N_{0,1}, \overline{G_0} \setminus \overline{N_{0,1}})$		
	$\downarrow$	redundant edges $S_{0,1}$	$\deg \overline{v} \leq 2$
1	$(G_1 = G_0/N_{0,1} \setminus S_{0,1},$ $\overline{G_1} = \overline{G_0} \setminus \overline{N_{0,1}/S_{0,1}})$		
	$\downarrow$	contraction kernel $N_{1,2}$	forest, depth 1
	$\vdots$		

13.3 The Representation Gap

The authors in [220, 423] (see, too, Chapter 8) asked the following question referring to several research issues: "How do we bridge the representational gap between image features and coarse model features?" They identify the one-to-one correspondence between salient image features (pixels, edges, corners,...) and salient model features (generalized cylinders, polyhedrons, invariant models,...) as **limiting assumption** that makes prototypical or generic object recognition impossible. They suggested to bridge and not to eliminate the representational gap, as it is done in the computer vision community for quite long, and to focus efforts on: **(i) region segmentation, (ii) perceptual grouping, and (iii) image abstraction.** Let us take these goals as a guideline to consider multiresolution representations under the special viewpoint of segmentation and grouping. In [236] the multiresolution representation was considered under the abstraction viewpoint.

Wertheimer [491] has formulated the importance of wholes (Ganzen) and not of its individual elements and introduced the importance of perceptual grouping and organization in visual perception. Regions as aggregations of primitive pixels play an extremely important role in nearly every image analysis task. Their internal properties (color, texture, shape, ...) help to identify them and their external relations (adjacency, inclusion, similarity of properties) are used to build groups of regions having a particular meaning in a more abstract context. The union of regions forming the group is again a region with both internal and external properties and relations.

Low-level cue image segmentation cannot and should not produce a complete final "good" segmentation, because there is no general "good" segmentation. Without prior knowledge, segmentation based on low-level cues will not be able to extract semantics in

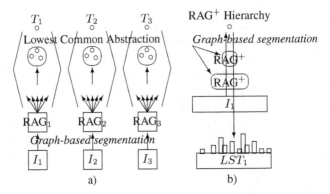

Fig. 13.3. a) The lowest common abstraction of a set of input exemplars [220] (see, too, Figure 8.2), and b) RAG+ hierarchy

generic images. The segmentation process results in "homogeneity" regions w.r.t the low-level cues using some similarity measures. Problems emerge because (i) homogeneity of low-level cues will not map to the semantics [220] and (ii) the degree of homogeneity of a region is in general quantified by threshold(s) for a given measure [138]. The low-level coherence of brightness, color, texture or motion attributes should be used to come up sequentially with hierarchical partitions [418]. Mid and high level knowledge can be used then to either confirm these groups or select some further attention. A wide range of computational vision problems could make use of segmented images, were such segmentation rely on efficient computation, e.g., motion estimation requires an appropriate region of support for finding correspondence. Higher-level problems such as recognition and image indexing can also make use of segmentation results in the problem of matching.

It is important that a grouping method has following properties [119]: (i) capture perceptually important groupings or regions, which reflect global aspects of the image, (ii) be highly efficient, running in time linear in the number of image pixels, and (iii) creates hierarchical partitions [418].

Authors in [220, 423] (see, too, Chapter 8) give a method how to bridge the representation gap. After the initial segmentation by an algorithm proposed in [119], they build the space of all possible region adjacency graphs formed by any sequence of merges of adjacent regions and form a lattice (Fig. 13.3a). Clearly the size of the lattice is exponential in the number of regions obtained after the initial segmentation. They define a *common abstraction* as a set of vertices (one per lattice) such that for any two vertices, their corresponding graphs are isomorphic. This allows them to define *the lowest common abstraction* (LCA) as the common abstraction whose underlying graph has maximal size. They were looking for a vertex (i.e. a region) that is common in input exemplar's lattice and that retains the maximum amount of structure common to exemplars. But in order to cope with the exponential size of lattices, they restrict the search for LCA to the intersection of lattices. The algorithm for finding the intersection of lattices is given in [220].

We propose an extended region adjacent graph ($RAG+$) hierarchy (Fig. 13.3b) to achieve partitioning of the image by using a minimum weight spanning tree (MST) in order to find region borders quickly and effortlessly in a bottom-up "stimulus-driven" approach based on local differences in a specific feature. A $RAG+$ is a RAG enhanced by non-redundant self loops or parallel edges. Rather than trying to have just one "good" segmentation the method produces a stack of (dual) graphs (a graph pyramid), which down-projected on the base level will give a multi-level segmentation, i.e. the labeled spanning tree (LST). The MST of an image is built by combining the advantage of regular pyramids (logarithmic tapering) with the advantages of irregular graph pyramids (their purely local construction and shift invariance). The aim is reached by using the selection method for contraction kernels proposed in [178] to achieve logarithmic tapering, local construction and shift invariance. Borůvka's minimum spanning tree algorithm [49] with dual graph contraction algorithm [233] builds in a hierarchical way a MST (of the region) preserving the proper topology. The topological relation seems to play an even more important role for vision tasks in natural systems than precise geometrical position.

13.4 A Hierarchy of Partitions

Hierarchies are a significant tool for image partitioning as they are naturally combined with homogeneity criteria. Horowitz and Pavlidis [196] define consistent homogeneity criteria over a set V as a boolean predicate P over its parts $\Phi(V)$ that verifies the consistency property: $\forall(x, y) \in \Phi(V) \quad x \subset y \Rightarrow (P(y) \Rightarrow P(x))$. In image analysis this states that the subregions of a homogeneous region are also homogeneous. It follows that if Pyr is a hierarchy and P a consistent homogeneity criterion on V then the set of maximal elements of Pyr that satisfy P defines a unique partition of V. Thus the combined use of a hierarchy and homogeneity criteria allows to define a partition in a natural way.

The goal is to find partitions of connected components $P_k = \{CC_1, CC_2, ..., CC_n\}$ such that these elements satisfy certain properties. We use the pairwise comparison of neighboring vertices, i.e. partitions to check for similarities [119, 126, 161]. A pairwise comparison function, $Comp(CC_i, CC_j)$ is true, if there is evidence for a boundary between CC_i and CC_j, and false when there is no boundary. Note that $Comp(CC_i, CC_j)$ is a boolean comparison function for pairs of partitions. The definition of $Comp(CC_i, CC_j)$ depends on the application.

The pairwise comparison function $Comp(\cdot, \cdot)$ measures the difference along the boundary of two components relative to the differences of the component's internal differences. This definition tries to encapsulate the intuitive notion of contrast: a contrasted zone is a region containing two components whose inner differences (**internal contrast**) are less then differences between them (**external contrast**). We define an **external contrast** between two components and an **internal contrast** of each component. These measures are defined in [119, 126, 161], analogously.

Every vertex $u \in G_k$ is a representative of a connected component $CC(u)$ of the partition P_k. The equivalent contraction kernel [233] of a vertex $u \in G_k$, $N_{0,k}(u)$ is a set of edges on the base level that are contracted, i.e. applying $N_{0,k}(u)$ on the base level contracts the subgraph $G' \subseteq G$ onto the vertex u. The **internal contrast** of the

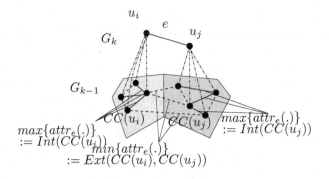

Fig. 13.4. Internal and external contrast

$CC(u) \in P_k$ is the **largest dissimilarity** inside the component $CC(u)$, i.e. the largest edge weight of the $N_{0,k}(u)$ of vertex $u \in G_k$,

$$Int(CC(u)) = max\{attr_e(e), e \in N_{0,k}(u)\}. \tag{13.1}$$

Let $u_i, u_j \in V_k, u_i \neq u_j$ be the end vertices of an edge $e \in E_k$. The **external contrast** between two components $CC(u_i), CC(u_j) \in P_k$ is the **smallest dissimilarity** between component $CC(u_i)$ and $CC(u_j)$, i.e. the smallest edge weight connecting $N_{0,k}(u_i)$ and $N_{0,k}(u_j)$ of vertices $u_i, u_j \in G_k$:

$$Ext(CC(u_i), CC(u_j)) = min\{attr_e(e), e = (v, w) : v \in N_{0,k}(u_i) \wedge w \in N_{0,k}(u_j)\}. \tag{13.2}$$

This definition is problematic since it uses only the "smallest" edge weight between the two components, making the method very sensitive to noise. But in practice this limitation works well as shown in Sec. 13.4.2. In Fig. 13.4 an example of $Int(\cdot)$ and $Ext(\cdot, \cdot)$ is given. The $Int(CC(u_i))$ of the component $CC(u_i)$ is the $maximum$ of weights of the solid edges (analogously for $Int(CC(u_j))$), whereas $Ext(CC(u_i), CC(u_j))$ is the $minimum$ of weights of the dashed edges connecting component $CC(u_i)$ and $CC(u_j)$. Vertices u_i and u_j are representative of the components $CC(u_i)$ and $CC(u_j)$. By contracting the edges $N_{0,k}(u_i)$ (see solid edges in Fig. 13.1c) one arrives to the vertex u_i, analogously $N_{0,k}(u_j)$ for u_j.

The pairwise comparison function $Comp(\cdot, \cdot)$ between two connected components $CC(u_i)$ and $CC(u_j)$ can now be defined as:

$$Comp(CC(u_i), CC(u_j)) = \begin{cases} \text{True} & \text{if} \\ \quad Ext(CC(u_i), CC(u_j)) > PInt(CC(u_i), CC(u_j)), \\ \text{False} & \text{otherwise,} \end{cases} \tag{13.3}$$

where the minimum internal contrast difference between two components, $PInt(\cdot, \cdot)$, reduces the influence of too small components and is defined as:

$$PInt(CC(u_i), CC(u_j)) =$$
$$min\{Int(CC(u_i)) + \tau(CC(u_i)), Int(CC(u_j)) + \tau(CC(u_j))\} \tag{13.4}$$

For the function $Comp(CC(u_i), CC(u_j))$ to be true, i.e. for the border to exist, the external contrast difference must be greater than the internal contrast differences. The reason for using a threshold function $\tau(CC(\cdot))$ is that for small components $CC(\cdot)$, $Int(CC(\cdot))$ is not a good estimate of the local characteristics of the data, in extreme case when $|CC(\cdot)| = 1$, $Int(CC(\cdot)) = 0$. Any non-negative function of a single component $CC(\cdot)$, can be used for $\tau(CC(\cdot))$. Choosing criteria other than minimum and maximum will lead to an NP-complete algorithm [119].

13.4.1 Building a Hierarchy of Partitions

The algorithm to build the hierarchy of partitions is shown in Alg. 2. Each vertex $u_i \in G_k$ defines a **connected region** $CC(u_i)$ on the base level of the pyramid, and since the presented algorithm is based on Borůvka's algorithm [49] it builds a $MST(u_i)$ of each region, i.e. $N_{0,k}(u_i) = MST(u_i)$ [179].

Algorithm 2 – Hierarchy of Partitions

Input: Attributed graph G_0.

1: $k := 0$
2: **repeat**
3:    **for all** vertices $u \in G_k$ **do**
4:        $E_{min}(u) := argmin\{attr_e(e) \mid e = (u, v) \in E_k \text{ or } e = (v, u) \in E_k\}$
5:    **for all** $e = (u_i, u_j) \in E_{min}$ with
       $Ext(CC(u_i), CC(u_j)) \leq PInt(CC(u_i), CC(u_j))$ **do**
6:        include e in contraction edges $N_{k,k+1}$
7:    contract graph G_k with contraction kernels, $N_{k,k+1}$: $G_{k+1} = C[G_k, N_{k,k+1}]$.
8:    **for all** $e_{k+1} \in G_{k+1}$ **do**
9:        set edge attributes $attr_e(e_{k+1}) := min\{attr_e(e_k) \mid e_{k+1} = C(e_k, N_{k,k+1})\}$
10:   $k := k + 1$
11: **until** $G_k = G_{k-1}$

Output: A region adjacency graph (RAG) pyramid.

The idea is to collect the smallest weighted edges e (4th step) that could be part of the MST, and then to check if the edge weight $attr_e(e)$ is smaller than the internal contrast of both of the components (MST of end vertices of e) (5th step). If these conditions are fulfilled then these two components are merged (7th step). Two regions will be merged if their internal contrast is larger than the external contrast, represented by the weight $attr_e(e)$ of the connecting edge. All the edges to be contracted form the contraction kernels $N_{k,k+1}$, which are then used to create the graph $G_{k+1} = C[G_k, N_{k,k+1}]$ [237]. In general $N_{k,k+1}$ is a forest. We update the attributes of those edges $e_{k+1} \in G_{k+1}$ with the minimum attribute of the edges $e_k \in E_k$ that are contracted into e_{k+1} ($9^t h$ step). The output of the algorithm is a pyramid where each level represents a RAG, i.e a partition. Each vertex of these $RAGs$ is the representative of a MST of a region in the image. The algorithm is greedy since it collects only the nearest neighbor with the minimum edge weights and merges them if the pairwise comparison (Eq. 13.3) evaluates to "false". Some properties of the algorithm are given in [180].

13.4.2 Experiments on Image Graphs

The base level of our experiments is the trivial partition, where each pixel is a homogeneous region. The attributes of edges are defined as the difference of its end point vertices. The attributes of edges can be defined as the difference between features of end vertices, $attr_e(u_i, u_j) := |F(u_i) - F(u_j)|$, where F is some feature. Other attributes could be used as well e.g. [418] $attr_e(u_i, u_j) := exp\{\frac{-||F(u_i)-F(u_j)||_2^2}{\sigma_I}\}$, where F is some feature, and σ_I is a parameter, which controls the scale of proximity measures of F. F could be defined as $F(u_i) := I(u_i)$, for gray value intensity images, or $F(u_i) := [v_i, v_i \cdot s_i \cdot \sin(h_i), v_i \cdot s_i \cdot \cos(h_i)]$, for color images in HSV color distance [418]. However the choice of the definition of the weights and the features to be used is in general a hard problem, since the grouping cues could conflict each other [276].

For our experiments we use, as attributes of edges, the difference between pixel intensities $F(u_i) := I(u_i)$, i.e. $attr_e(u_i, u_j) := |I(u_i) - I(u_j)|$. For color images we run the algorithm by computing the distances (weights) in RGB color space. We choose this simple color distances in order to study the properties of the algorithm. To compute the hierarchy of partitions we define $\tau(CC)$ to be a function of the size of CC, for example $\tau(CC) := \alpha/|CC|$, where $|CC|$ is the size of the component CC and α is a constant. The algorithm has one running parameter α, which is used to compute the function τ. A larger constant α sets the preference for larger components. More complex definition of $\tau(CC)$, which is large for certain shapes and small otherwise would produce a partitioning which prefers certain shapes. To speed up the computation, vertices are attributed ($attr_v$) with the internal differences, average color and the size of the region it represents. Each of these attributes is computed for each level of the hierarchy. Note that the height of the pyramid depends only on the image content.

We use indoor and outdoor RGB images. We found that $\alpha := 300$ produces the best hierarchy of partitions for the images *Monarch*[4], *Object*45 and *Object*11[5] shown in Fig. 13.5(I,III,IV) and $\alpha := 1000$ for the image in Fig. 13.5(II), after the average intensity attribute of vertices is down-projected onto the base grid. Fig. 13.5 show some of the partitions on different levels of a pyramid and the number of components. Note that in all images there are regions of large variability of intensity and gradient. This algorithm copes with this kind of variability of intensity and gradient and is capable of grouping perceptually important regions despite of large variability of intensity and gradient. In contrast to [119] the result is a hierarchy of partitions at multiple resolutions suitable for further goal driven, domain specific analysis. On lower levels of the pyramid the image is over-segmented whereas in higher levels it is under-segmented. Since the algorithm preserves details in low-variability regions, a noisy pixel would survive through the hierarchy, see Figure 13.5(Id). Image smoothing in low variability regions would overcome this problem. We do not smooth the images, as this would introduce another parameter into the method. The robustness of topology is discussed in Sec. 13.5.3.

The hierarchy of partitions can also be built from an over-segmented image to overcome the problem of noisy pixels. Note that the influence of τ in the decision criterion is smaller as the region gets bigger for a constant α. The constant α is used to produce a

---

[4] Waterloo image database
[5] Coil 100 image database

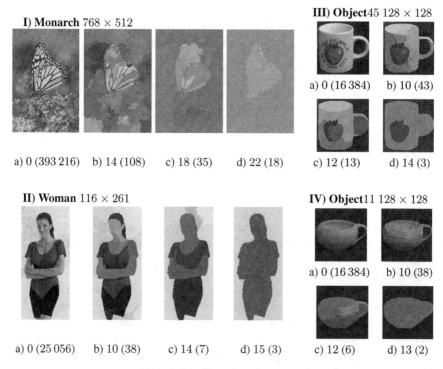

Legend: *Level (number of partitions)*

Fig. 13.5. Partitioning of images

kind of the over-segmented image and the influence of τ decays after each level of the pyramid. For an over-segmented image, where the size of regions is large, the algorithm becomes parameterless.

13.5 Preserving Topology

Objects mapped into images remain connected if they are not occluded by other objects nor disturbed by noise. Neither the projection nor the discretization separate the two corresponding adjacent regions in the image. A similar property holds for the adjacency of objects. Hence the **connectivity** and the **adjacency** of **regions** and of **boundary segments** is a very important property which should not be lost by abstraction. Several authors studied operations that allow the modification of the data structure, e.g. its reduction, while the topological properties of the represented objects and their background is preserved, e.g., [231, 316, 39, 234, 99, 61].

13.5.1 Preserving Topology in 2D

Table 13.1 summarizes the necessary primitive operations: The Euler number characterizes the topology of a description given in terms of points (P), lines (L) and faces (F). Since we aim at preserving its value the sum of the changes (Δ) must be zero:

Table 13.1. Topology Preserving Operations in 2D

	Points	Lines	Faces	Config.	PRE-CONDITION	CCL
Euler	P	$-L$	$+F$		$= const.$	
Incr.	ΔP	$-\Delta L$	$+\Delta F$		$= 0$	Euler
Contract(l, p_0)	-1	-1	0	(p_1, l, p_0)	$p_1 \neq p_0$	same label
Remove(l, f_0)	0	-1	-1	(f_x, l, f_0)	$f_x \neq f_0$	$\deg(f_0) \leq 2$
Any Incr.	$(-a$	$-b$	$-c)$		$b = a + c;$	
by a contr.	$(-1$	$-1)$		$\times a$		
by c remov.		$(-1$	$-1)$	$\times c$		

$$\Delta P - \Delta L + \Delta F = 0.$$

First we observe the changes introduced by **contracting an edge** l bounded by the two points p_0, p_1. This eliminates one of the points (i.e. p_0) and the edge l, hence it does not change the Euler characteristic. The only pre-condition is to avoid contracting a self-loop.

If we **remove an edge** l, the number of points remains the same, but two faces f_0, f_x are merged into one (f_x). That reduces the number of faces by one. If we would have the same face on both sides of the edge, i.e. $f_x = f_0$, the edge would be a bridge in G the removal of which would disconnect G. If one of the end points of l would have degree 1, the removal of its only connection to the remaining structure would isolate it. Both cases are excluded from removal by the pre-condition $f_x \neq f_0$. The second pre-condition $\deg(f_0) \leq 2$ identifies a redundant self-loop or a redundant multi-edge: in the later case f_0 is bounded by two parallel edges connecting the same end-points. This configuration is simplified in the second phase of dual graph contraction.

What about other operations? It is clear that the elimination of an edge must be accompanied by the removal of either a point or a face to preserve the Euler number. So we cannot have less elements involved in a topology preserving modification. But we can also show the following:

Contraction and removal are the ONLY operations needed to reduce the structure while preserving the topology. Any other topology-preserving operation can be achieved by appropriate combinations of contraction and removals. If we want to remove a number a of points and a number c of faces we have to remove also a number $b = a + c$ of edges to preserve the Euler number. This can be achieved by a contractions and c removals.

Pre-conditions for individual operations can be extended to sets of operations to allow a different order of execution or even parallelism: The requirement for contraction kernel to form a FOREST is such an extension. If the edges of a cycle would be contracted the last one need to be a self-loop which cannot be contracted. Hence sets of edges to be contracted must be acyclic.

13.5.2 What Remains After Repetitions?

We can repeat contracting edges the end point of which carry the same label and remove all unnecessary self-loops and multi-edges until no further contraction nor removal is possible. Note that a very similar strategy is used to create the border map in [37, 36] and the topological map in [92]. At convergence we have the following conditions:

1. All edges (p_1, l, p_2) with different end points have different labels: $lab(p_1) \neq lab(p_2)$.
2. A surviving self-loop (p, l, p) separates two different faces, (f_1, l, f_2) and the inner face has degree $\deg(f_1) > 2$. Since any tree of the dual graph would have been eliminated by the rule $\deg(f_1) \leq 2$ starting from the leafs up to the root, there must be a cycle $C \in \overline{G}$ and inside this cycle there exists a point $p_3 \in C : lab(p_3) \neq lab(p)$.
3. All faces have three or more sides: $\deg(f) \geq 3$.
4. **Pseudo or fictive edges** are self-loops ($p_0 = p_1$) which cannot be contracted in the primal graph and which separate two faces with $\deg(f_0) > 2$ and $\deg(f_1) > 2$. Such edges were first observed in [238] as an artifact of topology preserving contraction. They connect the boundary of a hole to the surrounding "main land". Holes can be equivalently represented by an inclusion tree as in [92].
5. Fictive edges appear arbitrarily placed and depend only on the order of contractions and removals. Similar observations can be found in the topological 3D-map [92] where fictive edges appear as the last ones before disconnecting a face or a boundary during the merging of faces and lines (for the process of successive region merging see [36, 37]).
6. For each hole there remains exactly one fictive edge (as indicated by the Betti number [132]).
7. Fictive edges are not delineated between two regions as all other edges. Hence they can be continuously deformed and their end points can be moved along the boundary as long as the edge remains fully embedded inside f. Other fictive edges are not excluded from being traversed by the end point! We conjecture that an arrangement of fictive edges can be transformed into any other legal arrangement of fictive edges. Algorithms for continuous deformation [380] or [134] may find a new application for re-arranging fictive edges.

13.5.3 Robustness of Graph Pyramids

There are several places in the construction of a graph pyramid where noise can affect the result:

1. the input data;
2. during selection of contraction kernels;
3. when summarizing the content of a reduction window by the reduction function.

The effects on the topology can be the following:

- a connected region falls into parts;
- two regions merge into one;
- break inclusion, create new inclusions;
- two adjacent regions become separated;
- two separated regions become adjacent.

All these changes reflect in the Euler number which we will use to judge the topological robustness of graph pyramids.

Let us start with the influence of a wrong pixel on the connectivity structure. A wrong pixel adjacent to a region can corrupt its connectivity (and the property of inclusion in $2D$) if it falls on a one pixel wide branch of the figure. The consequence can be that the region breaks into two parts which increases the Euler number by 1. A noise pixel inside a region creates a new connected component which is a topological change (e.g. a new inclusion) but it can be easily recognized and eliminated by its size. However the change is again not very drastic since one noise pixel can change the Euler number only by 1. If all regions of the picture both foreground and background are at least 2 pixels wide a single wrong pixel changes its size but not its connectivity.

For a branch of two pixels in width, two noise pixels in a particular spatial position relative to each other are needed to modify the topology. More generally to break the connectivity across an n-pixel wide branch of a region noise pixels are needed, forming a connected path from one side of the branch to the other. This can be considered as the consequence of the sampling theorem (see [228, 436]). All these topological modifications happen in the base of our pyramid. As long as we use topology-preserving constructions and/or consider identified noise pixels as non-survivors the topology is not changed in higher levels.

Different criteria and functions can be used for selecting contraction kernels and reduction, respectively. In contrast to data noise, errors are introduced by the specific operations and may be the consequence of numerical instabilities or quantization errors. There is no general property allowing to derive an overall property like robustness of all possible selection or reduction functions. Hence operational robustness needs to be checked for any particular choice.

13.6 Optimal Graph Contraction of Homogeneous Region

The reduction factor (see Sec. 13.2) determines the number of cells by which the reduced level shrinks after each reduction. The reduction factor can alternatively be expressed by the **diameter** L of the graph on base level. The diameter of a connected set of cells is defined as follows: Let $\text{dist}(u, v)$ denote the length of the shortest path between two cells u and v in terms of steps between nodes. Then the diameter is the maximum of all $\text{dist}(u, v)$ among all different pairs of cells u, v. If 4-connectivity is used, the image diameter of a rectangular $n \times m$ array is $n + m$. A reduction factor λ typically reduces the size of the array to $(n \times m)/\lambda = n/\sqrt{\lambda} \times m/\sqrt{\lambda}$ with a diameter of $L = (n + m)/\sqrt{\lambda}$.

Graph pyramids have a greater flexibility in allowing certain parts to shrink faster than others. Some subparts may even keep their size waiting for their surroundings to provide the necessary information to continue shrinking. Therefore it is not evident that graph pyramids have a similar computational complexity as regular image pyramids. Reduction in graph pyramids is a contraction process which is controlled by contraction kernels. Contraction kernels are subtrees of the graph that contract into a single vertex of the next higher pyramid level. Several successive contractions can be combined into a single contraction controlled by an equivalent contraction kernel (ECK)[235] which is a **tree spanning the receptive field** of the surviving vertex. This property allows us not only to achieve faster contraction rates by larger contraction kernels, but also to decompose large contraction kernels into smaller ones in a globally efficient way if no external constraint imposes a specific decomposition. This is the key idea for the present section. In images we often see large homogeneous regions without any specific substructure. These regions need to be shrunk into a single vertex of the region adjacency graph. In such cases it is important to summarize the properties of the large region in a small number of steps. In terms of graph contraction we search for a **decomposition of a tree** spanning the connected region into a number of local contraction kernels which can shrink the large region in a few parallel contraction steps into a single vertex. For this purpose each contraction kernel should form a maximal independent vertex set (MIS) like stochastic pyramids in [297]. The kernels span the whole region and consist of roots and leaves only, and roots are not allowed to be adjacent. This splits the problem into two:

1. Find a minimum spanning tree τ of the region.
2. Decompose τ into a minimal number of local MIS spanning forests, which contract the region by a few successive steps.

The first problem can be solved by several classical algorithms [49, 240, 357, 179]. For the second problem we propose the following algorithm called Recursive Decomposition of a Tree (RDT) [239] which aims at an efficient decomposition of a given tree τ (Alg. 3). This recursive decomposition actually stops after $\log(L)$ steps since the maximum diameter at iteration k is $L/2^k$.

Algorithm 3 – Recursive Decomposition of a Tree

Input: Tree τ.
1: Determine the diameter L and the "center" of τ ($center(tree)$).
2: Decompose tree τ into subtrees τ_i with diameter not greater than $L/2$.
3: Recurse steps 1 and 2 on the subtrees τ_i until their diameters $\tau_i \leq 2$ for all subtrees.
Output: Decomposed tree τ.

Algorithm 4 – Center of a Tree

Input: Tree $T(V, E)$
1: {Determine vertex degree:}
2: $\forall v \in V$ set $deg(v) := 0$.
3: $\forall t = (v, w) \in T \ deg(v) := deg(v) + 1$ and $deg(w) := deg(w) + 1$.
4: {Initialization of propagation front:}
5: $queue := \emptyset$.
6: **for all** $v \in V$ with $deg(v) := 1$ **do**
7:     $distance(v) := 0$.
8:     $append(v, queue)$.
9: **for all** $t = (v, w) \in T$ **do** {orient edges towards the center}
10:     **if** $deg(v) = 1$ **then**
11:         $father(v) := w$.

12:     **else if** $deg(w) = 1$ **then**
13:         $father(w) := v$.
14:     $append(v, queue)$.
15: **while** $|queue| > 1$ **do**
16:     $v := first(queue)$. {removes v from $queue$}
17:     $w := father(v)$.
18:     **if** $deg(w) = 1$ **then**
19:         $remove(w, queue)$.
20:     **else if** $deg(w) = 2$ **then**
21:         $dist(w) := dist(v) + 1$ and $deg(w) := 1$.
22:         $append(w, queue)$.
23:     **else**
24:         $decr(deg(w))$. {terminate shorter path at branchings e.g. if degree > 2}
25:     **for all** $t = (v, w) \in T$ **do** {orient edges towards the center}
26:         **if** $deg(v) = 1$ **then**
27:             $father(v) := w$.
28:         **else if** $deg(w) = 1$ **then**
29:             $father(w) := v$.
Output: Center of the tree, $L = dist(center)$ is the diameter.

The diameter of a (sub-)graph directly relates to the optimal height h of the pyramid, if contraction kernels are restricted to depth one: $h = \log(L)$. Hence, the optimal height of the pyramid is known in advance. From an apex of the pyramid with optimal height we can make down projection of the apex to the base level in optimal time. The RDT algorithm presented allows for contraction kernels of depth one and also higher depth, which enables us to construct pyramids of any height $h \geq 2$.

13.6.1 Building the Structure

Given a (non-rooted) tree $T = (V, E)$ we search for the longest path between any leafs of the tree. The center of the tree is located in the middle of the longest path. The following algorithm starts at the tree's leafs and proceeds towards the inside of the tree in a way similar to the well known distance transforms for binary shapes. Progression at branchings is held back until the longest path reaches the branching. This is the only difference to a distance transform. The algorithm finding the center is presented in Alg. 4. The output of the algorithm $Center(T(V, E))$ is the center (either a vertex or an edge) and the length of the longest path. This suffices for our purpose. However the longest path(s) can be determined by following the computed distances from the center by increments of -1 to the leafs.

13.6.2 Subdivide Diameter and Graph Pyramid with Optimal Height

Our strategy is to split the trees recursively into a forest with trees which have at most half the diameter of the original tree. Having determined the longest path through the tree and the center, we find edges of the tree the removal of which creates subtrees with the desired

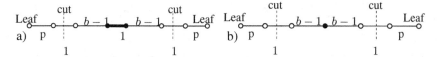

Fig. 13.6. The center is an edge a), and a vertex b)

property. Each of the subtrees becomes a single vertex when the respective subtrees are contracted. The vertices are connected with the center in the same manner as the subtrees were connected with each other by the removed edges. This is the configuration below the apex of the pyramid. Hence a single local contraction can produce the apex: It must be a tree with one root, the center becomes the apex, and a number of leafs connected with the root by edges. In order to determine where to cut the tree into subtrees, consider the subtrees that the longest path must traverse, like the examples in Figures 13.6. It will certainly cross the central subtree because it contains the center vertex. But there will also be two peripheral subtrees which intersect the longest path. Splitting the tree at edges having a given distance b from the center creates a central subtree which has diameter $2b - 2$ (or $2b - 1$ if the center falls on an edge). This is true not only for the longest path but for all paths between leaves newly created by the removed edges.

Next let us have a look at the diameter of the peripheral subtrees that are traversed by the longest path. Let p denote the length of the part of the diameter inside such a subtree. Note, that both peripheral parts must have the same length, we get the following relation for the total path length:

$$L = 2b + 2p \text{ (case: center is a vertex)} \tag{13.5}$$

$$L = 2b + 2p + 1 \text{ (case: center is an edge)} \tag{13.6}$$

Note further, that the peripheral subtree may have a diameter longer than p after cutting. In fact it can happen that two paths of the same length reach the vertex where the subtree has been split. The concatenation of these two equally long paths also connects two leaves. Consequently the diameter can be $2p$. Fortunately the diameter cannot be longer than this length otherwise we could construct another path through the original tree which is longer than our constructed diameter L. Requiring that the maximal possible diameter of the peripheral subtree after subdivision is equal to the diameter of the central subtree we can derive the distance of the cut edge from the center.

center is a vertex		center is an edge	
$2p$ =	$2b - 2$	$2p$ =	$2b - 1$
L =	$4b - 1$	L =	$4b$
$b - 1 = \lfloor (L-2)/4 \rfloor$		$b - 1 = \lfloor L/4 \rfloor - 1$	

$$\tag{13.7}$$

The resulting Algorithm 5 computes an optimal decomposition of a given tree. A particular decomposition by RDT is shown in Figure 13.7.

Algorithm 5 – Optimal Decomposition

Input: Tree τ.

1: Walk out from the center of the tree τ in $b-1$ steps in all directions.
2: Cut the tree τ at the edge b from the center.
3: Recursively decompose the central and all peripheral subtrees until trees have depth less than two.

Output: Optimally decomposed tree τ.

13.6.3 Experiments and Results

In [178, 177] contraction kernels are selected stochastically. In this section, they are constructed in a deterministic way using a recursive decomposition of τ into subtrees, contraction kernels of depth one are built.

Table 13.2 compares the height h of pyramids constructed by the RDT algorithm with three stochastic methods: MIS (maximal independent vertex set) [297], $MIES$ (maximal independent edge set) [178] and $MIDES$ (maximal independent directed edge set) [177]. Each method was tested with 100 randomized graphs with about 4000 nodes and 27700 edges which were generated by stochastic contraction of a given graph. The following values are compared: The minimum height $min(h)$ of the pyramids, the maximum height $max(h)$, the average height $\overline{h}$, and the variance $\sigma(h)$. All 100 pyramids constructed with RDT have a lower height than that of the competitors. In our experiments, the number of levels of the graph pyramid is always less or equal to $Log(Diameter)$ of the base level of a pyramid. For the same input graph the RDT algorithm gives us always the same graph pyramid which enables exact comparisons of successive runs on one set of input data.

Table 13.2. Comparison of the pyramids' height h

Algorithm	$min(h)$	$max(h)$	$\overline{h}$	$\sigma(h)$
Stochastic with MIS	9	20	12.39	2.4367
Stochastic with MIES	10	11	10.26	0.4408
Stochastic with MIDES	8	11	8.73	0.6172
Deterministic with RDT	7	8	7.94	0.0119

13.7 Conclusion and Outlook

In this paper we surveyed the construction and use of irregular pyramids which are hierarchies built on top of a geometrically well defined set of measurements, i.e. the pixels of a digital image. The higher levels of the hierarchy are derived by locally contracting groups of measurements belonging together depending on model dependent selection criteria while, at the same time, certain topological properties like adjacency and inclusion are preserved. This bottom-up pyramid construction derives gradually the scene topology and has the potential to bridge the representation gap. It can produce a

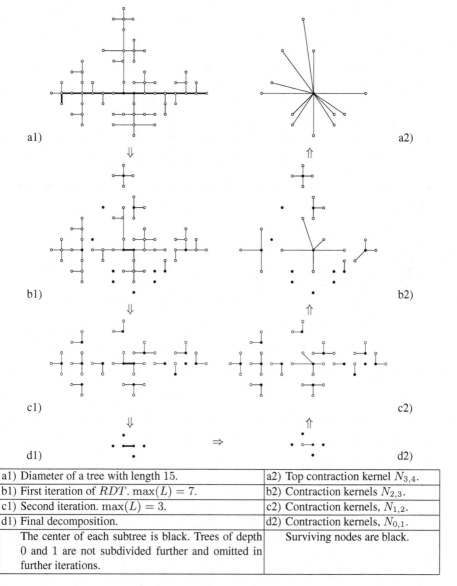

a1) Diameter of a tree with length 15.	a2) Top contraction kernel $N_{3,4}$.
b1) First iteration of RDT. $\max(L) = 7$.	b2) Contraction kernels $N_{2,3}$.
c1) Second iteration. $\max(L) = 3$.	c2) Contraction kernels, $N_{1,2}$.
d1) Final decomposition.	d2) Contraction kernels, $N_{0,1}$.
The center of each subtree is black. Trees of depth 0 and 1 are not subdivided further and omitted in further iterations.	Surviving nodes are black.

Fig. 13.7. Decomposition of the minimum spanning tree

hierarchy of partitions the ordered segments of which allow a higher level process to group, manipulate and modify objects at a high level of abstraction. Different topological data structures are needed depending on the dimension of the embedding space

- $2D$: planar graphs, combinatorial maps,
- $3D$: combinatorial maps, generalized maps,
- nD: generalized maps.

There are many ways to further develop the simple top-down decomposition strategy:

1. for finding the structure of a given shape:
   - using topology (recursively subdivide diameter),
   - using medial axis (geometrical shape),
   - using contrast (hierarchical segmentation).
2. for finding consistent structure of several aligned instances.

Variants of this strategy offer a great potential in context of learning cognitively meaningful entities and structures. E.g. in combining NON-aligned instances, identifying shapes by tracking, up-project data onto a common upper structure, assuming the higher levels do not change (in $3D$). As fields of applications we envision representations for articulated objects (e.g. person, hands), where the intrinsic $3D$ structure does not change at higher levels.

Acknowledgment

This paper has been supported by the Austrian Science Found under grants P14445-MAT, P14662-INF, and FSP-S9103-N04.

14

Cognitive Vision: Integrating Symbolic Qualitative Representations with Computer Vision

A.G. Cohn, D.C. Hogg, B. Bennett, V. Devin, A. Galata, D.R. Magee, C. Needham, and P. Santos

School of Computing, University of Leeds, LS2 9JT, UK
{agc|dch}@comp.leeds.ac.uk

Abstract. We describe the challenge of combining continuous computer vision techniques and qualitative, symbolic methods to achieve a system capable of *cognitive vision*. Key to a truly cognitive system, is the ability to learn: to be able to build and use models constructed autonomously from sensory input. In this paper we overview a number of steps we have taken along the route to the construction of such a system, and discuss some remaining challenges.

14.1 Introduction

To build an autonomous cognitive agent is a very challenging goal. Crucial to the ultimate attainment of this aim is an ability to perceive, understand, formulate hypotheses and act based on the agent's perceptions. In this paper we describe progress towards this challenge. This can be viewed as an update on our previous report [77].

A key focus of our work is to integrate quantitative and qualitative modes of representation; in particular we aim to exploit quantitative visual processing for tracking and motion analysis, and qualitative spatio-temporal representations to abstract away from unnecessary details, error and uncertainty. We use commonsense knowledge of the world as constraints on interpretations. Fundamental to our approach is our aim to learn as much as possible of any domain specific models required to understand and operate in a specific situation.

In the earliest days of AI, Computer Vision research already attempted to combine continuous and symbolic techniques; however during the last three decades Computer Vision and symbolic AI have grown apart. Each has made substantial progress, for example the former in the area of computing 3D Geometry from multiple views and model based tracking, and the latter in areas such as knowledge representation (e.g. work on qualitative spatial reasoning [76]), and learning [58, 79]. We follow Takeo Kanade's belief expressed in his IJCAI'03 Keynote Lecture that the time has now come to be able to combine pattern recognition in continuous feature spaces with relational models and reasoning.

Whereas it is clear that visual data is certainly acquired quantitatively, by forming qualitative models, we aim to abstract away from unnecessary details, noise, error and

H.I. Christensen and H.-H. Nagel (Eds.): Cognitive Vision Systems, LNCS 3948, pp. 221–246, 2006.
© Springer-Verlag Berlin Heidelberg 2006

uncertainty that are omnipresent in the visual domain. We view qualitative and quantitative representations as complementary; neither is sufficient on its own, but each is able to contribute to the overall system, as suggested by Forbus et al. [131]. At the quantitative level we are able to reason about low level features on texture vectors to form clusters of concepts by a fine grained analysis based on metric information. At the symbolic, qualitative level, we propose to exploit easily expressed, domain independent, commonsense knowledge as constraints on interpretations of the symbols formed from the low level clusters. Thus this research contributes to the *symbol grounding* issue [173], by showing how symbols can be formed and reasoned with, but remaining anchored directly to sensor inputs.

While it may be reasonable to impart some domain independent knowledge explicitly, ideally, an autonomous cognitive agent will acquire as much as possible of its models in an unsupervised manner. Moreover, it must be able to do this with real, noisy data. The work described later in this chapter will take up this challenge.

The structure of the rest of this chapter is as follows. Section 14.2 overviews a system which learned traffic behaviours using qualitative spatial relationships among close objects travelling along 'typical paths' (these paths being also learned) [122]; in later work we induced the set of qualitative spatial relationships rather than taking these as given a priori [139]. In section 14.3 we report on how it is possible to reason symbolically, using commonsense knowledge of continuity of physical objects, in order to refine ambiguous classifications from a statistical classifier [35]. Finally, in section 14.4, we describe ongoing work whose aim is to learn symbolic descriptions of intentional behaviours such as those found in simple table top games involving dice or cards, using *Inductive Logic Programming* [274]; we cluster sensor data to form symbols, and also indicate how overclustering can be handled at the symbolic level by forming equivalence classes [389].

14.2 Learning Traffic Behaviour Models

In [122], we have shown how qualitative spatio-temporal models of events in traffic scenes (e.g. following, overtaking) can be learnt. Using an existing tracking program which generates labelled contours for objects in every frame, the view from a fixed camera is partitioned statistically into semantically relevant regions based on the paths followed by moving objects. The paths are indexed with temporal information so objects moving along the same path at different speeds can be distinguished. A notion of proximity based on the speed of the moving objects is used as an attentional mechanism. The qualitative spatial relationship between close objects is described at every frame. Event models describing the behaviour of pairs of moving objects can then be built, using statistical methods: at each frame, for every pair of proximal objects, their relationship is described using a pair of qualitative values taken from two qualitative spatial calculi – see Figure 14.1.

Complete histories are then formed from the sequence of such descriptions which are then filtered using the continuity constraints imposed by *conceptual neighbourhoods* [76], eliminating very short interactions, and are abstracted to ignore the temporal length

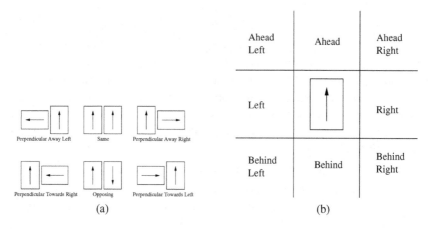

Fig. 14.1. A qualitative representation of relative orientation and direction of motion

during which each individual description holds. Each event type in the final event database thus comprises simply a sequence of qualitative spatial descriptions and can be readily transformed into a simple finite state machine to recognise the corresponding behaviour – see Figure 14.2 for example. The system has been tested on a traffic domain and learns various event models expressed in the qualitative calculus which represent human observable events, e.g. following and overtaking (see Figure 14.2 for a depiction of a simple overtaking event). The system can then be used to recognise subsequent selected event occurrences or unusual behaviours (i.e. inputs which do not correspond to the learned library of event types).

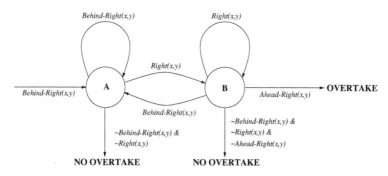

Fig. 14.2. A finite state machine generated to recognise a simple "overtaking" behaviour

In newer work [139], a data driven approach has been taken in order to automatically infer discrete and abstract representations (*symbols*) of primitive object interactions; this can be viewed as learning the basic qualitative spatial language, which was built-in to the earlier system [122]: we are able to learn a representation which maximises the discernability given a granularity (i.e. the number of relations desired). Figure 14.3 illustrates learnt primitive interaction patterns for the same traffic domain example application

[139]. These symbols are then used as an alphabet to infer the high level structure of typical interactive behaviour using variable length Markov models (VLMMs) [377, 163] (though we could also have used the event learning technique we used previously in [122]). The real time low level computer vision module [272] (which we describe in more detail below in section 14.3) detects and tracks moving objects within a scene and for each moving object extracts scene feature descriptors for its relative motion and spatial relationship to all moving objects that fall within its attentional window. These scene feature descriptors are invariant of the absolute position and direction of the interacting objects within a scene.

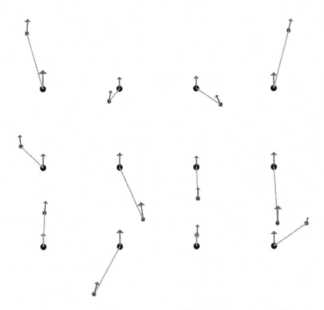

Fig. 14.3. Learnt primitive interaction patterns – traffic domain example. The two dots represent pairs of close vehicles (distinguished by the size of the dot). The arrows show their direction of movement and the connecting vector their relative orientation. These patterns represent typical "midpoints" as result of clustering the input data into n different conceptual "regions". Note how the 12 relations naturally cluster into virtually symmetric pairs, e.g. the middle two prototypes on the first line, which reflects the symmetry of the traffic domain.

14.3 Tracking and Classifying Objects

We assume that our domains of interest involve objects which move in space over time; thus the ability to track objects over time is critical. In this section we discuss an approach to this issue. However we do not wish to assume the existence of a ready made library of object models. At the lowest level therefore, our system relies on a tracker [272] which uses foreground, background and motion models. Each pixel is *explained* either as background, belonging to a foreground object, or as noise (c.f. [433]).

Calibrated ground-plane information can be used within the foreground model to strengthen object size and velocity consistency assumptions. Optionally, a learned model of direction and speed provides a prior estimate of object velocity, which is used to initialise object models. Our object models are based on position, size, colour, texture or other such features.

In brief, the process is as follows: blobs are tracked and features are extracted from a bounding box. Features (e.g. a colour histogram) are clustered in a learning phase to form a profile for each object from training data. These profiles can then be used to compute the *raw* likelihood of an object being one of these learned profiles.

However, in general, there is no certainty that the most likely hypothesis so computed will indeed be the correct object. Moreover, in the case of occlusion, the blob may in fact correspond to multiple objects. This is of course a classic computer vision problem. Our approach to this is to deliberately under-segment and then reason over space and time, applying commonsense notions of continuity to disambiguate the initial frame-by-frame low level classification hypotheses. In other words, we deliberately increase vagueness, by drawing bounding boxes sufficiently large to be sure that they enclose all spatially local objects (rather than risking cutting some in half), and then reason about box occupancy explicitly, relying on later (or possibly earlier) data in which the relevant objects are not occluding each other to provide more secure knowledge.

The lower level tracking and recognition systems explicitly model the possibility of ambiguity and error by assigning probabilities for the presence of objects within bounding boxes in each video frame. This output is passed to a reasoning engine which constructs a ranked set of possible models that are consistent with the requirements of object continuity. The final output is then a globally consistent spatio-temporal descrip-tion of the scene which is maximally supported by probabalistic information given by classifier.

A number of researchers have attempted to deal with object occlusion (and the resultant tracking problems) by attempting to track through occlusion. This involves reasoning about object ordering along the camera optical axis either using ground plane information [230, 203] or simply reasoning about relative spatial ordering [110]. Dy-namic models such as the Kalman filter are often used to model the position of occluded objects [370, 378], under the assumption of known dynamics (e.g. linear motion), when no visual information is available. Multiple cameras have also been used to bypass the occlusion problem [102], however this is not always possible or practicable.

Our approach to occlusion handling differs from this body of work and has more similarity with the methods of McKenna et al. [295] and Sherrah and Gong [417]. These works do not attempt to disambiguate occluding objects, but instead reason about the occlusion taking place. McKenna et al. track 'blobs' that may be groups or individuals. In their work it is initially assumed all objects are separate (an assumption we do not make); and when blobs merge the resultant blob is recorded as a 'group' made up of the contributing individuals. A dynamically updated model of global object colour is used to disambiguate objects at the point at which blobs split. This model is also used to reason about object occlusion within a group that makes up a single blob. This is useful when a split group consists of more than two individuals; however it relies on an assumption that no object is completely occluded during the split. Sherrah and Gong

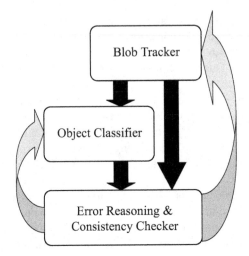

Fig. 14.4. An architecture for robust scene analysis

[417] present work in a highly constrained scenario where the head and hands of a single individual are tracked as blobs. The hands may occlude each other or the face (to form a single blob). A hand-built Bayesian network is used to perform frame-by-frame occlusion reasoning, based on available data (blob positions, velocities, number of blobs etc.). Perhaps the closest work to ours was presented recently by Yang et al. [501]. This system uses multiple cameras to provide a top view of the 'visual hull' of a crowd scene. Constraints on the number of pedestrians represented by each observed blob are determined according to the size of the blob's bounding box. These constraints are propagated from frame to frame to give an upper and lower limit on the number of objects present. All observed moving objects are assumed to be pedestrians, and no attempt is made to localise or identify individual pedestrians. Lipton et al. [261] present a system that uses simple object classification (pedestrian *vs.* car) to aid object tracking. Simple temporal consistency rules are used to prune transient objects resulting from noise. None of these systems performs more than frame-by-frame reasoning or allows for the possibility of error in the underlying low-level tracking and recognition algorithms. Our system performs long-term reasoning about object-blob associations over extended sequences of frames. By maintaining spatio-temporal consistency over sequences, many local imperfections and ambiguities in the low-level data are eliminated.

Our proposed architecture consists of three parts: i) the 'blob tracker' described above, ii) an object recognition/classification system, and iii) an error reasoning and consistency checking module. The relationship between these components is illustrated in Figure 14.4.

The grey arrows in Figure 14.4 represent the potential for feedback from the high-level reasoning system to the lower level modules. This feedback is not exploited in the system presented in this chapter; however this is an active area of research. In the rest of this section we summarise the error reasoning and consistency checking module, full details of which, along with further detail of the other two modules be found in [35].

The error reasoning and consistency checking module (Figure 14.4) is designed to reduce error and ambiguity in the output of the lower level modules by identifying a solution that both maximises statistical correlation with this output and is also globally consistent with respect to requirements of spatio-temporal continuity of objects.

Specifically, for a model to be physically possible, it must satisfy the following spatio-temporal constraints:

C1) *exclusivity* — an object cannot be in more than one place at the same time;

C2) *continuity* — an object's movement must be continuous (i.e. it cannot instantaneously 'jump' from one place to another).

In the output given by any statistical classifier, it is quite possible that an object is detected to a high degree of probability in two locations that are widely separated. This kind of error is fairly easy to eliminate on a frame by frame basis. We can consider all possible assignments of different objects to the tracked boxes in each frame and chose the combination that maximises the summed probabilities of object to box correspondences.[1]

The continuity of an object's position over time is much more difficult to model; and considerable problems arise in relating continuity constraints to tracker output. The main problem is that of occlusion: if an object moves behind another it is no longer detectable by the tracker; so, under a naive interpretation of the tracker and recognition system outputs, objects will appear to be discontinuous.

As well as ensuring spatio-temporal constraints are respected, we also want to find an object labelling which is maximally supported by the frame-by-frame tracker output and the probabilistic output of the object recogniser for each tracked box. However, a typical recognition system, such as the one we use, is trained to identify single objects, whereas in tracking a dynamic scene there will often be several objects in a box. This means that there is no completely principled way to interpret the output figures from the recogniser. Nevertheless, it seems reasonable to assume that although there is a large amount of error and uncertainty in the low-level output, it does give a significant indication of what objects may be present. We shall explain below how our system converts the low-level statistics into a metric of the likelihood of any given set of objects being in a box.

Local continuity information is provided by the low-level tracker module. The tracker output assigns to each blob's bounding box an identification tag (a number), which is maintained over successive frames. For newly split or merged boxes, new tags are assigned but the tag of their parent box in the previous frame is also recorded. Thus each box is associated with a set of *child* boxes in the next frame. Conversely each box can be associated with a set of its *parent* boxes in the previous frame. The parent/child relation determines a directed graph structure over the set of boxes, which we call a 'box continuity graph'. Such a graph is illustrated in Figure 14.5. Our algorithm depends on the structure of this graph, as we describe briefly below – see [35] for further details.

The continuity-based reasoning algorithm involves a somewhat complex restructuring of the available information, the details of which we omit here, but see [35].

---

[1] This assumes that the classifier is capable of identifying unique objects (such as particular people) rather than classes of similar objects. In situations where there may be multiple objects of the same class, the exclusivity constraint must be weakened.

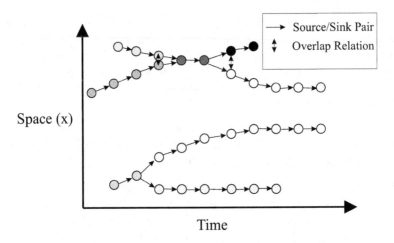

Fig. 14.5. Tracker output expressed as a 'box continuity' graph

14.3.1 Coarse Object Grouping with 'Envelopes'

Although the tracker output enables us to derive a graph representing temporal continuity between tracked boxes, this structure is only indirectly related to the trajectories of actual moving objects in the scene. There are several issues that complicate the relationship between tracker boxes and objects. Firstly, there is the basic problem caused by proximal and/or occluding objects, which means that a box may be occupied by several objects. This is compounded by the possibility that objects sometimes transfer between tracker boxes without themselves being independently tracked. This can occur because of occlusions among objects or because of limited resolution of the tracker (or a combination of the two). Hence, when a box containing more than one object is close to or overlaps another box, an object from the multiply occupied box can easily transfer to the neighbouring box without being detected.

A consideration of these problems led us to the idea that in order to get a more accurate identification of the locations and movements of closely grouped or occluding objects, we need to employ a representation in which the locations of objects are modelled at a coarser level than that of individual boxes. Hence, we introduced a higher level abstract data object that we call an *envelope*. The precise definition of these objects is quite complex, but is intuitively illustrated diagrammatically in Figure 14.6. The thicker lines indicate the positions of box boundaries over a sequence of frames. The dashed lines show the division of this structure into envelopes. See [35] for the precise definition of an envelope.

14.3.2 Enforcing Exclusivity and Continuity at the Envelope Level

Although envelopes give a coarser demarcation of object locations than do individual boxes, they provide a much more reliable basis for determining continuity. By definition, two different envelopes cannot spatially overlap (otherwise they would just be parts of a larger envelope). This means that there is an extremely low probability that an object

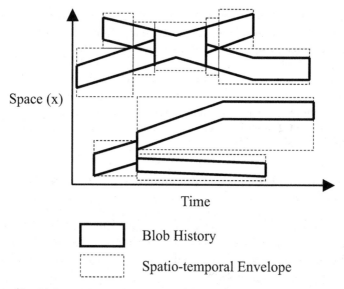

Fig. 14.6. Deriving spatio-temporal envelopes from tracker output

can transfer between envelopes without being detected. Hence, our algorithm makes the assumption that the occupancy of an envelope is constant throughout its existence.

The exclusivity constraint **C1**, corresponds to the requirement that no object can occupy two distinct spatio-temporal envelopes that overlap in time.

It will be seen in Figure 14.6 that the set of envelopes has a continuity graph structure similar to that of boxes. In fact an *envelope continuity graph* can be formed directly from the box continuity graph by collapsing all nodes derived from boxes in the same envelope into a single node, see Figure 14.7.

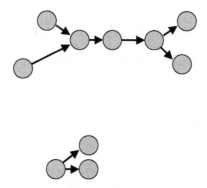

Fig. 14.7. Spatio-temporal envelopes form a directed graph

Because we allow objects to enter and leave the scene we also need to keep track of off-scene objects. We do this by introducing virtual, *off-scene envelopes* to our model. We could have different sets of off-scene envelopes for different entry/exit points but in the current implementation we assume there is only one off-scene location. Transfer to and from off-scene envelopes can only occur when a tracker box is either created or disappears.

Our algorithm will generate possible assignments of object labels to envelopes that satisfy both **C1** and **C2**. It will then choose the one that we consider 'best supported' by the classifier outputs.

14.3.3 Observational Likelihood of Box and Envelope Occupancy

There is a finite set of potential explanations for the output presented by the blob tracker and object classifier that are consistent with the continuity constraints described in the previous section. But the number of possible explanations is extremely large even in simple scenarios. A metric is required to rank these based on the symbolic and probabalistic output of these lower level processes.

The function we have chosen is as follows: for an envelope E and an object l, we compute for each blob history $C \in E$ the sum of the box votes for l over all frames for which C exists in E. To get the vote for the object to be in an envelope we take the maximum of its votes for each blob history in the envelope. This would be reasonable on the assumption that the object stays in the same blob history throughout its time within the envelope. This is not necessarily true, so the vote may be unreliable. Devising and evaluating more realistic voting functions is a subject of ongoing work. (Nevertheless, as will be seen below, our crude voting function is already a good enough metric to significantly enhance the reliability of recognition.)

In determining the support given by an envelope to a given set of labels, we impose a strong bias that favours the smallest possible number of objects being assigned to the box.

14.3.4 Selecting the Best Hypothesis for an Extended Frame Sequence

The previous subsection defined a method for calculating a metric for ranking potential explanations of the output of the lower level systems. In principle we could use this to evaluate all possible spatio-temporally consistent sequences of object labels. However, this would be infeasible for all but the shortest and simplest sequences. Whenever a tracker box splits into two, there are several possible assignments of the original box occupants to the newly created boxes. Thus the number of possible solutions grows exponentially with time (as well as being an exponential function of the number of objects involved). However, by taking a dynamic programming approach to the problem, the optimal solution can in fact be found by an algorithm whose complexity is linear in time. Thus, as long as the number of objects is relatively small, solutions for arbitrarily long sequences can be computed effectively.

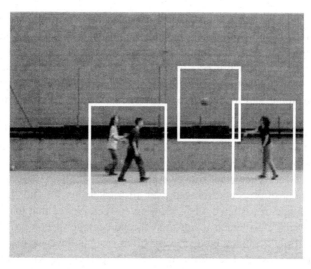

Fig. 14.8. A frame from the basketball scene, showing the bounding boxes around objects; notice that owing to partial occlusion, the tracker has enclosed two objects in a single box

14.3.5 Evaluation

The system was evaluated on approximately two and a half minutes of the basketball scene illustrated in Figure 14.8. This scene consists of four objects (three players and a ball), variable numbers of which may be in the scene at any one time. The movie contains much interaction and occlusion that a conventional object tracker would find hard to track with a single camera. The movie is tracked and classified at 25fps and the results fed into the reasoning engine. The system was applied to a sequence of 2200 frames (88 seconds real time) and took approximately 5 minutes to generate all possible spatio-temporally consistent labellings.[2] The model with the highest overall score was compared to a hand-annotated labelling which gives the ground truth at every 10th frame (plus some extra frames added at particularly dynamic parts of the video). Thus, over the length of the sequence, a total of 612 tracked boxes were compared.

Comparing the output of the consistency reasoning algorithm with the raw output of object recogniser is somewhat problematic, because the raw output does not give any indication of the number of objects that are in each box. The statistics given are just ranked probabilities of an individual object being present. However, for purposes of comparison, we must treat this data as somehow identifying a definite set of labels. To do this we use a rather rough heuristic: we say that the assignment includes any label which has the highest (or joint highest) probability of all those listed in the ouput, and also any other label identified with probability higher than 0.5. Figures computed from the resulting box-label assignments are given in the "Raw + Heuristic" column of our tables of statistics.

Another way of interpreting the raw output is to assume that the occupancy of each tracked box is somehow known by an independent procedure or oracle. The "Raw +

---

[2] All experiments were carried out on a 500 MHz Penium III; so real time performance is certainly possible on currently existing hardware.

Occ" column shows these figures. Here, when evaluating a box which we know (from human annotated ground-truth data) contains n objects, we take the n labels that are assigned the highest probabilites in the raw tracker/recogniser output.[3] Although there seems to be no obvious way this occupancy information could be obtained in practice, the statistics derived under this assumption may be useful for comparison. They show that the improvement gained by the reasoner goes well beyond that which could be obtained by simply being able to determine occupancy.

The table in Figure 14.9 compares the accuracy of assignments obtained using the "Raw + Heuristic" and "Raw + Occ" interpretations of the tracker/recogniser output with the optimal spatio-temporally consistent box labellings given by the model generation algorithm. The "Objects detected" row gives the number of correct labels as a percentage of the total number of objects (averaged over all tracker boxes). The "Labels correct" gives the percentage of assigned labels that are correct. Notice that the detection rate for "Raw + Heuristic" is much lower than the percentage of correct labels. This is because for multiply occupied boxes it very often assigns fewer labels than the acual number of objects present. The third row shows the percentage with which boxes are assigned the correct number of objects. This figure is not very informative for "Raw + Heuristic" (which nearly always returns a single assignment) or for "Raw + Occ" (which nearly always gives the correct occupancy). However, it does show how good the spatio-temporal reasoner is at working out box occupancy. The final row gives the percentage of all compared boxes, where the label assignment exactly matched the ground truth data. This is perhaps the most intuitive and best overall performance metric.

	Raw + Heuristic	Raw + Occ	Reasoner
Objects detected	44.0%	61.6%	82.5%
Labels correct	64.9%	62.3%	82.6%
Box occupancy correct	61.6%	98.5%	83.5%
Box labels all correct	39.5%	44.6%	68.6%

Fig. 14.9. Accuracy statistics for all sampled boxes

These figures show that use of the spatio-temporal consistency algorithm results in a significant improvement in the object recognition accuracy of the tracker. However, the enhancement obtained by this method is most effective in the case of multiply occupied boxes. Hence it is useful to divide up the statistics into single and multiple box cases. Of the 612 boxes compared, 377 contained a single object (i.e. a person or the ball) and 235 contained multiple objects. The single occupancy box statistics are presented in Figure 14.10.

This table is somewhat degenerate. This is because both raw data interpretations almost invariably assign a single label to single occupancy boxes. The reasoner is considerably more accurate, although it sometimes assigns more than one label to a single occupancy box.

---

[3] For multiple occupancy boxes, the raw output may occasionally give fewer labels than there are objects in the box (because it discards labels below a certain minimal threshold of probability). In this case we just take all labels in the raw output.

	Raw + Heuristic	Raw + Occ	Reasoner
Objects detected	64.2%	64.2%	84.1%
Labels correct	64.2%	64.2%	74.6%
Box labels all correct	64.2%	64.2%	73.7%

Fig. 14.10. Accuracy statistics for boxes containing one object (in ground truth)

The multiple box statistics in Figure 14.11 give a much more informative comparison. It will be seen in particular that the exact match score for the spatio-temporal consistency algorithm is over 60%; whereas, even when magically given the ground occupancy, the raw output of the recogniser rarely gives a completely correct labelling. Without being given the occupancy our heuristic interpretation did not give a single completely correct assignment for any multiply occupied box.

	Raw tracker	Raw + Occ	Reasoner
Objects detected	29.6%	59.8%	81.4%
Labels correct	66.1%	60.1%	89.8%
Box labels all correct	0%	13.2%	60.4%

Fig. 14.11. Accuracy statistics for boxes with more than one object (in ground truth)

14.4 Autonomous Learning for a Cognitive Agent

The major challenge we have been addressing is to design and prototype a framework for autonomous (human-level) learning of object, event and protocol models from audio-visual data, for use by an artificial "cognitive agent". This is motivated by the aim of creating a synthetic agent that can observe a scene containing unknown objects and agents and learn models of these objects and protocols sufficient to act in accordance with the implicit protocols presented to it. The framework we present below supports low-level (continuous) statistical learning methods, for object learning, and higher-level (symbolic) learning for sequences of events representing implicit temporal protocols (analogous to grammar learning). Symbolic learning is performed using the "Progol" Inductive Logic Programming (ILP) system [310, 311, 312] to generalise a symbolic data set, formed using the lower level (continuous) methods. The subsumption learning approach employed by the ILP system allows for generalisations of concepts such as equivalence and ordering, not easily formed using standard statistical techniques, and for the automatic selection of relevant configural and temporal information [389]. The system is potentially applicable to a wide range of domains, and is demonstrated in multiple simple game playing scenarios, in which the agent first observes a human playing a game (including vocal and/or facial expression), and then attempts game playing based on the low level (continuous) and high level (symbolic) generalisations it has formulated.

The perceived world may be thought of as existing on two levels; the sensory level (in which meaning must be extracted from patterns in continuous observations), and the conceptual level (in which the relationships between various discrete concepts are represented and evaluated). We suggest that making the link between these two levels is key to the development of artificial cognitive systems that can exhibit human-level qualities of perception, learning and interaction. This is essentially the classic AI problem of "Symbol Grounding" [173]. The ultimate aim of our work is truly autonomous learning of both continuous models, representing object properties, and symbolic (grammar like) models of temporal events, defining the implicit temporal protocols present in many structured visual scenes. Much work has been carried out in the separate areas of pattern recognition and model building in continuous data (see for example [107]) and symbolic learning in various domains such as robotics/navigation [58], bioinformatics [437] and language [218]. Several systems have been presented that link low-level video analysis systems with high-level (symbolic) event analysis in an end-to-end system, such as the work of Siskind [428] that uses a hand-crafted symbolic model of 'Pickup' and 'Putdown' events. This is extended in [121] to include a supervised symbolic event learning module, in which examples of particular event types are presented to the learner. Moore and Essa [309] present a system for recognising temporal events from video of the card game 'blackjack'. Multiple low level continuous temporal models (Hidden Markov Models), and object models (templates) are learned using a supervised procedure, and activity is recognised using a hand defined Stochastic Context-Free Grammar. A similar approach is used by Ivanov and Bobick [204] in gesture recognition and surveillance scenarios. However, none of these systems is capable of autonomous (unsupervised) learning of both continuous patterns and symbolic concepts. The motivation behind our research is to learn both low level continuous object models and high-level symbolic (grammar like) models from data in an arbitrary scenario with no human interaction. Systems capable of unsupervised learning of both continuous models of image patches and grammar-like (spatial) relations between image patches have been presented by the static image analysis community (e.g. [5]). These involve the use of general (non-scene specific) background knowledge of the type of relations that may be important (e.g near, far, leftof etc.). It is our aim to develop conceptually similar approaches for the analysis of dynamic video data. These would be similar to the grammars used in [309, 204], which are currently hand defined.

We separate learning into two parts: i) low level learning of patterns in continuous input streams, and ii) high level (symbolic) learning of spatial and temporal concept relationships. This separation of low level and high level processing has analogies in our understanding of the human brain's processing of visual information, as we discuss further in [274].

In our current approach, egocentric learning is carried out, meaning the models built are based on the behaviour of an agent with respect to the scenario, rather than being holistic models of the complete scenario. This allows the models to easily drive the behaviour of a synthetic agent that can interact with the real world in a near-natural way. Multiple derived features for each object identified by the attention mechanism are grouped into semantic groups representing real-world categories such as position, texture and colour. Clusters are formed for each semantic feature group separately using a clustering algorithm. Classifying models are then built using cluster membership as supervision. These models allow novel objects (identified by the attention mechanism) to be assigned a class label for each semantic group (texture, position, etc.). These symbolic labels are augmented by an annotation of the corresponding vocal utterances of the player(s), and used as input for symbolic learning (generalisation). The output of the continuous classification methods can be presented in such a way that instances of concepts such as ordering and equivalence may be induced, in addition to generalisations about behavioural protocols. An advantage of Progol's learning approach is that learning can be performed based on noisy (partially erroneous) data, using positive examples only.

Our prototype implementation has been applied to the learning of the objects, and protocols involved in various simple games including a version of "Snap", played with dice, and a version of the game "Paper, Scissors, Stone" played with cards. Typical visual input is shown in Figure 12(a)+12(b), and acoustic input is also possible, Figure 12(c).

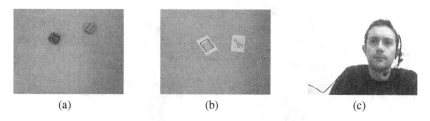

(a)   (b)   (c)

Fig. 14.12. Typical input data

14.4.1 Learning Framework

To facilitate autonomous (fully unsupervised) learning, a spatio-temporal attention mechanism is required to determine 'where' and 'when' significant object occurrences and interactions take place within the input video stream of the scenario to be learned from. The object models produced during low-level learning are used to produce a symbolic stream for use in the high-level learning. This symbolic stream is combined with a separate stream of symbols representing the vocal utterances issued by the player(s) participating in the game. These vocal utterances may either take the form of 'passive' reactions (e.g. "snap"), or 'active' statements of intent (e.g. "pickup-lowest"). The latter generates an implicit link between the vocal utterance and the subsequent action in the data stream. Our high-level system can learn this link, and thus an agent based on the learned model can generate these utterances as a command to actively participate in its environment by an 'amanuensis' (as currently our framework is implemented on a software only platform, with no robotic component). It should be noted that this approach relies on a direct link between the perception of a given vocal utterance and the generation of this utterance by the agent. In the implementation of our framework reported here and in [274], the vocal utterance is "perceived" by the agent via hand annotation of facial video sequences, and thus the link between the agent's perception and generation of an action is trivial. Automation of this process could be performed using standard speech recognition software, with the link between action perception and action generation (generation of speech using a standard speech generator) being made via a pre-defined vocabulary of words. Our aim is to learn our own vocabulary of utterances autonomously from the audio-visual face data. Such a system would have to make its own link between action perception and action generation. We have in fact very recently built our first such system, described in a paper under review, though a detailed description is beyond the scope of this paper. Figure 14.13 provides an overview of our learning framework.

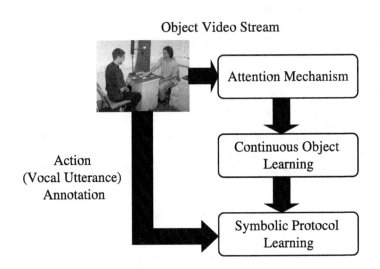

Fig. 14.13. Overview of the learning framework

It should be noted that conceptually the framework does not limit the perception and generation of action to vocal utterances; however a link is required between the perception and generation of individual agent actions for learned models to be used in an interactive agent. Vocal utterances are a good example of an action that can be perceived and generated without specialised hardware. It was for this reason they were chosen for our example implementation. The next three subsections will discuss attention, continuous object model learning, and higher level symbolic learning using Inductive Logic Programming.

14.4.2 Spatio-temporal Attention

Video streams of dynamic scenes contain large quantities of data, much of which is irrelevant to scene learning and interpretation. An attention mechanism is required to identify 'interesting' parts of the stream, in terms of spatial location ('where') and temporal location ('when'). For autonomous learning, models or heuristics are required to determine what is of interest, and what is not. Such models could be based on motion, novelty, high (or low) degree of spatial variation, or a number of other factors. In our framework it is merely important that an attention mechanism exists to identify interesting areas of space and time. For this reason we have chosen to use motion in our example implementation, as this is straightforward to work with. We make no claim that attention based on motion only is suitable in all scenarios; however it is appropriate in our chosen domains. It is highly likely that no single factor could provide a generic attention mechanism for learning and interpretation in all scenarios. In the view of the authors it is much more likely that multiple attention mechanisms would be required for fully generic learning and indeed that the attention mechanisms themselves might be subject to being learned.

The spatial aspect of our attention mechanism is based on the generic blob tracker described above in section 14.3. This identifies the centroid location, bounding box and pixel segmentation of any separable moving objects in the scene in each frame of the video sequence. If multiple objects are non-separable from the point of view of the camera they are tracked as a single object, until such time as they are separable (cf the system described in section 14.3). This is not a significant drawback in the example scenarios we present in this paper (and many others); however there are situations where a more complex spatial attention method would be required.

The temporal aspect of our attention mechanism identifies key-frames where there is qualitatively zero motion for a number of frames (typically three), which are preceded by a number of frames (typically three) containing significant motion. Motion is defined as a change in any object's centroid or bounding box above a threshold value (typically five pixels, determined from observed tracker positional noise). This method for temporal attention is based on the assumption that all objects remain motionless following a change in state (and that the process of change is not in itself important). This is valid for the example scenarios we present within this paper; we are actively researching more complex temporal attention mechanisms that do not make these assumptions.

14.4.3 Continuous Object Learning and Classification

In autonomous learning it is not in general possible to know *a-priori* what types of visual (and other) object properties are important in determining object context within a dynamic scene. For this reason, the use of multiple (in fact large numbers of) features such as colour, texture, shape, position etc. is proposed. We group sets of features together into hand defined semantic groups representing texture, position etc.[4] In this way, (initial) feature selection within these semantic groups is performed during continuous learning, and feature selection and context identification between the groups is performed during the symbolic learning stage.

For each semantic group, a set of example feature vectors is partitioned into classes using a graph partitioning method (an extension of [440]), which also acts as a feature selection method within the semantic group (see [273] for details). The number of clusters is chosen automatically based on a cluster compactness heuristic. There is a risk though, that the number of clusters is wrongly chosen; in section 14.5 we discuss

---

[4] In this article we use a 96D rotationally invariant texture description vector (based on the statistics of banks of Gabor wavelets and other related convolution based operations), and a 2D position vector only.

an approach to mitigate against this: the number of clusters is deliberately selected as overly large and cluster equivalence is determined during symbolic learning. This will be our preferred approach in future work, as temporal context (in additional to spatial appearance information) is taken into account.

Once a set of examples is partitioned, the partitions may be used as supervision for a conventional supervised statistical learning algorithm such as a Multi-layer perceptron, Radial Basis Function or Vector Quantisation based nearest neighbour classifier (we use the latter in our implementation). This allows for the construction of models that encapsulate the information from the clustering in such a way that they can be easily and efficiently applied to novel data. These models are used to generate training data suitable for symbolic learning. For each object identified by the attention mechanism, a property is associated with it for each semantic group. For example:

```
state([obj0,obj1],t1).
property(obj0,tex0).
property(obj1,tex1).
property(obj0,pos1).
property(obj1,pos0).
```

indicates that there are two objects present at time t1. The first belongs to texture class tex0 and position class pos1, and the second to texture class tex1 and position class pos0. These symbolic streams are a good representation of the input stream; however inevitably they are not noise free. Further details of the symbolic representation used is given in section 14.4.4.

14.4.4 Symbolic Learning Using Inductive Logic Programming

The previous section described how models are learned that can convert continuous sensory input into a symbolic data stream in an unsupervised way. We also wish to learn models of the spatio-temporal structure of the resultant (probably noisy) symbolic streams obtained. I.e. we wish to learn a model of any implicit temporal protocols presented by the scene and how these are anchored to objects, properties and spatial locations. (This is directly analogous to learning the grammar of a language by example.) Structure in such streams differs greatly from the structure learned by our lower level processes, in that the data consists of variable numbers of objects (and thus the state descriptions is of varying length). Progol allows a set of noisy positive examples to be generalised by inductively subsuming the data representations by more general data representations/rules.

Crucial in any inductive learning approach is the way in which data is represented. Progol aims to reduce representational complexity using a search procedure. In realistic scenarios, a search of all possible data representations is not possible, and Progol must be guided by rules that define the general form of the solution, and a suitable presentation of the data to be generalised. We represent the data in a scenario independent/neutral form using the generally applicable symbolic concepts of i) time points (time()), ii) object instances (object()), iii) object properties (proptype()), iv) actions/events (actiontype(), actionparametertype()), and v) relations between i)-iv). Each object instance is unique in space and time (subsequent symbolic reasoning may infer equivalences between objects at different times). Relations used in this work are: temporal succession (`successor(t2,t1)`, indicating `t2` directly follows `t1`), object-time relations (`state([obj0,obj1],t1)`, indicating `obj0` and `obj1` occur at time `t1`), action-time relations (`action(act1,[param1],t1)`, indicating action `act1`, with parameter `param1` occurred at time `t1`), and object-property relations (`property(obj0,p0)`, indicating `obj0` has property `p0`). It is also possible to use object-object relations (e.g., `leftof(obj1, obj2)`, indicating object `obj1` is to the left of object `obj2`), however these are not used in the examples we present below.

The final element required for Progol to generalise the data, is some guidance on the general form of the data generalisation required. As we wish to use the generalisation to generate facial-vocal behaviour it is desirable to force the generalisation to contain `action(utterance,...)` in the head of all rules, so that generalisations will all be of the form:

    action(utterance,...) :- ....

This is done through Progol's *mode declarations*. In this way the resultant generalisation can be fed into a Prolog interpreter as part of a program for an interactive cognitive agent (see later). We currently put little restriction on the form of the bodies of the rules.

The remainder of this section describes various experiments carried out using variations on the approach described.

Experiment 1

We define a simple, single player, two dice game based on the card game snap. The two dice are rolled one at a time. If the two dice show the same face the player shouts "snap" and utters the instruction "pickup-both". Both dice are picked up. Otherwise the player utters "pickup-lowest", and the dice showing the lowest value face is picked up. Before rolling the player utters the instruction "roll-both" or "roll-one", depending on if there is a dice already on the table. This is illustrated symbollically in Figure 14.14; we emphasise that learning was performed from actual visual data with real dice (cf Figure 12(a)) rather than the abstract diagrammatic representation in Figure 14.14.

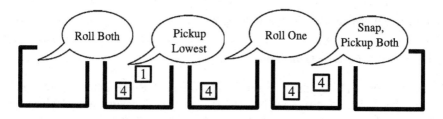

Fig. 14.14. Example of the game used in experiment 1

Experiment 2

In this experiment the utterances relating to the game in experiment 1 are made more specific by stating the face of significance as a second utterance (e.g. "pickup three" or "roll six"). Vocal utterances are represented as a one or two parameter utterance (depending on the number of words in the utterance), e.g.

```
action(utterance,[pickup,one],tN).
action(utterance,[snap],tN).
```

An example of this game is illustrated in Figure 14.15.

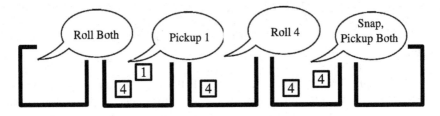

Fig. 14.15. Example of the game used in experiment 2

Experiment 3

An alternative game is used based on the game 'Paper, Scissors, Stone', in which two players simultaneously select one of these objects. Paper beats (wraps) stone, scissors beats (cuts) paper, and stone beats (blunts) scissors. Our version of this game is played with picture cards, rather than hand gestures for simplicity. Utterances ('I win', 'draw' and 'go') are represented as a different action for each player. Learning is performed for one player only, and, for simplicity, fixed absolute playing positions provide the link between players and cards. For example, output rules are of the form:

```
action(player1_utterance,[...],tN)  :-  .....
```

Figure 14.16 illustrates an example of this game.

14.4.5 Agent Behaviour Generation

The rules generated by symbolic learning with ILP, and the object models, are used to drive an interactive cognitive agent that can participate in its environment. With a small amount of additional Prolog code this program has been made to take its input from the lower level systems using network sockets, and output its results (via a socket) to a face utterance synthesis module (which simply replays a processed video of the appropriate response – i.e. a video sequence representing a typical example of the cluster from which the utterance symbol was formed). Figure 14.17 illustrates the operation of the interactive cognitive agent with the objects in the real world scene. A human participant

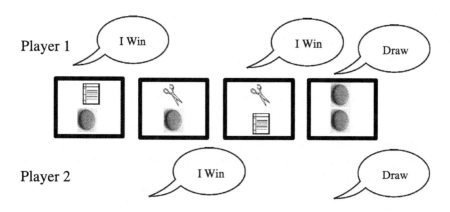

Fig. 14.16. Example of the game used in experiment 3

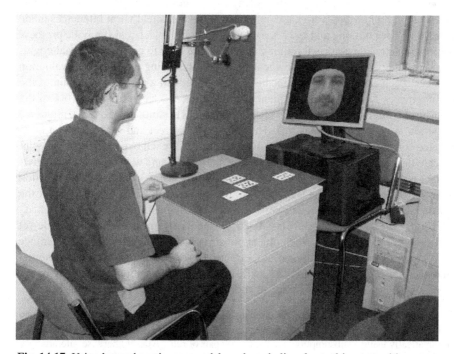

Fig. 14.17. Using learned continuous models and symbolic rules to drive a cognitive agent

```
action(utterance,[rollboth],A) :- state([],A).
action(utterance,[rollone],A) :- state([B],A).
action(utterance,[pickuplowest],A) :- state([B,C],A).
action(utterance,[snap],A) :- state([B,C],A), property(B,D),
                             property(C,D).
```

Fig. 14.18. Progol output for experiment 1a

is required to follow the instructions uttered by the synthetic agent (as the agent does not currently have any effectors).

The rules produced by Progol (ordered from most specific to most general if necessary[5]) directly form part of a Prolog program. We impose a limit of a single action generation per timestep in the (automatic) formulation of this program[6].

14.4.6 Evaluation and Results

Several minutes of footage of each game described previously (experiments 1-3) was recorded for training purposes, with separate sequences recorded for evaluation purposes. Training sequences were hand annotated[7] with the actual vocal utterances made (see table 14.1 for training and test set sizes). Continuous object, and symbolic protocol models were learned from each training sequence and used to drive an artificial cognitive agent. The performance of the agent was evaluated using the (unseen) evaluation sequences. Each experiment was repeated twice, once with a perfect annotation of the vocal utterances for the training sequence (experiment Na), and once with 10% of the utterances randomly replaced with erroneous utterances to simulate error in an utterance recognition system (experiment Nb). The number of correct and incorrect utterances generated for the evaluation sequences was recorded for each experiment/model with respect to the actual utterance made (table 14.1, column 5), and with respect to the utterance that would be expected, based on the (possibly erroneous) low-level classification of objects (table 14.1, column 6). These results are presented in Table 14.1, with the (intermediate) low-level classification performance (column 4) included for reference.

Although the low-level object classification models are imperfect, a perfect rule-set is generated for experiment 1 when object noise, and when object noise plus utterance noise, is present in the training data. A perfect rule-set is generated for experiment 3 with object noise; however some rules are lost with the introduction of utterance noise. Experiment 2 is more complex, due to the increased utterance possibilities, and so

---

[5] In the case that the body of one rule is a specialisation of another, the most general rule is moved below the most specific one in the ordering (if not the case already). This may be determined automatically using a subsumption check on each pair of rule bodies. Otherwise rule ordering is as output by Progol. Also, as already noted above, we are currently working on a stochastic rule-interpreter which will obviate the need for rule ordering and the direct use of Prolog as an interpreter.

[6] We have recently implemented a rule-interpreter, which can handle a wider range of scenarios (multiple simultaneous actions, non-deterministic/stochastic outcomes etc); however this is not necessary for the scenarios presented here so we omit the details.

[7] In more recent work, under review, we are able to acquire and integrate the vocal utterances automatically.

Table 14.1. Evaluation results. Note: Experiment Na: object identity noise, experiment Nb: object identity + vocal utterance noise. The columns represent: (a) the number of utterances in the training set, (b) the number of utterances in the test set, (c) the number of frames classified completely correctly, (d) the number of correct utterances compared to the actual utterances made, (e) the number of correct utterances compared to the (possibly erroneous) low-level classification.

	a	b	c	d	e
exp 1a	61	35	29 (83%)	32 (91%)	35 (100%)
exp 1b	61	35	29 (83%)	32 (91%)	35 (100%)
exp 2a	223	41	38 (93%)	31 (76%)	32 (78%)
exp 2b	223	41	38 (93%)	31 (76%)	32 (78%)
exp 3a	176	105	105 (100%)	105 (100%)	105 (100%)
exp 3b	176	105	105(100%)	71 (68%)	71 (68%)

requires more rules than the other two. Some rules are missing in both parts of this experiment, although performance is still reasonable. However, an accurate rule-set for experiment 2 was obtained using noise-free (synthetic) training data, indicating that it is noise in the symbolic data that results in the loss of rules (rather than the structure of the problem). These results demonstrate the graceful degradation of the ILP generalisation with noise. Less general rules are lost, rather than the entire process failing, when noise is introduced. This is essential for future work involving incremental and iterative learning. It is worth examining the rule-set generated by experiment 1 to illustrate the generalisation of the training data performed (Figure 14.18).

It can be seen from the snap rule in Figure 14.18 that the concept of property equality has been used in the generalisation of the training data. The rule-set perfectly and concisely represents the protocol of this game, despite errors in the classification of objects in the training data. This may be partially due to most of the erroneous classifications fitting the generalisation, owing to the nature of the utterances. It should be noted that the 'snap' rule is a specialisation of the 'pickuplowest' rule. Currently rules are ordered from most specific to most general for interpretation by the cognitive agent, allowing only the most specific rule to be activated. This works well for the scenarios presented in this paper; however work has commenced on a stochastic rule-interpreter that selects overlapping rules based on statistics from the training data (and obviates the need for explicit rule ordering). This will enable the modelling of more complex situations and non-deterministic outcomes. Figure 14.19 gives the generalisation from experiment 1b.

It is interesting to note that the generalisation given in Figure 14.19 is identical to the generalisation in Figure 14.18, apart from the addition of terms relating to (some of) the erroneous inputs[8]. These extra terms have no effect on the operation of a cognitive agent because, as grounded-assertions, they refer to specific times (which by definition will never recur).

---

[8] Progol retains these terms so that the generalisation represents the entire data set.

```
action(utterance,[rollboth],t600).
action(utterance,[rollone],t663).
action(utterance,[rollboth],t686).
action(utterance,[pickuplowest],t902).
action(utterance,[pickuplowest],t1072).
action(utterance,[rollboth],t1089).
action(utterance,[rollboth],A) :- state([],A).
action(utterance,[rollone],A) :- state([B],A).
action(utterance,[pickuplowest],A) :- state([B,C],A).
action(utterance,[snap],A) :- state([B,C],A), property(B,D),
                              property(C,D).
```

Fig. 14.19. Progol output for experiment 1b

14.5 Overclustering and Forming Equivalence Classes

We noted above the problems associated with automatically finding the right number of clusters when attempting to form a finite set of concepts from sensor data and suggested that one response to this problem would be to overcluster (i.e. to deliberately err on the generous side in choosing the number of clusters), and to reason explicitly about which apparently different concepts (i.e different clusters) should actually be regarded as equivalent[9]. In this section we explore this idea, which is reported in further detail in [388, 389]. The aim is to use Progol to induce axioms of equivalence for sets of objects which should be regarded as equivalent in the context they are being used. The experiment we performed was as follows.

The three objects of the paper-scissors-stone game were classified into 15 distinct classes. From the symbolic learning standpoint, this assumption is equivalent to showing, at each round of the game, one of 15 different shapes of papers, scissors and stones. Therefore, the axioms of equivalence might be obtained from analysing the states in which a draw occurs. It is worth noting that, in this experiment, we are not interested in inducing the rules of the game in question, but only in obtaining characteristics of the equivalence between objects in this context. Eight data sets (containing an average of 30 examples each) were utilised in this experiment.

In most cases, the sought axioms of equivalence were obtained as the first rules output. We could not find suitable mode declarations, however, that would allow Progol to find, on a single run, the reflexivity, symmetry and transitivity axioms. However, as we explain in [388, 389], by treating each of the eight data sets as a separate experiment, and giving most weight to rules found in more experiments, we were able to generate the formulae describing the appropriate equivalences between the symbols representing the 15 clusters, resulting in just three equivalence classes (as intuitively desirable).

---

[9] Strictly speaking, what we are doing is reasoning about property equivalence rather than object equivalence, although the former might be abduced from the latter.

14.6 Discussion, Current and Future Work

We have reported on our early work in combining continuous computer vision methods and high level symbolic representation and reasoning, and on a new technique for reasoning about occlusion. The main thrust of our current work reported here though is the framework for the autonomous learning of both low level (continuous) and high level (symbolic) models of objects and activity. It has been demonstrated that a set of object and temporal protocol models can be learned autonomously, that may be used to drive a cognitive agent that can interact in a natural (human-level) way with the real world. The application of this two-stage approach to learning means the symbolic representation learned through Inductive Logic Programming is explicitly grounded to the sensor data. Although our synthetic agent currently has no robotic capability, it can issue vocal instructions and thus participate in simple games through these actions. The combination of low-level statistical object models with higher level symbolic models has been shown to be a very powerful paradigm. It allows the learning of qualitative concepts and relations such as ordering and equivalence as well as relative spatial and temporal concepts.

We believe that the work reported here is the first application of inductive logic programming to visual protocol learning[10]. While the results reported here seem to represent a promising beginning, we are still a long way from where we want to be in terms of developing an agent with true human-level learning and interaction capabilities. Our system currently views the world it perceives as a whole, and cannot compartmentalise different experiences into different categories. As an example, if the training data contained two (or more) different games the system would try to generalise them as a single theory. While this will eliminate a lot of potential redundancy, this may not be the best, or most efficient, way of representing this information[11]. We would like to investigate learning in multiple scenarios, while allowing some generalisation between different scenarios (i.e. an idea of shared concepts between scenarios). We wish to use the non-generalised training instances from Progol output to feedback to, and improve, the lower level object models. In many scenarios this is essential, as some objects may not be easily discriminated using spatial appearance alone. In such cases temporal context is essential. The current system is based around single-shot 'observe and generalise' learning. In order for temporal information to be usefully included, learning must be extended to be iterative or incremental in nature. This is also an important goal if learning is to be more human-level (human learning continues throughout our entire life). We would like to make this natural extension to our system in due course. An advantage of incremental learning is that there is an existing model during (much of) the learning phase. This allows learning by experimentation, or "closed-loop" learning. This would require the formulation of a learning goal or motivation (e.g. the desire to map an environment in robotics [58]). Our current system has no such explicit motivation. However, the implicit

---

[10] Though we note other work on symbolic learning of event definitions from video exists, e.g. [121, 122].

[11] In the work reported in [389], we do describe how the system is able to generalise from multiple experiments; however we have not yet considered the issue of whether the experiments represent multiple instances of the same experience (i.e. game in the present scenario), or of different experiences (games).

motivation of accurate mimicry could be made explicit. This is an interesting avenue for research.

The practicalities of the ILP approach mean that the presentation of the symbolic data, and the output specification rules, determine the types of generalisations made. Informal experiments have shown us that different rules and input formulations may be required to learn different types of generalisations. How different output rule-sets are combined in the context of a cognitive agent is a subject of current research [388, 389]. We believe such combination of multiple generalisations is essential if learning in unconstrained scenarios is to be possible. In addition, as already noted above, we are currently building a rule-interpreter that deals with non-deterministic/stochastic scenarios (where a given input results in one of a range of actions) and overlapping rule-sets (where one rule takes precedence over another under similar conditions, as in experiment 1). This is based on recording statistics from the training set.

We plan to extend our system to include more object feature types (colour, spatial relationships, global and local shape etc.). It should be possible for the ILP system to learn which object features are relevant in a given scenario.

The task of building a truly cognitive agent, able to operate autonomously in multiple domains remains a significant challenge. Here, we have reported some progress towards this goal. Our overall approach has been to integrate high level logical reasoning with real visual data to compute scene descriptions and to recognise that one cannot rely on extensive hand built models – thus we have aimed to endow our system with the ability to learn as much as possible and only use non learned generic background knowledge (e.g. knowledge of spatio-temporal continuity). Although we have illustrated our work in game scenarios since this has allowed to concentrate on the cognitively interesting aspects of our approach, we believe our approach is more generally applicable to other domains and tasks (such as the robotic guide for the elderly [308], and the interactive room [46]).

Acknowledgements

The authors gratefully acknowledge the support of the EU FP5 Project, CogVis, IST-2000-29375 and of colleagues in the Vision and Qualitative Spatial Reasoning Groups at the University of Leeds.

15

On Scene Interpretation with Description Logics

Bernd Neumann[1] and Ralf Möller[2]

[1] Universität Hamburg
   neumann@informatik.uni-hamburg.de
[2] Technische Universität Hamburg-Harburg
   r.f.moeller@tuhh.de

Abstract. We examine the possible use of Description Logics as a knowledge representation and reasoning system for high-level scene interpretation. It is shown that aggregates composed of multiple parts and constrained primarily by temporal and spatial relations can be used to represent high-level concepts such as object configurations, occurrences, events and episodes. Scene interpretation is modelled as a stepwise process which exploits the taxonomical and compositional relations between aggregate concepts while incorporating visual evidence and contextual information. It is shown that aggregates can be represented by concept expressions of a Description Logic which provides feature chains and a concrete domain extension for quantitative temporal and spatial constraints. Reasoning services of the DL system can be used as building blocks for the interpretation process, but additional information is required to generate preferred interpretations. A probabilistic model is sketched which can be integrated with the knowledge-based framework.

15.1 Introduction

Interpreting a visual scene is a task which in general resorts to a large body of prior knowledge and experience of the viewer. Consider an every-day street scene as illustrated in Fig. 15.1.

Based on common-sense knowledge and experiences, we recognise that two persons are engaged with garbage collection while a third person is distributing mail. With visual evidence as sparse as a single snapshot, we obtain an interpretation which extends over time, supplements invisible objects outside the field of view, ignores uninteresting details, provides an estimate of daytime and season, and may even include assumptions about the intentions and emotions of the people in the scene. It is evident that scene interpretation is a knowledge-intensive process which is decisively shaped by the way common-sense knowledge and experiences are brought to bear.

While people seem to perform scene interpretations without effort, this is a formidable and as yet unsolved task for artificial vision systems. One reason is the often still unsatisfactory performance of low-level vision, in particular segmentation, tracking, 3D analysis, object recognition and categorisation. Often it is argued that the problem of complex scene interpretation cannot be tackled before reliable low-level results are available. However, low- level vision is not always the bottleneck. As the above example

H.I. Christensen and H.-H. Nagel (Eds.): Cognitive Vision Systems, LNCS 3948, pp. 247–275, 2006.
© Springer-Verlag Berlin Heidelberg 2006

Fig. 15.1. Street scene for scene interpretation

suggests, an even more important role may be played by high-level knowledge and experiences. Given suitable high- level knowledge structures, far-reaching interpretations may be obtained including propositions about parts of the scene for which there is no direct evidence at all.

Furthermore, high-level knowledge may provide top-down guidance to facilitate and improve low-level processes. This has been known for a long time (e.g. [215]), but there are few examples (e.g. [16]) where vision systems exploit high-level knowledge – beyond single-object descriptions – for low-level processing and decisions.

In view of the importance of knowledge for scene interpretation, it is useful to be aware of the rich body of research on knowledge representation and knowledge-based system methodology when designing a scene interpretation system. For an overview see the corresponding sections in AI textbooks such as [386, 333, 435]. Out of the many aspects of past and ongoing developments in knowledge representation, the following seem to be particularly significant for scene interpretation.

- Knowledge representation needs a sound formal basis when the body of knowledge becomes large and diverse. Many of the early representation formalisms such as semantic networks, early frame languages and rule systems suffer from the lack of precise semantics in the sense that the correct use of represented knowledge is partly based on intuitive notions which do not necessarily provide a consistent basis for large-scale knowledge processing.
- Knowledge representation systems may provide standardised inference services, which can be used (and reused) for application development. Typical inference services are consistency checking, inheritance, instance classification and model construction, but many more have been proposed and investigated, for example pattern matching services [22]. Inference services are interesting for scene interpretation as they may provide important functionality for the interpretation process in terms of existing software with well-defined properties.
- There is a growing body of research about spatial and temporal knowledge and related reasoning services [476, 438, 76]. Space and time play a dominant role in

visual scenes, and one may hope that spatial and temporal reasoning services provide useful support for scene interpretation. However, it is conspicuous that so far only few examples exist where spatial and temporal reasoning services have been integrated into a vision system [167, 317, 77]. One of the problems seems to be the mismatch between the quantitative spatial and temporal information arising from low-level vision and the mostly qualitative nature of spatial and temporal reasoning services.

- Description Logics (DLs) constitute a family of knowledge representation formalisms which have obtained much attention in the last decade. DLs provide object-oriented knowledge representation similar to frame systems used in many knowledge-based application systems, but based on formal semantics. DLs realise a subset of First Order Predicate Calculus. The subset is generally chosen as to guarantee the decidability of consistency checking and other key inference services. Furthermore, recent developments of sophisticated optimisation techniques have led to implemented DL systems which combine an expressive representation language with highly efficient services. [19] provides an excellent overview of the state-of-the-art of DL methodology.

In this contribution we report about an approach to using a DL for high-level scene interpretation. The insights and results are primarily based on long-standing work both on high-level vision and on formal knowledge representation in the Cognitive Systems Laboratory at Hamburg University, but certainly also try to reflect the development of the two fields in their respective research communities. The organisation of the following sections roughly mirrors the corresponding research history.

In Section 15.2 we examine the conceptual structures which are needed to represent knowledge for high-level vision. The guiding scenario is a living room, observed by a stationary smart-room camera. A typical scene is table-laying, when one or more human agents place dishes onto the table and the system has the task to recognise table-laying occurrences. Laying a table is, of course, only an exemplary task, and the goal is to develop a methodology which is applicable to high-level scene interpretation in greater generality. For example, based on this methodology, it should also be possible to recognise interesting occurrences in traffic scenes (as a possible task of a driver assistance system), team behaviour in soccer (or robocup) games, criminal acts in monitoring tasks, etc. Occurrences, object configurations and other high-level structures can be represented by aggregates which are introduced informally as representational units. Compositional and taxonomical hierarchies of aggregate concepts are proposed as the main structures of a high-level conceptual knowledge base. The aggregate structure represents the representational requirements which must be met by a DL system.

In Section 15.3 we discuss requirements for the interpretation process within the conceptual framework introduced before. In high-level vision, interpretation tasks may be highly context-dependent, involving prior information from diverse sources. Scene evidence may be incomplete, in particular in evolving time-varying scenes. Hence hypothesis generation and prediction become important issues. However, it is known that in the end, a valid scene interpretation must be a "model" (in the logical sense) of the conceptual knowledge and the scene data.

After having discussed knowledge representation requirements for high-level scene interpretation, we examine the potential of DL systems for this task. In Section 15.4 we give an introduction to the family of DLs and the conceptual expressions which can be formulated. As an extension important for scene interpretation, symbolic reasoning may be augmented by predicates over concrete domains such as real numbers representing temporal or spatial coordinates. We also introduce inference services offered by DL systems. They promise benefits both for knowledge-base maintenance and application development.

In Section 15.5 we examine the use of DL knowledge representation and inference services for scene interpretation. It is shown that the representational requirements for high-level vision aggregates can in fact be met by a particular DL called $\mathcal{ALCF(D)}$ (for the DL nomenclature see [19]). Regarding inference services for scene interpretation, logical model construction - which is a service provided by modern DL systems such as RACER or FaCT - is in principle a candidate. However, scene interpretation requires that the logical models not only satisfy all constraints expressed by conceptual knowledge and visual evidence, but also be most "plausible" or "preferred" with respect to a measure. Furthermore, the interpretation process must be flexible to adapt to a given focus of attention and other situational context. While this poses requirements which cannot be met by existing DL systems, such an interpretation process appears to be realisable in principle.

In Section 15.6 we shortly describe ongoing work towards an interpretation system where probabilistic information guides the interpretation process within the conceptual framework of a formal knowledge representation system.

Section 15.7, finally, summarises our findings and suggests directions for further research. One of the major impediments for decisive progress appears to be the prevailing segregation of the respective research communities of Computer Vision and Knowledge Representation. So far, the Computer Vision community has not succeeded in attracting significant attention of the Knowledge Representation community for research into high-level vision. But this is not really surprising in view of the enduring predominance of lower-level vision research.

15.2 Conceptual Structures for High-Level Scene Interpretation

In this section we first explain what we mean by "high-level interpretation". We then propose conceptual structures which can describe such "interpretations". We introduce "aggregates" as representational units for object configurations, occurrences, episodes, and other concepts which occur in high-level interpretations. We also discuss the interface between conceptual high-level descriptions and the data provided by lower-level processes.

15.2.1 High-Level Interpretations

We define high-level scene interpretation as the task of "understanding" a scene beyond single-object recognition. In a knowledge-based framework, a high-level interpretation is determined by constructing a description of the scene in terms of concepts provided in a conceptual knowledge base (Fig. 15.2). A scene is assumed to be a connected region of

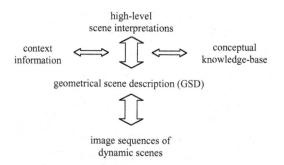

high-level
scene interpretations

context
information

conceptual
knowledge-base

geometrical scene description (GSD)

image sequences of
dynamic scenes

Fig. 15.2. Knowledge-based framework for high-level scene interpretation

the 4-dimensional space-time continuum. Our guiding example is a table-laying scene in a living-room where table-laying actions are observed over a certain time interval. We do not commit ourselves to a particular camera setup but simply assume that visual evidence is associated with the scene.

In order to be able to focus on high-level interpretation we will bypass lower-level image analysis issues and assume that a partial geometrical reconstruction of the scene in terms of objects and their properties is available which will constitute the input to high-level interpretation. This intermediate representation, called Geometrical Scene Description (GSD), has been introduced in earlier work [326] as a convenient separation between high-level and lower-level processes. In this work, however, we assume that high-level and lower-level processes will be able to interact. In fact, it is one of the goals of high-level processes to provide expectations and support for lower-level processes. Hence a GSD is not assumed to be complete and correct in any sense. In particular, objects in the GSD need not be fully classified, may be missing or may represent multiple scene objects. Imperfections at the level of the GSD will be a touchstone for robust high-level interpretion.

What are the requirements for describing scenes at a "high" conceptual level? From the examples given earlier we gather several characteristics. High-level scene interpretations typically

- involve several objects and occurrences;
- depend on the temporal and spatial relations between parts of the scene;
- describe scenes in qualitative terms, omitting geometrical detail;
- exploit contextual information;
- include inferred facts, unobservable in the scene;
- are based on conceptual knowledge and experiences about the world.

Consider, for example, the table-laying scene with a snapshot shown in Fig. 15.3. A high-level interpretation would express that a person is placing a cover onto a table. This is a qualitative summary of several individual occurrences involving different objects. The scene has a characteristic spatio-temporal structure. The final spatial configuration is described by the term "cover" referring to a priori knowledge about dish arrangements. Similarly, there is a typical temporal structure of the scene. For example, usually we would expect that the plate is placed before the saucer and the cup. Further expectations

Fig. 15.3. Snapshot of a table-laying scene

may arise from context information. If we know that it is early in the morning, we might infer that a breakfast table is laid and someone may intend to have breakfast soon.

From the example it is apparent that a scene interpretation may involve many conceptual levels above the level of single-object recognition, corresponding to different degrees of abstraction. At a low abstraction level we may talk about placing a fork beside a plate. At a higher level we may say that the table is laid for breakfast. It will be the task of the conceptual knowledge base to provide the corresponding conceptual structures.

Intuitively we may think of the elements of a high-level scene interpretation as "occurrences". The term emphasises the general case of a time-varying scene (ranging from simple object motions to large-scale episodes), but is not meant to exclude concepts for stationary situations such as a cover configuration on a table.

It has been mentioned that an interpretation should exploit contextual information. As "context" of a scene we denote any information at any abstraction level which is relevant for the interpretation of that scene but not observable. For vision, spatial and temporal context are particularly important. Spatial context is understood to influence the interpretation of a scene via spatial constraints. For example, context information about the location of the table border will constrain expected cover locations. Similarly, temporal context provides temporal constraints, for example, knowing the daytime may exclude certain interpretations such as "breakfast-table". The example suggests that it may be more appropriate to change certainty values rather than exclude an interpretation alltogether. Uncertainty management as an extension of a logic-based framework will be addressed in Section 15.6.

In general, context may be provided in terms of diverse kinds of information. For example, it may be known by verbal communication that the table is being laid. This top-down information may facilitate a detailed scene analysis and interpretation. Context may also be given in terms of known intentions of agents. For example, if it is known that an agent intends to have breakfast, but the table is covered with other items, say books, then it may be expected that the agent will clear the table and then place dishes.

Another kind of context may be given by focussed attention. In the smart-room setting of our example scenario, for example, attention may be directed by queries of a human user such as "Is there a plate on the table?". The query will restrict the space of interesting interpretations to those which include a plate.

15.2.2 Aggregates

We turn now to the task of describing occurrence concepts in a knowledge-representation framework. This will be done initially in a frame-based notation. In Section 15.5, we will rephrase the frame-based models as conceptual expressions of a Description Logic.

The main conceptual entities are called aggregates. An aggregate consists of a set of parts tied together to form a concept and satisfying certain constraints. There are no a priori assumptions about dependencies between parts or specific reasons to combine them into an aggregate. We simply assume that one is interested to recognise an aggregate as a whole.

As an example, consider the occurrence of placing a cover on a table. Fig. 15.4 shows the corresponding conceptual model. It is a crude conceptual description of a scene where a plate, a saucer and a cup are placed onto a table to form a cover. The place-cover aggregate includes a table top, three transport occurrences and a cover configuration as parts (the spatial constraints expressed by cover are not shown here). Parts are assumed to be existentially quantified. Furthermore, there are time marks which refer to the beginning and ending of the place-cover occurrence. In the constraints section, there are identity constraints, such as pc-tp1.tp-ob = pc-cv.cv-pl, which relate constituents of different parts to each other (the plate of the transport sub-occurrence is identical with the plate in the cover), and qualitative constraints on the time marks associated with sub-occurrences. For example, pc-tp3.tp-te $>=$ pc-tp2.tp-te denotes that the cup transport should end after the saucer transport. Aggregates involving mobile objects typically require that the objects fulfill certain temporal and spatial constraints.

```
name:         place-cover
parents:      :is-a agent-activity
parts:        pc-tt  :is-a table-top
              pc-tp1 :is-a transport with (tp-obj :is-a plate)
              pc-tp2 :is-a transport with (tp-obj :is-a saucer)
              pc-tp3 :is-a transport with (tp-obj :is-a cup)
              pc-cv  :is-a cover
time marks:   pc-tb, pc-te :is-a timepoint
constraints:  pc-tp1.tp-ob = pc-cv.cv-pl
              pc-tp2.tp-ob = pc-cv.cv-sc
              pc-tp3.tp-ob = pc-cv.cv-cp
                     . . .
              pc-tp3.tp-te >= pc-tp2.tp-te
              pc-tb <= pc-tp3.tb
              pc-te >= pc-cv.cv-tb
```

Fig. 15.4. Conceptual model of a place-cover scene

The example shows that an aggregate may have other aggregates as parts. Hence a compositional hierarchy is induced. The hierarchy is built on top of primitive occurrences which are generated as part of the GSD which will be discussed further down.

As indicated by the "parents" slot, aggregates are also embedded in a taxonomical hierarchy which is the usual organisational form for concepts at different abstraction levels.

Note that scene objects such as plate, saucer etc. are considered as aggregates composed of (i) a physical object or "body" in the 3D world and (ii) a "view" which is the visual evidence of the object in the camera view. As an example, Fig. 15.5 shows the conceptual model of a plate in a scene, where plate body and plate view are combined as an aggregate.

```
name:            plate
parents:         :is-a scene-object
parts:           pl-body :is-a body with pl-body-preds
                 pl-view :is-a view with pl-view-preds
constraints:     (constraints between pl-body-preds
                              and pl-view-preds)
```

Fig. 15.5. Conceptual model of a plate in a scene

The constraints section contains constraints which relate the parts to each other, e.g. ensuring that the view is compatible with the 3D shape of the physical object (which is, of course, not trivial). Note that the aggregate and its parts are embedded in distinct taxonomical hierarchies: scene-objects, bodies, and views. Only physically coherent objects will be modelled with a view, for example a candlestick. Aggregates with mobile parts, such as a cover, will in general not be described by views at the aggregate level.

The main motivating criterion for defining an aggregate is to provide a coherent description of entities which tend to co-occur in a scene. This is regardless of whether the entities are visible or not. In fact, aggregates provide the means to hypothesize parts without evidence. As an extreme example, aggregates may include mental states of agents along with occurrences in a scene, in particular desires or emotional states. The aggregate in Fig. 15.6 is a sketch of an "intended place-cover", specifying an agent along with the place-cover occurrence and a desired cover configuration as the mental state of the agent. Relational descriptions including mental states have also been used in [31] as a basis for situation semantics.

The view concepts associated with physical object concepts refer to the interface between high-level and lower-level vision, as instances of view concepts are provided by lower-level processes. The next subsection deals with this interface.

15.2.3 Interfacing High-Level and Lower-Level Representations

The main task of the interface between high-level and lower-level vision is to ground symbols of symbolic descriptions in data structures provided by lower-level vision processes. It is assumed that, from below, the scene is described in terms of segments or blobs, each

```
name:              intended-place-cover
parents:           :is-a intended-action
parts:             ipc-pc :is-a place-cover
                   ipc-ag :is-a agent
                   ipc-cv :is-a cover
constraints:       ipc-ag.desire = ipc-cv
                   (and other constraints)
```

Fig. 15.6. Conceptual model of an intended action

endowed with a rich quantitative description. As mentioned before, a similar scene description, denoted Geometrical Scene Description (GSD), has been introduced in earlier work [326]. Here, we do not require that objects of the GSD have been preclassified, but only postulate that view classes can be distinguished, e.g. "disk-shaped". A single view instance may be related to several object concepts, hence unambiguous recognition solely based on views may not be possible.

Blobs are mapped into instances of object views which are associated with object concepts of the conceptual knowledge base as described above. Basically, this mapping assigns symbols for qualitative subspaces of the quantitative blob descriptions. For example, a subspace of shape descriptions could be classified as "disk-shaped".

In addition to instances of object views, qualitative relations between object views are computed, for example topological relations such as "touch". There is a large set of relations which can in principle be computed from the GSD. From a cognitive perspective, qualitative predicates over distances and angles between suitable reference features, as well as temporal derivatives of distances and angles, are of primary importance. For example, qualitative spatial relations such as "right-of" or "parallel-to" are of this kind.

In general, it may not be feasible to compute distances and angles beween all pairs of objects. Utility measures and focus of attention come into play as well as verification requests of higher-level interpretation processes. It is therefore useful to think of instances of qualitative relations in terms of information which can be provided on demand.

In dynamic scenes, object motion and time-dependency of relations play an important part. The interface provides instances of views of *primitive occurrences* which are the basic building blocks for occurrences such as "place-cover" and other higher-level concepts. A primitive occurrence is defined as a conceptual entity where a qualitative relation is true over a time interval. Typical primitive occurrences are:

- object motion,
- straight object motion,
- approach or depart segment of an object motion relative to a second object,
- turning object motion,
- upward or downward motion.

If a predicate over a perceptual primitive is true throughout a scene, one usually does not talk about an occurrence. We will use the term *primitive relationship* instead, well aware that there is no inherent representational difference between a constancy which happens to change within the duration of a scene and one which does not.

15.3 Requirements for the High-Level Scene Interpretation Process

In this section we identify requirements which must be met by a high-level scene interpretation process. Further down, these requirements will be compared with existing inference services of DL systems.

15.3.1 Context-Based Interpretation

An interpretation of a scene is a partial description in terms of instances of concepts of the conceptual knowledge base. It is partial because only parts of the scene and a subset of the concepts are interesting in general, depending on the pragmatic context. This principle is well-known from work on Active Vision [43] and knowledge-based attention mechanisms [199]. In our knowledge-based framework, we allow an interpretation to be incomplete in three respects:

1. Objects need not be identified as parts of an aggregate. In particular, view objects may remain "unrecognized", i.e. not assigned to a scene-object aggregate.
2. An object which is an instance of a certain concept C need not necessarily be specialized to a known subconcept of C.
3. Aggregates need not be instantiated at the parts level.

Context information can enter the interpretation process in terms of instantiated aggregates which constrain other possible scene objects. For example, if the context of a breakfast scene is given, it is assumed that a corresponding aggregate is instantiated and possible parts - such as the occurrence "laying-the-breakfast-table" - are expected as constituents of the interpretation. Context-based instances are often not fully specified, with properties left open or partially constrained. For example, the begin and end times of an instance of "laying-the-breakfast-table" may initially be loosely constrained to the typical morning hours, e.g. to times between 6 and 11 a.m.

Spatial and temporal context plays a special part in scene interpretation, since spatial and temporal constraints provide important coherence in visual aggregates. The constraints section in aggregates will contain predominantly spatial and temporal constraints. In view of interpretation tasks under varying contextual conditions it is highly desirable that temporal and spatial constraints can be propagated between all constraint variables. For example, if a plate is interpreted as part of a cover, the plate location constrains other part locations, restricting possible choices and possibly even causing top-down guided image analysis in restricted areas.

As a consequence of context information, scene interpretation may be performed under diverse boundary conditions and the interpretation process must be influenced accordingly, in particular regarding the order in which possible hypotheses are tested. Hence one of the requirements for interpretation services must be flexibility to adjust to varying contexts.

15.3.2 Navigating in Hallucination Space

An interpretation may reach far beyond visual evidence, for example by including predictions about the temporal development of a dynamic scene or expectations about invisible objects. Hence instantiations with incomplete or no visual evidence are more the rule than the exception. This is aptly expressed by the sentence "Vision is controlled hallucination" attributed to Max Clowes (1971).

Considering the potentially large space of possible hallucinations and the flexibility required for varying contexts, it is useful to model the interpretation process as an incremental construction process with the goal to create and verify any instance which may be useful for the overall goals of the vision system. We know that logically, an instance of an aggregate C can only be verified if it is asserted by context information or its parts can be verified under the constraints specified in the concept definition of C. This recursive definition may eventually bring scene objects and hence visual evidence of the GSD into play. But scene objects cannot be verified - logically - from visual evidence alone as shown in Fig. 15.5, but would require assertions about the corresponding physical object. Hence logical verifiability cannot be a criterion for accepting an instance in an interpretation. However, it can be assured that interpretations are consistent with evidence and conceptual knowledge. Unfortunately, the space of consistent interpretations may be huge and the knowledge-representation framework does not offer a suitable criterion for preferring one consistent interpretation over the other. Hence additional information is required, for example in terms of likelihoods of interpretations. We will discuss preference measures for guiding the interpretation process in Section 15.6.

In [327] a repertoire of three basic interpretation steps has been identified: aggregate instantiation, instance refinement and instance merging. For clarity, it is useful to further distinguish two variants of instance refinement: instance specialisation and instance expansion. The interpretation steps are designed to move around freely in hallucination space, i.e. to allow the construction of any consistent interpretation. In the following, the four kinds of interpretation steps will be described.

Aggregate instantiation is the act of inferring an aggregate from parts, also known as part-whole reasoning. Given instances of (not necessarily all) parts of an aggregate and satisfied constraints, we want to establish an instance of the aggregate. The question when evidence in terms of parts justifies aggregate instantiation is, of course, related to the verification question raised above, and we note that aggregate instantiation requires guiding information.

The second kind of interpretation step is *instance specialisation*. Specialisation means tightening properties and constraints, either along the specialisation hierarchy or by checking objects for possible roles in aggregates. Hence instance specialisation steps are predetermined by the structure of the specialisation hierarchy and the aggregate definitions. As above, it must be noted that the conceptual structures do not specify preferred choices if alternative specialisations are possible.

The degree to which instances should be specialised depends on the overall task of the vision system, and no generally valid rule can be given. On the other hand, we know from Cognitive Science that "natural kinds" play an important role in human thinking and communication. Roughly, a natural kind is a concept which describes essential visual properties of its instances [208]. In our domain, "plate" is a natural kind whereas "dish" is not. Asserting natural kinds could be a useful guiding goal for specialisation steps.

Instance expansion is the step of instantiating the parts of an aggregate if the aggregate itself is already instantiated. Logically, asserting an aggregate instance would generally imply the assertion of part instances. But for a task-oriented and context-dependent interpretation it is useful to be able to suppress details. Hence it will not be required that parts are instantiated if an aggregate is instantiated. A typical reason for instance expansion is the need to connect higher-level aggregates to visual evidence.

The fourth kind of interpretation step, *instance merging,* is required because of the distributed nature of interpretation activities. New instances may be generated at any level and in any branch of the compositional hierarchy depending on visual evidence, context information and current interpretation state. Hence different sequences of interpretation steps may lead to identical instances which must be merged. This will happen in particular when instantiations are initiated both bottom-up and top-down, for example caused by visual evidence on one side and strong context-based expectations on the other. In our domain, context information such as "the table is laid" may have led to the top-down instantiation of a cover and its parts. Visual evidence about a plate and other items must then be merged with these instances. Again, we note that there may be many choices, and guiding information is needed.

15.3.3 Scene Interpretation as Model Construction

As shown by [369] and further elaborated in [289, 406, 405], image interpretation can be formally described as constructing a partial model. "Model" is used here in the logical sense and means a mapping from the symbols of logical formulae into a domain such that the formulae are true.

Applied to scene interpretation, there are three sets of formulae, (i) generic knowledge about the world, (ii) knowledge about a specific scene in terms of visual evidence and context, and (iii) propositions which are generated as the scene interpretation. Model construction means connecting constant, predicate and function symbols of the formulae with corresponding individuals, predicates and functions of a real world domain. The fact that the third set of formulae, the scene interpretation, is not given but incrementally constructed, is one of the differences to the notion of interpretation as used in formal knowledge representation.

The constructed model is "partial" in that neither all possible nor all implied conceptualisations of the scene must be expressed as formulae, and in particular that image analysis must not be perfect.

In addition to these general properties of a model, Schröder postulates that two requirements must be fulfilled. First, it must be possible to extend the partial model to a complete model. This ensures consistency of any scene interpretation since it is always part of a model. Second, disjunctions must be resolved. This ensures completeness with respect to specialisation.

It is interesting to transfer Schröder's criteria for scene interpretation [405] into the conceptual framework introduced above, although this is not (yet) formulated in a precise logical language. Scene interpretation as outlined in Subsections 15.3.1 and 15.3.2 is an interpretation in the logical sense, i.e. the scene interpretation process determines a mapping from symbolic expressions into the real world, by connecting symbolic constants to individual entities in the scene via sensory input and computational procedures. For example, instantiating a place-cover aggregate connects the corresponding formula with the real-world scene via spatio-temporal constraints and whatever visual evidence is related to the occurrence.

The mapping is a model, if it causes all symbolic expressions of the conceptual knowledge and the scene-specific knowledge to become true. For example, if a plate is on the table in the scene, then a corresponding symbolic relation ON should hold for symbolic tokens PLATE1 and TABLE1 assigned to the scene objects. This is the case if the real-world meaning is correctly represented by the computational procedure which determines the ON-relation for the scene object.

Sometimes, our intuitive notions may differ from what is being computed and one might argue that in those cases a vision system does not compute a model. Discrepancies may range from obvious mistakes (e.g. interpreting a shadow as a physical object) to disputable propositions where even people might disagree (e.g. calling a spatial relation "near"). For a formal analysis, it is therefore useful to avoid references to intuition and accept the operational semantics realised by the conceptual models and computational procedures. In this sense consistent scene interpretations always correspond to logical models.

Schröder's consistency requirement makes sure that a partial model is always the kernel of a potentially complete model. In our framework, requirements for scene interpretations have been introduced without this condition, and it is not apparent at this stage how one could ensure that a partial scene interpretation remains consistent if it is completed by further image analysis. As an example, imagine a scene where a plate is placed onto an empty table. The vision system may come up with the interpretation of "table-laying" including predictions about future actions. The continuation of the scene, however, may show that the plate is picked up again and put elsewhere. Hence the premature interpretation cannot be completed to be consistent with the scene.

In view of the fact that visual evidence is ambiguous as a rule (and not as an exception), we expect that Schröder's consistency requirement cannot be met in practice. Rather, we must be prepared to (i) withdraw an interpretation if it becomes inconsistent with additional information, and (ii) provide guiding information which helps to select between multiple possible models.

Let us now consider Schröder's specialisation requirement which calls for interpretations without unresolved disjunctions. Disjunctions occur naturally in conceptual descriptions where choices are left open, for example, when a concept may be specialised further according to the taxonomy, or when a property may have several values. Requiring interpretations without disjunctions is equivalent to enforcing interpretations at the lowest possible abstraction level. This is clearly not the right answer for all vision tasks and pragmatic contexts which one can think of. For example, in an obstacle avoidance task the vision system could well do without the most specific classification of obstacles as long as their geometry is recognised properly.

In summary, we see that model construction, although the right logical framework for scene interpretation, leaves several questions unanswered regarding a practically useful interpretation process. These questions will be brought up again when we examine DLs for possible interpretation services, and will also be addressed in Section 15.6.

15.4 Knowledge Representation and Reasoning with Description Logics

Description Logics (DLs), also called terminological logics, originated from the work of several researchers who tried to replace the intuitive semantics of semantic networks by formal logic-based semantics [498, 50, 181, 499]. It was soon realised that semantic networks and frames do not require full first-order logic, but fragments suffice for typical representation and reasoning tasks. Moreover, since inference problems are found to be decidable in these fragments, reasoning can be operationalised by sound, complete, and terminating algorithms. This is a clear advantage compared to theorem provers for full first-order logic or theorem provers for Horn clauses with function symbols (e.g., PROLOG).

DLs have taken a remarkable development as both solid theoretical foundations and successful operational systems have been achieved. The interest of using DL systems for practical applications is due to several attractive aspects.

- The family of DLs comprises a variety of representation languages ranging from languages with polynomial complexity such as CLASSIC [51] to highly expressive languages which - in the worst case - are no longer polynomial, such as $\mathcal{SHIQ}(D_n)^-$ [197, 169].
- DL systems offer various kinds of inference services which can be used for application development. Systems are available off the shelf and are based on international standards for web based system development (e.g., OWL [466]). An excellent presentation of the history and current state of DL technology is offered in [19]. One example for a current DL system is RACER [168]. RACER supports the logic $\mathcal{SHIQ}(D_n)^-$ and provides extensive support OWL.
- The representation language is object-based and supports frame-like representations.

For the purpose of this contribution it is useful to introduce DLs in terms of a repertoire of language features which are potentially important for scene interpretation, rather than focussing on particular DLs. In Section 15.5, we will then examine how to meet the knowledge representation requirements for scene interpretation. Unfortunately, not all features of the repertoire can be combined in a single language without losing decidability, so a careful analysis is necessary and a restricted use may be imposed. Note that decidability was not an issue in related work such as [385].

15.4.1 Syntax and Semantics of Description Logics

Knowledge representation in DLs is based on unary predicates called concepts (or concept terms), binary predicates called roles (or role terms), and so-called individuals. A concept is interpreted in a Tarski-style set-theoretic semantics as a set of elements from a domain of discourse (also called universe), a role is interpreted as a set of pairs of elements from the domain, and an individual denotes an element of the domain. The elements in the second position of a role pair are called role fillers. Functional roles which map each first argument into at most one role filler are called features.

Building Blocks

For each application one has to fix a set of concept names (so-called atomic concepts), a set of role names (also called atomic roles), and a set of individuals. Names can be used to build complex concept and role terms. This is accomplished with the help of operators whose meaning is precisely defined in terms of the set-theoretical semantics. Below we present the language for building complex concept terms. We rely on a notation with the following abbreviations (possibly used with index):

C concept term	CN concept name
R role term	RN role name
F feature	n natural number
I individual	

Concept terms may be formed as follows:

$C \longrightarrow$	CN	concept name
	`*top*`	universal concept (containing all other concepts)
	`*bottom*`	empty concept
	`(not` C`)`	negation of a concept
	`(and` C_1 `...` C_n`)`	intersection of concepts
	`(or` C_1 `...` C_n`)`	union of concepts
	`(some` R C`)`	existential quantification
	`(all` R C`)`	value restriction
	`(at-least` n R C`)`	qualified at-least number restriction
	`(at-most` n R C`)`	qualified at-most number restriction
	`(exactly` n R C`)`	qualified exact number restriction
	`(same-as` F_1 F_2`)`	feature (chain) agreement
	`(subset` R_1 R_2 `)`	role-value map
	`(one-of` I_1 `...` I_n`)`	singleton set

For the roles used in qualified number restrictions addtional restrictions apply: They must be neither transitive nor must there exist a transitive subrole (see below). Role terms may be formed as follows:

$R \longrightarrow$	RN	role name
	`**top**`	universal role (containing all other roles)
	`**bottom**`	empty role
	`(inverse` R`)`	inverse role
	`(and` R_1 `...` R_n`)`	intersection of roles
	`(or` R_1 `...` R_n`)`	union of roles
	`(compose` F_1 `...` F_n`)`	feature chain
	`(compose` R_1 `...` R_n`)`	role composition

The concept expressions involving roles may require some explanations. The value restriction `(all` R C`)` denotes a class of objects where all role fillers of R, if there are any, belong to the concept C. Hence `(and plate (all has-shape oval))` describes plates whose shapes are oval (but specific instances of oval shapes are not necessarily known). To express that a candlestick must have at least one candle, one can use the existential role restriction (and candlestick (some has-candle candle)). Several forms of number restrictions can be used to further restrict the role-fillers for a class of objects. For example, (and candlestick (at-least 2 has-candle candle) (at-most 2 has-candle candle)) describes the candlesticks with exactly two candles.

With so-called feature (chain) agreements one can describe elements of the domain which possess the same fillers for (possibly different) feature chains. Consider the definition of a cover which requires that plate and saucer have the same colour. This restriction could be expressed as

```
(same-as (compose has-plate has-colour)
         (compose has-saucer has-colour))
```

For (compose R_1 R_2) we also write $R_1 \circ R_2$ in the sequel. Feature chain agreement is one of those constructs which cannot be combined with other critical constructs without jeopardizing decidability. In particular, feature chain agreement is part of the CLASSIC language, however it cannot be used in a language as expressive as $\mathcal{SHIQ}(D_n)^-$ [21]. Another critical construct not supported in $\mathcal{SHIQ}(D_n)^-$ is the role-value map (subset with role chains). In general, this construct cannot be integrated even into the (less expressive) CLASSIC language without losing decidability [398]. But as can be seen from the previous example and some other examples shown below, both constructs appear to play a natural role in human concept formation.

$\mathcal{SHIQ}(D_n)^-$ is an example of a DL language that does not only support the description of abstract objects (in the universe) but also supports additional domains with objects for which, for instance, an order is defined and certain algebraic operators (functions) such as addition and multiplication are specified. An additional domain plus a set of predicates syntactically constructed with reference to a set of predefined operators is called a concrete domain.

Concrete domains were introduced with the language $\mathcal{ALC}(D)$ [20]. The (D) part stands for concrete domains. The language $\mathcal{ALC}$ [399] comprises the first eight concept constructors from the grammar shown above. Another important extension of DLs in terms of predicates over concrete domains was established by [20] with the language $\mathcal{ALCFP}(D)$ (i.e., $\mathcal{ALC}$ with feature agreements (same-as), feature composition, and concrete domains). The integration of concrete domain predicates allows to include predicates which are evaluated outside the Description Logic reasoner. Examples of concrete domain predicates interesting for scene interpretation are inequalities over real numbers, Allen's interval calculus [7], or the RCC-8 calculus about spatial regions [363].

At the time of this writing RACER is the only optimized DL system which supports concrete domains with the language $\mathcal{SHIQ}(D_n)^-$. In particular, the concept language offers operators for forming concepts based on predicates involving (in)equalities over the integers and the reals. The following shows the syntax for concrete domain concept expressions (CDCs) which extend the list of concept terms presented earlier. AN denotes an attribute name which specifies an integer- or real-valued variable.

$$\begin{array}{rll}
CDC \longrightarrow & \text{(a } AN\text{)} \quad \text{(an } AN\text{)} & \text{attribute filler exists restriction} \\
& \text{(no } AN\text{)} & \text{no attribute filler exists restriction} \\
& \text{(min } AN \ integer\text{)} & \text{integer predicate exists restriction} \\
& \text{(max } AN \ integer\text{)} & \\
& \text{(equal } AN \ integer\text{)} & \\
& \text{(> } aexpr \ aexpr\text{)} & \text{real predicate exists restriction} \\
& \text{(>= } aexpr \ aexpr\text{)} & \\
& \text{(< } aexpr \ aexpr\text{)} & \\
& \text{(<= } aexpr \ aexpr\text{)} & \\
& \text{(= } aexpr \ aexpr\text{)} & \\
aexpr \longrightarrow & AN & \\
& real & \\
& \text{(+ } aexpr1 \ aexpr1^*\text{)} & \\
& aexpr1 & \\
aexpr1 \longrightarrow & AN & \\
& real & \\
& \text{(}\star \ real \ AN\text{)} &
\end{array}$$

It can be seen that concrete domain predicates offer an interesting way to integrate quantitative data from low-level vision with symbolic reasoning in high-level vision. As an example, we could define an integer-valued attribute size for the number of pixels of a plate-view and express a conceptual restriction on the size of the plate-view by means of the concept expression:

```
(and (min size 13) (max size 20))
```

Conceptual Knowledge

The language for building concept terms as introduced above can be used to describe subsets of the universe. Concept definitions and logical relationships between concepts are introduced by so-called terminological axioms. The general forms of terminological axioms are given as follows (for definitions, C_1 is a concept name):

(equivalent $C_1 \ C_2$) (identity relationship between sets associated with C_1 and C_2)
(implies $C_1 \ C_2$) (subset relationship between the sets associated with C_1 and C_2)
(disjoint $C_1 \ \ldots \ C_n$) (the sets associated with C_1 and C_2 are disjoint)

Similar to concept definitions, relationships between roles can be enforced:

$$\begin{array}{l}
\text{(equivalent } R_1 \ R_2\text{)} \\
\text{(implies } R_1 \ R_2\text{)}
\end{array}$$

In addition, in the language $\mathcal{SHIQ}(D_n)^-$ roles may be declared to be functional or have other properties such as transitivity or symmetry. For historical reasons, a set of axioms is referred to as a TBox (terminological box).

It is apparent that n-ary predicates (or in set terminology: n-ary relations) cannot be directly represented. However, there is a well-known way around by reifying n-tuples. Let

$$R \subseteq C_1 \times C_2 \times \ldots \times C_n$$

be an n-ary relation. Define C as the set of all n-tuples of R and R_i as the binary relation between an n-tuple and its ith component.

$$R_i \subseteq C \times C_i \, , i = 1 \ldots n$$

The concepts C and $C_1 \ldots C_n$ together with the roles $R_1 \ldots R_n$ represent the n-ary relation R. Reification will be used extensively for defining concepts for high-level scene interpretation which typically relate many components to each other.

Assertional Knowledge

So far, we have presented constructs for representing conceptual knowledge in a TBox. DL syntax also includes constructs for representing factual (assertional) knowledge about individuals. This body of knowledge is called an ABox. Let IN, IN1 and IN2 be individual names, then the following constructs express concept membership and role membership, respectively:

(instance *IN C*)	IN is instance of C
(related *IN1 IN2 R*)	IN1 is related to IN2 via role R

The following ABox constructs are provided for concrete domain extensions:

(constrained IN ON AN)

A concrete domain object ON is the filler for an attribute AN with respect to an individual IN.

(constraints *constraint-expr1* ... *constraint-exprN*)

Constraint expressions describe relationships between objects of a concrete domain.

A knowledge base is a pair of TBox and ABox. Practical systems such as RACER support multiple knowledge bases. In particular, one TBox can be referred to by multiple ABoxes.

15.4.2 Reasoning Services of Description Logics

In addition to providing the framework for knowledge bases, a DL system offers specific kinds of reasoning services. They are logical inferences based on the formal semantics, similar to inferences in first-order predicate logic. From an application-oriented point of view, the reasoning services are useful for two main purposes, (i) organizing and maintaining a potentially large knowledge base, and (ii) providing complete and correct procedures as building blocks for application systems. Typical reasoning services of a DL system determine

- whether a concept is consistent (i.e., satisfiable),
- whether a concept is subsumed by another concept,
- whether two concepts are disjoint,
- whether a TBox is coherent (i.e. contains no inconsistent concept names),

- what are the parents (children) of a concept,
- whether an ABox is consistent w.r.t. a TBox,
- whether an individual is an instance of a certain concept,
- what are the most-specific concept names of which an individual is an instance,
- what are the instances of a given concept,
- what are the individuals filling a role for a specified individual,
- general queries for tuples of individuals mentioned in ABoxes that satisfy certain predicates (so-called conjunctive queries).

It can be shown that, in general, all of these services can be reduced to consistency checking of an ABox w.r.t. a TBox. Hence, in implemented DL systems, a premium is on efficient and optimised algorithms for consistency checking. One way to do this is by model construction as this is an elegant way to define an algorithm for proving satisfiability. Many DL systems are based on model construction techniques (they use so-called tableau provers). This is interesting because model construction has been shown to be one of the building blocks for the logical paraphrase of scene interpretation (Section 15.3.3).

Usually, inference services of most DL systems are based on the open-world assumption (OWA) as opposed to the closed-world assumption (CWA). Employing the CWA means that if a fact does not follow from a knowledge base, then the negation is assumed to hold. As a consequence of the OWA, in DL systems, inferences are drawn to the extent that they are not affected by additional information. This precludes intuitive inferences which might be useful for scene interpretation. For example, if there is evidence for two dinner covers on a table, the interpretation of a "dinner-for-two" cannot be logically inferred as additional covers may be added to the knowledge base. Note however, that the DL system RACER supports a very expressive query language for ABoxes (conjunctive queries) that also allows for CWA-based inferences (see below).

In the DL literature, there are also so-called non-standard inference services investigated, which have been introduced mainly in support of knowledge engineering, for example providing normalised forms for concept definitions. Some of the non-standard inferences may also be interesting for scene interpretation, for example, the generalisation operation LCS which computes the most specific concept subsuming several specified concepts [75]. However, due to space restrictions we cannot report on details here.

15.5 Scene Interpretation with Description Logics

We now examine in detail how scene interpretation - according to the ideas and requirements put forth in the previous sections - can be supported by knowledge representation and reasoning with a DL system. We will first deal with representational requirements and then with the interpretation process.

15.5.1 Representing Aggregates with DL Concepts

The main representational unit which has been identified for conceptual knowledge representation is an aggregate. An aggregate expresses the properties and constraints which make a particular set of objects worth being recognised as a whole. As shown in Section 15.2, aggregates can be described informally by frames, and it is straightforward to translate basic frame notation into DL notation: Slot identifiers become role names, concept expressions for slot values become role value restrictions, and the whole frame is represented as a union of role restrictions.

The assignment of role names deserves some consideration. One might be tempted to represent all roles connecting an aggregate to parts with a single role type "has-part" (or some other standard name). This would ignore that, in general, parts "play different roles" in an aggregate, and unwanted inheritance relations may result if these roles are not distinguished. It is useful to think of an aggregate as a reified n-ary relation where the roles relate components to corresponding positions in the n-tuples, as pointed out in Section 15.4.1. Hence role names within an aggregate should in general be distinct.

On the other hand, there may be aggregates related to one another by specialisation, for example "cover" and "breakfast-cover". Here, parts in different aggregates could play identical roles and should have identical names so that the specialisation relation between "cover" and "breakfast-cover" can be deduced.

In order to function within a vision system, individuals in the ABox of a DL system must interface to lower-level vision. Mechanisms to feed concrete data into the ABox are common-place for DL applications, so this is no serious challenge. In the framework presented in Section 15.2, lower-level processes will supply data for instances of view concepts which are modelled as parts of scene objects. Also, context information may be entered into the ABox in terms of instantiated aggregates.

Representing the constraints section of aggregates is a more difficult issue. In the following simple example a DL concept is defined for a cover consisting of a plate, a saucer near the plate, and a cup on the saucer.

```
(equivalent cover
        (and configuration
            (exactly 1 cv-pl plate)
            (exactly 1 cv-sc (and saucer (some near plate)))
            (exactly 1 cv-cp (and cup (some on saucer)))
            (subset cv-pl (compose cv-sc near))
            (subset cv-sc (compose cv-cp on))))
```

Fig. 15.7. DL concept for a simple cover

The requirement that the saucer is located near the same plate as referred to by the role cv-pl is expressed by the subset construct which relates the filler of the role cv-pl and the filler of the role chain (compose cv-sc near). The requirement that the cup is located on the same saucer as referred to by the role cv-sc is expressed in a similar way. Concept terms involving the subset and same-as operator as well as role and feature chains often seem to be appropriate representation means in aggregates for scene interpretation.

A special task of the constraint section of an aggregate is to express spatial and temporal constraints. In principle, this could be done in a manner similar to the example in Fig. 15.7 where the symbolic roles "near" and "on" do the job. For example, in a (simplified) place- cover aggregate one could express the temporal "before" relation between the place-saucer and the place-cup occurrences as follows:

```
(equivalent place-cover
 (and agent-activity
   (exactly 1 pc-tp1 (and transport (some tp-obj plate)))
   (exactly 1 pc-tp2
    (and transport
     (some tp-obj saucer)
     (some before (and transport (some tp-obj cup)))
      (exactly 1 pc-tp3 (and transport (some tp-obj cup)))))
   (subset pc-tp3 (compose pc-tp2 before)))))
```

Fig. 15.8. Simplified DL concept for place-cover

This would require that qualitative temporal and spatial relations needed for conceptual modelling (such as "on" or "before") must be instantiated bottom-up by processes outside of the DL system. Assuming separate control structures of high-level and low-level processes, this would lead to bottom-up computation of a potentially very large number of pairwise spatial and temporal relations, from which only a small number may play a part in a high-level interpretation.

By integrating quantitative computations into the high-level concepts, a more efficient and also more transparent solution may be achieved. This can be made possible by concrete-domain concept terms as introduced in Section 15.4.1. As a convenient shorthand for feature composition we now use the concatenation operator o (see Fig. 15.9).

```
(equivalent place-cover
  (and agent-activity
    (exactly 1 pc-tp1 (and transport (some tp-obj plate)))
    (exactly 1 pc-tp2 (and transport (some tp-obj saucer)))
    (exactly 1 pc-tp3 (and transport (some tp-obj cup)))
    (<=  pc-tp2 o tp-end  pc-tp3 o tp-end)
    (=   pc-beg (minim pc-tp1 o tp-beg
                       pc-tp2 o tp-beg
                       pc-tp3 o tp-beg))
    (=   pc-end (maxim pc-tp1 o tp-end
                       pc-tp2 o tp-end
                       pc-tp3 o tp-end))
    (<=  (- pc-end pc-beg) max-duration)))))
```

Fig. 15.9. DL concept of place-cover with temporal constraints

Four temporal constraints are specified:

1. The end of the place-saucer occurrence must be before the end of the place-cup occurrence.

2. The begin of the `place-cover` occurrence is the minimum of the begins of its constituent occurrences.
3. The end of the `place-cover` occurrence is the maximum of the ends of its constituent occurrences.
4. The overall duration must not exceed a given maximal duration.

The constraints involve attributes relating an occurrence to its begin and end time, expressed in terms of values of the concrete domain of integers. Different from the first formulation with qualitative roles, the content of the constraints is now part of high-level concepts. This opens up the way for flexible interpretation strategies where constraints are propagated in order to restrict possible instantiations at choice points. In particular, constraints pertaining to hypothesized objects without visual evidence can be used to constrain lower-level processes. For example, if evidence for a plate has led to instantiating a cover, spatial constraints between plate and missing cover parts, such as cup and saucer, can be exploited for top-down guided image analysis at the constrained locations. Our approach differs from temporal or spatial logic approaches in that it does not attempt to integrate inherent properties of space and time into the symbolic realm, but rather exploits the computational facilities of a metric space. The need for a metric space between signal and symbol processing has also been pointed out in [141].

Note that the minim and maxim operators are not part of a regular DL syntax. But the intended semantics can also be expressed by a disjunction of inequalities between pairs of variables.

In summary, we have shown that the basic structure of an aggregate as introduced in Section 15.2 can be modelled by a DL system using the following scheme:

```
(equivalent <concept-name>
    (and <parent-concept1> ... <parent-conceptN>
        (<number-restriction1> <role-name1> <part-concept1>)
        . . .
        (<number-restrictionK> <role-nameK> <part-conceptK>)
        <constraints between parts>))
```

Currently, at the TBox level, the expressivity of RACER is not sufficiently developed to allow for concise and intuitive formulations. The problems are mainly due to decidability problems in the general case. Note that for special cases of representations problems, such as the ones discussed above, usually, developing decidability proofs and developing optimized implementations is too much work. So if a general inference system such as RACER is to be used, TBox axioms must be "too weak" in a sense. In subsequent sections we will explain how the expressive RACER query language allows us to cope with this situation appropriately. Before this can be explained, however, we consider how scene interpretation processes can be modeled using standard inference services as explained above.

15.5.2 Supporting the Scene Interpretation Process with a DL System

Support of the interpretation process has already been an important aspect for choosing particular constraint representations in the previous subsection. We now examine in more generality how the interpretation process can be supported by reasoning services of a

DL system. As pointed out earlier, the use of DL reasoning services would offer two main advantages:

1. The formal semantics of a DL language helps to avoid misunderstandings which often arise if knowledge bases and inference procedures are constructed intuitively.
2. Correct inference procedures may obviate the need for developing parts of application-specific programs.

Looking at the list of services presented in Section 15.4.2 we see that the first group deals with concept terms only and is mainly useful for the construction and maintenance of a knowledge base. The key inference service of this group is a satisfiability test from which all other concept-related services can be derived, for example concept subsumption, which tests whether one concept is more general than another, and concept classification, which determines the parent concepts for a given concept term.

The second group deals with ABoxes and TBoxes together and hence is more directly relevant for scene interpretation. It should be clear from the preceding that the TBox of a DL takes the role of the conceptual knowledge base and the ABox of a container for concrete scene data. Referring to Fig. 15.2, the ABox contains (i) visual evidence in terms of the GSD, (ii) context information in terms of partially specified concept instances, and (iii) the high-level scene description generated by the interpretation process. A DL system always checks consistency of the ABox w.r.t. the TBox, hence the ABox formally corresponds to a (partial) model of the TBox and - given its role in the scene interpretation framework - is a (partial) scene interpretation. We conclude that DL consistency checking can be used to ensure consistent scene interpretations.

Another key inference service is the instance check, which determines whether an individual is an instance of a given concept w.r.t. the current ABox and the TBox. The most-specific atomic concepts of which an individual is an instance can be derived by instance classification (which, internally, is based on instance checks). The set of most-specific atomic concepts computed by instance classification is also known as the set of direct types. If the direct types are computed for all individuals in advance, this is known as ABox realization. All inference services require deduction, i.e., multiple models have to be considered.

At first glance, instance classification appears to be an inference service which is immediately applicable for scene interpretation. Given an image segment represented as an individual in an ABox, this service would deliver the most specific concept applicable to this individual. But this will not work in general because of two main reasons:

(i) Scene interpretation (and image interpretation in general) cannot be solely modelled as deduction. It is well-known that image evidence is generally not conclusive regarding a classification because of the many-to-one nature of the imaging process. Hence an inference service which infers a class membership cannot solve the full interpretation problem. As elaborated earlier, it appears to be more adequate to model image interpretation as a (logical) model-construction task.

(ii) Individuals do not yet exist for aggregates which must be discovered. Hence instance checking cannot be applied. As a work-around, random aggregate individuals could be created, but this would turn interpretation into a top-down trial-and-error procedure which cannot be efficient in general. However, if aggregate individuals are determined by part-whole reasoning as described below, they are educated guesses based on parts, and a classification step could become obsolete in many cases.

We now turn to the interpretation steps identified in Section 15.3. The first kind is aggregate instantiation, also known as part-whole reasoning. Given an individual in an ABox, what are the possible aggregates supported by this individual, and which aggregate should be chosen first? Assuming that aggregates are modelled by DL concepts as explicated above, we can exploit the special syntax of aggregate concept definitions which allows to identify parts by specific roles. The idea behind this syntactic construction is to provide a way for distinguishing roles which model spatio-temporal co-occurrence aggregate. This way we can identify the concept terms which describe the respective role fillers, and what remains to be done for part-whole reasoning is instance checking of the individual against each concept terms. This can be done with a readily available reasoning service. A concrete solution for part-whole reasoning in RACER will be presented in the next subsection.

However, no support can be given for the strategic decision which aggregate - out of possibly many candidates - should be tried first. This requires a preference measure which is outside the scope of current DL systems. It must be expected that uneducated choices will lead to backtracking and hence inefficiency of the interpretation process. The development of a preference measure for part-whole reasoning must be considered a prerequisite for the employment of DL systems in practical scene interpretation applications.

The second kind of interpretation step required for scene interpretation is instance specialisation. One of the main advantages of a DL system is the specialisation network automatically generated for all concept definitions. Hence all specialisations of a given (atomic) concept can be efficiently retrieved. To compute the possible specialisations of an individual, the most specific atomic concepts of which an individual is an instance (i.e., the so-called direct types) can be determined by a service called instance classification, and then more specific concepts can be found by consulting the specialisation hierarchy. In general, there will be alternative choices, and it is useful to have guidance for a "best" choice. As with part-whole reasoning, such guidance is outside the scope of current DL systems.

Instance expansion is a step applied to instantiated aggregates and causing its parts to be instantiated. This operation is completely determined by the concept definition of the aggregate, and extending an existing DL system to include this new service should be possible without serious problems.

The fourth kind of interpretation step needed for scene interpretation is instance merging. As pointed out earlier, this step is typically required when a top-down generated hypothetical instance has to be connected with bottom-up evidence. Formally, the reasoning service required here is to determine whether it is consistent with the TBox and the current ABox to unify the descriptions of two individuals. Unification requires specialising the role fillers of the individuals until the most general common representation is found. This must be applied recursively to the instances of parts of aggregates and terminates at the level of instances of primitive concepts.

As observed for other kinds of interpretation steps, DL systems do not offer guidance when alternative choices are possible and an order of preference becomes important.

In summary, the logical structure of DL concepts can be exploited for constraining possible choices of interpretation steps to those which lead to a logical model, i.e. to a description consistent with visual evidence, context and conceptual knowledge. But in general, there are many models, and degrees of freedom are left open regarding choices among alternatives. The decisive question is which model to prefer in the face of several possiblities. From an answer to this question one can expect criteria regarding the preferred order for interpretation steps and other choices. Our understanding of vision suggests that these choices are critical for the practically useful performance of a vision system.

15.5.3 Scene Interpretation Using RACER's Query Language

In previous sections we have discussed how necessary scene interpretation knowledge could be modelled using Description Logics in terms of TBoxes and ABoxes. One important insight was that the TBox language provided by current DL systems such as RACER appears to be "too weak". In this section we show how we can compensate for the deficiencies using a sophisticated query language for ABox individuals. Recently, the RACER query language nRQL (new RACER Query Language) has been developed [168]. It provides an extension to existing ABox query services in terms of query expressions with variables. In the following we will show how nRQL can be conveniently used to support the scene interpretation process.

The retrieval operator of nRQL has the general format

```
(retrieve <list-of-objects> <query-body>)
```

where the list-of-objects may contain variables (beginning with "?") and individuals. The query-body is essentially a boolean combination of ABox assertions (see above) with individuals (possibly) replaced by variables. Actually, nRQL is very expressive (non-recursive datalog with negation) and cannot be explained in detail here. A query can be seen as a template which is applied to the ABox and delivers all variable bindings satisfying the template. RACER provides for an optimized implementation of nRQL.

As an example for the use of nRQL in our image interpretation scenario, let us assume that the current ABox contains various plates, cups and saucers. The following query will retrieve all combinations of parts which satisfy the aggregate definition of a cover given in Fig. 15.7.

```
(retrieve (?x ?y ?z) (and (?x plate)
                          (?y saucer)
                          (?z cup)
                          (?x ?y near)
                          (?z ?y on)))
```

Note that the same-as relation can be expressed by using the same variable name. The result of the query is a list of all possible bindings of the variables to individuals of the ABox. For the fictitious ABox of this example, the result could be

```
(((?x plate1) (?y saucer3) (?z cup2))
 ((?x plate4) (?y saucer2) (?z cup4)))
```

indicating two combinations of plate, saucer and cup which satisfy the constraints of the cover definition.

This opens up an interesting way to support part-whole reasoning for scene interpretation. The query mechanism can be used to efficiently retrieve combinations of ABox individuals which justify the assertion of an aggregate instance. Furthermore, such queries can be automatically generated from the aggregate definitions. To establish an aggregate for each set of bindings retrieved by the query, a new individual must be entered into the ABox as an instance of the aggregate concept and related to the retrieved individuals via the roles of the aggregate concept. For the first set of bindings shown above, the new ABox entries would be:

```
(instance cover1 cover)
(related cover1 plate1 cv-pl)
(related cover1 saucer3 cv-sc)
(related cover1 cup2 cv-cp)
```

As a convenient service of the DL system, the new individual cover1 will be automatically classified w.r.t. all TBox concepts and implicit subsumption by other concepts - e.g. by specialisations of cover - will be discovered.

In order to be able to assert aggregate instances also in cases of partial evidence, it is necessary to provide "partial" queries for subsets of parts, in addition to the "complete" query for all parts of the aggregate. For the cover in our example, one could generate queries involving any two of the three parts of a cover. For aggregates with many parts, the number of possible queries could become very large, however, and additional considerations are required to control query invocation. This points to the need of a preference measure based on the expected success of a query. This is the subject of the next section.

15.6 Preferred Models for Scene Interpretation

It has been shown at several points in the previous sections that stepwise interpretation needs guidance for selecting the most "plausible" or preferred partial interpretation among alternatives. In AI, various approaches have been developed to augment a knowledge base with preference rules of some sort [386]. In earlier work we have explored extensions of DLs using default rules [307]. The main drawback of rule-based approaches is the need to handcraft the rules, so it is worthwhile to look for preference measures which can possibly be learnt. This has led us to investigate probabilistic approaches and ways to combine probabilistic information with a structured knowledge base. The basic idea is to compare alternative interpretation steps by the probabilities of the resulting (partial) interpretations given current evidence, and to choose the interpretation step which maximises this probability.

Intuitively, the probability of a particular scene follows from statistics about scenes in a given domain, and it is not implausible to assume that such statistics can be obtained, at least qualitatively. For example, the statistics would tell that in a table-laying scene a saucer is more likely to be part of a cover than part of a candlestick. Similarly, typical locations of cutlery relative to a plate could be distinguished from less typical locations.

Let us go one step further and assume that the cases giving rise to the statistics are available in a case-base. Then a partial interpretation can be viewed as a set of assertions which matches a subset of the cases in the case-base. Turned into a query of the RACER query language nRQL, the partial interpretation would retrieve this subset from the case-base. Hence, the probability of a partial interpretation can be viewed as the fraction of cases matching the interpretation. Furthermore, preferring an interpretation step which leads to a most probable interpretation means preferring the interpretation which is least restrictive regarding the number of remaining cases. Note that this is a strategy of least commitment.

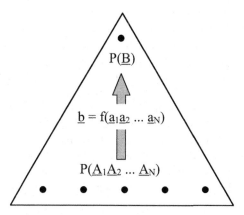

Fig. 15.10. Probabilistic structure of an aggregate (the upper node, described by a Joint Probability Distribution (JPD) $P(\underline{B})$, represents export features. The lower nodes, described by a JPD $P(\underline{A}_1 \underline{A}_2 \ldots \underline{A}_n)$, represent import features of the parts. f is a deterministic mapping between import and export features.)

Different from approaches which try to model the space of interpretations by a Bayesian Net [42, 373] with aggregate nodes "causing" part nodes, we model a scene probabilistically at the level of primitive visual events provided by the GSD. Descriptions at higher abstraction levels are assigned probabilities according to the constituting primitive events. This motivates the following probabilistic structure for aggregates.

Each aggregate is described probabilistically in terms of a Joint Probability Distribution (JPD) over part features ("import features") and a JPD over aggregate features ("export features") which are derived from the part features (Fig. 15.10). For example, the aggregate "cover" is described probabilistically by a JPD over part features such as location, size, colour, and a JPD over the export features of a cover, e.g., size and location of a enclosing rectangle.

The JPDs are fragments as each JPD only represents probabilities for the subspace of features for positive occurrences. So if the aggregate in Fig. 15.10 describes a cover, then $P(\underline{B})$ is actually the fragment describing $P(\underline{B}, cover = yes)$. This is equivalent to specifying the prior $P(cover = yes)$ and the conditional $P(\underline{B}|cover = yes)$. Similar structures have been proposed in [245] and [165].

There are no particular independency assumptions about part features within a single aggregate. However it is assumed that dependencies between different aggregates can be modelled exclusively with export features which then describe the aggregates as parts in a higher-level aggregate. For example, a "romantic-cover" could be defined as an aggregate consisting of a cover and a candlestick. Then it is assumed that the export features of cover suffice to model dependencies between the candlestick and all parts of the cover.

As a consequence, the probabilistic dependencies between aggregates remain tree-shaped when partial interpretations are constructed from several aggregates. Within an aggregate, the JPD may not always be representable by a tree-shaped Bayes Net, as typical dependencies in our table-setting scenario show. But the computational complexity is limited by the number of parts and features combined in one aggregate.

To compute a measure of preference for an interpretation decision, for example of a part-whole reasoning step, the probabilities of competing choices given evidence and context are computed by a propagation algorithm similar to inferencing in a tree-shaped Bayesian Network [343] except of the structures within aggregates. It is beyond the scope of this contribution to present the inferencing procedure in detail. Instead, we will illustrate a typical preference computation by an example.

Consider a scene with a plate and a saucer as visual evidence and context knowledge to the effect that a lonely-dinner table has been laid (Fig. 15.11). Let us assume that the current interpretation step is to assign the saucer either to the aggregate "cover" or the aggregate "candlestick". Hence the probabilities of the two alternatives must be compared:

$$P(alt1) = P(cv\text{-}saucer = saucer|lonely\text{-}dinner = yes, plate\text{-}view, saucer\text{-}view)$$
$$P(alt2) = P(cs\text{-}saucer = saucer|lonely\text{-}dinner = yes, plate\text{-}view, saucer\text{-}view)$$

Depending on the visual evidence, in particular on the locations of plate and saucer, and the JPD relating cover and candlestick in the aggregate cover, one alternative will be more likely than the other and determine the interpretation step (see Fig. 15.11).

Summarising this section, we have sketched a probabilistic inference scheme which provides preferences for choices left open by consistency-based interpretation. While probabilistic inferencing for scene interpretation has been proposed before, the new aspect in this research is the combination of probabilistic information with logic-based knowledge representation.

15.7 Conclusions and Future Research

We have presented a conceptual framework for knowledge-based scene interpretation and examined how it could be realised with a DL system. It has been shown that the conceptual structure of multiple-object occurrences, in particular temporal and spatial relations, can be expressed in a DL which meets specific representational requirements, including feature chains, the same-as construct, and a concrete domain extension for the representation of temporal and spatial constraints. Currently, there is no operational DL

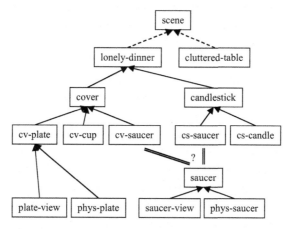

Fig. 15.11. Partial interpretation with two choices for assigning the saucer to an aggregate (dotted lines denote specialisations, solid lines parts)

system which offers all of these language features. For a possible extension of an existing language such as RACER, decidability would need to be examined carefully. Instead of extending the expressivity of a DL language for the sake of more expressive TBox definitions, another approach would be to use a more expressive query language as a tool for scene interpretation. As the example of RACER's query language nRQL shows, feature chaining and other requirements for scene interpretation can be expressed intuitively and operationalised efficiently by a query system with capabilities beyond the concept declarations in the TBox. This opens up a way for accomplishing scene interpretation with the combined power of concept definitions and queries. It is interesting to note that this is in accord with the active vision paradigm where task-oriented approaches have been proposed rather than completely generic mechanisms.

It has also been shown that the knowledge-based framework leaves several degrees of freedom regarding the selection of possible interpretations. A probabilistic approach has been sketched which provides guidance by preferring the most probable interpretation at choice points in the interpretation process. Further research on combining the probabilistic information with the conceptual units of the knowledge representation system is in progress.

Part V

Control and Systems Integration

16

A Framework for Cognitive Vision Systems or Identifying Obstacles to Integration*

Markus Vincze, Michael Zillich, and Wolfgang Ponweiser

Institute of Automation and Control, Vienna University of Technology
Gusshausstr. 27-29/376, 1040 Vienna, Austria
vincze@acin.tuwien.ac.at

Abstract. Cognitive Vision Systems (CVS) attempt to provide solutions for tasks such as exploring the environment, making robots act autonomously or understanding actions of people. What these systems have in common is the use of a large number of models and techniques, e.g., perception-action mapping, recognition and categorisation, prediction, reaction and symbolic interpretation, and communication to humans. Within this contribution these cognitive vision functionalities of a CVS are encapsulated in components. To arrive at the level of building a system from these functionalities it is considered essential to provide a framework that coordinates the components. Two principles organise the components: (1) the service principle uses a "yellow pages" directory to announce its capabilities and to select other components, and (2) the hierarchy principle orders components along data abstraction from signal to symbolic levels and ascertains that system response is reactive. ActIPret shows the interpretation of a person handling tools involving functionalities such as tracking, object and gesture recognition, spatial-temporal object relationships and reasoning to extract the symbolic description. To move towards other multi-task CVS we invite researchers to exchange components and framework.

16.1 Introduction

Computer vision has reached a state where it becomes possible to derive conceptual information from basic visual input streams. Applications in the area of mobile robots, surveillance or vehicle steering are some examples. This advance led to the use of terms such as Cognitive Vision, CVS and, finally, Cognitive Systems, where emphasis on vision as the sole or main sensor is removed. As argued in the introduction to this seminar, such "systems", and in particular, Cognitive *Vision* Systems become possible with the advance of computing power, the availability of techniques to handle the vast amount of video data, the development of reasoning techniques to approach the semantic level, and finally the advances in robotics and other forms of active vision and active embodiment. As a consequence, a CVS or a Cognitive System comprises processes ranging from low-level (data) to high-level (semantic) processing including a large number of models and techniques (e.g., perception-action mapping, recognition and categorisation, prediction,

* This work is supported by the EU-Project ActIPret under grant IST-2001-32184 and project S9101 of the Austrian Science Foundation.

H.I. Christensen and H.-H. Nagel (Eds.): Cognitive Vision Systems, LNCS 3948, pp. 279–293, 2006.

reaction and symbolic interpretation) and feedback and interaction mechanisms and embodiment to fulfil a task (e.g., navigating to goals, finding objects and communication to humans).

The ultimate driving force of developing such systems is to obtain systems that are applicable to a wide range of tasks, robust to changing and possibly new environments and situations, and which execute the tasks within reasonable time limits (see "Introductory Remarks" to this book). These expectations in a CVS impose a number of constraints:

- The system is *on-line* with the observed scene. Therefore the system has to *react* in the temporal order of activities observed and with appropriate time delay (*data-driven*).
- The system has to solve several tasks *concurrently*, tasks must be executed on *restricted resources*, tasks are *complex* in terms of the methods and combinations applied and require *control and integration* of (nowadays) *probabilistic* methods to fulfil the demands of cognitive processes. Therefore the system has to enable *task-driven* processes.
- Additionally all practical aspects of software engineering have to be taken into account such as *scalability, ease of use* and *software reuse.*[2]

To comply with all these requirements vision scientists have been investigating different architectures and frameworks. Early examples are the VAP project (Vision as Process, [86]), which basically enabled data-driven processes and active vision, or the Khoros software development environment [232]. Later examples are DACS [124] or RAVL [13]. Recent attempts have been made in the robotics, multi-agent and software engineering areas, each area with different approaches and fulfilling a slightly different spectrum of requirements (for details see Section 16.1.1).

This work wants to foster the use of a software framework as a tool to build Cognitive Vision *Systems*. This framework has been devised specifically for CVS to study the interaction between low-level and high-level processes. It exploits experience of software engineering to build complex systems based on the component principle [444]. The idea is to develop components individually and to endow the component with a service description that enables other components to *reuse* individual functionalities (or cognitive vision skills) already developed and to focus on studying the interaction in the *system*.

Two aspects greatly support a component-based approach. First, experience in software engineering found this as the best solution to reuse software and to build larger systems. And second, it will be shown below that the component structure forces scientists and engineers to clearly specify what their vision function can do under certain circumstances. This description will use the notion of Quality of Service (QoS), which, for the first time, makes computer vision developers specify in formal terms what their algorithm really can do. We see this need to be objective about vision capabilities as a big step forward to advance the science of computer vision and cognitive vision.

After reviewing in more detail related work (Section 16.1.1) and approaches presented in this volume (Section 16.1.2) the software framework is introduced in detail

---

[2] The latter two have been often underestimated but they are critical for successful application and everyday use.

in Section 16.2. It has been designed for CVS applications, in particular, the ActIPret project, which sets out to interpret activities of persons handling tools and involves skills such as tracking, object and gesture recognition, spatial-temporal object relationships and reasoning to extract the symbolic description. We will exemplify the use of the framework with two examples from this project (Section 16.3) and finalise with a discussion of the usefulness of such a framework (Section 16.4).

16.1.1 Related Work

To comply with all these requirements it is proposed to use a software framework that provides the basic functionalities for these requirements. One such attempt has been made in the European IST Project ActIPret, which has the goal to interpret activities of a person handling objects. To study the interaction between low-level and high-level processes, a software framework has been developed based on the component principle [444]. The coordination requirements of component based programming are related to distributed artificial intelligence and multi-agent theory [84], [500], [420], [225], [358]. Multi-agent systems use negotiation to determine a configuration. Such an approach is too time consuming for a reactive system that must respond with a fixed delay.

Some architectures for robotics and perception cope with this constraint and are related to component-based system programming (e.g., [6], [18], [257]). Such architectures provide mechanisms to configure a system set-up during compile or start-up time. Dynamic component selection and activation is not permitted in such systems. E.g., the OROCOS project (www.orocos.org) provides basic common principles for frameworks for developing robot control software (e.g., fusion and reactive behaviour).

Other tools to develop frameworks can be separated into the communication middleware, e.g., RPC (Sun Microsystems), DCOM or CORBA, and higher-level framework tools and concepts such as SAPHIRA (SRI), AYLLU (ActivMedia), BERRA [257], OSCAR [45], SMARTSOFT [394]. However, the API's (application programming interface) of these tools provide little or no temporal dynamics in the sense of on-line changes in the component set-up and trivial or specific API's for sensory processes.

The ActIPret framework sets out to resolve these shortcomings. It is presented in Section 16.2 and examples are given in Section 16.3.

16.1.2 Functionalities of Cognitive Vision Systems

At the seminar several approaches to cognitive vision systems have been given. From the view point of building future CVS that can solve several tasks, it is interesting to scrutinise the (cognitive vision) functionalities that a framework needs to accommodate. While this work is based on the requirements specific to the ActIPret project, the framework is intended to support other CVS.

Within ActIPret the vision functionalities have been ordered according to the data abstraction from the 2D image data to textual descriptions of activities. Vision functionalities are detection, tracking (hand and objects), recognition (motion gestures and objects), handling spatio-temporal relationships and reasoning about activities. In a learning phase the individual functionalities are trained, while the execution phase presents the final system with on-line learning limited to adaptation (this is also true for all the other systems described below).

G. Granlund (see Chapter 4) structured the system in three layers also following data abstraction: perception-action mapping (which is again subdivided into the layers: deliberation, vehicle and view control, reactive layer), symbolic representation layer (scene, objects, knowledge), and the language interpretation layer.

The system presented by Cohn et al. (see Chapter 14) is also split into the learning and execution phase. The latter distinguishes a tracking, a classification and a reasoning layer. The real power of the system is a "meta learning" component, which selects rules to link data instances to learn at the classification as well as reasoning level.

J. Tsotsos (see Chapter 3) presented a system that is built on attention and the natural cycles of perception. In the sense considered here it also structures into levels, with the next higher level being search strategies and knowledge and on top of the system the task-orientation.

Finally, the work by Hans-Hellmut Nagel (see Chapter 5) gives a systematic view of ingredients to a CVS. It starts from resource limitations due to actuators, sensors and computing power and leads over system states and relations (as the main form of abstraction) to reasoning, planning functionalities that cope with the system's purpose.

The purpose of highlighting system structures is to analyse the requirements of CVS from the view point of providing a tool for structuring the functionalities to obtain systems that are widely applicable, robust, rapid and where previous developments can to a large extent be reused. The final item is a point of obvious need if CVS shall move from very few engineered systems to a large number of systems applied in different domains.

16.2 A Software Framework for Cognitive Vision Systems

One of the goals of ActIPret is to develop a general-purpose framework for CVS that can be used not only for the ActIPret demonstrator but also in other CVS applications, i.e., other machine vision systems and also in robotic systems.

This section summarises the important design goals that are derived from the essential elements of cognitive vision demands as reviewed in Section 1 (Section 16.2.1). We then give the design decisions to realise the framework (Section 16.2.2), outline the two particular principles the framework builds on, namely the 'service principle' and the 'hierarchy principle' (Section 16.2.3), and introduce the structure of the individual components (Section 16.2.4) and the mechanism to select components (Section 16.2.5). Finally, Section 16.2.7 presents important implementation details.

16.2.1 Requirements on a Software Framework for CVS

The realisation of the CVS goals listed in the Introduction and of systems reviewed impose a series of specific requirements on a software framework. First, computer (and cognitive) vision implies image data of multiple redundancies: temporal redundancy from data streams, stereo or multiple views, within each image many cues and a vast number of features and an even larger number of feature operators, and a multiple of representations to store and formalise the image content. And second, the vision functionalities are not alone. There are many other sensors, e.g., speech, sonar, laser rangers, to name only a few, that contribute to the systems. The system is embodied, in the minimum with the restrictions to camera views. It is embedded in a task and the situations deriving from this, and it may contain knowledge representations or even a kind of commonsense knowledge to better cope with these situations. Finally, a CVS is expected to contain linguistic components that can present knowledge semantically.

To summarise, a software framework for CVS should support to build a system with the following specifications.

- Proactivity: an on-line software system, such as a CVS and in particular the ActIPret system, has to deal with limited resources. Hence the system has to focus its resources (processing power, views, etc.) according to task relevancy. Proactivity subsumes goal and task orientation, taking the initiative to control resources and to generate appropriate sub-tasks [500].
- Reactivity: the system has to react to the sensor input provided by the cameras. The goal is to build a CVS that reacts and responds to human actions. Hence reactions must take place in a time scale appropriate to human activity.
- Scalability: this should be linear or as close as possible to linear. In practice this means that duplication of any component should result in (as near as possible) a duplication of the associated service assuming the existence of similarly duplicated resources.
- Control: scalability also implies distributed control throughout the system (a single control component would not scale). Hence, each component has its own "control policy" (albeit at different scales of task relevance) to control the services requested and the results or data obtained.
- Modularity: the development effort for CV software can be limited by reusing software segments. Modularity forms the basis for software reuse and a dynamic system structure.
- Independence of components: a component only needs to know about the functionality (the service) of another component and not about their implementations. Hence, every component has the control of the services it provides to other components and the services it requests from other components.

Several of these requirements aim at fulfilling a point that is often neglected: (re)usability by the researcher and engineer. Project success depends to a larger extend than generally acknowledged on a fast learning curve, the support to evaluate components and the whole system, transparent use of the tool (e.g., interface specifications), and a certain flexibility to enable modifications without the need to adapt the complete system. Experience from software engineering advocates programming based on *components* the present most successful approach in this respect [444].

16.2.2 Design Decisions

To realise the framework, some design decisions had to be taken. The decisions are driven by the list of requirements given previously.

- The system is distributed: vision and interpretation require significant processing power. In order to achieve scalability the system has to be distributed over several machines. Distribution into distinct modules (components) simplifies parallel development.
- The components of the framework run asynchronously: the effort required to synchronise a distributed system outweighs the simplification in the integration process. Furthermore, synchronisation is pointless for components having different temporal behaviours such as tracking and recognition.
- Data consistency: control over service responses from other components assumes that the data received is consistent. For example, if two detectors on different cameras are asked to find a hand, the responses must be fused in the component that requested those two services.

16.2.3 Design Principles

As a consequence of the requirements and following the design decisions, the framework is built according to two major design principles: (1) the "service principle" and (2) the "hierarchy principle". These two terms are explained subsequently. The underlying software concept is founded on a component-based approach [445], which is faster than classical agent systems to guarantee reactivity and enables easier distribution than conventional object oriented approaches whose scalability ends at the one-computer border.

Our first goal for the CV framework is to build a task driven system, so every distributed component is task driven. From the point of view of a component, it has to provide one or more interfaces to make its functionality accessible. Using this interface other components can initiate one or more tasks. Components can be regarded as black boxes and so according to the goal of component independence these interfaces have to describe all of the component's capabilities. Because of the task related nature these interfaces are called *services*, which are derived from the CORBAservices ([335]). They form a "Yellow Pages" dynamic look-up directory that makes it possible to select on-line the best service available according to a formalised performance characterisation. The component itself builds the frame for the service provider.

Any component or service provider can use the services of other components. In this case the component or service provider establishes the interface of the service requested. This interface object is called service requester. Every component 'presents' its own abilities by providing services via the service provider and every component makes use of the abilities of other components by requesting services via the service requester. Using the service principle the implementation is hidden outside of the component.

The "hierarchy principle" resolves the problem of building a reactive system. Fully agent-based systems do not use a hierarchy. All agents negotiate until a configuration is reached. This is thought too time consuming for a reactive system. To reduce administrative communication overheads during decision-making (service selection) a strict hierarchical structure of components is used. Hence every link between components has a higher-level component and a lower-level component. The higher-level component always orders the task (service), the lower-level component has to process (provide/deliver) it.

16.2.4 Component Structure

At this point it is appropriate to define a component [474].

- The inside of a SW-component is a piece of software with some properties. It is a unit or entity that can be reused.
- The outside of a SW-component is an interface with some properties. It provides a good or service to humans or other SW-components.

From the view point of a CVS, a component encapsulates (that is the relation between inside and outside) the cognitive vision (or other system) function, and provides the means for communication with other components. The function itself encompasses all aspects typical of today's vision functions. This includes memory up to the point of a separate component (such as a model server), mechanisms for self-evaluation (e.g., reporting confidence measures, expected accuracy, and resource demands), the necessary control to execute the function, which entails control of processing as well as views and embodiment and the use of other components, and finally techniques to exploit and report context.

The context states how the software is to be managed and used, within a defined process for software development and maintenance. If the context is not stated (and it usually isn't), then concepts such as encapsulation and reuse are ambiguous [474].

The last point leads to a side effect of using a framework to build a CVS: the contextual relationships, that is how to use the component and what it can do under the contextual circumstances, need to be formalised. While it might be considered cumbersome, this enforces to clearly specify what a vision function can do. And it can be said, with justified self criticism, that scientific work in computer vision has not addressed this issue sufficiently (with the noticeable exception of work in performance evaluation).

In conclusion, using the two design principles (16.2.3) a component is made up of three elements (see Fig. 16.1):

- The component itself that is the frame for all other building units. The component unit is responsible for managing services. This includes offering of services that can be provided, reception of service requests and establishing of service providers. Also long term memory of common data or other functionality all providers share is placed in the component.
- The service provider contains the real functionality that provides the service. The component establishes the service provider as an instantiation of a service.
- The service requester is the access point for all responses from a service provider. It can be established by a component or a service provider that requires other services.

16.2.5 Service Selection

In order to fulfil task orientation and to optimise resource allocation it is necessary to manage service requests. Otherwise components might be activated that cannot obtain the necessary resources. The critical issue is the method of selecting a service. Service selection serves the purpose of selecting resources efficiently. [226] presents an overview of options of making the preferences of the requester and the properties of the provider

Fig. 16.1. Structure of a component

known to the other components and/or a middle agent. Often used approaches are black-board systems, where the preferences are known by all others, or a broker system, where the middle agent knows about both preferences and properties and negotiates to select a service.

The mechanism introduced here is derived from the CORBA trader service [335]. It adheres to the yellow-pages principle, where the provider makes his properties known to the middle agent and the requester. The following sequence describes the process for registering a service in the service list and selecting the service(s). Also refer to Fig. 16.2 for an example sequence to set-up a component connection.

1. During the component start-up every component registers its services in a global service list, (i.e., they export a service offer). A service list entry consists of the service name, the ID of the component providing the service and an abstract description of the service (i.e., Quality of Service, costs, constraints, etc.). If due to changes in the environment properties of the component change, this is reflected in an updated service list entry.
2. If a component or service provider needs a service of another component it creates a service requester to establish a connection. All selection, configuration and communication is done by the service requester.
3. The service requester starts the search for a service in the service list (it asks for service "S1" in Figure 2). The component description (QoS, constraints, etc.) makes it possible to select the relevant subset of all components providing the service "S1". The service list returns the list of corresponding service offers (in our example, for components 2, 3 and 4). The service requester can now use the service properties to select the service that is most suited to the demand, in this example the service of Component 3.
4. The service requester selects one of the service offers received and establishes a link to the provider selected. This completes the process of service selection.

16.2.6 Quality of Service, Utility and Costs

The goal of a CVS is to fulfil a task by using appropriate components. The appropriateness can be measured as the Utility (U) of a service. The Cost (C) of running a service is the Utility of the disabled service(s). This stems from the fact that for a given computing power services need to be negotiated according to the utility they offer versus cancelling other services (and their utilities).

The obvious system goal is to optimise system utility, that is, select the service that has the property

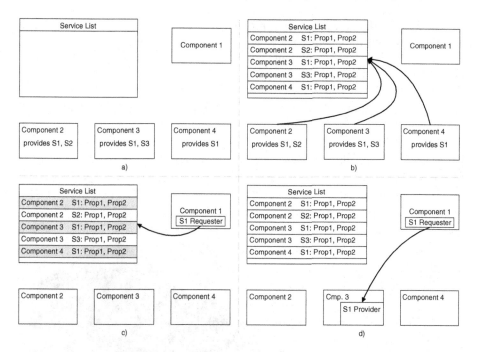

Fig. 16.2. a) A system state before any services are offered. b) The components offered their services with current properties. c) The service requester asks for services with specific properties. d) The service requester establishes a link to the selected service provider.

$$\max(U - C). \tag{16.1}$$

Using the notion of Quality of Service (QoS), the utility of one component is a function of QoS. The QoS defines the properties of components in terms of (1) execution time (as expected or inferred from previous use), (2) accuracy (spatial, 2D or 3D) and (3) the confidence or certainty in a correct match or correct result of the function (also see [354]). As a start the simple relation

$$U = f(QoS) = f(\text{execution time}) + f(\text{accuracy}) + f(\text{confidence}) \tag{16.2}$$

is proposed. Work in the ActIPret project has shown that formalising vision functions to this extent is already cumbersome. It also indicates that the science of computer vision did not yet settle enough to reward work in this area.

16.2.7 Implementation: zwork and Its Graphical User Interface (GUI)

The software implementation of the framework is based on RPC (Remote Procedure Call) under the operating system Linux. RPC has been chosen because it is very established, standardised, light weight, fast and easy to use. CORBA as an alternative networking layer imposes a larger overhead and is generally tailored to other uses, such as web-services rather than a real-time vision system. Moreover CORBA is still developing and different implementations are not interchangeable.

The framework implementation is referred to as zwork. It provides the communication mechanisms to establish and request services. Deliverable D1.3, available from the ActIPret home-page (actipret.infa.tuwien.ac.at), gives more details about zwork, an installation and a programmer's guide.

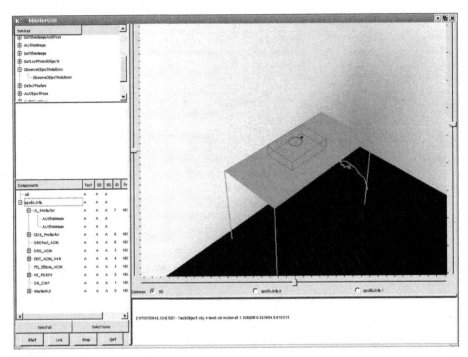

Fig. 16.3. GUI of the Cognitive Vision Framework developed in ActIPret. In the 3D display (top right), the green (bright) trajectory is the 3D hand trajectory. The ellipses are the two CDs recognised, also marked with an "f" for found. This 3D rendering can be viewed from different angles using the sliders in the GUI.

In order to control such a framework and give the user, and especially the developer, feedback of the results of various components, a graphical user interface (GUI) is mandatory. Results of different vision modules should be superimposed on the original image to indicate correct operation at a glance.

A GUI with the capability to display text and drawing primitives as an overlay of the processed 2D images and a 3D graphical display was implemented, see Fig. 16.3. It provides the following functions:

- Display of the original 2D images from the cameras together with an overlay of vision processing results. A button just below the image selects this alternate display.
- Display of 3D representation of the objects (see Figure 16.3 for an example), trajectories and other spatial information. The three sliders to the left, right and below the image allow zoom in and spherical angle change for the view of the 3D scene.
- Display all services available at present (box to the left top).

- Display of all components (box to the left centre) and currently running services. Graphical output for each component can be enabled or disabled.
- Display of textual information (box to the bottom right) to output symbolic information, e.g., recognised gesture or activity concepts.
- Various functions for debugging and presentation (bottom left), e.g., for logging data and images, and to make a snap shot of the GUI (such as presented in Fig. 16.3).

16.3 Experiments in the ActIPret Project

Fig. 16.4 gives on overview of the ActIPret Demonstrator architecture. The system was rigorously tested by the ActIPret partners in an integration meeting at a partners site (Fig. 16.5). For these tests, there were no Activity Planner and User HMI components available. As a result the internal ARE (Activity Reasoning Engine, see Fig. 16.4) output was displayed at the GUI.

Of particular interest is the study of the interaction between components. Two examples are given. The first example is the automatic initialisation of tracking using detection. The second is the contextual use of hand tracking to limit the area to search for potential objects that might be grasped.

Ellipse detection is used to initialise ellipse tracking. Fig. 16.6 shows this coupling of two components for a lamp, Fig. 16.7 for a CD object. The technique of detection is based on a hierarchical grouping method that is very efficient in computing [507]. By exploiting an ordering according to most likely ellipse arcs, arc groupings and, finally, ellipses, it also produces reliable results. Computing time is less than 500 ms on an

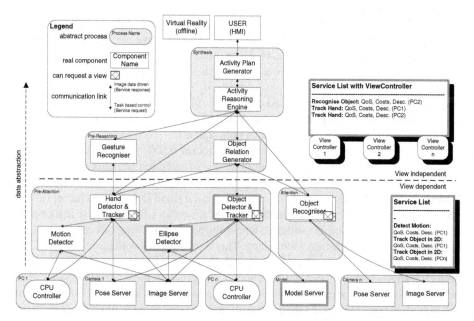

Fig. 16.4. The components of the ActIPret demonstration system

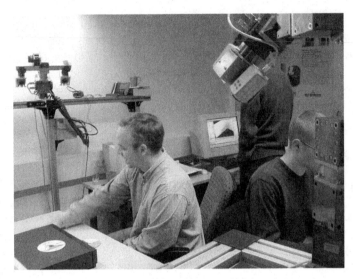

Fig. 16.5. A live demonstration of the ActIPret framework in the laboratory at PROFACTOR. Top left is the active fixed stereo system, top right the stereo system on the robot arm. The screen in the background shows the GUI of the framework while Jon Howell (from the ActIPret partners from the University of Sussex) is placing a CD in the player.

Athlon 1.880+ PC for the full image (768x576 pixels) and only 50 ms when used in a ROI (Region of Interest) provided by hand tracking (exemplified in the second example). Tracking exploits the technique described in detail in [477]. In the Fig. 16.6 only the first frame is shown.

An example of using context in ActIPret is the exploitation of the hand trajectory to narrow the SOI (Space of Interest) for computational expensive components like object detection and object recognition. Fig. 16.8 is an instant where the hand is tracked (ellipses around the hand) and the motion direction indicates the image region where potential grasp objects, in this case CDs, might be detected. The search region on the top of the cd-player is caused by a previous hand motion. The ellipses reported are generated using the method of hierarchical grouping presented in [507]. It can be seen that the most likely hypothesis, marked with "0", is the CD in both squares.

In the first example, the Object Detector & Tracker (ODT, please refer to Fig. 16.4) needs external help to provide the promised service of detection and calls the Ellipse Detector (ED) to detect the lamp object. In the second example it is the Object Relationship Generator (ORG) that establishes the context between Hand Detector & Tracker (HDT) and ODT. The ODT then again selects the service from an ED to initialise tracking. In this case a second option is available, where the service of Object Recognition (OR) could provide object locations for tracking. This is investigated with partner CMP (Center for Machine Perception, Czech Technical University, Prague) within the ActIPret project. It shows that with a growing number of components, more versatile systems can be built and that there are several routes to fulfil a task, which adds to the robustness of the overall system. This later aspect is the ultimate driving force to build the framework and it is seen as a promising method to approach building widely applicable CVS.

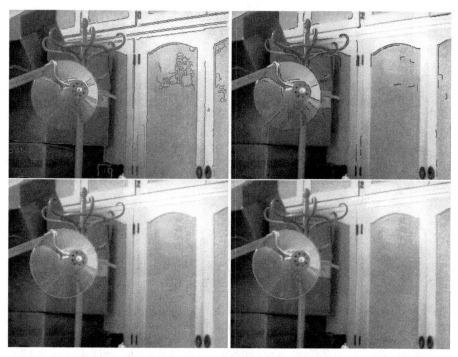

Fig. 16.6. Detecting all ellipses in the scene to track the object. Top left shows the edges, top right the grouped arcs, bottom left the only detected ellipse and the final image the first step of tracking using the technique of [477].

Fig. 16.7. The same technique of Fig. 16.6 used in another context: detecting all ellipses in the scene to track the CD.

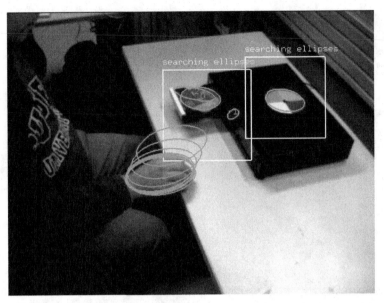

Fig. 16.8. Display of information from Hand Tracker and Ellipse Detector overlaid on the original image. The green ellipses represent the hand tracked over the last images. The two squares contain information on ellipse detection within this ROI. Each time the ellipses detected are displayed and the number gives the ranking, with number 0 being the highest ranking and indicating that both CDs have been found correctly.

16.4 Conclusions

The intention of this paper is to raise the awareness that building CVS includes many facets of science for fulfilling the tasks intended. The argument is that embodiment, multiple modes of sensing with vision as a powerful yet demanding sense (in terms of resources as well as methods) and reasoning about the percepts as well as the situation and goals, call for a supporting software framework.

The paper then outlined one tool, zwork, to provide such a framework for the ActIPret project. This framework will be further used and improved in the ActIPret project. The main project goal is to study the interaction of vision functionalities for activity interpretation. The central theme of work is to use contextual information to increase the robustness of the interpretation. The framework is the necessary tool to do so easily. zwork operates with a quick component start-up, a data transfer time of one millisecond and it has, due to its simple design, a short learning phase for the vision researcher. The developers plan to make the framework tool zwork publicly available. Please contact the authors.

The notion of QoS was introduced to formalise the properties of vision function-alities encapsulated in the components. While recent work on performance evaluation started to aid such a formalisation, computer vision methods elucidate such a scientific formalisation far more than methods in other engineering sciences. It is therefore thought essential to work along this line to arrive at clearly defined properties of methods for given context and use. The component-based approach enforces this development and the advantages gained from building components (reuse in other applications, easy use of methods by other, formal comparison of methods) will have the effect to seriously evaluate the advance of vision methods.

The current demonstrations work with intermediate functionality of the components. While simple options for redundant components (finding CDs either with recognition or ellipse detection) have been realised, the full power of a component-based approach becomes visible if *many* components offer similar or competing services. Hence, we want to encourage other vision researchers to exchange their developments and components with our framework to build more powerful and versatile Cognitive Vision Systems.

17

Visual Capabilities in an Interactive Autonomous Robot

James J. Little, Jesse Hoey, and Pantelis Elinas

Department of Computer Science
University of British Columbia
little@cs.ubc.ca

Abstract. We build visually guided mobile robots that collaborate with us in dynamic unstructured environments. While engineering these embodied agents we discover what visual information is relevant for a variety of tasks. When we build systems that interact with the world, with humans, and with other agents, we rely upon all of the aspects of cognitive vision.

Our Robot Partners project at UBC focuses on the design and implementation of interacting autonomous mobile robots. The capabilities of the robots that permit collaboration in a variety of roles include mapping and localization, recognizing people, interpreting gestures and expression, naming scenes and interacting with people.

The roles the robots can play include *José*, the robot waiter, and HOMER, the Human Oriented Messenger Robot, both of which involve human-robot interaction. Our recent work aims to extend these roles and to learn useful categories of visual signals in the context of particular tasks.

17.1 Introduction

When we build systems that interact with the world, with humans, and with other agents, we rely upon all of the aspects of cognitive vision, including knowledge representation, descriptions of the scene and its constituent objects, models of agents and their intentions, learning, adaptation to the world and other agents, reasoning about events and about structures, interpretation of other agents' and users' interactions, and recognition and categorization.

We intend our work to be collaboration with an autonomous agent, where the agent's autonomy is circumscribed within a restricted set of goals organized around a task. We choose to work with embodied agents (see Fig. 17.1) to determine what visual information is relevant in dynamic, unstructured environments that exercise both sensing and planning. Robotic agents are *embodied*: the structure of the action space and perception space reflect the physical realization of the agent, i.e., there are constraints from the world and the agent that limit the operations of the agent's sensors and actuators. They are also *situated*: they must act and respond to dynamic, unstructured, often unpredictable environments.

We will describe the capabilities of our mobile robots. A visual *capability* is a collection of processes that derives specific information about the objects, events or activities

H.I. Christensen and H.-H. Nagel (Eds.): Cognitive Vision Systems, LNCS 3948, pp. 295–312, 2006.

(a)   (b)

Fig. 17.1. (a) HOMER the messenger robot (b) closeup of HOMER's head, which is mounted on a pan-tilt unit and equipped with a PGR Bumblebee binocular stereo head (from [113]).

in the robot's environment, at a variety of semantic levels. The visual capabilities are broadly grouped into two categories: mobility and human-robot interaction (HRI). Most of these depend primarily on visual inputs. Mobility includes mapping, localization and navigation, while HRI includes speech synthesis and speech recognition, face recognition, people finding, and facial expressions. We will also describe our recent work that develops new capabilities such as user modeling, interpretation of gestures and actions, and interaction with human agents.

Granlund argues (see Chapter 4) for a bootstrap learning phase in which invariants of the world and the connections between perception and action are learned. Our capabilities are built upon the product of this learning phase. Granlund's argument can be contrasted with the extensive recent interest in learning to categorize image content where the labels are supplied at a high semantic level divorced from action.

A task can be described either by specifying the goal state that is its desired outcome or, more commonly, specifying a series of steps by which the desired outcome is achieved. The former is declarative, the latter procedural. If the goal state only is specified, the steps by which the goal is achieved must be arrived at by reasoning [59], or by policy creation [359], or by learning [414]. Procedural specification of tasks can be engineered, as is typical in mobile robotics.

As the activities of robotics systems increase in scope, both methods of constructing task solvers become cumbersome. In the declarative mode, the structure of the capabilities of the robot and the semantics of the world must be encoded somehow. For example, the Situation Graph [16] is an example of a structural description of the semantics of a scene that is used both in the understanding of an image sequence and the generation of descriptions of the sequences. Learning seems to avoid these difficulties but has only been applied to the simplest of tasks.

Thonnat [275] details the knowledge needed for a knowledge-based vision system: domain knowledge, image-to-scene mapping knowledge, and image processing knowledge. These latter two describe the appearance of the scene in the image, combining information about optics, photometrics, geometry, and the specifics of objects. This knowledge is *generative*; it models how the scene *generates* images.

[64] provides an excellent account of the use of generative models in describing visual input and adapting to new situations, in the context of understanding dynamic scene activity.

We show later how our recent work [190], by situating learning in the context where utilities (reward functions) are made explicit, can learn relevant structure adaptively, without *a priori* conceptions of the salient information.

A *role* is a collection of tasks unified by a high level goal. Each of the tasks in itself assembles a set of goals. In our case the roles include the high level tasks of waiting and message delivery. In each role there are a variety of subtasks, each of which requires information about the current state of the world. By using the term "role" we emphasize that the robot's basic capabilities do not change, only the way the information is assembled and used, as well as the fact that the role brings along a style of interaction, perhaps even a personality, associated with the tasks.

Of course, to make progress, we often increase the structure of the experimental situation, reduce the uncertainty, or limit the semantic complexity of the scene. Roles are such limited sets of tasks. Within a role we can explore the performance of elements that may play a part in a more complete future system.

We can also distinguish between situations where the task is accomplished by reactive or deliberative or mixed systems. Purely reactive systems rely on a simple mapping between sensor inputs and actions, and many have learned the association between sensor input and action by methods such as reinforcement learning [414]. Another aspect of the structure of systems arises from modeling a dynamic unstructured world, for which the components of effective intelligent systems must combine discrete and continuous components [504].

There are a variety of compelling reasons to include a cognitive component in a robot. First, interactive input from human users, beyond simple signals, needs the capacity to refer to objects and activities in the environment, as well as to state the intentions and desires of the users. The robot generates speech to explain its interpretation of actions/situations [145] and to communicate its intentions. Humans eventually wish systems to be able to acquire new tasks as a result of interaction, so the robot needs names and recognition of entities in the world. It should be able to learn these verbal descriptions. Also, deliberative systems need to mirror some of the structure of the scene to consider their alternatives and weigh the outcomes. Reasoning allows one to specify necessary, not just low probability, elements of an interpretation[77, 140]. In the context of the robots, this permits diagnosis of events.

17.1.1 Mobile Robots

Building service robots to help people has been the subject of much recent research. The challenge is to achieve reliable systems that operate in highly dynamic environments and have easy to use interfaces. This involves solving both the more traditional robot problems of navigation and localization and the more recent problems in human-robot interaction. Another challenge arises from the large scope of these systems and the many pieces that must be integrated together to make them work. RHINO [59], one of the most successful service robots ever built, was designed as a museum tour guide. RHINO successfully navigated a very dynamic environment using laser sensors and interacted with people using pre-recorded information; a person could select a specific tour of the museum by pressing one of many buttons on the robot. RHINO's task planning was specified using an extension to the GOLOG language called GOLEX; GOLEX is an extension of first order calculus, but with the added ability to generating hierarchical plans and a run-time component monitoring the execution of those plans. MINERVA [449], the successor of RHINO, could generate tours in real-time. MINERVA also improved on the interaction by incorporating a steerable head capable of displaying different emotional states.

More recently, [308] designed PEARL, a robot for assisting the elderly. PEARL's main task is to escort people around an assisted living facility. Its navigation and localization uses probabilistic techniques with laser sensors. PEARL is more focused on the interaction side with an expressive face and a speech recognition engine. PEARL's largest contribution is the use of a partially observable Markov decision process for modeling uncertainty at the highest level of task specification.

GRACE [427], Graduate Robot Attending a ConferencE, is an example of system designed for a task with many advanced mobile robotics elements, including extensive navigation and interaction ability. However, in GRACE, substantial portions of the system are still engineered at a detailed level in languages designed for agent programming [426].

In the following sections, we will discuss how we have progressed in building effective interactive mobile robots, from engineered systems that incorporate multiple layers, to our recent robots with complex interaction ability, again engineered, to those built more on sounder probabilistic methods. First we will describe the capabilities of our vision-based mobile robots, and then the roles that the robots have embodied. Finally we will detail our recent work in learning visual actions, which suggests ways that learning can discover relevant perceptual events for interactive robot partners.

17.2 Capabilities

Visual capabilities provide information about the progress toward the robot's goal and information about the world that the robot needs to make decisions and act. We have assembled a range of capabilities that we use to implement the roles that the robots play.

17.2.1 Mobility

Localization and Mapping

In order to collaborate with its partners, i.e., other robots and humans, a robot needs to determine its location, especially when it has developed a model of the location of

(a)   (b)

Fig. 17.2. (a) SIFT features found, with scale and orientation indicated by the size and orientation of the squares. (b) Stereo matching result, where horizontal and vertical lines indicate the horizontal and vertical disparities respectively (from [411]).

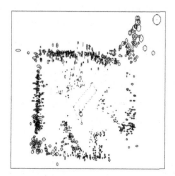

Fig. 17.3. Bird's eye view of the 3D SIFT database map, showing the uncertainty ellipses of the landmarks, and the robot trajectory during the map building. Note that the smallest ellipses represent the most reliable and useful landmarks (from [410]).

people, their activities, and the objects they may need. Depending on the task, the map may be purely topological, combined metric and topological, or fully metric.

Many mobile robots have used sonar, infrared, or lasers for mapping and localization. Our robots are equipped with a Point Grey Research [1] Bumblebee^{TM} stereo vision camera that delivers real-time stereo and color images. Previous versions of the robots used the Digiclops trinocular stereo camera. Simultaneous Localization and Mapping (SLAM) [249, 450] provides a map built from observations acquired by a moving platform; map construction needs localization of the observer which is in turn dependent on the map.

We use visual features of the environment as landmarks for building re-usable maps[410, 412], as have Sim and Dudek [425], who learn generative models of scene features, which can then be used to estimate pose. The features we use are Lowe's Scale-Invariant Feature Transform (SIFT) image descriptors [266], in which image content is

---
[1] www.ptgrey.com

transformed into local feature coordinates that are invariant to translation, rotation, scale, and other imaging parameters. Figure 17.2 shows the SIFT features from a vantage point in our lab. Since the features are observed in stereo, we can link SIFT image features with 3D landmarks.

In SIFT-based localization, the 3D map is continuously built over time. In Figure 17.3 we show the bird's eye view of the SIFT database as well as the robot trajectory after 148 frames with 4828 landmarks in the database. The uncertainty of each 3D landmark is represented as an ellipsoid. In the bird's eye view projection, error ellipses covering a region of 1 standard deviation in either sides of X and Z directions are shown. Once we have built a map of the robot's environment, we can anchor the rich stereo data that the robot acquires [315] to the map's coordinate system, enabling modeling and tele-operation.

Navigation

Real-time stereo supplies coarse information about the location of surfaces nearby the robot. As well, it supports detection of objects such as people. We rely only on the stereo data to supply us with information about obstacles during navigation. Figure 17.4 shows the process by which stereo data is transformed from images to occupancy grids [109], used for obstacle identification and navigation. Given a goal location, the robot position, and the occupancy grid map, we want to find the shortest and safest path connecting the two. We find the path by a potential field method that mixes distance to the goal location with repulsion fields around obstacles [314].

Local 3D Map

A robot also requires sensing and representation of nearby objects. It would be best to have a scene description with labeled scene elements localized in the local map, but lacking the ability to perform such recognition, we build a local 3D map of the occupied volume elements (voxels) in the vicinity of the robot. The occupancy grid used by the robot is limited to 2D because of the space requirements and computational load imposed by the 3D map; a typical room of 10m by 10m by 3m at 5cm resolution needs 200x200x60 or 2.4M voxels.

We map only the local space around the robot and carry that volume along with the robot, merging newly viewed locations with the current map. The known movement of the robot is computed from its odometry updated by the localization provided by the SIFT map. The local map of the 3D volume surrounding the robot supports interaction with people and nearby objects (Figure 17.5). The robot could use a 3D map to assist it to recognize where people are, and to improve navigation.

17.2.2 Human Robot Interaction

To provide a personal interface to the robot, we need to recognize both the faces (or the whole body) of its partners, their gestures, or even the activity of the partners. When in addition the robot knows its location and the activities and people associated with

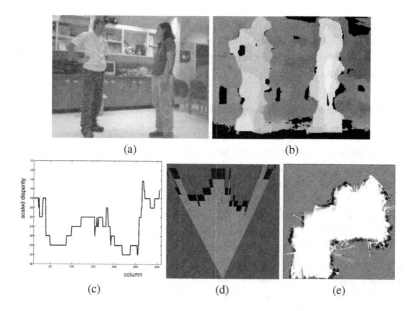

Fig. 17.4. From stereo images to radial maps. (a) greyscale image (b) disparity image (black indicates invalid, otherwise brighter indicates closer to the cameras) (c) depth vs columns graph (d) the resultant estimate of clear, unknown and occupied regions (light grey is clear, black is occupied and dark grey is unknown), which is then merged into the occupancy grid (e) (from [113]).

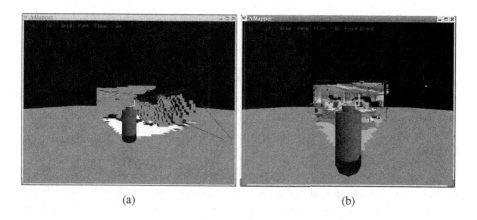

Fig. 17.5. Local 3-D occupancy grids generated during local operation (a) and the voxels painted with the current image (b). Green voxels marks cells that have occupancy of 60% or more. The blue lines represent the field of view.

the location it opens up many opportunities for collaboration and interaction. Speech recognition yields significant benefits in interaction, but is very difficult unless the robot is quite close, while speech synthesis and presenting facial expressions on the robot make the robot's intentions and actions more evident.

Recently, progress has supplied some of the infrastructure needed to enable substantial interaction: recognizing context [452, 322], recognizing particular objects [268], identifying instances of particular classes such as faces [479] and pedestrians [480], as well as collections of classes [120].

Speech Recognition and Sound Localization

Sound signals localized with an array of microphones permits the agent to turn to its partner [111] so that visual recognition of gesture can proceed. In [114] we show how to use gestures with speech for a more useful interface, for example, to direct a robot in exploration tasks. Speech input also offers the possibility of attaching names to locations and objects indicated by gestures. Speech, however, is difficult to recognize in the noisy environment of the robot, which is itself a noise source.

In conjunction with speech, facial expressions are displayed on our robot (see Fig. 17.1) with an animated face on a laptop screen mounted on a pan-tilt unit. The animated face lends expressiveness to the speech, thus making interactions with the robot more interesting. When interacting with a robot, people inevitably act as if the robot were a person [368, 351], however little the robot resembles a human. These expectations can lead to unsatisfactory or frustrating interactions if the robot is slow or inappropriate. It is important for an interactive robot to make its capabilities clear to human users to alleviate this problem.

Finding People and Face Recognition

In Section 17.3 the robot's capability for finding people is described. Further details can be found in [112].

Our simple face detection and recognition process (see [113]) uses skin color segmentation, followed by connected components analysis. Then, the region found is compared with a set of color templates of people's faces in a database, and a simple Bayesian decision procedure is applied. We have found that this method works relatively well with a small database of few people.

Activities

Locations can be determined by localization. Activities are associated with particular locations, for example, the printer in our lab. In general, however, the robot must be able to identify activities, which are groups or sequences of related actions, typically with a goal or purpose. Our work on recognizing people has focused on motion characteristics ([262] studies gait identification) but there are many biometrics [205] for recognizing persons by fingerprint, retinal scan, iris, as well as motion. Likewise there are many methods for categorizing motion and activity [64, 187].

In our work we need to represent estimates of instantaneous motion derived from optical flow fields. The representation could be learned from examples, but we have selected an *a priori* basis, the Zernike polynomials, that express the flow over a compact region. In particular we use these polynomials for representation and recognition of complex human motion [187].

Recognizing gestures and activities requires representation of articulated, non-rigid motion at many scales. [189] develops a model based on Coupled Hidden Markov Models (CHMMs). These methods have been developed outside the robot context but are now ready to be incorporated in the robots; their structure and use will be treated in Section 17.4.

Associating Words with Objects in Images

de Freitas and his coworkers [66] continue to establish the possibilities of learning the association between the names of scene objects and images, begun in part in Duygulu et al. [29]. As first steps toward constructing the necessary mapping between scene elements and words, Carbonetto and de Freitas [65] developed a statistical model for learning the probability that a word is associated with an object in a scene. They learn these relationships without access to the correct associations between image elements and words. Instead they learn associations from collections of labels of images together with segmentations, either simple or sophisticated, of the images. Of course, contextual translation improves the results, since the assumption of independence is far too weak. A more expressive model takes context into account and can better learn the model parameters.

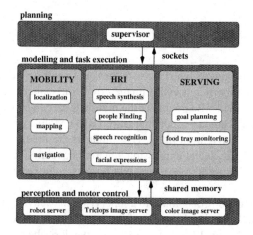

Fig. 17.6. Control Architecture of *José* (from [112])

17.3 Roles for Robots

The role of *José* [112] uses our visual processes, localization, mapping, navigation and human-robot interaction, in the context of a particular robotic task: serving food to a gathering of people. To accomplish this task, a robot must reliably navigate around a room populated by groups of people, politely serving appetizers to humans. The robot must also monitor the food it has available to serve, and return to a home base location to refill when the food is depleted. Problems specific to the serving task were also solved using vision, including finding people to serve and monitoring food. As well, the robot's success depends significantly on its interaction with users, its "persona", and its ability to generate appropriate speech.

José is driven by a hierarchical behavior-based control architecture [18], as shown in Figure 17.6. The system divides the robot's behaviors into three levels, each of which contains simple, independent, modules. The modularity of the system makes implementation and testing simple and efficient.

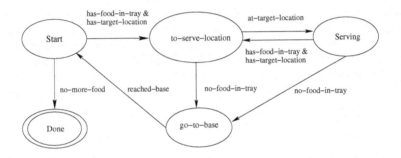

Fig. 17.7. The State Diagram for *José*'s Serving Behaviors (from [112])

The lowest level behaviors interface with the robot's sensors and actuators, relaying commands to the motors or retrieving images from the camera. These are described more fully elsewhere [114]. Behaviors at the middle level can be grouped in two broad categories: mobility and human-robot interaction (HRI). Mobility modules perform mapping, localization and navigation [314]. HRI modules are for face recognition, people finding, speech synthesis, facial expression generation, sound localization and gesture recognition [114]. Each middle level module outputs some aspect of the state of the environment.

The highest level of control belongs to a supervisor that activates mid-level behaviors to achieve the task at hand. The behavior of the supervisor is modeled with a finite state automaton, depicted in Fig. 17.7. In the following we describe how the system utilizes several capabilities to enable itself to complete the task of serving people.

As part of situation awareness, a robot must find people (Fig. 17.8), i.e., it must determine the "target location" mentioned in the state diagram (Fig. 17.7). It must detect locations in the occupancy grid where people are standing and which coincide with results of skin color segmentation, resulting in a "desirability map". This map assigns a measure of likelihood for finding people to each location in the map, and serves as a guide for the supervisor to plan locations to attend. Several serving capabilities are included in *José*'s architecture: goal planning and food tray monitoring. The former more properly would be in the supervisory control but in *José* it is simplified by using the iconic "desirability map" so that planning, like navigation, can be accomplished by

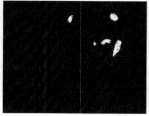

Fig. 17.8. A view of *José*'s environment from the home base as seen though the color camera (left) and corresponding skin segmentations (middle) and stereo depth images (right) (from [112]).

following gradients in the map. To encourage visits to multiple locations and because people move around, desirability decreases over time (Fig. 17.9).

Food tray monitoring [112] uses simple thresholded images of the black tray. The food stands out against the background so detection is simple, but like planning for finding and visiting people, this visual task more directly connects with interaction and progress in the task, and is therefore given special treatment. For example, food must be present to be offered, and if taken when not offered, the robot expresses its disappointment at the rudeness of the customers.

Ideally the robot should be able also to record the movement of identified people in its vicinity. This would require identification of individuals, determining their location and monitoring their movement over time.

17.3.1 HOMER: Human Oriented MEssenger Robot

The second role we have implemented on this set of capabilities is a messenger robot, HOMER, the Human Oriented MEssenger Robot, a mobile robot that communicates messages between humans in a workspace. The message delivery task is a challenging domain for an interactive robot. It presents all the difficulties associated with uncertain navigation in a changing environment, as well as those associated with exchanging information and taking commands from humans using a natural interface. In designing HOMER, however, we are concerned with the more general problem of building mobile robotic systems with capacities to interact with humans independently of the task they are asked to perform. Such robots need the visual capabilities we have implemented, as well as the ability to present clear, simple and natural interactive interfaces, which enable easy exchanges of information between robot and human. The capabilities can be linked to modules in the software organization.

In HOMER, for example, the face recognition module reports a distribution over people's faces in its database, while the navigation module reports the current location of the robot with respect to the maps. These outputs are typically reported to the highest level modules. Each module further offers a set of possible actions the module can effect.

Crucial to the design of a human-interactive mobile robot is the ability to rapidly and easily modify the robot's behavior, specifying the changes in a clear and simple language of high-level concepts. For example, we may wish to modify our message delivery robot so that it also delivers coffee. The robot will need new hardware (an actuator to grab the

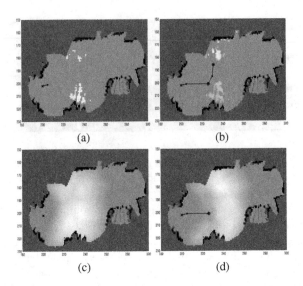

(a)   (b)

(c)   (d)

Fig. 17.9. Occupancy grids (a), (b), during a serving run. *José*'s trajectory is shown, with an 'x' marking the home base, and 'o's marking serving locations. White pixels show the location of people determined from the fusion of the stereo data and the skin-color segmentation. Desirability maps (c), (d), change over time as the robot visits serving locations; the brightness of a pixel is proportional to the probability that people are at that location. The robot combines proximity and the people probability to determine its goal location (from [112]).

coffee with) and new sensors (to operate the new actuators, to recognize cash money,...). Further it will need to be able to plan solutions to deal with the extended state space of coffee delivery. For example, it now needs to plan for the situation in which one buys for and receives a coffee from an attendant.

In [113] we discuss the software issues arising from these concerns in the design of HOMER. Independently operating modules from the core of HOMER's architecture are shown in Figure 17.10. They report their states to a manager, who collects information from all the robot's modules, and synthesizes a current world state, which is reported to a planning engine. The planning engine returns an optimal action, which the manager delegates to one or more modules.

In *José* we implemented the manager and planner together in the supervisor as a finite state machine. In HOMER we separate planning and management tasks, and use a Markov decision process (MDP) domain representation for the planner. Markov decision processes (MDPs) have become the semantic model of choice for decision theoretic planning (DTP) in the AI planning community [359]. Fully-observable MDPs model the domain of interest with a finite set of (fully observable) states S. Actions of an agent, drawn from a finite set $\mathcal{A}$, induce stochastic state transitions, with $P(S_t|A_t, S_{t-1})$ denoting the probability with which state $S_t \in S$ is reached when action $A_t \in \mathcal{A}$ is executed at state $S_{t-1} \in S$. A real-valued reward function R associates with each state, s, and action, a, its immediate utility $R(s, a)$. Figure 17.11 shows the Bayesian network representation of an MDP. Specification of a domain in this way is simpler and more

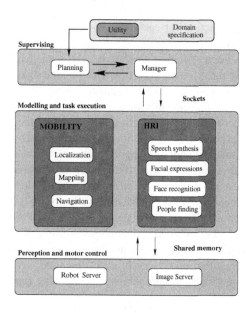

Fig. 17.10. Control Architecture for HOMER (from [113])

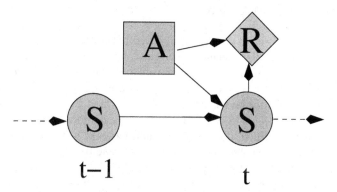

Fig. 17.11. Two time slices of a Markov decision process MDP as a Bayesian network. The full network involves infinitely many time slices. Actions, A, induce transitions between states, S. A reward function, R, gives the utility of taking an action in a state.

intuitive, particularly for large domains. Further, it makes explicit the independence of the different modules as factors in the MDP. Finally, MDPs can be learned from data, allowing the robot to adapt its planning model to changing environments or tasks.

An MDP can be solved to yield a optimal policy of action. This computation uses dynamic programming to propagate values from the reward function at some time in the future backwards through the probabilistic state transition function. The result is an assignment of value to any state of the domain, and an action which is optimal to take for each state in that it will lead to the achievement of most value for the robot. We use a factored, structured, MDP solver, SPUDD [191], which takes as input the conditional probabilities, Pr, and the reward function $R(s)$, and computes an optimal infinite-horizon policy of action for each state, assuming a *expected total discounted reward* as our optimality criterion.

Once an MDP has been specified and solved, the manager must simply map the output of the modules to the representation of environmental state used by the MDP. The current outputs of all the modules (and the manager's state) comprise the current state of the robot. The manager presents this state to the planning engine, which consults a policy of action and recommends some action. The manager then delegates this action to whatever modules respond to it. The policy maps world states to actions.

In general, the modules will not only report their state, but also some variance information about the measurement of the state. If this information is passed on to the planner, the planner, to take best advantage of all information available, should use a partially observable Markov decision process (POMDP), as shown in Figure 17.12(a). Unfortunately, policy computation is intractable in general for POMDPs, although approximate solutions are possible, and often yield satisfactory solutions. A POMDP planner could be easily fit into HOMER's architecture if needed. In our current implementation, we use a planner which requires full observability of the state, and so the manager may be responsible for compressing the probabilistic belief state reported by a module by choosing a maximum value.

17.4 Learning Visual Actions

Our work with HOMER shows that we can build a robot system over a set of modularized capabilities by connecting the manager module to a planner whose policies are computed from the utility and domain specification relevant to the specifics of the task.

In our recent work [189] we develop a vision-based, adaptable, decision-theoretic model of human facial displays in interactions. The model is a partially observable Markov decision process, or POMDP. The video observations are integrated into the POMDP using a hierarchical dynamic Bayesian network, which creates spatial and temporal abstractions amenable to decision making. The parameters of the model are learned from training data. However, the training does not require labeled data, since we do not train classifiers for individual facial actions, and then integrate them into the model. Rather, the learning process *discovers* clusters of facial motions and their relationship to the context automatically. As such, it can be applied to any situation in which non-verbal gestures are purposefully used in a task.

The visual capabilities of this system are not separated from the task performance. Rather they are tightly connected throughout the Bayesian network. Moreover, their focus is not specified beforehand, although the visual channel, optical flow, is fixed. But the particular elements that are salient to the task are determined from the task itself. This is an entirely new method of learning the visual capabilities. In the following we describe in detail some elements of the model to demonstrate its workings and how it relates to the previous description of the robot's roles.

Figure 17.12(b) shows the POMDP model for facial display understanding as Bayesian network in the context of a robot, here named "Bob", and a human with whom the robot is interacting, here named "Ann". In this figure the blue (in B/W prints: grey) circles are observable, while the white circles are the hidden state variables. The reward function $R(s)$ is shown in a yellow (grey) diamond; this is similar to the reward used in computing the policy for HOMER.

The state of the model is factored into Bob's private internal state, Bs, Ann's observable action, $Aact$, and Ann's unobservable facial display, $Acom$, all of which are discrete-valued and finite. The observations of Ann's displays, O, are sequences of video frames containing Ann's face, and are conditioned on the high level display descriptor, $Acom$. For example, a particular assignment of a value to $Acom$, say "smile", will correspond with an observation, O, which is a video sequence in which Ann smiles. The model describes how Bob's action at time t, $Bact_t$, changes the state, $S_t = \{Bs_t, Aact_t, Acom_t\}$, from time $t-1$ to time t through a conditional probability distribution, $P(S_t|Bact, S_{t-1})$. This distribution is factored into three terms as shown in Figure 17.12(a). The first involves only fully observable variables, and is the conditional probability of the state at time t under the effect of both player's actions: $P(Bs_t|Aact_t, Bact)$. The second is Bob's distribution over Ann's actions given his action, the previous state, her previous action, and her previous display: $P(Aact_t|Bact, Acom_{t-1}, Aact_{t-1}, Bs_{t-1})$. The third describes Bob's expectation about Ann's displays given his action, the previous state and her previous display: $P(Acom_t|Bact, Bs_{t-1}, Acom_{t-1})$. These last two distributions involve the unobservable display state, $Acom$, and are what must be learned from data.

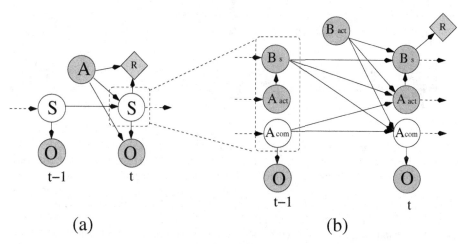

Fig. 17.12. (a) Two time slices of general POMDP. (b) Two time slices of factored POMDP for facial display understanding. The state, S, has been factored into $\{Bs, Aact, Acom\}$, and conditional independencies have been introduced: Ann's actions do not depend on her previous actions and Ann's display is independent of her previous action given the state and her previous display. These independencies are not strictly necessary, but simplify our discussion, and are applicable in the simple game we analyse (from [189]).

The observation function, $P(O|D) \equiv P(O|Acom)$, is shown as a Bayesian network in Figure 17.13. In this case, we have relabeled $D \equiv Acom$ for ease of exposition. The model is being used to assess a sequence in which a person smiles, in an imitation task where the person is asked to imitate a facial display. The reward function in this simple game is just the correct matching of the interpretation of the face by the system and the expression displayed for imitation.

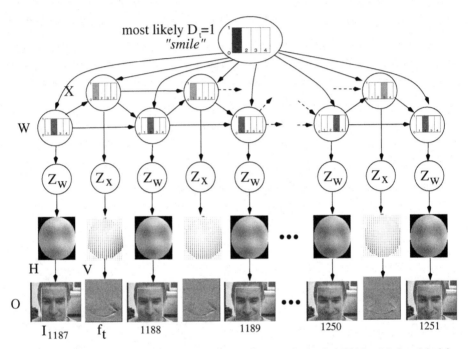

Fig. 17.13. A person smiling is analysed by the mixture of Coupled Hidden Markov Models. Observations, O, are sequences of images, I, and image temporal derivatives, f_t, both of which are projected over the facial region to a set of basis functions, yielding feature vectors, Z_x and Z_w. The image regions, H, are projected directly, while it is actually the optical flow fields, V, related to the image derivatives which are projected to the basis functions [188]. The class distributions, X and W, are temporally modeled as a mixture, D, of coupled Markov chains. The probability distribution over D is at the top. The most likely state, $D = 2$, can be associated with the concept "smile". Probability distributions over X and W are shown for each time step. All other nodes in the network show their expected value given all evidence (from [189]).

Spatially abstracting a video frame during a human facial display involves modeling both the current configuration and dynamics of the face. Our observations consist of the video images, I, and the temporal derivatives, f_t, between pairs of images. The task is first to spatially summarise both of these quantities, and then to temporally compress the entire sequence to a distribution over high level descriptors, $Acom$. The optical flow field over the facial region is projected to the Zernike polynomial basis [187]. The resulting feature vector, Z_x, is then conditioned on a set of discrete states, X, parametrised by normal distributions. The raw (greyscale) images are projected to the same basis functions, resulting in a feature vector, Z_w, which is also modeled using a mixture of normal distributions with mixture coefficients W. During learning the model automatically selects a small subset of the basis functions that represent the variation well.

At each time frame, we have a discrete dynamics state, X, and a discrete configuration state, W, which are abstract descriptions of the instantaneous dynamics and configuration of the face, respectively. These are temporally abstracted using a mixture of coupled hidden Markov models (CHMM), in which the dynamics and configuration states are interacting Markovian processes. The conditional dependencies between the X and W chains are chosen to reflect the relationship between the dynamics and configuration. This mixture model can be used to compute the likelihood of a video sequence given the facial display descriptor, $P(\mathbf{O}|D)$. The mixture components, D, are a set of discrete abstractions of facial behavior. It is important to remember that there are no labels associated with these states at any time during the training. Labels can be assigned after training, as is done in Figure 17.13, but these are only to ease exposition.

The adaptive dynamic Bayesian model of human facial displays is trained directly on a set of video sequences, and does not need any prior knowledge about the expected types of displays. Without any behavior labels, the model discovers classes of video sequences and their relationship with actions, utilities and context. These relationships define, or give meaning to, the discovered classes of displays. The method learns the relevant classes from videos of humans playing a computer game. The model is conducive to intelligent decision making or prediction.

17.5 Discussion

We have begun with simple engineered supervisors to implement visually guided robots, built on a set of capabilities. We then showed how an MDP based robot could use the expressivity of the POMDP representation to construct the manager and planner. Finally we see how the same decision theoretic framework can be extended to accommodate learning of classes of visual signals, leading to adaptive systems that can be developed in a more rigorous fashion.

Our most recent work on human facial displays demonstrates benefits of embedding the learning problem in a decision-theoretic framework [190]. The learned values of states are used to discover the number of display classes which are important for achieving value in the context of the interaction. This type of value-directed structure learning allows an agent to only focus resources on necessary distinctions.

Still, the semantics of the environment and human activity are complex. Communication of structure of activities and scenes to a robot is necessary for extensible robots. Many elements in the scene description can be learned. In contrast, many activities are most easily expressed in a declarative logical form; amassing the necessary knowledge for competent robots remains a formidable task.

Learning word-to-image association provides a means of expanding the reach of robotic domain knowledge in addition to the process of attaching spoken names to objects indicated by gestures. Integration with the rapidly improving recognition and categorization methods should lead to enhanced robot abilities.

Acknowledgements

Many members of the Robot Partners project have participated in the research described here, including Don Murray, Nando de Freitas, David Lowe, and Alan Mackworth, all of UBC, James J. Clark of McGill University, and Stephen Se of MDRobotics.

This work was supported by grants from the Natural Sciences and Engineering Research Council of Canada and from the Institute for Robotics and Intelligent Systems, a Canadian Network of Centres of Excellence.

Part VI

Conclusions

18

On Sampling the Spectrum of Approaches Toward Cognitive Vision Systems

H.-H. Nagel

Institut für Algorithmen und Kognitive Systeme,
Fakultät für Informatik, Universität Karlsruhe (TH),
76128 Karlsruhe, Germany
nagel@iaks.uni-karlsruhe.de

In a collection of scientific contributions like this one, it is usually *left for the reader to create* a coherent internal representation of the topical area discussed, based on the different aspects treated by the authors and on their points of view. The overall picture thus has to be constructed by integrating individual presentations with differing centers of emphasis.

18.1 Introductory Considerations

The advantage of such a procedure consists in the ease with which a reader can reconfigure an assessment in the light of later developments or if (s)he prefers to look at the problem area from a different point of view. Considerable efforts have been spent to facilitate such endeavors with this text – by insertion of cross-references between chapters, by the inclusion of backreferences to quotations from the literature, and by the addition of a detailed list of index terms. Access to an electronic version of this text will ease the exploitation of these supporting tools.

The challenge remains, though, for each reader to decide whether the preceding chapters constitute a random selection of topics or a sample characterizing an emerging area of *coherent* scientific activity. An attempt – favoring the latter alternative – follows to *explicate relations between contributions* incorporated into this volume while still acting with care not to impose a particular point of view onto this exercise at the detriment of others.

18.2 Foundations of Cognitive Vision Systems

In Chapter 2, D. Vernon paints a broad and diverse background picture which could be seen as a framework accommodating the more specialized subsequent contributions. J. Tsotsos in Chapter 3 then establishes a link to developments in brain research, both regarding experimental neurophysiology and theoretical investigations which look towards

H.I. Christensen and H.-H. Nagel (Eds.): Cognitive Vision Systems, LNCS 3948, pp. 315–319, 2006.

a more encompassing interpretation compatible with established methods in computer vision. Although the topic of attention does not yet play a dominant role in investigations reported later in this volume, an algorithmic analogue to attention will become more prominent once categorization has to be applied to a larger and more varied set of categories in images and image sequences. So far, computational resources roughly suffice for the experiments to be performed – or the experiments are tacitly matched to the resources available. This may no longer be possible in the future, in particular if real-time constraints will have to be obeyed. Such a consideration will become even more important if a CogVS has to analyze not only static images, but videos recording time-varying scenes where the task consists in characterizing the *behavior* and in finding out the *intentions* of agents. It can be found already – albeit somewhat veiled as a specific design problem – in Chapter 12 on 'Things that See' by J.L. Crowley. Investigators may thus be well advised to keep an eye on attention-related research.

The two subsequent contributions by G. Granlund and H.-H. Nagel approach the discussion of a CogVS-architecture from almost diametrically opposing directions. Chapter 2 by D. Vernon already mentioned the existence of significantly differing points of departure towards the discussion of a CogVS. The existence of such differences should not only be attributed to an early stage of the discussion about the concept of a CogVS, but in addition to the large range of subtopics which have to be taken into account for a CogVS. From this point of view, it appears more significant that different system concepts exhibit commonalities in areas which do not constitute the focus of detailed emphasis by different authors. As an example, the reader is invited to compare Figure 4.4 from Granlund's contribution with Figure 5.1 in Nagel's exposition. Both – rather coarse – schematic structures of a CogVS comprise a component devoted to the interaction between a 'sensor/actuator-centered' subsystem and some system-external communication partner, in many cases a human operator. At least in the case where such a communication becomes varied enough to justify the use of a (restricted natural) language, a (bi-)directional transition between entities treated by the sensor/actuator-centered subsystem and a symbolic representation will become necessary.

18.3 Adaptation, Learning, Recognition, and Categorization

A symbolic representation may remain restricted to identifiers for 'classes' or 'categories', without attempts to associate such classes or categories with concepts used by a Natural Language Understanding or Generation process *within* the CogVS. Approaches associated with recognition or categorization address the intertwined problems to detect, segment, categorize, possibly even track, recognize and identify the image of relevant (parts of) bodies in the recorded scene. The verbs serialized in the preceding sentence are frequently used in a colloquial manner with the tendency to obscure rather than emphasize the specifics of different processing steps.

The detection step should establish an hypothesis that the image of a relevant body could be found at a particular location in the image frame to be analysed. Segmenting the image of a relevant body ('figure') from the remainder of the current frame ('ground') will ease, if not enable in the first place, the assignment of the segmented figure to a category identifier, i.e. establish this figure as an element of a set denoted by a category identifier. A category may comprise different subcategories or 'classes': elements of a class are expected to differ only with respect to characteristics which are considered irrelevant for the task at hand whereas different classes within a category may exhibit relevant – i.e. not to be treated as being due to noise – differences. The *intra-category* variation is thus expected to be much larger than the *intra-class* variation. Whereas the intra-class variation may be modeled by a purely stochastic process, the intra-category variation will in general comprise non-stochastic characteristics. Correct assignment of a figure to a category opens the road to two options: (i) the activation of category-specific 'classification' steps, e.g., the use of cascaded classifiers in case of single image frames, and (ii) the initialisation of a tracking phase during a subsequence of consecutive image frames in order to obtain more information about the hypothesized element. The coherent acquisition of information about an hypothesis during a tracking phase may facilitate to identify a particular individuum and to associate it with additional – possibly even time-varying – attributes. This latter potential is illustrated in Chapter 9 by V. Krüger and co-authors.

In the case of single frame analysis, the contributions by D. Hall (Chapter 6) and by Leibe & Schiele (Chapter 10) both acquire category characteristics from a learning sample, but can be looked at as emphasizing two different 'dimensions' of processing within a CogVS. Hall estimates the 'scale' of features. This enables her to determine feature characteristics more precisely with the effect that subsequent processing steps proceed on a firmer basis which in turn results in a more robust approach. Leibe & Schiele study a different alternative to make categorization more robust. Their approach sort of 'leapfrogs' an initial segmentation in the usual 'detection-segmentation-recognition' sequence of processing steps by linking the detection results directly to a tentative categorization step. Knowledge about category appearance can then be exploited to start a category-specific *segmentation* step whose results are subjected to a verification process. Taken together, the approaches discussed in Chapters 6, 9, and 10 nicely illustrate means to increase the versatility and robustness of processing steps which link signals with concepts. Obviously, it appears tempting to combine their complementary advantages in future system implementations.

Whereas the contributions discussed in the preceding paragraph emphasize different assumptions about how to exploit characteristics of input images, Chapter 7 and Chapter 8 address *methodological* aspects of processing signals and features. The contribution by Franc & Hlavac (Chapter 7) investigates a trade-off between speed and approximation errors during machine learning steps based on large learning samples. Dickinson et al. in Chapter 8 study *many-to-many* feature matching. CogVS tend to become large and encompassing. It thus will be advantageous if component modules can be selected and integrated on the basis of established 'quality assurances' regarding computational expenses and precision – see, too, Section 18.5 on 'Integrated Systems'.

Chapter 11 by Niemann and co-workers exemplifies in two different ways the kinds of transition which are likely to be encountered increasingly in a CogVS. The learning process in this case exploits conceptual representations and it addresses the learning of an *analysis strategy* rather than of category or class characteristics. In addition, it exemplifies the feedback from higher levels of representation to control, e.g., camera pose, i.e. sensor characteristics as discussed in connection with Figure 4.4 from Granlund's contribution or Figure 5.1 in Nagel's contribution. The approach discussed in this Chapter 11 will be taken up again in Section 18.5 on 'Integrated Systems'.

18.4 Representation and Inference

The incorporation of conceptual processing levels based on formal logic characterizes, too, the experimental systems described by Crowley in Chapter 12, by Cohn et al. in Chapter 14, by Vincze et al. in Chapter 16, and by Little et al. in Chapter 17. Perspectives for future research regarding such approaches become especially evident in Chapter 15 by Neumann & Möller who investigate the use of 'Description Logic (DL)' as a representational tool for image interpretation. These investigations are guided by the desire to gradually transform the image interpretation process from the use of heuristics into formally verifiable logical inferences. In this context, Description Logic studies restrictions of First Order Predicate Logic in order to guarantee the decidability of logical expressions constructed according to the DL-constraints. The challenge consists in finding a balance between the expressiveness of a formal language and the need to limit computational expenses for the evaluation of formal representations expressed in this manner. One may look at such investigations as aiming at system components with proven 'quality' – or 'Quality of Service (QoS)' (see, e.g., the introductory section of Chapter 16) – assurances, in this case for *conceptual (qualitative)* rather than numerical (quantitative) processing as discussed in Chapters 7 and 8.

18.5 Integrated Systems

As mentioned already, CogVS are likely to become large and complex in comparison with experimental systems devoted to the study of a particular (sub-)problem. The discussion in the introductory section of Chapter 16 by Vincze et al. expands on related considerations. Various subsets of chapters in this volume illustrate different aspects regarding the initial design, continuous development, and maintenance of entire CogVS. One such aspect refers to approaches which assemble system components based on a *conceptual* characterisation of the subtask to be handled by a component. This aspect is mentioned explicitly, e.g., in Chapter 11 by Niemann and co-workers and in the contribution by Vincze et al. in Chapter 16. It should be noted that a connection between conceptual characterisations of component characteristics and natural language expressions may not only improve the interface between a CogVS and its human users, but can simplify considerably the further expansion of system capabilities and their maintenance.

A different aspect is concerned with assurances regarding 'quality' or 'Quality of Service (QoS)' of a component which become the more important the larger and more complex a system becomes. This necessity gradually shifts the emphasis of researchers from an heuristic exploitation of new ways to accomplish an effect towards the analysis of algorithms with respect to computational expenses, guaranteed termination, and proven statements about properties of computed results. As mentioned already, Chapters 7 and 8 are relevant here regarding processing steps closer to signal representations whereas

Chapter 15 can be seen in this context as treating analogous questions at the level of conceptual representations and their evaluation based on formal logic.

Chapter 13 by Kropatsch and co-workers clearly has to be mentioned in this context, too. It should not be a surprise that this work heavily relies on graph theory to analyse, represent and combine geometrical relations. Hierarchies of pyramids are studied in order to cope with systematic variations of representational resolution. The associated problem formulations and solution approaches are introduced in abstract terms and subsequently are used to treat image segmentations. It is expected that a comparison with different uses of graph theory in Chapters 6 and 8 will be stimulating.

Independently of the particular emphasis a reader is inclined to assign to the concept of a CogVS, the contributions to this volume constitute a sample which is encompassing enough to let the coherence of scientific activities in this area become visible.

Acknowledgment

My sincere thanks go to the participants of the Dagstuhl Seminar 03441 on Cognitive Vision Systems (26-30 October 2003) who devoted their time to patiently correct my misunderstandings of what they had presented in the lecture hall.

Part VII

References, Subject Index, Author Index

References

1. S. Agarwal and D. Roth. Learning a Sparse Representation for Object Detection. In A. Heyden, G. Sparr, M. Nielsen, and P. Johansen, editors, *Computer Vision - ECCV 2002, Part IV*, volume 2353 of *Lecture Notes in Computer Science*, pages 113–127, Copenhagen, Denmark, 28–31 May 2002. Springer-Verlag Berlin·Heidelberg·New York/NY. *(Quoted on pages 73, 81, 148, 151, 153, 154, and 155)*

2. R. Agarwala, V. Bafna, M. Farach, M. Paterson, and M. Thorup. On the Approximability of Numerical Taxonomy (Fitting Distances by Tree Metrics). *SIAM Journal on Computing*, 28(2):1073–1085, 1999. *(Quoted on page 119)*

3. U. Ahlrichs. *Wissensbasierte Szenenexploration auf der Basis erlernter Analysestrategien*. Studien zur Mustererkennung, Bd. 5. Logos Verlag, Berlin, Germany, 2002. *(Quoted on pages 166 and 179)*

4. R.K. Ahuja, T.L. Magnanti, and J.B. Orlin. *Network Flows: Theory, Algorithms, and Applications*, pages 4–7. Prentice Hall, Englewood Cliffs, New Jersey, 1993. *(Quoted on page 122)*

5. S. Aksoy, C. Tusk, K. Koperski, and G. Marchisio. Scene Modeling and Image Mining with a Visual Grammar. In *Frontiers of Remote Sensing Information Processing*, Singapore, 2003. World Scientific. *(Quoted on page 234)*

6. J.S. Albus. 4-D/RCS: A Reference Model Architecture for Demo III. In *IEEE ISIC/ CIRA/ ISAS International Symposium on Intelligent Control*, pages 634–639, September 1998. *(Quoted on page 281)*

7. J.F. Allen. Maintaining Knowledge About Temporal Intervals. *Communications of the ACM*, 11(26):832–843, 1983. *(Quoted on page 262)*

8. J.F. Allen. Towards a General Theory of Action and Time. *Artificial Intelligence*, 23(2):123–154, 1984. *(Quoted on page 190)*

9. J. Aloimonos, I. Weiss, and A. Bandyopadhyay. Active Vision. In *Proc. First Int. Conf. on Computer Vision*, pages 35–54, London, UK, 8–11 June 1987. *(Quoted on page 166)*

10. J. Aloimonos, I. Weiss, and A. Bandyopadhyay. Active Vision. *International Journal of Computer Vision*, 1(4):333–356, 1988. *(Quoted on page 184)*

11. S. J. Anderson, N. Yamagishi, and V. Karavia. Attentional Processes Link Perception and Action. *Proc. Royal Society London B Biol Sci.*, 269(1497):1225–1232, 2002. *(Quoted on pages 44 and 46)*

12. Anonymous. ECVision: European Research Network for Cognitive Computer Vision (Network Website). Technical report, European Commission, Brussels, 2003. http://www.ecvision.org. *(Quoted on page 8)*

13. Anonymus. Recognition and Vision Library. Technical report, Centre for Vision, Speech, and Signal Processing (CVSSP) at the University of Surrey, 2003. http://ravl.sourceforge.net. *(Quoted on page 280)*

14. S. Ansaldi, L. de Floriani, and B. Falcidieno. Geometric Modeling of Solid Objects by Using a Face Adjacency Graph Representation. *Computer Graphics*, 19(3):131–139, 1985. *(Quoted on page 200)*

15. M. Arens. SGTEditor v1.2 Reference Manual v1.3. Technical report, Institut für Algorithmen und Kognitive Systeme, Fakultät für Informatik der Universität Karlsruhe (TH), October 2003. http://cogvisys.iaks.uni-karlsruhe.de/Vid-Text. *(Quoted on page 64)*

16. M. Arens and H.-H. Nagel. Behavioral Knowledge Representation for the Understanding and Creation of Video Sequences. In A. Günter, R. Kruse, and B. Neumann, editors, *Proceedings of the 26th German Conference on Artificial Intelligence (KI–2003)*, volume 2821 of *Lecture Notes in Artificial Intelligence (LNAI)*, pages 149–163, Hamburg, Germany, 15–18 September 2003. Springer-Verlag Berlin·Heidelberg·New York/NY. *(Quoted on pages 64, 248, and 296)*

17. M. Arens, A. Ottlik, and H.-H. Nagel. Using Behavioral Knowledge for Situated Prediction of Movements. In S. Biundo, T. Frühwirth, and G. Palm, editors, *Proceedings of the 27th German Conference on Artificial Intelligence (KI–2004)*, volume 3238 of *Lecture Notes in Artificial Intelligence (LNAI)*, pages 141–155, Ulm, Germany, 20–24 September 2004. Springer-Verlag Berlin·Heidelberg·New York/NY. *(Quoted on page 64)*

18. R.C. Arkin. *Behaviour Based Robotics*. The MIT Press, Cambridge, MA, 1998. *(Quoted on pages 281 and 304)*

19. F. Baader, D. Calvanese, D. MacGuinness, D. Nardi, and P.F. Patel-Schneider, editors. *The Description Logic Handbook*. Cambridge University Press, Cambridge, UK, 2003. *(Quoted on pages 249, 250, and 260)*

20. F. Baader and P. Hanschke. A Schema for Integrating Concrete Domains into Concept Languages. In *Proc. 12th International Joint Conference on Artificial Intelligence (IJCAI-91)*, pages 452–457, Sydney, Australia, 24-30 August 1991. *(Quoted on page 262)*

21. F. Baader and P. Hanschke. Extensions of Concept Languages for a Mechanical Engineering Application. In H.J. Ohlbach, editor, *'Advances in Artificial Intelligence'*, 16th German Conference on Artificial Intelligence (KI-92), volume 671 of *Lecture Notes in Computer Science*, pages 132–143, Bonn (Germany), 31 August–3 September 1992. Springer-Verlag Berlin·Heidelberg·New York/NY. *(Quoted on page 262)*

22. F. Baader and R. Küsters. Matching in Description Logics with Existential Restrictions. In A.G. Cohn, F. Giunchiglia, and B. Selman, editors, *Proceedings 7th Intern. Conf. on Principles of Knowledge Representation and Reasoning (KR 2000)*, pages 261–272, Breckenridge, CO, 11–15 April 2000. Morgan Kaufmann Publishers, San Mateo, CA. *(Quoted on page 248)*

23. R. Bajcsy. Image Filtering – a Context Dependent Process. *IEEE Trans. Circuits Systems*, CAS-22:463—474, 1975. *(Quoted on page 7)*

24. R. Bajcsy. Active Perception. *Proc. IEEE*, 76(8):996–1005, 1988. *(Quoted on pages 166 and 184)*

25. D. Ballard. Generalizing the Hough Transform to Detect Arbitrary Shapes. *Pattern Recognition*, 13(2):111–122, 1981. *(Quoted on pages 151, 153, and 154)*

26. D.H. Ballard. Animate Vision. *Artificial Intelligence*, 48(1):57–86, 1991. *(Quoted on page 17)*

27. S. Baluja and D. Pomerleau. Dynamic Relevance: Vision-Based Focus of Attention Using Artificial Neural Networks. *Artificial Intelligence*, 97(1-2):381–395, 1997. *(Quoted on page 26)*

28. H.B. Barlow. Single Units and Cognition: a Neurone Doctrine for Perceptual Psychology. *Perception*, 1:371–394, 1972. *(Quoted on page 34)*
29. K. Barnard, P. Duygulu, D. Forsyth, N. de Freitas, D.M. Blei, and M.I. Jordan. Matching Words and Pictures. *J. Mach. Learn. Res.*, 3:1107–1135, 2003. *(Quoted on page 303)*
30. H.G. Barrow and J.M. Tenenbaum. Recovering Intrinsic Scene Characteristics from Images. In A. R. Hanson and E. M. Riseman, editors, *Computer Vision Systems*, pages 3–26, New York, NY, 1978. Academic Press. *(Quoted on page 7)*
31. J. Barwise and J. Perry. *Situations and Attitudes*. The MIT Press, Cambridge, MA, USA, 1983. *(Quoted on page 254)*
32. B. Baumgart. A Polyhedron Representation for Computer Vision. In *AFIPS National Computer Conferenc Proc.*, volume 44, pages 589–596, Anaheim, CA, May 1975. *(Quoted on page 200)*
33. S. Belongie, J. Malik, and J. Puchiza. Matching Shapes. In *Proc. Eighth International Conference on Computer Vision (ICCV-2001)*, volume I+II, pages I:454–461, Vancouver, BC, Canada, 9–12 July 2001. IEEE Computer Society: Los Alamitos, CA. *(Quoted on page 149)*
34. S. Belongie, J. Malik, and J. Puchiza. Shape Matching and Object Recognition Using Shape Contexts. *IEEE Transactions on Pattern Analysis and Machine Intelligence*, 24(4):509–522, April 2002. *(Quoted on page 149)*
35. B. Bennett, D.R. Magee, A.G. Cohn, and D.C. Hogg. Using Spatio-Temporal Continuity Constraints to Enhance Visual Tracking of Moving Objects. In R. López de Mántaras and L. Saitta, editors, *Proc. 16th European Conference on Artificial Intelligence (ECAI-04)*, pages 922–926, Valencia, Spain, 22–27 August 2004. IOS Press: Amsterdam, NL. *(Quoted on pages 222, 226, 227, and 228)*
36. Y. Bertrand, G. Damiand, and C. Fiorio. Topological Encoding of 3D Segmented Images. In G. Borgefors, I. Nyström, and G. S. di Baja, editors, *International Conference on Discrete Geometry for Computer Imagery*, volume 1953 of *Lecture Notes in Computer Science*, pages 311–324. Springer-Verlag Berlin·Heidelberg·New York/NY, Germany, 2000. *(Quoted on pages 200 and 213)*
37. Y. Bertrand, C. Fiorio, and Y. Pennaneach. Border Map: A Topological Representation for nD Image Analysis. In Y. Bertrand, M. Couprie, and L. Perroton, editors, *International Conference on Discrete Geometry for Computer Imagery*, volume 1568 of *Lecture Notes in Computer Science*, pages 242–257. Springer-Verlag Berlin·Heidelberg·New York/NY, Germany, 1999. *(Quoted on page 213)*
38. D. Beymer and T. Poggio. Image Representations for Visual Learning. *Science*, 272:1905–1909, June 1996. *(Quoted on page 48)*
39. J.C. Bezdek and N.R. Pal. An Index of Topological Preservation for Feature Extraction. *Pattern Recognition*, 28(3):381–391, March 1995. *(Quoted on page 211)*
40. I. Biederman. Recognition by Components: A Theory of Human Image Understanding. *Psychol. Review*, 94:115–147, 1987. *(Quoted on pages 146 and 150)*
41. T.O. Binford. Visual Perception by Computer. In *Proc. IEEE Conference on Systems and Control*, Miami, FL, December 1971. *(Quoted on page 146)*
42. T.O. Binford, T.S. Levitt, and W.B. Mann. Bayesian Inference in Model-Based Machine Vision. In L. N. Kanal, T.S. Levitt, and J. F. Lemmer, editors, *Uncertainty in Artificial Intelligence*, volume 3, pages 73–95. North-Holland, Amsterdam, The Netherlands, 1989. *(Quoted on page 273)*
43. A. Blake and A. Yuille, editors. *Active Vision*. The MIT Press, Cambridge/MA and London/UK, 1992. *(Quoted on pages 166 and 256)*
44. V. Blanz and T. Vetter. Face Recognition Based on Fitting a 3D Morphable Model. *IEEE Trans. Pattern Analysis and Machine Intelligence*, 25(9):1063–1074, 2003. *(Quoted on page 149)*

45. S. Blum. Oscar - Eine Systemarchitektur für den autonomen mobilen Roboter MAR-VIN. In R. Dillmann, H. Wörn, and M. von Ehr, editors, *Autonome Mobile Systeme*, Informatik aktuell, pages 218–230, Karlsruhe, Germany, November 2000. Springer-Verlag Berlin·Heidelberg·New York/NY. *(Quoted on page 281)*

46. A. Bobick, S. Intille, J. Davies, F. Baird, C. Pinhanez, L. Campbell, Y. Ivanov, A. Schutte, and A. Wilson. "The Kidsroom": A Perceptually-based Interactive and Immersive Story Environment. *Presence: Teleoperators and Virtual Environments*, 8:367–391, 1999. *(Quoted on page 246)*

47. D.G. Bobrow and T. Winograd. An Overview of KRL, a Knowledge Representation Language. *Cognitive Science*, 1(1):3–46, 1977. *(Quoted on page 184)*

48. E. Borenstein and S. Ullman. Class-Specific, Top-Down Segmentation. In A. Heyden, G. Sparr, M. Nielsen, and P. Johansen, editors, *Computer Vision - ECCV 2002, Part II*, volume 2351 of *Lecture Notes in Computer Science*, pages 109–122, Copenhagen, Denmark, 28–31 May 2002. Springer-Verlag Berlin·Heidelberg·New York/NY. *(Quoted on pages 147, 152, 156, and 157)*

49. O. Borůvka. O Jistém Problému Minimálnim. Práce Mor. Přírodvěd. Spol. v Brně (Acta Societ. Scienc. Natur. Moravicae), III(3):37–58, 1926. *(Quoted on pages 207, 209, and 215)*

50. R.J. Brachman. On the Epistemological Status of Semantic Networks. In N.V. Findler, editor, *Associative Networks - Representation and Use of Knowledge by Computer*, pages 3–50. Academic Press, Inc., New York, NY, USA·London, UK, 1975. *(Quoted on page 260)*

51. R.J. Brachman, D.L. McGuinness, P.F. Patel-Schneider, L.A. Resnick, and A. Borgida. Living with CLASSIC: When and How to Use a KL-ONE-like Language. In J. F. Sowa, editor, *Principles of Semantic Networks*, pages 401–456. Morgan Kaufmann, San Mateo, CA, USA, 1991. *(Quoted on page 260)*

52. R.J. Brachman and J.G. Schmolze. An Overview of the KL-ONE Knowledge Representation System. *Cognitive Science*, 9:171–216, 1985. *(Quoted on page 167)*

53. E. Brisson. Representing Geometric Structures in D Dimensions: Topology and Order. *Discrete and Computational Geometry*, 9:387–426, 1993. *(Quoted on page 200)*

54. R.A. Brooks, R. Greiner, and T.O. Binford. The ACRONYM Model-Based Vision System. In *Proc. Sixth Intern. Joint Conf. on Artificial Intelligence (IJCAI-79)*, volume I, pages 105–113, Tokyo, Japan, 20-23 August 1979. *(Quoted on page 7)*

55. P.J. Brown. The Stick-e Document: a Framework for Creating Context Aware Applications. In *Electronic Publishing*, pages 259–272, 1996. *(Quoted on page 184)*

56. L. Brun and W.G. Kropatsch. Introduction to Combinatorial Pyramids. In G. Bertrand, A. Imiya, and R. Klette, editors, *Digital and Image Geometry: Advanced Lectures*, volume 2243 of *Lecture Notes in Computer Science*, pages 108–128. Springer-Verlag Berlin·Heidelberg·New York/NY, 2001. *(Quoted on page 205)*

57. L. Brun and W.G. Kropatsch. Contraction Kernels and Combinatorial Maps. *Pattern Recognition Letters*, 24(8):1051–1057, 2003. *(Quoted on page 205)*

58. C. Bryant, S. Muggleton, C. Page, and M. Sternberg. Combining Active Learning with Inductive Logic Programming to Close the Loop in Machine Learning. In *Proc. AISB Symposium on AI and Scientific Creativity*, Division of Informatics, University of Edinburgh and Edinburgh College of Art, 8–9 April 1999. *(Quoted on pages 221, 234, and 245)*

59. W. Burgard, A.B. Cremers, D. Fox, D. Hahnel, G. Lakemeyer, D. Schulz, W. Steiner, and S. Thrun. The Interactive Museum Tour-guide Robot. In *Proceedings of the Fifteenth National Conference on Artificial Intelligence (AAAI '98)*, pages 11–18, Madison, Wisconsin, July 1998. *(Quoted on pages 296 and 298)*

60. C.J. Burges. Simplified Support Vector Decision Rule. In *13th Intl. Conf. on Machine Learning*, pages 71–77, San Mateo, 1996. Morgan Kaufmann. *(Quoted on page 89)*

61. J. Burguet and R. Malgouyres. Strong Thinning and Polyhedrization of the Surface of a Voxel Object. In G. Borgefors, I. Nyström, and G. S. di Baja, editors, *International Conference on Discrete Geometry for Computer Imagery*, volume 1953 of *Lecture Notes in Computer Science*, pages 222–234. Springer-Verlag Berlin·Heidelberg·New York/NY, Germany, 2000. *(Quoted on page 211)*

62. M.C. Burl, M. Weber, and P. Perona. A Probabilistic Approach to Object Recognition using Local Photometry and Global Geometry. In H. Burkhardt and B. Neumann, editors, *Computer Vision – ECCV'98*, volume 1407 of *LNCS*, pages 628–641, Freiburg, Germany, 2-6 June 1998. Springer-Verlag Berlin·Heidelberg·New York/NY. *(Quoted on pages 148 and 150)*

63. P.J. Burt and E.H. Adelson. The Laplacian Pyramid as a Compact Image Code. *IEEE Trans. on Communication*, 31(4):532–540, April 1983. *(Quoted on page 202)*

64. H. Buxton. Learning and Understanding Dynamic Scene Activity: a Review. *IVC*, 21(1):125–136, January 2003. *(Quoted on pages 297 and 302)*

65. P. Carbonetto and N. de Freitas. Why Can't José Read? The Problem of Learning Semantic Associations in a Robot Environment. In R. Barzilay, E. Reiter, and J.M. Siskind, editors, *Human Language Technology Conference Workshop on Learning Word Meaning from Non-Linguistic Data*, Edmonton, Canada, 31 May 2003. *(Quoted on page 303)*

66. P. Carbonetto, N. de Freitas, and K. Barnard. A Statistical Model for General Contextual Object Recognition. In *Proc. 8th European Conference on Computer Vision (ECCV 2004), Part I*, volume 3021 of *Lecture Notes in Computer Science*, pages 350–362, Prague, Czech Republic, 11–14 May 2004. Springer-Verlag Berlin·Heidelberg·New York/NY. *(Quoted on page 303)*

67. P. Cavalcanti, P. Carvalho, and L. Martha. Non-manifold Modeling: An Approach Based on Spatial Subdivision. *Computer-Aided Design*, 29(3):209–220, 1997. *(Quoted on page 200)*

68. A. Chella, M. Frixione, and S. Gaglio. A Cognitive Architecture for Artificial Vision. *Artificial Intelligence*, 89(1–2):73–111, 1997. *(Quoted on page 39)*

69. Y. Cheng. Mean Shift Mode Seeking and Clustering. *IEEE Transactions on Pattern Analysis and Machine Intelligence (PAMI)*, 17(8):790–799, August 1995. *(Quoted on page 154)*

70. K. Cheverest, N. Davies, and K. Mitchel. Developing a Context Aware Electronic Tourist Guide: Some Issues and Experiences. In *ACM CHI*, pages 17–24. ACM Press, 2000. *(Quoted on page 184)*

71. T. Choudhury, B. Clarkson, T. Jebara, and A. Pentland. Multimodal Person Recognition Using Unconstrained Audio and Video. In R. Chellappa and J. Phillips, editors, *Proc. 2nd Int. Conf. on Audio- and Video-based Biometric Person Authentication*, pages 176–181, Washington, D.C., 22-23 March 1999. *(Quoted on pages 127 and 129)*

72. C.K. Chow. An Optimum Character Recognition System Using Decision Functions. *IRE Trans. Electronic Computers*, 6:247–254, 1957. *(Quoted on page 166)*

73. H.I. Christensen and H.-H. Nagel. *Report on Dagstuhl Seminar 03441: Cognitive Vision Systems*. Dagstuhl, 2003. http://www.dagstuhl.de/03441/Report/. *(Quoted on pages 9 and 24)*

74. S. Cohen and L. Guibas. The Earth Mover's Distance under Transformation Sets. In *Proc. 7th International Conference on Computer Vision*, pages 1076–1083, Kerkyra, Greece, 20-27 September 1999. *(Quoted on page 122)*

75. W.W. Cohen, A. Borgida, and H. Hirsh. Computing Least Common Subsumers in Description Logics. In W. Swartout, editor, *Proc. AAAI-92*, pages 754–760, San Jose, CA, 12–16 July 1992. AAAI Press, Menlo Park, CA USA. *(Quoted on page 265)*

76. A.G. Cohn and S.M. Hazarika. Qualitative Spatial Representation and Reasoning: An Overview. *Fundamenta Informaticae*, 46(1-2):1–29, 2001. *(Quoted on pages 221, 222, and 248)*

328   References

77. A.G. Cohn, D.R. Magee, A. Galata, D.C. Hogg, and S. Hazarika. Towards an Architecture for Cognitive Vision Using Qualitative Spatio-Temporal Representations and Abduction. In C. Freksa, W. Brauer, C. Habel, and K.F. Wender, editors, *Spatial Cognition III, Routes and Navigation, Human Memory and Learning, Spatial Representation and Spatial Learning*, volume 2685 of *Lecture Notes in Computer Science*, pages 232–248. Springer-Verlag Berlin·Heidelberg·New York/NY, 2003. *(Quoted on pages 221, 249, and 297)*

78. V. Colin de Verdière. *Représentation et Reconnaissance d'Objets par Champs Réceptifs.* PhD Thesis. Institut National Polytechnique de Grenoble, France, 1999. *(Quoted on page 79)*

79. S. Colton, A. Bundy, and T. Walsh. Automatic Identification of Mathematical Concepts. In P. Langley, editor, *Proc. Seventeenth International Conference on Machine Learning (ICML-2000)*, pages 183–190, Stanford University, Stanford, CA, USA, 29 June–2 July 2000. Morgan Kaufmann. ISBN 1-55860-707-2. *(Quoted on page 221)*

80. D. Comaniciu and P. Meer. Distribution Free Decomposition of Multivariate Data. *Pattern Analysis and Applications*, 2(1):22–30, 1999. *(Quoted on page 154)*

81. T.F. Cootes, G.J. Edwards, and C.J. Taylor. Active Appearance Models. In H. Burkhardt and B. Neumann, editors, *Proc. 5th European Conference on Computer Vision, Vol. II*, volume 1407 of *LNCS*, pages 484–498, Freiburg, Germany, 2-6 June 1998. Springer-Verlag Berlin·Heidelberg·New York/NY. *(Quoted on pages 7, 149, and 152)*

82. I.J. Cox, editor. *Autonomous Robot Vehicles.* Springer-Verlag Berlin·Heidelberg·New York/NY, Berlin, New York, 1990. *(Quoted on page 166)*

83. G.A. Crocker and W.F. Reinke. An Editable Nonmanifold Boundary Representation. *Computer Graphics and Applications*, 11(2):39–51, 1991. *(Quoted on page 200)*

84. J.L. Crowley. Integration and Control of Reactive Visual Processes. *Robotics and Autonomous Systems*, 16(1):17–27, December 1995. *(Quoted on pages 183 and 281)*

85. J.L. Crowley and F. Bérard. Multi–Modal Tracking of Faces for Video Communications. In *IEEE Conference on Computer Vision and Pattern Recognition, CVPR '97*, pages 640–645, San Juan, Puerto Rico, 17–19 June 1997. IEEE Computer Society Press: Los Alamitos, CA. *(Quoted on page 187)*

86. J.L. Crowley and H.I. Christensen, editors. *Vision as Process.* Springer-Verlag Berlin·Heidelberg·New York/NY, 1995. *(Quoted on pages 184 and 280)*

87. J.L. Crowley, J. Coutaz, and F. Berard. Things that See: Machine Perception for Human Computer Interaction. *Communications of the ACM*, 43(3):54–64, March 2000. *(Quoted on page 195)*

88. J.L. Crowley, J. Coutaz, G. Rey, and P. Reignier. Perceptual Components for Context Aware Computing. In *4th Intern. Conference on Ubiquitous Computing (UBICOMP 2002)*, volume 2498 of *Lecture Notes in Computer Science*, pages 117–134, Göteborg, Sweden, 29 September–1 October 2002. Springer-Verlag Berlin·Heidelberg·New York / NY. *(Quoted on page 193)*

89. J.L. Crowley and Y. Demazeau. Principles and Techniques for Sensor Data Fusion. *Signal Processing*, 32(1-2):5–7, May 1993. *(Quoted on page 187)*

90. S.M. Culhane and J.K. Tsotsos. An Attentional Prototype for Early Vision. In G. Sandini, editor, *Proc. Second European Conference on Computer Vision*, volume 588 of *LNCS*, pages 551–560, Santa Margherita Ligure, Italy, 19–22 May 1992. Springer-Verlag Berlin·Heidelberg·New York/NY. *(Quoted on page 32)*

91. *CVPR-2000: Proc. IEEE Conference on Computer Vision and Pattern Recognition*, Hilton Head Island, SC, 13–15 June 2000. IEEE Computer Society: Los Alamitos, CA. *(Quoted on pages 346 and 347)*

92. G. Damiand. *Définition et étude d'un modèle topologique minimal de représentation d'images 2d et 3d.* PhD thesis, LIRMM, Université de Montpellier, 2001. *(Quoted on page 213)*

93. R. Davis, H. Shrobe, and P. Szolovits. What is a Knowledge Representation? *AI Magazine*, 14(1):17–33, 1993. *(Quoted on page 11)*

94. L. De Floriani, E. Puppo, and P. Magillo. A Formal Approach to Multiresolution Hypersurface Modeling. In W. Straber, R. Kein, and R. Rau, editors, *Geometric Modeling: Theory and Practice*, pages 302–323. Springer-Verlag Berlin·Heidelberg·New York/NY, 1997. *(Quoted on page 200)*

95. J. Denzler. *Probabilistische Zustandsschätzung und Aktionsauswahl im Rechnersehen.* Habilitationsschrift. Technische Fakultät, Univ. Erlangen–Nürnberg, 2003. *(Quoted on page 166)*

96. J. Denzler, C.M. Brown, and H. Niemann. Optimal Camera Parameter Selection for State Estimation With Applications in Object Recognition. In B. Radig and S. Florczyk, editors, *Pattern Recognition, Proc. 23rd DAGM Symposium*, volume 2191 of *Lecture Notes in Computer Science (LNCS)*, pages 305–312, München, Germany, 2001. Springer-Verlag Berlin·Heidelberg·New York/NY. *(Quoted on page 166)*

97. J. Denzler and D.W.R. Paulus. Active Motion Detection and Object Tracking. In *Proceedings of the International Conference on Image Processing (ICIP)*, volume 3, pages 635–639, Austin, TX, USA, 1994. IEEE Computer Society Press. *(Quoted on page 166)*

98. A.K. Dey. Understanding and Using Context. *Personal and Ubiquitous Computing*, 5(1):4–7, 2001. *(Quoted on page 185)*

99. T.K. Dey, H. Edelsbrunner, S. Guha, and D.V. Nekhayev. Topology Preserving Edge Contraction. Technical Report RGI-Tech-98-018, Raindrop Geomagic Inc., Research Triangle Park, North Carolina, 1998. *(Quoted on page 211)*

100. E.D. Dickmanns. A General Dynamic Vision Architecture for UGV and UAV. *Applied Intelligence*, 2:251–270, 1992. *(Quoted on page 26)*

101. D. Dobkin and M. Laszlo. Primitives for the Manipulation of Three-dimensional Subdivisions. *Algorithmica*, 4(1):3–32, 1989. *(Quoted on page 200)*

102. S.L. Dockstader and A.M. Tekalp. Multiple Camera Fusion for Multi-Object Tracking. In *Proc. IEEE Intern. Workshop on Multi-Object Tracking*, pages 95–102, Vancouver, Canada, 8 July 2001. *(Quoted on page 225)*

103. G. Dorkó and C. Schmid. Selection of Scale-Invariant Parts for Object Class Recognition. In *Proc. 9th International Conference on Computer Vision, Vol. I*, pages 634–640, Nice, France, 13-16 October 2003. *(Quoted on page 76)*

104. A. Doucet, S. Godsill, and C. Andrieu. On Sequential Monte Carlo Sampling Methods for Bayesian Filtering. *Statistics and Computing*, 10(3):197–208, July 2000. *(Quoted on pages 128, 129, 132, and 138)*

105. B.A. Draper, R.T. Collins, J. Brolio, A.R. Hansen, and E.M. Riseman. The Schema System. *International Journal of Computer Vision*, 2(3):209–250, 1989. *(Quoted on page 184)*

106. H.L. Dreyfus. From Micro-Worlds to Knowledge Representation. In J. Haugland, editor, *Mind Design: Philosophy, Psychology, Artificial Intelligence*, pages 161–204, Cambridge, Massachusetts, 1982. Bradford Books, MIT Press. Excerpted from the Introduction to the second edition of the author's *What Computers Can't Do*, Harper and Row, 1979. *(Quoted on page 17)*

107. R.O. Duda, P.E. Hart, and D.G. Stork. *Pattern Classification.* John Wiley & Sons, New York, NY, 2nd edition, 2001. *(Quoted on page 234)*

108. W. Eichhorn and H. Niemann. A Bidirectional Control Strategy in a Hierarchical Knowledge Structure. In *Proc. Int. Conference on Pattern Recognition*, pages 181–183, Paris, France, 1986. *(Quoted on page 165)*

109. A. Elfes. Using Occupancy Grids for Mobile Robot Perception and Navigation. *IEEE Computer*, 22(6):46–67, June 1989. *(Quoted on page 300)*

110. A. Elgammal and L.S. Davis. Probabilistic Framework for Segmenting People Under Occlusion. In *Proc. International Conference on Computer Vision*, volume II, pages 145–152, Vancouver, B.C., Canada, 9-12 July 2001. *(Quoted on page 225)*

111. P. Elinas. Interactive Direction Exploration for Mobile Robots. Master's thesis, The University of British Columbia, Vancouver, BC, 2002. M.Sc., supervisor J.J. Little. *(Quoted on page 302)*

112. P. Elinas, J. Hoey, D. Lahey, J. Montgomery, D. Murray, S. Se, and J.J. Little. Waiting with *José*, a Vision Based Mobile Robot. In *Proc. ICRA*, pages 3698–3705, Washington, D.C., May 2002. *(Quoted on pages 302, 303, 304, 305, and 306)*

113. P. Elinas, J. Hoey, and J.J. Little. HOMER: Human Oriented Messenger Robot. In *AAAI Spring Symposium on Human Interaction with Autonomous Systems in Complex Environments*, pages 45–51, March 2003. *(Quoted on pages 296, 301, 302, 306, and 307)*

114. P. Elinas and J.J. Little. A Robot Control Architecture for Guiding a Vision-based Mobile Robot. In *Proc. of AAAI Spring Symposium in Intelligent Distributed and Embedded Systems*, pages 11–17, Stanford, CA, March 2002. *(Quoted on pages 302 and 304)*

115. H. Elter and P. Lienhardt. Cellular Complexes as Structured Semi-simplicial Sets. *International Journal of Shape Modeling*, 1(2):191–217, 1994. *(Quoted on page 200)*

116. J. Estublier, P.Y. Cunin, and N. Belkhatir. Architectures for Process Support System Interoperability. In *Proc. Fifth Intern. Conf. on the Software Process (ICSP5)*, Lisle, IL, June 1998. *(Quoted on pages 183 and 191)*

117. O.D. Faugeras. *Three-Dimensional Computer Vision*. MIT Press, Cambridge, MA, 1993. *(Quoted on page 7)*

118. D. Felleman and D. Van Essen. Distributed Hierarchical Processing in the Primate Visual Cortex. *Cerebral Cortex*, 1:1–47, 1991. *(Quoted on page 34)*

119. P.F. Felzenszwalb and D.P. Huttenlocher. Image Segmentation Using Local Variation. In *IEEE Conference on Computer Vision and Pattern Recognition (CVPR-98)*, pages 98–104, Santa Barbara, CA, 23–25 June 1998. *(Quoted on pages 109, 206, 207, 209, and 210)*

120. R. Fergus, P. Perona, and A. Zisserman. Object Class Recognition by Unsupervised Scale-Invariant Learning. In *IEEE Conference on Computer Vision and Pattern Recognition (CVPR-2003)*, pages 264–271, Madison, USA, July 2003. *(Quoted on pages 73, 76, 146, 148, 150, and 302)*

121. A. Fern, R. Givan, and J.M. Siskind. Specific-to-general Learning for Temporal Events with Application to Learning Event Definitions from Video. *Journal of Artificial Intelligence Research (JAIR)*, 17:379–449, July–December 2002. *(Quoted on pages 234 and 245)*

122. J. Fernyhough, A.G. Cohn, and D.C. Hogg. Constructing Qualitative Event Models Automatically from Video Input. *Image and Vision Computing*, 18(2):81–103, January 2000. *(Quoted on pages 222, 223, 224, and 245)*

123. V. Ferruci and A. Paoluzzi. Extrusion and Boundary Evaluation for Multidimensional Polyhedra. *Computer-Aided Design*, 23(1):40–50, 1991. *(Quoted on page 200)*

124. G.A. Fink, N. Jungclaus, F. Kummert, H. Ritter, and G. Sagerer. A Distributed System for Integrated Speech and Image Understanding. In *International Symposium on Artificial Intelligence*, pages 117–126, Cancun, Mexico, 1996. *(Quoted on page 280)*

125. A. Finkelstein, J. Kramer, and B. Nuseibeh, editors. *Software Process Modeling and Technology*. Research Studies Press, John Wiley and Sons Inc, 1994. *(Quoted on page 183)*

126. B. Fischer and J.M. Buhmann. Data Resampling for Path Based Clustering. In L. Van Gool, editor, *24th DAGM-Symposium*, volume 2449 of *Lecture Notes in Computer Science*, pages 206–214, Zurich, Switzerland, 16-18 September 2002. Springer-Verlag Berlin·Heidelberg·New York/NY. *(Quoted on page 207)*

127. V. Fischer and H. Niemann. A Parallel Any–Time Control Algorithm for Image Understanding. In *Proc. Int. Conference on Pattern Recognition*, pages 141–145 of Vol. I Track A 'Computer Vision', Vienna, Austria, 1996. IEEE Computer Society. *(Quoted on page 167)*

128. M.A. Fischler and T.A. Strat. Recognising Objects in a Natural Environment; A Contextual Vision System (CVS). In *DARPA Image Understanding Workshop*, pages 774–796, Palo Alto, CA, 23–26 May 1989. Morgan Kaufmann, San Mateo, CA, USA. *(Quoted on page 184)*

129. K. Fleischer. *Interpretation innerstädtischer Straßenverkehrsszenen durch modellgestützte Bildfolgenauswertung.* 'Berichte aus der Informatik' (in German). Shaker Verlag: Aachen, Germany, 2002. Dissertation, Fakultät für Informatik der Universität Karlsruhe (TH). *(Quoted on page 63)*

130. K. Fleischer, H.-H. Nagel, and T.M. Rath. 3D-Model-Based-Vision for Innercity Driving Scenes. In *Proc. IEEE Intelligent Vehicle Symposium (IV'2002)*, pages 477–482, Versailles, France, 18-20 June 2002. IEEE Operations Center, 455 Hoes Lane, P.O. Box 1331, Piscataway, NJ 09955-1331, USA. *(Quoted on page 63)*

131. K. Forbus, P. Nielsen, and B. Faltings. Qualitative Kinematics: A Framework. In *Proceedings IJCAI-87*, pages 430–436, 1987. *(Quoted on page 222)*

132. R. Forman. Combinatorial Differential Topology and Geometry. *New Perspectives in Geometric Combinatorics*, 38:177–206, 1999. *(Quoted on page 213)*

133. D. Forsyth and M. Fleck. Body Plans. In *CVPR'97*, pages 678–683, 1997. *(Quoted on page 150)*

134. S. Fourey and R. Malgouyres. Intersection Number of Paths Lying on a Digital Surface and a New Jordan Theorem. In Y. Bertrand, M. Couprie, and L. Perroton, editors, *International Conference on Discrete Geometry for Computer Imagery*, volume 1568 of *Lecture Notes in Computer Science*, pages 104–117. Springer-Verlag Berlin·Heidelberg·New York/NY, Marne-la-Vallée, France, March 1999. *(Quoted on page 213)*

135. V. Franc and V. Hlaváč. Greedy Algorithm for a Training Set Reduction in the Kernel Methods. In N. Petkov and M.A. Westenberg, editors, *Computer Analysis of Images and Patterns*, pages 426–433, Berlin, Germany, August 2003. Springer-Verlag Berlin·Heidelberg·New York/NY. *(Quoted on page 89)*

136. B.J. Frey and N. Jojic. Learning Graphical Models of Images, Videos, and Their Spatial Transformations. In C. Boutilier and M. Goldszmidt, editors, *Proc. 16th Conf. Uncertainty in Artificial Intelligence (UAI'00)*, pages 184–191, Stanford, CA, 30 June–3 July 2000. Morgan Kaufmann: San Francisco, CA. *(Quoted on page 136)*

137. B. Fritzke. Growing Cell Structures – a Self-organizing Network for Unsupervised and Supervised Learning. *Neural Networks*, 7(9):1441–1460, 1994. *(Quoted on page 137)*

138. C.-S. Fu, S.-W. Cho, and K. Essig. Hierarchical Color Image Region Segmentation for Content-Based Image Retrieval System. *IEEE Trans. on Image Processing*, 9(1):156–162, 2000. *(Quoted on page 206)*

139. A. Galata, A.G. Cohn, D. Magee, and D.C. Hogg. Modeling Interaction Using Learnt Qualitative Spatio-Temporal Relations and Variable Length Markov Models. In F. van Harmelen, editor, *Proc. 15th European Conference on Artificial Intelligence (ECAI'02)*, pages 741–745, Lyon, France, 21-26 July 2002. IOS Press: Amsterdam, NL. *(Quoted on pages 222, 223, and 224)*

140. A. Galata, N. Johnson, and D.C. Hogg. Learning Variable-Length Markov Models of Behavior. *Computer Vision and Image Understanding*, 81(3):398–413, March 2001. *(Quoted on page 297)*

141. P. Gärdenfors. *Conceptual Spaces - The Geometry of Thought.* MIT Press, Cambridge, MA, USA, 2000. *(Quoted on page 268)*

142. M.S. Gazzaniga. *The Social Brain. Discovering the Networks of the Mind.* Basic Books, New York, 1985. *(Quoted on page 44)*

143. R. Gerber and H.-H. Nagel. 'Occurrence' Extraction from Image Sequences of Road Traffic Scenes. In L. van Gool and B. Schiele, editors, *Proc. Workshop on Cognitive Vision*, pages 1–8, ETH Zurich, Switzerland, 19-20 September 2002. http://www.vision.ethz.ch/cogvis02/finalpapers/gerber.pdf. *(Quoted on page 66)*

144. R. Gerber and H.-H. Nagel. Fuzzy Metric-Temporal Logic Representation of 'Occurrences' for Road Vehicle Traffic, 2004. Institut für Algorithmen und Kognitive Systeme der Universität Karlsruhe (TH), 76128 Karlsruhe, Germany. *(Quoted on page 66)*

145. R. Gerber, H.-H. Nagel, and H. Schreiber. Deriving Textual Descriptions of Road Traffic Queues from Video Sequences. In F. van Harmelen, editor, *Proc. 15th European Conference on Artificial Intelligence (ECAI–2002)*, pages 736–740, Lyon, France, 21-26 July 2002. IOS Press: Amsterdam, NL. *(Quoted on pages 64 and 297)*

146. G. Ghose and J. Maunsell. Specialized Representations Review in Visual Cortex: A Role for Binding? *Neuron*, 24:79–85, 1999. *(Quoted on page 34)*

147. J.J. Gibson. *The Perception of the Visual World*. Houghton Mifflin, Boston, 1950. *(Quoted on page 14)*

148. J.J. Gibson. *The Ecological Approach to Visual Perception*. Houghton Mifflin, Boston, 1979. *(Quoted on page 14)*

149. M.A. Giese and T. Poggio. Morphable Models for the Analysis and Synthesis of Complex Motion Patterns. *International Journal of Computer Vision*, 38(1):59–73, 2000. *(Quoted on page 149)*

150. R. Glantz and W.G. Kropatsch. Plane Embedding of Dually Contracted Graphs. In G. Borgefors, I. Nyström, and G. S. di Baja, editors, *International Conference on Discrete Geometry for Computer Imagery*, volume 1953 of *Lecture Notes in Computer Science*, pages 348–357. Springer-Verlag Berlin·Heidelberg·New York/NY, 2000. *(Quoted on page 203)*

151. G.H. Golub and C.F. Van Loan. *Matrix Computations*. The John Hopkins University Press, Baltimore, MD · London, UK, second edition, 1989. *(Quoted on page 91)*

152. G.H. Granlund. The Complexity of Vision. *Signal Processing*, 74(1):101–126, April 1999. Invited paper. *(Quoted on pages 17, 39, 42, and 52)*

153. G.H. Granlund. Does Vision Inevitably Have to be Active? In *Proceedings of the 11th Scandinavian Conference on Image Analysis (SCIA)*, pages 11–19, Kangerlussuaq, Greenland, 7–11 June 1999. Also as Technical Report LiTH-ISY-R-2247. *(Quoted on pages 17, 42, and 48)*

154. G.H. Granlund. An Associative Perception-Action Structure Using a Localized Space Variant Information Representation. In *Proceedings of Algebraic Frames for the Perception-Action Cycle (AFPAC)*, Kiel, Germany, September 2000. *(Quoted on pages 40 and 54)*

155. G.H. Granlund. Cognitive Vision. Background and Research Issues. Technical report, ECVision Research Planning. Background Documents, 2002. *(Quoted on page 17)*

156. G.H. Granlund and H. Knutsson. *Signal Processing for Computer Vision*. Kluwer Academic Publishers, 1995. ISBN 0-7923-9530-1. *(Quoted on page 49)*

157. G.H. Granlund and A. Moe. Unrestricted Recognition of 3D Objects for Robotics Using Multilevel Triplet Invariants. *Artificial Intelligence Magazine*, 25(2):51–67, Summer 2004. *(Quoted on page 54)*

158. J. Grezes, M. Tucker, J. Armony, R. Ellis, and R.E. Passingham. Objects Automatically Potentiate Action: an fMRI Study of Implicit Processing. *Eur J Neurosci*, 17(12):2735–2735, 2003. *(Quoted on pages 44 and 46)*

159. W. E. L. Grimson. *Object Recognition by Computer: The Role of Geometric Constraints*. MIT Press, Cambridge, MA, USA, 1990. *(Quoted on pages 48 and 151)*

160. L. Guibas and J. Stolfi. Primitives for the Manipulation of General Subdivisions and the Computation of Voronoi Diagrams. *ACM Trans. on Graphics*, 4(2):74–123, 1985. *(Quoted on page 200)*

161. L. Guigues, L.M. Herve, and J.-P. Cocquerez. The Hierarchy of the Cocoons of a Graph and its Application to Image Segmentation. *Pattern Recognition Letters*, 24(8):1059–1066, 2003. *(Quoted on page 207)*

162. A. Gupta, I. Newman, Y. Rabinovich, and A. Sinclair. Cuts, Trees and l_1 Embeddings. In *Proceedings of Symposium on Foundations of Computer Science*, pages 399–409, 1999. *(Quoted on page 119)*

163. I. Guyon and F. Pereira. Design of a Linguistic Postprocessor Using Variable Memory Length Markov Models. In *International Conference on Document Analysis and Recognition*, pages 454–457, 1995. *(Quoted on page 224)*

164. A. Guzman. *Computer Recognition of Three-Dimensional Objects in a Visual Scene*. Ph.D. Thesis. MIT, Cambridge, Massachusetts, 1968. *(Quoted on page 7)*

165. E. Gyftodimos and P. Flach. Hierarchical Bayesian Networks: A Probabilistic Reasoning Model for Structured Domain. In E. de Jong and T. Oates, editors, *Proceedings ICML-2002 Workshop on Development of Representations*, pages 23–30, Sydney, Australia, 9 July 2002. *(Quoted on page 274)*

166. M. Haag and H.-H. Nagel. Combination of Edge Element and Optical Flow Estimates for 3D-Model-Based Vehicle Tracking in Traffic Image Sequences. *International Journal of Computer Vision*, 35(3):295–319, December 1999. *(Quoted on page 65)*

167. M. Haag, W. Theilmann, K. Schäfer, and H.-H. Nagel. Integration of Image Sequence Evaluation and Fuzzy Metric Temporal Logic Programming. In G. Brewka, Ch. Habel, and B. Nebel, editors, *KI-97: Advances in Artificial Intelligence*, volume 1303 of *Lecture Notes in Artificial Intelligence*, pages 301–312, Freiburg, Germany, 1997. Springer-Verlag Berlin·Heidelberg·New York/NY. *(Quoted on page 249)*

168. V. Haarslev and R. Möller. RACER System Description. In R. Goré, A. Leitsch, and T. Nipkow, editors, *Proceedings International Joint Conference on Automated Reasoning (IJCAR 2001)*, volume 2083 of *Lecture Notes in Computer Science*, pages 701–705, Siena, Italy, 18–23 June 2001. Springer-Verlag Berlin·Heidelberg·New York/NY. *(Quoted on pages 260 and 271)*

169. V. Haarslev, R. Möller, and M. Wessel. The Description Logic $\mathcal{ALCNH}_{R+}$ Extended with Concrete Domains: A Practically Motivated Approach. In R. Goré, A. Leitsch, and T. Nipkow, editors, *Proceedings International Joint Conference on Automated Reasoning (IJCAR 2001)*, volume 2083 of *Lecture Notes in Computer Science*, pages 29–44, Siena, Italy, 18–23 June 2001. Springer-Verlag Berlin·Heidelberg·New York/NY. *(Quoted on page 260)*

170. D. Hall, V. Colin de Verdière, and J.L. Crowley. Object Recognition Using Colored Receptive Fields. In D. Vernon, editor, *Proc. European Conference on Computer Vision (ECCV-2000)*, volume 1842 of *Lecture Notes in Computer Science*, pages 164–177, Dublin, Ireland, 26 June–1 July 2000. Springer-Verlag Berlin·Heidelberg·New York/NY. *(Quoted on pages 75, 147, and 187)*

171. A.R. Hanson and E.M. Riseman. VISIONS: A Computer System for Interpreting Scenes. In A.R. Hanson and E.M. Riseman, editors, *Computer Vision Systems*, pages 303–334. Academic Press, New York, NY, 1978. *(Quoted on pages 7 and 184)*

172. R.M. Haralick and L.G. Shapiro. *Computer and Robot Vision*. Addison-Wesley Publ. Co., Reading, MA, 1992. *(Quoted on page 40)*

173. S. Harnad. The Symbol Grounding Problem. *Physica D*, 42:335–346, 1990. *(Quoted on pages 222 and 234)*

174. C.J. Harris and M. Stephens. A Combined Corner and Edge Detector. In *Proceedings of 4th Alvey Vision Conference*, pages 147–151, Manchester, UK, 31 August–2 September 1988. *(Quoted on pages 148 and 153)*

175. R. Hartley and A. Zisserman. *Multiple View Geometry in Computer Vision*. Cambridge University Press, 2000. *(Quoted on page 7)*

176. J. Haugland. Semantic Engines: An Introduction to Mind Design. In J. Haugland, editor, *Mind Design: Philosophy, Psychology, Artificial Intelligence*, pages 1–34, Cambridge, Massachusetts, 1982. Bradford Books, MIT Press. *(Quoted on page 11)*

177. Y. Haxhimusa, R. Glantz, and W.G. Kropatsch. Constructing Stochastic Pyramids by MIDES
    - Maximal Independent Directed Edge Set. In E. Hancock and M. Vento, editors, *Proc.
    4th IAPR-TC15 on Graph Based Representations in Pattern Recognition*, volume 2726 of
    Lecture Notes in Computer Science, pages 35–46, York, UK, June-July 2003. Springer-
    Verlag Berlin·Heidelberg·New York/NY. *(Quoted on page 218)*

178. Y. Haxhimusa, R. Glantz, M. Saib, G. Langs, and W.G. Kropatsch. Logarithmic Tapering
    Graph Pyramid. In L. Van Gool, editor, *Pattern Recognition, Proc. 24th DAGM Sym-
    posium (DAGM-2002)*, volume 2449 of *Lecture Notes in Computer Science*, pages 117–
    124, Zurich, Switzerland, 16–18 September 2002. Springer-Verlag Berlin·Heidelberg·New
    York/NY. *(Quoted on pages 203, 207, and 218)*

179. Y. Haxhimusa and W.G. Kropatsch. Hierarchical Image Partitioning with Dual Graph Con-
    traction. In B. Michaelis and G. Krell, editors, *Pattern Recognition, Proc. 25th DAGM
    Symposium (DAGM-2003)*, volume 2781 of *Lecture Notes in Computer Science*, pages 338–
    345, Magdeburg, Germany, 10–12 September 2003. Springer-Verlag Berlin·Heidelberg·New
    York/NY. *(Quoted on pages 209 and 215)*

180. Y. Haxhimusa and W.G. Kropatsch. Hierarchical Image Partitioning with Dual Graph
    Contraction. Technical Report TR-81, PRIP, Vienna University of Technology, July 2003.
    http://www.prip.tuwien.ac.at/ftp/pub/publications/trs/tr81.pdf.
    (Quoted on page 209)

181. P.J. Hayes. The Logic of Frames. In D. Metzing, editor, *Frame Conception and Text
    Understanding*, pages 46–61. Walter de Gruyter & Co., Berlin, Germany, 1979. *(Quoted on
    page 260)*

182. B. Heigl, D. Paulus, and H. Niemann. Tracking Points in Sequences of Color Images. In
    B. Radig, H. Niemann, Y. Zhuravlev, I. Gourevitch, and I. Laptev, editors, *Pattern Recog-
    nition and Image Understanding*, pages 70–77, Herrsching, Germany, 1999. (infix, Sankt
    Augustin, ISBN 3-89601-016-6). *(Quoted on page 170)*

183. F. Heimes and H.-H. Nagel. Towards Active Machine-Vision-Based Driver Assistance for
    Urban Areas. *International Journal of Computer Vision*, 50(1):5–34, October 2002. *(Quoted
    on page 63)*

184. B. Heisele, T. Serre, M. Pontil, and T. Poggio. Component-Based Face Detection. In
    *Proc. IEEE Computer Society Conference on Computer Vision and Pattern Recognition
    (CVPR-2001)*, volume 1, pages 657–662, Kauai, Hawaii, 8–14 December 2001. *(Quoted on
    page 150)*

185. F. Heitz, P. Perez, and P. Bouthemy. Multiscale Minimization of Global Energy Functions
    in Some Visual Recovery Problems. *Computer Vision, Graphics, and Image Processing*,
    59:125–134, 1994. *(Quoted on page 166)*

186. H. v. Helmholtz. *Treatise on Physiological Optics*. The Optical Society of America,
    Rochester, NY, 1924. (Southall, Trans. from 3rd German ed. of 1909, ed.). *(Quoted on
    page 26)*

187. J. Hoey and J.J. Little. Representation and Recognition of Complex Human Motion. In
    Proceedings IEEE Conf. on Computer Vision and Pattern Recognition (CVPR '00), pages
    I: 752–759, Hilton Head Island, SC, 13–15 June 2000. *(Quoted on pages 302 and 310)*

188. J. Hoey and J.J. Little. Bayesian Clustering of Optical Flow Fields. In *Proc. Ninth IEEE
    International Conference on Computer Vision (ICCV-2003)*, volume II, pages 1086–1093,
    Nice, France, 13–16 October 2003. *(Quoted on page 310)*

189. J. Hoey and J.J. Little. Decision Theoretic Modeling of Human Facial Displays. In *Proc.
    8th European Conference on Computer Vision (ECCV 2004), Part III*, volume 3023 of
    Lecture Notes in Computer Science, pages 26–38, Prague, Czech Republic, 11–14 May
    2004. Springer-Verlag Berlin·Heidelberg·New York/NY. *(Quoted on pages 303, 308, 309,
    and 310)*

190. J. Hoey and J.J. Little. Value Directed Learning of Gestures and Facial Displays. In *IEEE Conf. on Computer Vision and Pattern Recognition*, Washington DC, June 2004. *(Quoted on pages 297 and 311)*

191. J. Hoey, R. St-Aubin, A. Hu, and C. Boutilier. SPUDD: Stochastic Planning Using Decision Diagrams. In *Proceedings of International Conference on Uncertainty in Artificial Intelligence (UAI '99)*, pages 279–288, Stockholm, 1999. *(Quoted on page 307)*

192. J.E. Hoffman. Visual Attention and Eye Movements. In H. Pashler, editor, *Attention*, pages 119–154. University College London Press, London, UK, 1998. *(Quoted on page 26)*

193. B.K.P. Horn and B.G. Schunck. Determining Optical Flow. *Artificial Intelligence*, 17(1-3):185–203, 1981. *(Quoted on page 7)*

194. J. Hornegger and H. Niemann. Statistical Learning, Localization, and Identification of Objects. In *Proceedings of the 5th International Conference on Computer Vision (ICCV)*, pages 914–919, Boston, Massachusetts, USA, 1995. (IEEE Computer Society Press). *(Quoted on page 166)*

195. J. Hornegger and H. Niemann. Probabilistic Modeling and Recognition of 3–D Objects. *Int. Journal of Computer Vision*, 39(3):229–251, 2000. *(Quoted on page 166)*

196. S.L Horowitz and T. Pavlidis. Picture Segmentation by a Tree Traversal Algorithm. *Journal of the ACM*, 23(2):368–388, 1976. *(Quoted on pages 169 and 207)*

197. I. Horrocks, U. Sattler, and S. Tobies. Reasoning with Individuals for the Description Logic $\mathcal{SHIQ}$. In D. McAllester, editor, *Proceedings 17th International Conference on Automated Deduction (CADE-17)*, volume 1831 of *Lecture Notes in Computer Science*, pages 482–496, Pittsburgh, PA, 17–20 June 2000. Springer-Verlag Berlin·Heidelberg·New York/NY. *(Quoted on page 260)*

198. P.V.C. Hough. Method and Means of Recognizing Complex Patterns, December 1962. U.S. Patent 3 069 654 18. *(Quoted on pages 151 and 153)*

199. R. Howarth. Interpreting a Dynamic and Uncertain World: High-level Vision. *Artificial Intelligence Review*, 9:37–63, 1995. *(Quoted on page 256)*

200. A.J. Howell and H. Buxton. Face Recognition Using Radial Basis Function Neural Network. In R.B. Fisher and E. Trucco, editors, *Proc. British Machine Vision Conference*, pages 455–464, Edinburgh, UK, 9-12 September 1996. British Machine Vision Association. *(Quoted on pages 129 and 137)*

201. M.H. Huffman. Impossible Objects and Nonsense Sentences. In D. Meltzer and D. Michie, editors, *Machine Intelligence 6*, pages 295–323, New York, 1971. American Elsevier Publishing Company. *(Quoted on page 7)*

202. M. Isard and A. Blake. Contour Tracking by Stochastic Propagation of Conditional Density. In B. Buxton and R. Cipolla, editors, *Computer Vision – ECCV '96*, volume 1064 of *Lecture Notes in Computer Science*, pages 343–356, Cambridge, UK, 15-18 April 1996. Springer-Verlag Berlin·Heidelberg·New York/NY. *(Quoted on pages 128 and 131)*

203. M. Isard and A. Blake. Condensation – Conditional Density Propagation for Visual Tracking. *International Journal of Computer Vision*, 29(1):5–28, August 1998. *(Quoted on pages 129, 138, and 225)*

204. Y. Ivanov and A. Bobick. Recognition of Visual Activities and Interactions by Stochastic Parsing. *IEEE Trans. on Pattern Analysis and Machine Intelligence*, 22(8):852–872, 2000. *(Quoted on page 234)*

205. A.K. Jain, A. Ross, and S. Prabhakar. An Introduction to Biometric Recognition. *IEEE Transactions on Circuits and Systems for Video Technology, Special Issue on Image- and Video-Based Biometrics*, 14(1):4–20, January 2004. *(Quoted on page 302)*

206. M. Jeannerod. *The Cognitive Neuroscience of Action*. Blackwell Publishers Ltd, Oxford, UK, 1997. *(Quoted on page 44)*

207. O. Jesorsky, K. Kirchberg, and R. Frischholz. Robust Face Detection Using the Hausdorff Distance. In *Audio and Video based Person Authentication AVBPA 2001*, pages 90–95, 2001. *(Quoted on pages 81 and 82)*

208. P.N. Johnson-Laird. *Mental Models*. Cambridge University Press, Cambridge, UK, 1983. *(Quoted on page 257)*

209. J.-M. Jolion and A. Rosenfeld. *A Pyramid Framework for Early Vision*. Kluwer Academic Publishers, Dordrecht, The Netherlands, 1994. *(Quoted on page 202)*

210. M. Jones and D. Vernon. Using Neural Networks to Learn Hand-Eye Co-ordination. *Neural Computing and Applications*, 2(1):2–12, 1994. *(Quoted on page 13)*

211. M.J. Jones and T. Poggio. Multidimensional Morphable Models. In *ICCV'98*, pages 683–688, 1998. *(Quoted on page 149)*

212. M.J. Jones and T. Poggio. Multidimensional Morphable Models: A Framework for Representing and Matching Object Classes. *International Journal of Computer Vision*, 29(2):107–131, August/September 1998. *(Quoted on page 149)*

213. T. Kadir and M. Brady. Scale, Saliency, and Image Description. *Int. Journal of Computer Vision*, 45(2):83–105, 2001. *(Quoted on page 148)*

214. R. Kalman. A New Approach to Linear Filtering and Prediction Problems. *Transactions of the ASME – Journal of Basic Engineering*, 82(Series D):35–45, 1960. *(Quoted on page 187)*

215. T. Kanade. Region Segmentation: Signal vs. Semantics. In *Proc. International Joint Conference on Pattern Recognition (IJCPR '78)*, pages 95–105, Kyoto, Japan, 7-10 November 1978. *(Quoted on pages 61, 62, and 248)*

216. L.C. Katz and C.J. Shatz. Synaptic Activity and the Construction of Cortical Circuits. *Science*, 274:1133–1138, 15 November 1996. *(Quoted on page 42)*

217. K. Kawamura and M. Iskarous. Trends in Service Robots for the Disabled and the Elderly. In *Intelligent Robots and Systems*, pages 1647–1654, Piscataway, NJ, 1994. IEEE Computer Society. *(Quoted on page 166)*

218. D. Kazakov and S. Dobnik. Inductive Learning of Lexical Semantics with Typed Unification Grammars. In *Oxford Working Papers in Linguistics, Philology, and Phonetics*. Oxford University Press, Oxford, UK, 2003. *(Quoted on page 234)*

219. J.A.S. Kelso. *Dynamic Patterns – The Self-Organization of Brain and Behaviour*. M.I.T. Press, 3rd edition, 1975. *(Quoted on pages 10, 11, 13, and 14)*

220. Y. Keselman and S. Dickinson. Generic Model Abstraction from Examples. In *Proc. IEEE Conf. Computer Vision and Pattern Recognition (CVPR-2001)*, volume 1, pages 856–863, Kauai, Hawaii, 8–14 December 2001. *(Quoted on pages 108, 109, 111, 112, 205, and 206)*

221. Y. Keselman, A. Shokoufandeh, M. Demirci, and S. Dickinson. Many-to-many Graph Matching via Metric Embedding. In *Proc. IEEE Conf. Computer Vision and Pattern Recognition (CVPR-2003)*, pages 850–857, Madison, WI, June 2003. *(Quoted on pages 108, 122, and 123)*

222. J.F. Kihlstrom. The Cognitive Unconscious. *Science*, 237(4821):1445–1452, 18 September 1987. *(Quoted on page 11)*

223. B.B. Kimia, A. Tannenbaum, and S.W. Zucker. Shape, Shocks, and Deformations I: The Components of Two-Dimensional Shape and the Reaction-Diffusion Space. *International Journal of Computer Vision*, 15:189–224, 1995. *(Quoted on page 116)*

224. G. Kitagawa. Monte Carlo Filter and Smoother for Non-Gaussian Nonlinear State Space Models. *J. Computational and Graphical Statistics*, 5(1):1–25, March 1996. *(Quoted on pages 128, 129, and 138)*

225. M. Klusch, S. Bergamaschi, P. Edwards, and P. Petta. *Intelligent Information Agents: The AgentLink Perspective*, volume 2586 of *Lecture Notes in Artificial Intelligence*. Springer-Verlag Berlin·Heidelberg·New York/NY, 2003. *(Quoted on page 281)*

226. M. Klusch and K. Sycara. Brokering and Matchmaking for Coordination of Agent Societies: A Survey. In A. Omicini et al., editor, *Coordination of Internet Agents*. Springer-Verlag Berlin·Heidelberg·New York/NY, 2001. *(Quoted on page 285)*

227. J.J. Koenderink and A.J. van Doorn. Generic Neighborhood Operators. *IEEE Transactions on Pattern Analysis and Machine Intelligence*, PAMI-14(6):597–605, June 1992. *(Quoted on page 74)*

228. U. Koethe and P. Stelldinger. Shape Preserving Digitization of Ideal and Blurred Binary Images. In I. Nyström, G. S. di Baja, and S. Svensson, editors, *International Conference on Discrete Geometry for Computer Imagery (DGCI)*, volume 2886 of *Lecture Notes in Computer Science*, pages 82–91. Springer-Verlag Berlin·Heidelberg·New York/NY, 2003. *(Quoted on page 214)*

229. W. Köhler. *Dynamics in Psychology*. Liveright, New York, 1940. *(Quoted on page 14)*

230. D. Koller, J. Weber, and J. Malik. Robust Multiple Car Tracking with Occlusion Reasoning. In J.-O. Eklundh, editor, *Proc. Third European Conference on Computer Vision (ECCV '94)*, volume 800 of *Lecture Notes in Computer Science*, pages I:189–196, Stockholm, Sweden, 2–6 May 1994. Springer-Verlag Berlin·Heidelberg·New York/NY. *(Quoted on page 225)*

231. T. Kong and A. Rosenfeld. Digital Topology: A Comparison of the Graph-based and Topological Approaches. In G. Reed, A. Roscoe, and R. Wachter, editors, *Topology and Category Theory in Computer Science*, pages 273–289. Oxford University Press, Oxford, UK, 1991. *(Quoted on page 211)*

232. K. Konstantinides and J.R. Rasure. The Khoros Software Development Environment for Image and Signal Processing. *IEEE Transactions on Image Processing*, 3(3):243–252, May 1994. *(Quoted on page 280)*

233. W.G. Kropatsch. Building Irregular Pyramids by Dual Graph Contraction. *IEE-Proc. Vision, Image and Signal Processing*, 142(6):366–374, 1995. *(Quoted on pages 200, 202, 203, and 207)*

234. W.G. Kropatsch. Property Preserving Hierarchical Graph Transformations. In C. Arcelli, L.P. Cordella, and G. S. di Baja, editors, *Advances in Visual Form Analysis*, pages 340–349. World Scientific Publishing Company, Singapore, 1997. *(Quoted on page 211)*

235. W.G. Kropatsch. From Equivalent Weighting Functions to Equivalent Contraction Kernels. In E. Wenger and L.I. Dimitrov, editors, *Digital Image Processing and Computer Graphics (DIP-97): Appl. in Human. and Nat. Sci.*, volume 3346 of *SPIE*, pages 310–320, 1998. *(Quoted on page 214)*

236. W.G. Kropatsch. Abstract Pyramid on Discrete Representations. In I.J.O. Lachaud, A. Braquelaire, and A. Vialard, editors, *International Conference on Discrete Geometry for Computer Imagery*, volume 2301 of *Lecture Notes in Computer Science*, pages 1–21. Springer-Verlag Berlin·Heidelberg·New York/NY, 2002. *(Quoted on page 205)*

237. W.G. Kropatsch, A. Leonardis, and H. Bischof. Hierarchical, Adaptive and Robust Methods for Image Understanding. *Survey on Mathematics for Industry*, 9:1–47, 1999. *(Quoted on pages 202, 203, and 209)*

238. W.G. Kropatsch and H. Macho. Finding the Structure of Connected Components Using Dual Irregular Pyramids. In D. Richard, editor, *Cinquième Colloque International Conference on Discrete Geometry for Computer Imagery*, pages 147–158. Laboratoire de Logique, Algorithmique et Informatique de Clermont I, LLAIC1, Université d'Auvergne, 1995. *(Quoted on page 213)*

239. W.G. Kropatsch, M. Saib, and M. Schreyer. The Optimal Height of a Graph Pyramid. In F. Leberl and F. Fraundorfer, editors, *26th Workshop of the Austrian Association for Pattern Recognition*, pages 87–94, Graz, A, September 2002. Austrian Computer Society. *(Quoted on page 215)*

240. J.B.J. Kruskal. On the Shortest Spanning Subtree of a Graph and the Travelling Salesman Problem. *Proc. Amer. Math. Soc.*, 7:48–50, 1956. *(Quoted on page 215)*

241. F. Kummert, H. Niemann, R. Prechtel, and G. Sagerer. Control and Explanation in a Signal Understanding Environment. *Signal Processing*, 32:111–145, 1993. *(Quoted on page 166)*

242. M. Lades, J.C. Vorbrüggen, J. Buhmann, J. Lange, C. von der Mahlsburg, R.P. Würz, and W. Konen. Distortion Invariant Object Recognition in the Dynamic Link Architecture. *Transactions on Computers*, 42(3):300–311, March 1993. *(Quoted on pages 78 and 79)*

243. Y. Lamdan, J.T. Schwartz, and H.J. Wolfson. Object Recognition by Affine Invariant Matching. In *CVPR88*, pages 335–344, Ann Arbor, MI, June 1988. *(Quoted on pages 148 and 151)*

244. Y. Lamdan and H.J. Wolfson. Geometric Hashing: A General and Efficient Model-Based Recognition Scheme. In *ICCV88*, pages 238–249, Tampa, Florida, Dec 1988. *(Quoted on page 151)*

245. K.B. Laskey, S.M. Mahoney, and E. Wright. Hypothesis Management in Situation-Specific Network Construction. In J.S. Breese and D. Koller, editors, *Proceedings Seventeenth Conference on Uncertainty in Artificial Intelligence*, pages 301–309, Seattle, Washington, USA, 2–5 August 2001. Morgan Kaufmann, Publ.: San Mateo, CA, USA. *(Quoted on page 274)*

246. T.S. Lee and D. Mumford. Hierarchical Bayesian Inference in the Visual Cortex. *Optical Society of America*, 20(7):1434–1448, July 2003. *(Quoted on page 40)*

247. B. Leibe and B. Schiele. Analyzing Appearance and Contour Based Methods for Object Categorization. In *CVPR03*, Madison, WI, June 2003. *(Quoted on pages 146, 147, and 153)*

248. B. Leibe and B. Schiele. Interleaved Object Categorization and Segmentation. In *BMVC'03*, 2003. *(Quoted on pages 147, 148, and 153)*

249. J.J. Leonard and H.F. Durrant-Whyte. Simultaneous Map Building and Localisation for an Autonomous Mobile Robot. In *Proceedings of IEEE/RSJ International Conference on Intelligent Robots and Systems (IROS'91)*, pages 1442–1447, New York, USA, 1991. *(Quoted on page 299)*

250. T.K. Leung, M.C. Burl, and P. Perona. Finding Faces in Cluttered Scenes Using Random Labelled Graph Matching. In *International Conference on Computer Vision*, pages 637–644, Cambridge, MA, 1995. *(Quoted on page 78)*

251. B. Li and R. Chellappa. Simultaneous Tracking and Verification via Sequential Posterior Estimation. In *Proc. IEEE Conf. on Computer Vision and Pattern Recognition*, volume 2, pages 110–117, Hilton Head Island, SC, 13-15 June 2000. IEEE Computer Society. *(Quoted on page 129)*

252. C.-E. Liedtke, J. Bückner, O. Grau, S. Growe, and R. Tönjes. AIDA: A System for the Knowledge Based Interpretation of Remote Sensing Data. In *Proc. of the Third International Airborne Remote Sensing Conference and Exhibition*, Copenhagen, 1997. *(Quoted on page 165)*

253. P. Lienhardt. Topological Models for Boundary Representation: A Comparison with n-dimensional Generalized Maps. *Computer-Aided Design*, 23(1):59–82, 1991. *(Quoted on page 200)*

254. P. Lienhardt. N-dimensional Generalized Combinatorial Maps and Cellular Quasi-manifolds. *Int. J. of Comp. Geom. and Appl.*, 4(3):275–324, 1994. *(Quoted on page 200)*

255. T. Lindeberg. Edge Detection and Ridge Detection with Automatic Scale Selection. *International Journal of Computer Vision*, 30(2):117–154, 1998. *(Quoted on page 75)*

256. T. Lindeberg. Feature Detection with Automatic Scale Selection. *International Journal of Computer Vision*, 30(2):79–116, 1998. *(Quoted on page 148)*

257. M. Lindström, A. Orebäck, and H.I. Christensen. Berra: Research Architecture for Service Robots. In *Proc. IEEE International Conference on Robotics and Automation (ICRA 2000)*, volume 4, pages 3278–3283, San Francisco, CA, 24-28 April 2000. *(Quoted on page 281)*

258. N. Linial, E. London, and Y. Rabinovich. The Geometry of Graphs and Some of its Algorithmic Applications. In *Proceedings of 35th Annual Symposium on Foundations of Computer Science*, pages 557–591, 1994. *(Quoted on page 119)*

259. N. Linial, A. Magen, and M.E. Saks. Trees and Euclidean metrics. *Proceedings of the Thirtieth Annual ACM Symposium on the Theory of Computing*, pages 169–175, 1998. *(Quoted on page 121)*

260. R. Linsker. Self-Organization in a Perceptual Network. *Computer*, 21(3):105–117, March 1988. *(Quoted on page 13)*

261. A. Lipton, H. Fujiyoshi, and R. Patil. Moving Target Classification and Tracking from Real-time Video. In *Proc. IEEE Workshop on Applications of Computer Vision*, pages 8–14, Princeton, NJ, 19-21 October 1998. *(Quoted on page 226)*

262. J.J. Little and J. Boyd. Recognizing People by Their Gait: the Shape of Motion. *Videre*, 1(2):1–32, 1998. *(Quoted on page 302)*

263. J.S. Liu and R. Chen. Sequential Monte Carlo Methods for Dynamic Systems. *Journal of the American Statistical Association*, 93(443):1032–1044, September 1998. *(Quoted on pages 128, 129, 131, 132, 138, and 144)*

264. H. Loos and C. von der Malsburg. 1-Click Learning of Object Models for Recognition. In H.H. Bülthoff, S.-W. Lee, T.A. Poggio, and C. Wallraven, editors, *Proc. Second International Workshop on Biologically-Motivated Computer Vision (BMCV 2002)*, volume 2525 of *Lecture Notes in Computer Science (LNCS)*, pages 377–386, Tübingen, Germany, 22-24 November 2002. Springer-Verlag Berlin·Heidelberg·New York/NY. *(Quoted on page 149)*

265. D.G. Lowe. Radial Basis Function Networks. In M. Arbib, editor, *The Handbook of Brain Theory and Neural Networks*, pages 779–782. The MIT Press, Cambridge, MA, 1995. *(Quoted on page 136)*

266. D.G. Lowe. Object Recognition from Local Scale-Invariant Features. In *Proc. Seventh International Conference on Computer Vision (ICCV '99)*, pages 1150–1157, Kerkyra, Greece, 20-27 September 1999. *(Quoted on pages 75, 148, 154, and 299)*

267. D.G. Lowe. Local Feature View Clustering for 3D Object Recognition. In *Proc. IEEE Conf. Computer Vision and Pattern Recognition (CVPR 2001)*, volume 1, pages 682–688, Kauai, Hawaii, 8–14 December 2001. *(Quoted on pages 148 and 151)*

268. D.G. Lowe. Distinctive Image Features from Scale-invariant Keypoints. *International Journal of Computer Vision*, 60(2):91–110, 2004. *(Quoted on pages 148, 151, and 302)*

269. A. Lux. The Imalab Method for Vision Systems. In J.L. Crowley, J.H. Piater, M. Vincze, and L. Paletta, editors, *3rd International Conference on Computer Vision Systems (ICVS 2003)*, volume 2626 of *Lecture Notes in Computer Science*, pages 314–322, Graz, Austria, 1-3 April 2003. Springer-Verlag Berlin·Heidelberg·New York/NY. *(Quoted on page 185)*

270. D. Macrini. Indexing and Matching for View-Based 3-D Object Recognition Using Shock Graphs. Master's thesis, Department of Computer Science, University of Toronto, 2003. *(Quoted on page 116)*

271. D. Macrini, A. Shokoufandeh, S. Dickinson, K. Siddiqi, and S.W. Zucker. View-Based 3-D Object Recognition Using Shock Graphs. In *Proc. International Conference on Pattern Recognition*, volume 3, pages 24–28, Quebec, August 2002. *(Quoted on page 116)*

272. D.R. Magee. Tracking Multiple Vehicles Using Foreground, Background and Motion Models. *Image and Vision Computing*, 22(2):143–155, 2004. *(Quoted on page 224)*

273. D.R. Magee, D.C. Hogg, and A.G. Cohn. Autonomous Object Learning Using Multiple Feature Clusterings in Dynamic Scenarios. Technical Report School of Computing Research Report 2003.15, University of Leeds, UK, 2003. *(Quoted on page 237)*

274. D.R. Magee, C. Needham, P. Santos, A.G. Cohn, and D.C. Hogg. Autonomous Learning for a Cognitive Agent Using Continuous Models and Inductive Logic Programming from Audio-visual Input. In S. Coradeschi and A. Saffiotti, editors, *Proc. AAAI Workshop on Anchoring Symbols to Sensor Data*, pages 17–24. AAAI Press, 2004. *(Quoted on pages 222, 234, and 235)*

275. N. Maillot, M. Thonnat, and A. Boucher. Towards Ontology Based Cognitive Vision. In J.L. Crowley, J.H. Piater, M. Vincze, and L. Paletta, editors, *Third Intern. Conference on Computer Vision Systems (ICVS 2003)*, volume 2626 of *Lecture Notes in Computer Science LNCS*, pages 44–53, Graz, Austria, 1–3 April 2003. Springer-Verlag Berlin·Heidelberg·New York/NY. *(Quoted on page 297)*

276. J. Malik, S. Belongie, T. Leung, and J. Shi. Contour and Texture Analysis for Image Segmentation. *International Journal of Computer Vision*, 43(1):7–27, June 2001. *(Quoted on pages 76, 152, and 210)*

277. S.G. Mallat. A Theory for Multiresolution Signal Decomposition: The Wavelet Representation. *IEEE Trans. on Pattern Analysis and Machine Intelligence*, 11(7):674–693, July 1989. *(Quoted on page 202)*

278. D. Marr. Early Processing of Visual Information. *Phil. Trans. Royal Society London*, B 275:483–524, 1976. *(Quoted on page 7)*

279. D. Marr. Artificial Intelligence – A Personal View. *Artificial Intelligence*, 9(1):37–48, 1977. *(Quoted on page 11)*

280. D. Marr. Representing Visual Information. In A.R. Hanson and E.M. Riseman, editors, *Computer Vision Systems*, pages 61–80, New York, NY, 1978. Academic Press. *(Quoted on page 7)*

281. D. Marr. *Vision: A Computational Investigation into the Human Representation and Processing of Visual Information*. W.H. Freeman, San Francisco, CA, 1982. *(Quoted on pages 7, 145, 146, 150, and 152)*

282. D. Marr and E. Hildreth. Theory of Edge Detection. *Proc. Royal Society London*, B 207:187–217, 1980. *(Quoted on page 7)*

283. D. Marr and H.K. Nishihara. Representation and Recognition of the Spatial Organization of Three Dimensional Structure. *Proc. Royal Society London*, B 200:269–294, 1978. *(Quoted on page 7)*

284. D. Marr and T. Poggio. A Theory of Human Stereo Vision. *Proc. Royal Society London*, B 204:301–328, 1979. *(Quoted on page 7)*

285. T. Martinetz and K. Schulten. Topology Representing Networks. *Neural Networks*, 7(3):505–522, 1994. *(Quoted on page 137)*

286. J. Matas, O. Chum, U. Martin, and T. Pajdla. Robust Wide Baseline Stereo from Maximally Stable Extremal Regions. In P.L. Rosin and D. Marshall, editors, *Proc. British Machine Vision Conference*, pages 384–393, Cardiff, Wales, 2-5 September 2002. *(Quoted on page 148)*

287. J. Matoušek. On Embedding Trees into Uniformly Convex Banach Spaces. *Israel Journal of Mathematics*, 237:221–237, 1999. *(Quoted on pages 119, 120, and 121)*

288. K. Matsumoto, W. Suzuki, and K. Tanaka. Neuronal Correlates of Goal-Based Motor Selection in the Prefrontal Cortex. *Science*, 301(5630):229–232, 2003. *(Quoted on page 44)*

289. T. Matsuyama and V. Hwang. *SIGMA: A Knowledge–based Aerial Image Understanding System*. Plenum Press, New York, 1990. *(Quoted on pages 165 and 258)*

290. H. Maturana. Biology of Cognition. Technical Report BCL 9.0, University of Illinois, Urbana, Illinois, 1970. *(Quoted on page 15)*

291. H. Maturana. The Organization of the Living: a Theory of the Living Organization. *International Journal of Man-Machine Studies*, 7(3):313–332, 1975. *(Quoted on page 15)*

292. H. Maturana and F.J. Varela. *The Tree of Knowledge – The Biological Roots of Human Understanding*. New Science Library, Boston & London, 1987. *(Quoted on pages 15 and 16)*

293. H.R. Maturana and F.J. Varela. *Autopoiesis and Cognition*, volume 42 of *Boston Studies on the Philosophy of Science*. D. Reidel Publishing Company, 1980. *(Quoted on page 15)*

294. W.S. McCulloch and W. Pitts. A Logical Calculus of the Ideas Immanent in Nervous Activity. *Bulletin of Mathematical Biophysics*, 5:115–133, 1943. *(Quoted on page 10)*

295. S. McKenna, S. Jabri, Z. Duric, A. Rosenfeld, and H. Wechsler. Tracking Groups of People. *Computer Vision and Image Understanding*, 80(1):42–56, 2000. *(Quoted on page 225)*

296. S.J. McKenna and S. Gong. Non-intrusive Person Authentication for Access Control by Visual Tracking and Face Recognition. In J. Bigün, G. Chollet, and G. Borgefors, editors, *Proc. First Int. Conf. on Audio- and Video-based Biometric Person Authentication*, volume 1206 of *Lecture Notes in Computer Science*, pages 177–183, Crans-Montana, Switzerland, 12–14 March 1997. *(Quoted on page 129)*

297. P. Meer. Stochastic Image Pyramids. *Computer Vision, Graphics, and Image Processing (CVG&IP)*, 45(3):269–294, March 1989. *(Quoted on pages 203, 215, and 218)*

298. B.W. Mel. MURPHY: A Robot that Learns by Doing. In *Neural Information Processing Systems*, pages 544–553. American Institute of Physics, 1988. *(Quoted on pages 13 and 21)*

299. S. Mika, G. Rätsch, J. Weston, B. Schölkopf, and K.-R. Müller. Fisher Discriminant Analysis with Kernels. In Y.-H. Hu, J. Larsen, E. Wilson, and S. Douglas, editors, *Neural Networks for Signal Processing IX*, pages 41–48. IEEE, 1999. *(Quoted on page 87)*

300. K. Mikolajczyk and C. Schmid. Indexing Based on Scale Invariant Interest Points. In *Proc. Eighth International Conference on Computer Vision*, volume 1, pages 525–531, Vancouver, Canada, 9-12 July 2001. *(Quoted on pages 76 and 148)*

301. K. Mikolajczyk and C. Schmid. An Affine Invariant Interest Point Detector. In A. Heyden, G. Sparr, M. Nielsen, and P. Johansen, editors, *Computer Vision - ECCV 2002, Part I*, volume 2350 of *Lecture Notes in Computer Science*, pages 128–142, Copenhagen, Denmark, 28–31 May 2002. Springer-Verlag Berlin·Heidelberg·New York/NY. *(Quoted on page 148)*

302. K. Mikolajczyk and C. Schmid. A Performance Evaluation of Local Descriptors. In *CVPR'03*, Madison, WI, June 2003. *(Quoted on page 148)*

303. K. Mikolajczyk, A. Zisserman, and C. Schmid. Shape Recognition with Edge-Based Features. In *BMVC'03*, pages 779–788, September 2003. *(Quoted on page 148)*

304. M. Minsky. A Framework for Representing Knowledge. In P. Winston, editor, *The Psychology of Computer Vision*, pages 211–277. McGraw Hill, New York, NY, 1975. *(Quoted on page 184)*

305. B. Moghaddam. Principal Manifolds and Probabilistic Subspaces for Visual Recognition. *IEEE Transactions on Pattern Analysis and Machine Intelligence*, 24(6):780–788, June 2002. *(Quoted on pages 130, 132, and 133)*

306. A. Mohan, C. Papageorgiou, and T. Poggio. Example-based Object Detection in Images by Components. *IEEE Transactions on Pattern Analysis and Machine Intelligence (PAMI)*, 23(4):349–361, April 2001. *(Quoted on page 150)*

307. R. Möller, B. Neumann, and M. Wessel. Towards Computer Vision with Description Logics - Some Recent Progress. In G. Sagerer and S. Wachsmuth, editors, *Proc. Workshop on Integration of Speech and Image Understanding*, pages 101–115, Corfu, Greece, 21 September 1999. IEEE Computer Society, Los Alamitos, CA, USA. *(Quoted on page 272)*

308. M. Montemerlo, J. Pineau, N. Roy, S. Thrun, and V. Verma. Experiences with a Mobile Robotic Guide for the Elderly. In *Proc. Eighteenth AAAI National Conference on Artificial Intelligence (AAAI '02)*, pages 587–592, Edmonton, Alberta, Canada, 28 July–1 August 2002. American Association for Artificial Intelligence. ISBN 0-262-51129-0. *(Quoted on pages 246 and 298)*

309. D. Moore and I. Essa. Recognizing Multitasked Activities from Video Using Stochastic Context-Free Grammar. In *Proc. 18th National Conference on Artificial Intelligence (AAAI-02)*, pages 770–776, Edmonton, Alberta, Canada, 28 July – 1 August 2002. *(Quoted on page 234)*

310. S. Muggleton. Inverse Entailment and Progol. *New Generation Computing, Special issue on Inductive Logic Programming*, 13(3-4):245–286, 1995. *(Quoted on page 233)*

311. S. Muggleton. Learning from Positive Data. In S. Muggleton, editor, *ILP96*, volume 1314 of *Lecture Notes in Artificial Intelligence (LNAI)*, pages 358–376. Springer-Verlag Berlin·Heidelberg·New York/NY, 1996. *(Quoted on page 233)*

312. S. Muggleton and J. Firth. Relational Rule Induction with CProgol4.4: A Tutorial Introduction. In S. Dzeroski and N. Lavrac, editors, *Relational Data Mining*, pages 160–188. Springer-Verlag Berlin·Heidelberg·New York/NY, September 2001. *(Quoted on page 233)*

313. H. Murase and S.K. Nayar. Visual Learning and Recognition of 3D Objects from Appearance. *International Journal of Computer Vision*, 14(1):5–24, 1995. *(Quoted on page 146)*

314. D. Murray and J.J. Little. Using Real-time Stereo Vision for Mobile Robot Navigation. *Autonomous Robots*, 8:161–171, 2000. *(Quoted on pages 300 and 304)*

315. D.R. Murray. *Patchlets: a Method of Interpreting Correlation Stereo 3D Data*. PhD thesis, Computer Science, The University of British Columbia, 2004. *(Quoted on page 300)*

316. P.F. Nacken. Image Segmentation by Connectivity Preserving Relinking in Hierarchical Graph Structures. *Pattern Recognition*, 28(6):907–920, June 1995. *(Quoted on page 211)*

317. H.-H. Nagel. From Video to Language - a Detour via Logic vs. Jumping to Conclusions. In G. Sagerer and S. Wachsmuth, editors, *Proc. Integration of Speech and Image Understanding*, pages 79–100, Corfu, Greece, 21 September 1999. IEEE Computer Society, Los Alamitos, CA, USA. *(Quoted on page 249)*

318. H.-H. Nagel. Image Sequence Evaluation: 30 Years and Still Going Strong. In A. Sanfeliu, J.-J. Villanueva, M. Vanrell, R. Alquézar, J.-O. Eklundh, and Y. Aloimonos, editors, *Proc. 15th Intern. Conference on Pattern Recognition*, volume 1, pages 149–158, Barcelona, Spain, 3-7 September 2000. IEEE Computer Society: Los Alamitos, CA. *(Quoted on pages 60 and 61)*

319. H.-H. Nagel. Steps Towards a Cognitive Vision System. *AI Magazine*, 25(2):31–50, Summer 2004. *(Quoted on pages 62 and 65)*

320. H.-H. Nagel and M. Arens. 'Innervation des Automobils' und Formale Logik (in German). In M. Maurer and Ch. Stiller, editors, *Fahrerassistenzsysteme mit maschineller Wahrnehmung*, pages 89–116. Springer-Verlag Berlin·Heidelberg·New York/NY, 2005. *(Quoted on page 64)*

321. H.-H. Nagel, F. Heimes, K. Fleischer, M. Haag, H. Leuck, and S. Noltemeier. Quantitative Comparison Between Trajectory Estimates Obtained from a Binocular Camera Setup within a Moving Road Vehicle and from the Outside by a Stationary Monocular Camera. *Image and Vision Computing*, 18(5):435–444, April 2000. *(Quoted on page 63)*

322. V. Nair and J.J. Clark. Automated Visual Surveillance Using Hidden Markov Models. In *VI02*, page 88, 2002. *(Quoted on page 302)*

323. A. Needham. Object Recognition and Object Segregation in 4.5-month-old Infants. *J. Exp. Child Psych.*, 78(3):3–24, 2001. *(Quoted on pages 146 and 152)*

324. R.C. Nelson and A. Selinger. A Cubist Approach to Object Recognition. In *ICCV-1998: Sixth International Conference on Computer Vision*, pages 614–621, Bombay, India, 4–7 January 1998. Narosa Publishing House, New Delhi, India. *(Quoted on pages 146, 148, and 150)*

325. R.C. Nelson and A. Selinger. Large-Scale Tests of a Keyed, Appearance-Based 3-D Object Recognition System. *Vision Research*, 38(15-16):2469–2488, August 1998. *(Quoted on pages 148 and 150)*

326. B. Neumann. Description of Time-Varying Scenes. In D. Waltz, editor, *Semantic Structures – Advances in Natural Language Processing*, pages 167–206. Lawrence Erlbaum Assoc., Hillsdale, NJ · Hove and London, UK, 1989. *(Quoted on pages 251 and 255)*

327. B. Neumann and T. Weiss. Navigating Through Logic-based Scene Models for High-level Scene Interpretations. In J.L. Crowley, J.H. Piater, M. Vincze, and L. Paletta, editors, *3rd International Conference on Computer Vision Systems - ICVS 2003*, volume 2626 of *Lecture Notes in Computer Science*, pages 212–222, Graz, Austria, 1-3 April 2003. Springer-Verlag Berlin·Heidelberg·New York/NY. *(Quoted on page 257)*

328. H. Niemann. *Pattern Analysis and Understanding*, volume 4 of *Springer Series in Information Sciences*. Springer-Verlag Berlin·Heidelberg·New York/NY, 2 edition, 1990. *(Quoted on page 174)*

329. H. Niemann. Knowledge–Based Interpretation of Images. In B. Jähne, H. Haußecker, and P. Geißler, editors, *Handbook of Computer Vision and Applications*, volume 2, pages 855–874. Academic Press, San Diego, 1999. *(Quoted on pages 165 and 167)*

330. H. Niemann, H. Bunke, I. Hofmann, G. Sagerer, F. Wolf, and H. Feistel. A Knowledge Based System for Analysis of Gated Blood Pool Studies. *IEEE Trans. on Pattern Analysis and Machine Intelligence*, 7:246–259, 1985. *(Quoted on page 165)*

331. H. Niemann, G. Sagerer, S. Schröder, and F. Kummert. ERNEST: A Semantic Network System for Pattern Understanding. *IEEE Trans. on Pattern Analysis and Machine Intelligence*, 9:883–905, 1990. *(Quoted on page 167)*

332. N.J. Nilsson. *Problem Solving Methods in Artificial Intelligence*. McGraw Hill, New York, 1971. *(Quoted on page 174)*

333. N.J. Nilsson. *Artificial Intelligence - A New Synthesis*. Morgan Kaufmann, San Mateo, CA, 1998. *(Quoted on page 248)*

334. Y. Ohta. *Knowledge-Based Interpretation of Outdoor Natural Colour Scenes*. Pitman Books, Boston, MA, 1985. *(Quoted on page 165)*

335. Object Management Group (OMG). *CORBAservices: Common Object Service Specification*. Object Management Group, Inc., Needham, U.S.A., March 1995. *(Quoted on pages 284 and 286)*

336. A. Ottlik and H.-H. Nagel. On Consistent Discrimination Between Directed and Diffuse Outdoor Illumination. In B. Michaelis and G. Krell, editors, *Proc. 25th DAGM–Symposium (DAGM'03)*, volume 2781 of *Lecture Notes in Computer Science*, pages 418–425, Magdeburg, Germany, 10-12 September 2003. Springer-Verlag Berlin·Heidelberg·New York/NY. *(Quoted on pages 65 and 66)*

337. A. Paoluzzi, F. Bernardini, C. Cattani, and V. Ferrucci. Dimension Independent Modeling with Simplicial Complexes. *ACM Trans. on Graphics*, 12(1):56–102, 1993. *(Quoted on page 200)*

338. C. Papageorgiou and T. Poggio. A Trainable System for Object Detection. *Int. Journal of Computer Vision*, 38(1):15–33, 2000. *(Quoted on pages 146, 149, and 150)*

339. J. Pascoe. Adding Generic Contextual Capabilities to Wearable Computers. In *Proc. 2nd International Symposium on Wearable Computers (ISWC 98)*, pages 92–99, Pittsburgh, PA, 19–20 October 1998. *(Quoted on page 185)*

340. J. Pauli and G. Sommer. Perceptual Organization with Image Formation Compatibilities. *Pattern Recognition Letters*, 23(7):803–817, May 2002. *(Quoted on page 11)*

341. D. Paulus. *Aktives Bildverstehen*. Der andere Verlag, Osnabrück, 2001. *(Quoted on page 165)*

342. J. Pearl. *Heuristics. Intelligent Search Strategies for Computer Problem Solving*. Addison–Wesley Publ. Co., Reading, Mass., 1984. *(Quoted on page 174)*

343. J. Pearl. *Probabilistic Reasoning in Intelligent Systems - Networks of Plausible Inference*. Morgan Kaufmann, Publ.: San Mateo, CA, USA, 1988. *(Quoted on page 274)*

344. M. Pelillo and E.R. Hancock, editors. *Proc. International Workshop on Energy Minimization Methods in Computer Vision and Pattern Recognition*, volume 1223 of *Lecture Notes in Computer Science*. Springer-Verlag Berlin·Heidelberg·New York/NY, Venice, Italy, 21–23 May 1997. *(Quoted on page 166)*

345. G. Peters. *A View-based Approach to Three-dimensional Object Perception*. PhD Thesis. Universität Bielefeld, Germany, December 2001. *(Quoted on page 78)*

346. M.A. Peterson. Object Recognition Processes Can and Do Operate Before Figure-Ground Organization. *Current Directions in Psychological Science*, 3:105–111, 1994. *(Quoted on pages 146 and 152)*

344   References

347. D. Philipona, J.K. O'Regan, and J.-P. Nadal. Is There Something Out There? Inferring Space from Sensorimotor Dependencies. *Neural Computation*, 15(9):2029–2049, 2003. *(Quoted on pages 17 and 44)*

348. D. Philipona, J.K. O'Regan, J.-P. Nadal, and O.J.-M.D. Coenen. Perception of the Structure of the Physical World Using Unknown Multimodal Sensors and Effectors. In S. Thrun, L. Saul, and B. Schölkopf, editors, *NIPS 2003*, volume 16 of *Advances in Neural Information Processing Systems*. MIT Press, 2003. *(Quoted on page 17)*

349. P.J. Phillips, H. Moon, S.A. Rizvi, and P.J. Rauss. The FERET Evaluation Methodology for Face-Recognition Algorithms. *IEEE Transactions on Pattern Analysis and Machine Intelligence*, 22(10):1090–1104, 2000. *(Quoted on pages 129 and 134)*

350. J. Piater and J.L. Crowley. Event-based Activity Analysis in Live Video Using a Generic Object Tracker. In *Proc. Third IEEE Intern. Workshop on Performance Evaluation of Tracking and Surveillance*, pages 1–8, Copenhagen, Danmark, 1 June 2002. *(Quoted on page 187)*

351. R. Picard. *Affective Computing*. MIT Press, 1997. *(Quoted on page 302)*

352. S. Pinker. Visual Cognition: An Introduction. *Cognition*, 18:1–63, 1984. *(Quoted on page 11)*

353. T. Poggio and S. Edelman. A Network that Learns to Recognize Three-dimensional Objects. *Nature*, 343:263–266, 1990. *(Quoted on page 48)*

354. W. Ponweiser, G. Umgeher, and M. Vincze. A Reusable Dynamic Framework for Cognitive Vision Systems. In *Proc. Workshop on Computer Vision System Control Architectures at ICVS'03*, pages 31–34, Graz, 31 March 2003. *(Quoted on page 287)*

355. A.R. Pope and D.G. Lowe. Probabilistic Models of Appearance for 3-D Object Recognition. *International Journal of Computer Vision*, 40(2):149–167, November 2000. *(Quoted on page 7)*

356. L. Priese and V. Rehrmann. On Hierarchical Color Segmentation and Applications. In *IEEE Conference on Computer Vision and Pattern Recognition, CVPR'93*, pages 633–634, New York City, NY, 15–17 June 1993. IEEE Computer Society Press: Los Alamitos, CA. *(Quoted on page 169)*

357. R.C. Prim. Shortest Connection Networks and Some Generalizations. *Bell Systems Technical Journal*, 36:1389–1401, 1957. *(Quoted on page 215)*

358. K.-V. Prouskas and J.V. Pitt. A Real-time Architecture for Time-aware Agents. *IEEE Transactions on System, Man and Cybernetics (Part B)*, SMC–34(3):1553–1568, June 2004. *(Quoted on page 281)*

359. M.L. Puterman. *Markov Decision Processes: Discrete Stochastic Dynamic Programming*. Wiley, New York, NY, 1994. *(Quoted on pages 296 and 306)*

360. Z.W. Pylyshyn. *Computation and Cognition*. Bradford Books, MIT Press, 2nd edition, 1984. *(Quoted on page 10)*

361. M.R. Quillian. Semantic Memory. In M. Minsky, editor, *Semantic Information Processing*, pages 227–270. MIT Press, Cambridge, MA and London, UK, 1968. *(Quoted on page 184)*

362. J. Quintana and J.M. Fuster. From Perception to Action: Temporal Integrative Functions of Prefrontal and Parietal Neurons. *Cereb. Cortex*, 9(3):213–221, 1999. *(Quoted on page 44)*

363. D.A. Randell, Z. Cui, and A.G. Cohn. A Spatial Logic Based on Regions and Connections. In B. Nebel, C. Rich, and W. Swartout, editors, *Principles of Knowledge Representation and Reasoning*, pages 165–176, Cambridge, MA, USA, 25-29 October 1992. Morgan Kaufman, Publ.: San Mateo, CA, USA. *(Quoted on page 262)*

364. R.P.N. Rao and D.H. Ballard. An Active Vision Architecture Based on Iconic Representations. Technical Report TR548, 1995. *(Quoted on page 39)*

365. R.P.N. Rao and D.H. Ballard. An Active Vision Architecture Based on Iconic Representations. *Artificial Intelligence*, 78(1–2):461–505, 1995. *(Quoted on page 75)*

366. R.P.N. Rao and D.H. Ballard. Object Indexing Using an Iconic Sparse Distributed Memory. In *ICCV'95*, pages 24–31, 1995. *(Quoted on pages 146 and 147)*

367. J. Rasure and S. Kubica. The Khoros Application Development Environment. In J.L. Crowley and H.I. Christensen, editors, *Experimental Environments for Computer Vision and Image Processing*, volume 11 of *Machine Perception Artificial Intelligence Series*, pages 1–32. World Scientific Press, Singapore, 1994. *(Quoted on page 183)*

368. B. Reeves and C. Nass. *The Media Equation: How People Treat Computers, Television, and New Media Like Real People and Places*. Cambridge University Press, Cambridge, UK, 1996. *(Quoted on page 302)*

369. R. Reiter and A.K. Mackworth. The Logic of Depiction. Technical Report TR 87-23, Dept. Computer Science, Univ. of British Columbia, Vancouver, BC, Canada, September 1987. *(Quoted on page 258)*

370. P. Remagnino, A. Baumberg, T. Grove, D. Hogg, T. Tan, A. Worrall, and K. Baker. An Integrated Traffic and Pedestrian Model-Based Vision System. In A.F. Clark, editor, *Proc. British Machine Vision Conference (BMVC 1997)*, volume 2, pages 380–389, Colchester, UK, 8–11 September 1997. *(Quoted on page 225)*

371. S.W. Reyner. An Analysis of a Good Algorithm for the Subtree Problem. *SIAM J. Comput.*, 6:730–732, 1977. *(Quoted on page 115)*

372. M. Riesenhuber and T. Poggio. Computational Models of Object Recognition in Cortex: A Review. Technical Report 1695, Artificial Intelligence Laboratory and Department of Brain and Cognitive Sciences, Massachusetts Institute of Technology, Aug. 2000. *(Quoted on pages 48 and 50)*

373. R.D. Rimey. *Control of Selective Perception Using Bayes Nets and Decision Theory*. PhD thesis, Computer Science Dept., University of Rochester, December 1993. *(Quoted on page 273)*

374. L.G. Roberts. Machine Perception of Three-Dimensional Solids. In J.T. Tippett et al., editor, *Optical and Electro-Optical Information Processing*, pages 159–197. M.I.T. Press: Cambridge, MA, 1965. *(Quoted on page 7)*

375. E.M. Robertson, J.M. Tormos, F. Maeda, and A. Pascual-Leone. The Role of the Dorsolateral Prefrontal Cortex during Sequence Learning is Specific for Spatial Information. *Cereb. Cortex*, 11(7):628–635, 2001. *(Quoted on page 44)*

376. T. Rodden, K. Chervest, N. Davies, and A. Dix. Exploiting Context in HCI Design for Mobile Systems. In C. Johnson, editor, *1st Workshop on Human Computer Interaction with Mobile Devices*, Glasgow, Scotland, UK, 22 May 1998. *(Quoted on page 184)*

377. D. Ron, S. Singer, and N. Tishby. The Power of Amnesia. In *Advances in Neural Information Processing Systems*, volume 6, pages 176–183. Morgan Kaufmann, 1994. *(Quoted on page 224)*

378. R. Rosales and S. Sclaroff. Improved Tracking of Multiple Humans with Trajectory Prediction and Occlusion Modeling. In *Proc. IEEE Workshop on the Interpretation of Visual Motion*, Santa Barbara, CA, 22 June 1998. *(Quoted on page 225)*

379. A. Rosenfeld, editor. *Multiresolution Image Processing and Analysis*, volume 12 of *Springer Series in Information Sciences*. Springer-Verlag Berlin·Heidelberg·New York/NY, 1984. *(Quoted on page 202)*

380. A. Rosenfeld and A. Nakamura. Local Deformations of Digital Curves. *Pattern Recognition Letters*, 18(7):613–620, July 1997. *(Quoted on page 213)*

381. A. Roskies. The Binding Problem. *Neuron*, 24:7–9, 1999. *(Quoted on page 33)*

382. J. Rossignac and M. O'Connor. SGC: a Dimension-independent Model for Pointsets with Internal Structures and Incomplete Boundaries. In M.J. Wozny, J. Turner, and K. Preiss, editors, *Geometric Modeling for Product Engineering*, pages 145–180. Elsevier Science, 1989. *(Quoted on page 200)*

383. H. Rowley, S. Baluja, and T. Kanade. Neural Network-based Face Detection. *IEEE Transactions on Pattern Analysis and Machine Intelligence*, 20(1):23–38, 1998. *(Quoted on pages 146 and 149)*

384. Y. Rubner, C. Tomasi, and L.J. Guibas. The Earth Mover's Distance as a Metric for Image Retrieval. *International Journal of Computer Vision*, 40(2):99–121, 2000. *(Quoted on page 122)*

385. T.A. Russ, R.M. MacGregor, B. Salemi, K.E. Price, and R. Nevatia. VEIL: Combining Semantic Knowledge with Image Understanding. In O. Firschein and T.M. Strat, editors, *Radius: Image Understanding for Imagery Intelligence*, pages 409–418. Morgan Kaufmann, 1997. *(Quoted on page 260)*

386. S. Russell and P. Norvig. *Artificial Intelligence - A Modern Approach*. Prentice-Hall, Upper Saddle River, NJ, 2003. *(Quoted on pages 248 and 272)*

387. G. Sagerer and H. Niemann. *Semantic Networks for Understanding Scenes*. Advances in Computer Vision and Machine Intelligence. Plenum Press, New York and London, 1997. *(Quoted on pages 165, 167, and 173)*

388. P. Santos, D.R. Magee, and A.G. Cohn. Looking for Logic in Vision. In *Proc. Eleventh Workshop on Automated Reasoning*, pages 61–62, University of Leeds, Leeds, UK, 31 March–1 April 2004. *(Quoted on pages 244 and 246)*

389. P. Santos, D.R. Magee, A.G. Cohn, and D.C. Hogg. Combining Multiple Answers for Learning Mathematical Structures from Visual Observation. In R. López de Mántaras and L. Saitta, editors, *Proc. 16th European Conference on Artificial Intelligence (ECAI-04)*, pages 544–548, Valencia, Spain, 22–27 August 2004. IOS Press: Amsterdam, NL. *(Quoted on pages 222, 233, 244, 245, and 246)*

390. K.H. Schäfer. *Unscharfe zeitlogische Modellierung von Situationen und Handlungen in Bildfolgenauswertung und Robotik*, volume 135 of '*Dissertationen zur Künstlichen Intelligenz (DISKI)*'. infix Verlag: Sankt Augustin, Juli 1996. (in German). *(Quoted on page 64)*

391. R.C. Schank and R.P. Abelson. *Scripts, Plans, Goals and Understanding*. Lawrence Erlbaum Associates, Hillsdale, NJ, USA, 1977. *(Quoted on page 184)*

392. B. Schiele and J.L. Crowley. Recognition without Correspondence Using Multidimensional Receptive Field Histograms. *Int. Journal of Computer Vision*, 36(1):31–52, January 2000. *(Quoted on pages 146 and 147)*

393. B. Schilit and M. Theimer. Disseminating Active Map Information to Mobile Hosts. *IEEE Network*, 8(1):22–32, 1994. *(Quoted on page 184)*

394. C. Schlegel and R. Wörz. The Software Framework SmartSoft for Implementing Sensorimotor Systems. In *Proc. IROS'99*, pages 1610–1616, Kyongju, Korea, 17-21 October 1999. IEEE/RSJ, IEEE Press. *(Quoted on page 281)*

395. C. Schmid. Constructing Models for Content-based Image Retrieval. In *IEEE Conference on Computer Vision and Pattern Recognition*, volume 2, pages 39–45, Kauai, Hawaii, USA, December 2001. *(Quoted on pages 75 and 76)*

396. C. Schmid and R. Mohr. Combining Greyvalue Invariants with Local Constraints for Object Recognition. In *IEEE Conference on Computer Vision and Pattern Recognition (CVPR'96)*, pages 872–877, San Francisco, CA, 18–20 June 1996. *(Quoted on pages 146 and 147)*

397. C. Schmid and R. Mohr. Local Greyvalue Invariants for Image Retrieval. *IEEE Transactions on Pattern Analysis and Machine Intelligence*, PAMI-19(5):530–534, 1997. *(Quoted on page 75)*

398. M. Schmidt-Schauß. Subsumption in KL-ONE is Undecidable. In R.J. Brachman, H.J. Levesque, and R. Reiter, editors, *First International Conference on Principles of Knowledge Representation (KR'89)*, pages 421–431, Toronto, ON, Canada, 15-18 May 1989. Morgan Kaufmann, Publ.: San Mateo, CA, USA. *(Quoted on page 262)*

399. M. Schmidt-Schauß and G. Smolka. Attributive Concept Descriptions with Unions and Complements. Technical Report SR-88-21, Fachbereich Informatik, Universität Kaiserslautern, Kaiserslautern (Germany), 1988. *(Quoted on page 262)*

400. H. Schneiderman and T. Kanade. A Statistical Method of 3D Object Detection Applied to Faces and Cars. In CVPR-2000 [91], pages 746–751. *(Quoted on pages 146 and 149)*

401. H. Schneiderman and T. Kanade. Object Detection Using the Statistics of Parts. *International Journal of Computer Vision*, 56(3):151–177, 2004. *(Quoted on pages 146 and 149)*

402. B. Schölkopf. *Support Vector Learning*. GMD–Bericht Nr. 287. Oldenbourg, München, 1997. *(Quoted on page 166)*

403. B. Schölkopf, P. Knirsch, A. Smola, and C.J. Burges. Fast Approximation of Support Vector Kernel Expansions, and an Interpretation of Clustering as Approximation in Feature Spaces. In P. Levi, R.-J. Ahlers, F. May, and M. Schanz, editors, *Mustererkennung 1998 - 20. DAGM-Symposium*, pages 124–132, Stuttgart, Germany, 29 Sept.–1 Oct. 1998. Springer-Verlag Berlin·Heidelberg·New York/NY. *(Quoted on page 89)*

404. B. Schölkopf, A. Smola, and K.R. Müller. Nonlinear Component Analysis as a Kernel Eigenvalue Problem. *Neural Computation*, 10(5):1299–1319, 1998. *(Quoted on page 89)*

405. C. Schröder. *Bildinterpretation durch Modellkonstruktion: Eine Theorie zur rechnergestützten Analyse von Bildern*, volume DISKI 196 of *Dissertationen zur Künstlichen Intelligenz*. infix: Sankt Augustin, Germany, 1999. Dissertation (in German), 4. Dezember 1998, Fachbereich Informatik der Universität Hamburg, Hamburg, Germany. ISBN 3-89601-196-0. *(Quoted on page 258)*

406. C. Schröder and B. Neumann. On the Logics of Image Interpretation: Model-Construction in a Formal Knowledge-Representation Framework. In *Proc. International Conference on Image Processing (ICIP-96)*, volume 2, pages 785–788, 16-19 September 1996. *(Quoted on page 258)*

407. A.B. Schwartz, D.W. Moran, and G.A. Reina. Differential Representation of Perception and Action in the Frontal Cortex. *Science*, 303(5656):380–383, 2004. *(Quoted on page 44)*

408. K. Schwerdt and J.L. Crowley. Robust Face Tracking Using Color. In *Proc. 4th IEEE International Conference on Automatic Face and Gesture Recognition*, pages 90–95, Grenoble, France, 28-30 March 2000. IEEE Computer Society, Los Alamitos, CA. *(Quoted on page 186)*

409. S. Sclaroff. Deformable Prototypes for Encoding Shape Categories in Image Databases. *Pattern Recognition*, 30(4):627–641, April 1997. *(Quoted on page 149)*

410. S. Se, D.G. Lowe, and J.J. Little. Local and Global Localization for Mobile Robots Using Visual Landmarks. In *Proceedings of the IEEE/RSJ International Conference on Intelligent Robots and Systems (IROS '01)*, pages 414–420, Maui, Hawaii, October 2001. *(Quoted on page 299)*

411. S. Se, D.G. Lowe, and J.J. Little. Vision-based Mobile Robot Localization and Mapping Using Scale-invariant Features. In *Proceedings of the IEEE International Conference on Robotics and Automation (ICRA)*, pages 2051–2058, Seoul, Korea, May 2001. *(Quoted on page 299)*

412. S. Se, D.G. Lowe, and J.J. Little. Mobile Robot Localization and Mapping with Uncertainty Using Scale-Invariant Landmarks. *Intl. Journal of Robotics Research*, 21(8):735–758, August 2002. *(Quoted on page 299)*

413. E. Sharon, A. Brandt, and R. Basri. Fast Multiscale Image Segmentation. In CVPR-2000 [91], pages 70–77. *(Quoted on page 152)*

414. H. Shatkay and L.P. Kaelbling. Learning Topological Maps with Weak Local Odometric Information. In *Proc. 15th International Joint Conference on Artificial Intelligence (IJCAI-97)*, pages 920–929, Nagoya, Japan, 23-29 August 1997. *(Quoted on pages 296 and 297)*

415. M. Shaw and D. Garlan. *Software Architecture: Perspectives on an Emerging Disciplines*. Prentice Hall, 1996. *(Quoted on page 183)*

416. R.N. Shepard and S. Hurwitz. Upward Direction, Mental Rotation, and Discrimination of Left and Right Turns in Maps. *Cognition*, 18:161–193, 1984. *(Quoted on page 12)*

417. J. Sherrah and S. Gong. Resolving Visual Uncertainty and Occlusion through Probabilistic Reasoning. In M. Mirmehdi and B. Thomas, editors, *Proc. British Machine Vision Con-*

ference (BMVC-2000), pages 252–261, Bristol, UK, 11-14 September 2000. *(Quoted on pages 225 and 226)*

418. J. Shi and J. Malik. Normalized Cuts and Image Segmentation. In *IEEE Conference on Computer Vision and Pattern Recognition (CVPR-1997)*, pages 731–737, San Juan, Puerto Rico, 17–19 June 1997. IEEE Computer Society Press: Los Alamitos, CA. *(Quoted on pages 152, 206, and 210)*

419. Y. Shirai. A Context-sensitive Line Finder for Recognition of Polyhedra. *Artificial Intelligence*, 4:95–119, 1973. *(Quoted on page 7)*

420. Y. Shoham. What We Talk About When We Talk About Software Agents. *IEEE Intelligent Systems*, 14(2):28–31, March/April 1999. *(Quoted on page 281)*

421. A. Shokoufandeh, S. Dickinson, C. Jönsson, L. Bretzner, and T. Lindeberg. On the Representation and Matching of Qualitative Shape at Multiple Scales. In A. Heyden, G. Sparr, M. Nielsen, and P. Johansen, editors, *Computer Vision - ECCV 2002, Part III*, volume 2352 of *Lecture Notes in Computer Science*, pages 759–775, Copenhagen, Denmark, 28–31 May 2002. Springer-Verlag Berlin·Heidelberg·New York/NY. *(Quoted on page 114)*

422. A. Shokoufandeh, S.J. Dickinson, K. Siddiqi, and S.W. Zucker. Indexing Using a Spectral Encoding of Topological Structure. In *IEEE Conference on Computer Vision and Pattern Recognition (CVPR'99)*, pages 491–497, Fort Collins, CO, 23–25 June 1999. *(Quoted on page 116)*

423. A. Shokoufandeh, Y. Keselman, F. Demirci, D. Macrini, and S. Dickinson. Many-to-many Feature Matching in Object Recognition. In H.I. Christensen and H.-H. Nagel, editors, *(this volume)*. Springer-Verlag Berlin·Heidelberg·New York/NY, 2005. *(Quoted on pages 205 and 206)*

424. K. Siddiqi, A. Shokoufandeh, S.J. Dickinson, and S.W. Zucker. Shock Graphs and Shape Matching. *International Journal of Computer Vision*, 30(1):1–24, 1999. *(Quoted on pages 108, 111, 116, and 123)*

425. R. Sim and G. Dudek. Learning Generative Models of Scene Features. In *Proc. IEEE Conf. Computer Vision and Pattern Recognition (CVPR 2001)*, volume 1, pages 406–412, Kauai, Hawaii, 8–14 December 2001. *(Quoted on page 299)*

426. R. Simmons and D. Apfelbaum. A Task Description Language for Robot Control. In *Proceedings of Conference on Intelligent Robotics and Systems*, Vancouver, 1998. *(Quoted on page 298)*

427. R. Simmons, D. Goldberg, A. Goode, M. Montemerlo, N. Roy, B. Sellner, C. Urmson, A. Schultz, M. Abramson, W. Adams, A. Atrash, M. Bugajska, M. Coblenz, M. MacMahon, D. Perzanowski, I. Horswill, R. Zubek, D. Kortenkamp, B. Wolfe, T. Milam, and B. Maxwell. GRACE: an Autonomous Robot for the AAAI Robot Challenge. *AI Magazine*, 24(2):51–72, 2003. *(Quoted on page 298)*

428. J.M. Siskind. Visual Event Classification via Force Dynamics. In *Proc. National Conference on Artificial Intelligence (AAAI-2000)*, pages 149–155, Austin, TX, 30 July – 3 August 2000. *(Quoted on page 234)*

429. A.W.M. Smeulders, M. Worring, S. Santini, A. Gupta, and R. Jain. Content-based Image Retrieval at the End of the Early Years. *IEEE Trans. Pattern Analysis and Machine Intelligence*, 22(12):1349–1380, December 2000. *(Quoted on page 11)*

430. A. Smola and B. Schölkopf. Sparse Greedy Matrix Approximation for Machine Learning. In *Proc. 17th International Conf. on Machine Learning*, pages 911–918. Morgan Kaufmann, San Francisco, CA, 2000. *(Quoted on page 89)*

431. R.W. Sperry. *Science and Moral Priority: Merging Mind, Brain and Human Values*. Praeger, New York, NY, 1985. *(Quoted on page 44)*

432. S.P. Springer and G. Deutsch. *Left Brain, Right Brain*. Freeman, New York, 1993. *(Quoted on page 44)*

433. C. Stauffer and W.E.L. Grimson. Adaptive Background Mixture Models for Real-time Tracking. In *Proc. IEEE Computer Society Conference on Computer Vision and Pattern Recognition (CVPR '99)*, pages 246–252, Fort Collins, CO, 23–25 June 1999. *(Quoted on page 224)*

434. J. Steffens, E. Elagin, and H. Neven. Personspotter – Fast and Robust System for Human Detection, Tracking and Recognition. In M. Yachida and S. Morishima, editors, Proc. 3rd Int. Conf. on Automatic Face and Gesture Recognition (FG'98), pages 516–521, Nara, Japan, 14-16 April 1998. IEEE Computer Society Washington, DC, USA. *(Quoted on page 129)*

435. M.J. Stefik. *Introduction to Knowledge Systems*. Morgan Kaufmann, San Francisco, CA, 1995. *(Quoted on page 248)*

436. P. Stelldinger and U. Koethe. Shape Preservation during Digitization: Tight Bounds Based on the Morphing Distance. In B. Michaelis and G. Krell, editors, *Pattern Recognition, Proc. 25th DAGM Symposium (DAGM-2003)*, volume 2781 of *Lecture Notes in Computer Science*, pages 108–115, Magdeburg, Germany, 10–12 September 2003. Springer-Verlag Berlin·Heidelberg·New York/NY. *(Quoted on page 214)*

437. M. Sternberg, R. King, R. Lewis, and S. Muggleton. Application of Machine Learning to Structural Molecular Biology. *Philosophical Transactions of the Royal Society B*, 344:365–371, 1994. *(Quoted on page 234)*

438. O. Stock, editor. *Spatial and Temporal Reasoning*. Kluwer Academic Publishers, Dordrecht, NL, 1997. *(Quoted on page 248)*

439. M. Störring, H.J. Andersen, and E. Granum. Skin Color Detection Under Changing Lighting Conditions. *Journal of Autonomous Systems*, June 2000. *(Quoted on page 186)*

440. A. Strehl and J. Ghosh. Cluster Ensembles - A Knowledge Reuse Framework for Combining Multiple Partitions. *Journal of Machine Learning Research*, 3:583–617, 2002. *(Quoted on page 237)*

441. G. Sumbre, Y. Gutfreund, G. Fiorito, T. Flash, and B. Hochner. Control of Octopus Arm Extension by a Peripheral Motor Program. *Science*, 293:1845–1848, 2001. *(Quoted on page 45)*

442. R.S. Sutton and A.G. Barto. *Reinforcement Learning*. A Bradford Book, Cambridge, London, 1998. *(Quoted on page 175)*

443. M.J. Swain and D.H. Ballard. Color Indexing. *International Journal of Computer Vision*, 7(1):11–32, 1991. *(Quoted on pages 146, 147, and 170)*

444. C. Szyperski. *Component Software*. Addison Wesley, Boston, MA, 1999. *(Quoted on pages 280, 281, and 283)*

445. C. Szyperski and C. Pfister. Workshop on Component-Oriented Programming, Summary. In M. Mühlhäuser, editor, *Special Issues in Object-Oriented Programming - ECOOP96 Workshop Reader*. dpunkt Verlag, Heidelberg, 1996. *(Quoted on page 284)*

446. J.M. Tenenbaum and H.G. Barrow. Experiments in Interpretation Guided Segmentation. *Artificial Intelligence*, 8:241–274, 1977. *(Quoted on page 7)*

447. E. Thelen and L.B. Smith. *A Dynamic Systems Approach to the Development of Cognition and Action*. MIT Press / Bradford Books Series in Cognitive Psychology. MIT Press, Cambridge, Massachusetts, 1994. *(Quoted on pages 10, 11, 14, and 18)*

448. M. Thonnat and A. Bijaoui. Knowledge-based Galaxy Classification Systems. In A. Heck and F. Murtagh, editors, *Knowledge-based Systems in Astronomy*, volume 329 of *Lecture Notes in Physics*. Springer-Verlag Berlin·Heidelberg·New York/NY, 1989. *(Quoted on page 165)*

449. S. Thrun, M. Bennewitz, W. Burgard, A.B. Cremers, F. Dellaert, D. Fox, D. Hahnel, C. Rosenberg, N. Roy, J. Schulte, and D. Schulz. MINERVA: A Second-generation Museum Tour-Guide Robot. In *Proceedings of IEEE International Conference on Robotics and Automation (ICRA'99)*, pages 1999–2005, Detroit, Michigan, May 1999. *(Quoted on page 298)*

450. S. Thrun, W. Burgard, and D. Fox. A Probabilistic Approach to Concurrent Mapping and Localization for Mobile Robots. *Machine Learning and Autonomous Robots (joint issue)*, 31(5):1–25, 1998. *(Quoted on page 299)*

451. C. Tomasi and T. Kanade. Detection and Tracking of Point Features. Technical Report CMU-CS-91-132, Carnegie Mellon University, Pittsburgh, PA, 1991. *(Quoted on page 170)*

452. A. Torralba, K.P. Murphy, W.T. Freeman, and M.A. Rubin. Context-Based Vision System for Place and Object Recognition. In *Proc. Ninth IEEE International Conference on Computer Vision (ICCV-2003)*, volume I, pages 273–280, Nice, France, 13–16 October 2003. *(Quoted on page 302)*

453. K. Toyama and A. Blake. Probabilistic Tracking in a Metric Space. In *Proc. Eighth International Conference on Computer Vision*, volume 2, pages 50–59, Vancouver, BC, Canada, 9-12 July 2001. *(Quoted on page 136)*

454. A. Treisman and G. Gelade. A Feature-integration Theory of Attention. *Cognitive Psychology*, 12:97–136, 1980. *(Quoted on page 34)*

455. A. Treisman and H. Schmidt. Illusory Conjunctions in the Perception of Objects. *Cognitive Psychology*, 14:107–141, 1982. *(Quoted on page 34)*

456. J.K. Tsotsos. A 'Complexity Level' Analysis of Vision. In *Proc. First International Conference on Computer Vision (ICCV-1987)*, pages 346–355, London, UK, 8-11 June 1987. *(Quoted on pages 25 and 27)*

457. J.K. Tsotsos. The Complexity of Perceptual Search Tasks. In *Proc. International Joint Conference on Artificial Intelligence*, pages 1571–1577, Detroit, 1989. *(Quoted on pages 25, 27, and 34)*

458. J.K. Tsotsos. Analyzing Vision at the Complexity Level. *Behavioral and Brain Sciences*, 13(3):423 – 445, 1990. *(Quoted on pages 25 and 27)*

459. J.K. Tsotsos. On the Relative Complexity of Passive vs. Active Visual Search. *International Journal of Computer Vision*, 7(2):127 – 141, 1992. *(Quoted on pages 26 and 27)*

460. J.K. Tsotsos, S.M. Culhane, W. Wai, Y. Lai, N. Davis, and F. Nuflo. Modeling Visual Attention via Selective Tuning. *Artificial Intelligence*, 78(1–2):507–547, 1995. *(Quoted on pages 27, 30, and 32)*

461. J.K. Tsotsos, M. Pomplun, Y. Liu, J.-C. Martinez-Trujillo, and E. Simine. Attending to Motion: Localizing and Classifying Motion Patterns in Image Sequences. In H.H. Bülthoff, S.-W. Lee, T.A. Poggio, and C. Wallraven, editors, *Proc. Second International Workshop on Biologically-Motivated Computer Vision (BMCV 2002)*, volume 2525 of *Lecture Notes in Computer Science (LNCS)*, pages 439–452, Tübingen, Germany, 22-24 November 2002. Springer-Verlag Berlin·Heidelberg·New York/NY. *(Quoted on page 32)*

462. S. Ullman and R. Basri. Recognition by Linear Combinations of Models. *IEEE Trans. on Pattern Analysis and Machine Intelligence (PAMI)*, 13(10):992–1006, Oct. 1991. *(Quoted on page 48)*

463. S. Ullman, M. Vidal-Naquet, and E. Sali. Visual Features of Intermediate Complexity and Their Use in Classification. *Nature Neuroscience*, 5(7):682–687, Jul 2002. *(Quoted on page 151)*

464. S. Umeyama. Least-Squares Estimation of Transformation Parameters Between Two Point Patterns. *IEEE Transactions on Pattern Analysis and Machine Intelligence*, 13(4):376–380, April 1991. *(Quoted on page 123)*

465. T.J. van Gelder and R.F. Port. It's About Time: An Overview of the Dynamical Approach to Cognition. In R.F. Port and T.J. van Gelder, editors, *Mind as Motion – Explorations in the Dynamics of Cognition*, pages 1–43, Cambridge, MA, 1995. Bradford Books, MIT Press. *(Quoted on pages 12, 13, 14, and 15)*

466. F. van Harmelen, J. Hendler, I. Horrocks, D.L. McGuinness, P.F. Patel-Schneider, and L.A. Stein. OWL Web Ontology Language Reference, http://www.w3.org/TR/owl-guide/, 2003. *(Quoted on page 260)*

467. L.J. van Vliet, I.T. Young, and P.W. Verbeek. Recursive Gaussian Derivative Filters. In *International Conference on Pattern Recognition*, pages 509–514, August 1998. *(Quoted on pages 75 and 76)*

468. V. Vapnik. *The Nature of Statistical Learning Theory*. Springer-Verlag Berlin · Heidelberg · New York/NY, 1995. *(Quoted on page 87)*

469. V. Vapnik. *Statistical Learning Theory*. John Wiley & Sons, Inc., 1998. *(Quoted on page 87)*

470. F.J. Varela. *Principles of Biological Autonomy*. Elsevier North Holland, New York, NY, 1979. *(Quoted on page 15)*

471. F.J. Varela. Whence Perceptual Meaning? A Cartography of Current Ideas. In F.J. Varela and J.-P. Dupuy, editors, *Understanding Origins – Contemporary Views on the Origin of Life, Mind and Society*, volume 130 of *Boston Studies in the Philosophy of Science*, pages 235–263. Kluwer Academic Publishers, 1992. *(Quoted on pages 11, 12, 15, and 18)*

472. S.P. Vecera and R.C. O'Reilly. Figure-Ground Organization and Object Recognition Processes: An Interactive Account. *J. Exp. Psych.: Human Perception and Performance*, 24(2):441–462, 1998. *(Quoted on pages 146 and 152)*

473. D. Vernon. A Vision on Cognitive Vision. In *Dagstuhl Seminar 03441*. Schloss Dagstuhl, Germany, 26-30 October 2003. `ftp://ftp.dagstuhl.de/pub/Proceedings/03/03441/03441.VernonDavid.Slides.pdf`. *(Quoted on page 25)*

474. R. Veryard. *Component-Based Business: Plug and Play*. Springer-Verlag Berlin · Heidelberg · New York/NY, 2001. *(Quoted on page 285)*

475. M. Vidal-Naquet and S. Ullman. Object Recognition with Informative Features and Linear Classification. In *Proc. Ninth IEEE International Conference on Computer Vision (ICCV-2003)*, volume I, pages 281–288, Nice, France, 13–16 October 2003. *(Quoted on page 151)*

476. L. Vila. A Survey on Temporal Reasoning in Artificial Intelligence. *AI Communications*, 7(1):4–28, 1994. *(Quoted on page 248)*

477. M. Vincze, M. Ayromlou, W. Ponweiser, and M. Zillich. Edge Projected Integration of Image and Model Cues for Robust Model-Based Object Tracking. *Int. Journal of Robotics Research*, 20(7):533–552, 2001. *(Quoted on pages 290 and 291)*

478. P. Viola and M. Jones. Rapid Object Detection Using a Boosted Cascade of Simple Features. In *Proceedings IEEE Conference on Computer Vision and Pattern Recognition (CVPR 2001)*, volume 1, pages 511–518, Kauai, Hawaii, 8–14 December 2001. *(Quoted on pages 146, 149, and 150)*

479. P. Viola and M.J. Jones. Robust Real-Time Face Detection. In *Proc. Eighth International Conference on Computer Vision (ICCV-2001)*, volume II, page 747, Vancouver, BC, Canada, 9-12 July 2001. *(Quoted on page 302)*

480. P. Viola, M.J. Jones, and D. Snow. Detecting Pedestrians Using Patterns of Motion and Appearance. In *Proc. Ninth IEEE International Conference on Computer Vision (ICCV-2003)*, volume II, pages 734–741, Nice, France, 13–16 October 2003. *(Quoted on pages 146, 150, and 302)*

481. C. von der Malsburg. The What and Why of Binding: Review The Modeler's Perspective. *Neuron*, 24:95–104, 1999. *(Quoted on page 34)*

482. W. Wai and J.K. Tsotsos. Directing Attention to Onset and Offset of Image Events for Eye-head Movement Control. In *Proc. IAPR International Conference on Pattern Recognition*, volume A, pages 274–279, Jerusalem, 1994. *(Quoted on page 32)*

483. D.L. Waltz. *Generating Semantic Descriptions from Drawings of Scenes with Shadow*. Ph.D. dissertation, Artificial Intelligence Laboratory. Massachusetts Institute of Technology, Cambridge, MA, 1972. *(Quoted on page 7)*

484. A. Ward, A. Jones, and A. Hopper. A New Location Technique for the Active Office. *IEEE Personal Comunications*, 4(1):42–47, 1997. *(Quoted on page 184)*

485. W.H. Warren. Perceiving Affordances: Visual Guidance of Stairclimbing. *Journal of Experimental Psychology: Human Perception and Performance*, 10:683–703, 1984. *(Quoted on page 14)*

486. M. Weber, M. Welling, and P. Perona. Towards Automatic Discovery of Object Categories. In *Proceedings IEEE Conf. on Computer Vision and Pattern Recognition (CVPR '00)*, pages II:101–108, Hilton Head Island, SC, 13–15 June 2000. *(Quoted on pages 146, 148, and 150)*

487. M. Weber, M. Welling, and P. Perona. Unsupervised Learning of Models for Recognition. In D. Vernon, editor, *Proc. European Conference on Computer Vision (ECCV-2000)*, volume 1842 of *Lecture Notes in Computer Science*, pages I:18–32, Dublin, Ireland, 26 June–1 July 2000. Springer-Verlag Berlin·Heidelberg·New York/NY. *(Quoted on pages 148 and 150)*

488. H. Wechsler, V. Kakkad, J. Huang, S. Gutta, and V. Chen. Automatic Video-based Person Authentication Using the RBF Network. In J. Bigün, G. Chollet, and G. Borgefors, editors, *Proc. First Int. Conf. on Audio- and Video-based Biometric Person Authentication*, volume 1206 of *Lecture Notes in Computer Science*, pages 85–92, Crans-Montana, Switzerland, 12–14 March 1997. *(Quoted on pages 129 and 137)*

489. K. Weiler. Edge-Based Data Structures for Solid Modeling in Curved-Surface Environments. *Computer Graphics and Applications*, 5(1):21–40, January 1985. *(Quoted on page 200)*

490. K. Weiler. The Radial-edge Data Structure: A Topological Representation for Non-manifold Geometry Boundary Modeling. In J.L. Encarnacao, M.J. Wozny, and H.W. McLaughlin, editors, *Geometric Modelling for CAD Applications*, pages 3–36. Elsevier Science Publishers B. V. (North-Holland), Amsterdam, NL, 1988. *(Quoted on page 200)*

491. M. Wertheimer. Über Gestalttheorie. *Philosophische Zeitschrift für Forschung und Aussprache*, 1:30–60, 1925. *(Quoted on page 205)*

492. R. Wilson and G.H. Granlund. The Uncertainty Principle in Image Processing. *IEEE Transactions on Pattern Analysis and Machine Intelligence*, PAMI–6(6):758–767, November 1984. Report LiTH-ISY-I-0576, Computer Vision Laboratory, Linköping University, Sweden, 1983. *(Quoted on page 52)*

493. T. Winograd. Architectures for Context. *Human-computer Interaction*, 16(2-4):401–419, 2001. *(Quoted on page 184)*

494. T. Winograd and F. Flores. *Understanding Computers and Cognition – A New Foundation for Design*. Addison-Wesley Publishing Company, Inc., Reading, Massachusetts, 1986. *(Quoted on pages 11, 14, 15, 21, and 22)*

495. L. Wiskott, J.M. Fellous, N. Krüger, and C. von der Mahlsburg. Face Recognition by Elastic Bunch Graph Matching. In L.C. Jain, editor, *Intelligent Biometric Techniques in Fingerprint and Face Recognition*, pages 355–396. CRC Press, 1999. *(Quoted on pages 75 and 78)*

496. L. Wiskott, J.M. Fellous, N. Krüger, and C. von der Malsburg. Face Recognition by Elastic Bunch Graph Matching. *IEEE Transactions on Pattern Analysis and Machine Intelligence*, 19(7):775–779, 1997. *(Quoted on page 149)*

497. H. Wolfson. Model-Based Object Recognition by Geometric Hashing. In *ECCV'90*, volume 427 of *Lecture Notes in Computer Science (LNCS)*, pages 526–536. Springer-Verlag Berlin·Heidelberg·New York/NY, 1990. *(Quoted on page 151)*

498. W.A. Woods. What's in a Link? Foundations for Semantic Networks. In D.G. Bobrow and A. Collins, editors, *Representation and Understanding*, pages 35–82. Academic Press, Inc., New York, NY, USA · London, UK, 1975. *(Quoted on page 260)*

499. W.A. Woods and J.G. Schmolze. The KL-ONE Family. In F. Lehmann, editor, *Semantic Networks in Artificial Intelligence*, pages 133–178. Pergamon, 1992. *(Quoted on page 260)*

500. M. Wooldridge and N. Jennings. Intelligent Agents: Theory and Practice. *Knowledge Engineering Review*, 10(2):115–152, 1995. *(Quoted on pages 281 and 283)*

501. D.B. Yang, H.H. González-Baños, and L.J. Guibas. Counting People in Crowds with a Real-Time Network of Simple Sensors. In *Proc. Ninth IEEE International Conference on*

Computer Vision (ICCV-2003), volume I+II, pages I:122–129, Nice, France, 13–16 October 2003. IEEE Computer Society: Los Alamitos, CA. *(Quoted on page 226)*

502. S.X. Yu and J. Shi. Object-Specific Figure-Ground Segregation. In *CVPR'03*, June 2003. *(Quoted on pages 147 and 152)*

503. A.L. Yuille, D.S. Cohen, and P.W. Hallinan. Feature Extraction from Faces Using Deformable Templates. In *CVPR-1989: Proc. IEEE Conference on Computer Vision and Pattern Recognition*, pages 104–109, San Diego, CA, 4–8 June 1989. IEEE Computer Society: Los Alamitos, CA. *(Quoted on pages 149 and 152)*

504. Y. Zhang and A.K. Mackworth. Constraint Nets: a Semantic Model for Hybrid Dynamic Systems. *Theoretical Computer Science*, 138(1):211–239, 1995. *(Quoted on page 297)*

505. S. Zhou, V. Krüger, and R. Chellappa. Face Recognition from Video: A CONDENSATION Approach. In *Proc. Fifth Intern. Conf. on Automatic Face and Gesture Recognition*, pages 212–217, Washington, DC, USA, 20-21 May 2002. IEEE Computer Society, Washington DC, USA. *(Quoted on pages 138 and 139)*

506. U. Ziemann. Sensory-motor Integration in Human Motor Cortex at the Pre-Motoneurone Level: Beyond the Age of Simple MEP Measurements. *J Physiol (Lond)*, 534(3):625–, 2001. *(Quoted on pages 44 and 45)*

507. M. Zillich and J. Matas. Ellipse Detection Using Efficient Grouping of Arc Segments. In Beleznai and Schlögl, editors, *Proc. 27th Workshop of the Austrian Association of Pattern Recognition ÖAGM/AAPR*, pages 143–148, Wien, 2003. Oldenburg Publisher. *(Quoted on pages 289 and 290)*

508. V. Zýka. *Verification and Refinement of Local Surface Models for Geometrical Stereo-reconstruction (In Czech)*. PhD thesis, Department of Cybernetics, Faculty of Electrical Engineering, Czech Technical University, Prague, Czech Republic, September 2003. *(Quoted on page 103)*

Subject Index

Author Index

Lecture Notes in Computer Science

For information about Vols. 1–3941

please contact your bookseller or Springer